W9-CRQ-186

Quicken® User's Guide

Version 3 for Windows

New version created by
Eli Abbe
Paul Gentry
Tim Villanueva
Joe Wells
Daryl Yee

Intuit™

First Printing, September 1993.
ISBN: 0-929804-52-X

Intuit Inc.
P. O. Box 3014
Menlo Park, California 94026

Manuals, Help, Qcards, and tutorials
Kathryn Berg
Mervyn Lewis
Nicolette ter Rele

Development team
Jill Baird
John Baldwin
Li Chan
Jim Del Favero
Gila Karash
Jacqueline Maartense
John Pattinson
Rowena Pelayo
Hermanese Sims
Dave Stewart
Erik Torres

Special thanks to
Dan Gordon
Bruce Hertzfeld
Suna Kneisley
Ray Kundra
Elizabeth Lagman
Eleanor Mayfield
Martin Runneals
Wade Temple
Anna Van Gordon
Lisa Yee

Contents

Setting up your finances

Entering your data

Working with accounts

Analyzing your finances

Taking control of your finances

Managing your files

Appendixes

Setting up accounts

You've set up at least one checking account in Quicken. Now you can add more accounts to your Quicken file to track your finances in more detail.

Quicken has six account types with features tailored to different tracking needs:
bank
cash
credit card
asset
liability
and **investment**.

Follow the same basic steps to create and use any account type.

Setting up additional Quicken accounts

With Quicken, you can create up to 64 related accounts in a single Quicken file. (This number can be increased up to a maximum of 255 by copying the file; see page 338.) The steps to set up additional accounts are basically the same as those you followed to set up your first Quicken account.

If you have not already set up your first Quicken account, see "Setting up your first bank account" on page 18 of the *Getting Started Guide*.

1   **If you have more than one file, be sure to open the one you want before setting up the new account.**

In most cases, you'll want to set up all your accounts in the same file so you can create reports based on data from all of them. However, in some cases you might want separate Quicken files. When you set up a new account, Quicken adds it to the current Quicken file. For information about when and how to create more than one Quicken file, see "Setting up additional files" on page 332.

2   **From the Activities menu, choose Create New Account.**

Or, from the Account list, click New.

3   **Click a button to select the type of account to create, and then click OK.**

Quicken displays information about each account type below the account type name.

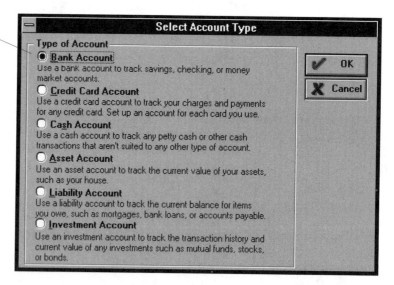

Liability accounts:
If you intend to set up a liability account to track an amortized loan such as a house mortgage, please read Chapter 23, *Tracking loans and mortgages*, beginning on page 315 first. That chapter explains how Quicken sets up a liability account for you as part of setting up the loan.

4   **Enter the account name, opening balance (except for investment accounts) and date, and optional account information.**

Enter a unique name for the account, up to 15 characters long. Use your own name, your bank name, or a descriptive name such as Checking, VISA, or Mortgage. The name can include letters, numbers, spaces, and any characters except these: / : [ ]

It's important that you enter the balance and date correctly. See the table on this page to enter the correct information in these fields.

New Account Information

A̲ccount Name: MasterCard

B̲alance: 890.76   as of: 3/19/94
(Enter the amount you owe on your credit card)

☐ I̲ntelliCharge

D̲escription: 5191 3200 0194 5329

Credit L̲imit (opt.): 1500

✓ OK
✗ Cancel
📁 Info

The description in this box is optional. You can enter up to 21 characters.

(Optional) Click Info to enter some background details about the account.

Account type	Balance	Date
Bank	Enter the ending balance shown on your last bank statement	Enter the date of your last bank statement
Cash	Enter the amount of cash you have on hand	Enter today's date
Credit card	Enter the balance due shown on your last credit card statement	Enter the date of your last credit statement
Asset	Enter the current value of the asset	Enter today's date
Liability	Enter the current principal amount owed on the loan	Enter today's date
Investment	Not applicable	Not applicable

Windows tip

To move to the next box in a window, click the box or press Tab.

5 Enter other information in the New Account Information window.

- To enable electronic payments for a bank account, see Chapter 9, *Paying bills electronically,* beginning on page 111.

- To enable IntelliCharge for a credit card account, see "Setting up a credit card account to use IntelliCharge" on page 140.

- To use an asset account to track a savings goal, see "Setting up savings goals" on page 297.

- To enter additional information about the account for your own benefit (for example, the account number or interest rate), click Info. Fill in the boxes of the Additional Account Information window and click OK to close the window.

Windows tip

You can press Enter instead of clicking OK.

6 Click OK.

7 (Optional) If this is a liability account, Quicken asks if you would like to set up an amortized loan. If you click Yes, be sure to read Chapter 23, *Tracking loans and mortgages,* beginning on page 315.

Quicken creates the new account and opens the register for it.

Selecting an account to use

You can work with many accounts at one time by opening multiple account windows on your desktop. There are three ways to open the Account list:

- From the Lists menu, choose Account.
- Press Ctrl+A.
- Click the Accts (Accounts) icon on the iconbar.

The Account list includes detailed information about the accounts in the current file. It shows the name, type, description, number of transactions in the account, and the ending balance for each account. If you have checks to be printed, the Account list also displays a checkmark in the Chks column for that account.

There are three ways to access the account you want to use:

- To open an account, choose it from the Account list.

Double-click the account you want to open.

OR

Select the account and then click Use. (To select an account, either click its name or move the highlight bar using the Up Arrow and Down Arrow keys.)

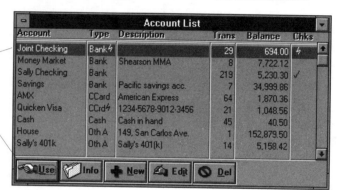

- If the account is already open, click on it to make it active.

In this example, the Category & Transfer List window is active. (The title bar of an active window is highlighted.) Click anywhere in the Bank Account window to make it active and see its register.

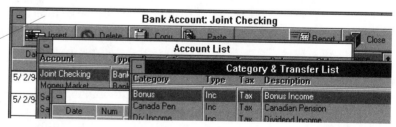

- If the account is already open, but obscured by other windows, choose the account name from the bottom half of the Window menu.

The bottom part of the Window menu lists all the Quicken windows that are open.

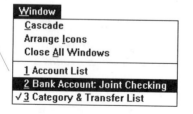

When you click on an account name, Quicken opens the register for the account. Quicken displays the account type (such as Bank Account) and the account name (such as Joint Checking) in the title bar of the register.

Editing account information

After setting up and using an account, you can change its name, description, or opening balance.

Using the Edit Account Information window, you can:

- Rename a Quicken account
- Change its description or other information
- Change the credit limit for a credit card account

Or press Ctrl+A

1 **From the Lists menu, choose Account.**

2 **Select the account you want to edit.**

The savings account is selected in this Account list.

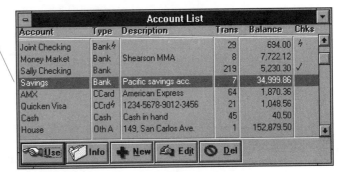

Account	Type	Description	Trans	Balance	Chks
Joint Checking	Bank⌂		29	694.00	⌂
Money Market	Bank	Shearson MMA	8	7,722.12	
Sally Checking	Bank		219	5,230.30	✓
Savings	Bank	Pacific savings acc.	7	34,999.86	
AMX	CCard	American Express	64	1,870.36	
Quicken Visa	CCrd⌂	1234-5678-9012-3456	21	1,048.56	
Cash	Cash	Cash in hand	45	40.50	
House	Oth A	149, San Carlos Ave.	1	152,879.50	

Use   Info   New   Edit   Del

Or press Ctrl+E

3 **Click Edit.**

Enter up to fifteen characters for an account name.

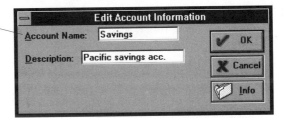

Edit Account Information

Account Name: Savings

Description: Pacific savings acc.

✓ OK
✗ Cancel
Info

Windows tip
To move to the next field in the window, click the field or press Tab.

4 **Change the account name or description.**

If you change the name of an account, Quicken automatically updates any transactions linked to this account through transfers to show the new name. (For more information about account transfers, see "Transferring money between accounts" on page 24.)

5 **(Optional) If this is a credit card account, change the credit limit and click OK.**

6 **(Optional) Click Info to change the additional information about the account, then return to the Edit Account Information window.**

Windows tip
You can press Enter instead of clicking OK.

7 **Click OK.**

Quicken makes any changes to the account information and updates the name of the account in the Account list and in the Category & Transfer list.

See Chapter 3, *Using the register,* beginning on page 17, for details of how to enter and edit transactions in the register.

- You can also change the opening balance.

  It's important to enter the correct opening balance for an account when you are setting up the account. However, if you need to change the opening balance for an account after the account is set up, you can go directly to the Opening Balance transaction in the register and change the date or amount of the transaction. Enter the revised opening balance into the deposit column over the previous amount. The next time you reconcile this account, Quicken displays an opening balance difference. See "Having Quicken adjust for differences" on page 80.

- You may need to change the account from one type to another.

  For example, you might want to turn a bank account into a credit card account. It's important to enter the correct account type when you are setting up the account. However, if you want to change the type of the account, you need to export the old account to a QIF file, set up a new account, and then import transactions from the QIF file into the new account. See "Copying data from one account to another" on page 340 for instructions.

Deleting an account

Deleting a Quicken account permanently removes all of that account's records from your file. Once you delete an account, there is no way to recover it. Be certain you want to delete an account before doing so.

Or press Ctrl+A

1 **From the Lists menu, choose Account.**

2 **Select the account you want to delete in the Account list.**

Or press Ctrl+D

3 **Click Del.**

Quicken warns that you are about to permanently remove this account from your file. If Quicken deletes the account, it also deletes the account name from the Category field of any transfer transactions.

Windows tip
You can press Enter instead of clicking OK. Or you can back out by pressing Esc instead of clicking Cancel.

4 **Type YES and click OK if you are certain you want to delete the account.**

Quicken permanently removes the account from your file.

Setting up categories and classes

Categories and classes are labels that you can apply to transactions to track how much you are spending on particular items, such as Rent, Groceries, or Dining Out.

When you "categorize" and "classify" transactions, Quicken can give you insight into your finances through financial reports, graphs, and budgets.

About categories

Quicken categories are flexible and easy to use. You can name your categories using words, numbers, or characters in any combination. You can set up categories before you categorize transactions, or set them up "on the fly" as you enter transactions. You can enter categories in some or all of your transactions.

For home uses, you might have expense categories for expenses such as groceries, mortgage interest paid, medical fees, and utilities. Your income categories might include items such as salary, bonuses, interest income, and dividends.

You can also categorize different parts of the same transaction with multiple category names. Categorizing one transaction with multiple categories or classes is called "splitting" a transaction. For example, if you spend $220 at a department store, you may not spend the entire amount on one item. A split transaction allows you to track more specifically where the money went: $17 on books, $139 on clothing, and $64 on housewares.

Whether you want to modify the standard Quicken list of home or business categories or start from scratch, think about what questions you would like Quicken reports and graphs to answer.

If you are tracking your home finances, you probably want reports and graphs to tell you:

- How much you spend each month on food, mortgage interest, tuition, or charity. These items are your *expense categories*.

- How much you receive each month in salary and bonuses, dividends, interest income, or rent from investment properties. These items are your *income categories*.

When you categorize your transactions, you can:

- Prepare for your tax returns by printing a report that lists all tax-related income and expenses.* (See "Tax summary" on page 213.)

- Set up budget amounts for each category and quickly compare your actual expenses with your budget amounts by creating a budget report or budget variance graph. (See 21, *Budgeting your income and expenses,* beginning on page 289.)

- Export your transaction data to tax software. (See "Transferring Quicken data to tax preparation software" on page 273.)

---

*   🍁 Canadian users: You will notice that the standard home category list includes GST and PST categories for tracking amounts you spend towards these taxes. If you need to track these taxes as part of your business, however, we recommend that you set up liability accounts instead of using categories, as described in the separate booklet included in your package.

Setting up categories and subcategories

Quicken maintains a category list that includes the names of all the categories in the current Quicken file. Whenever you set up a new category, Quicken adds it to the list.

You can set up your category names before you enter transactions, or you can set them up as you enter transactions. Whenever you type a new category name in a transaction, Quicken offers to set up the new category and add it to the list.

You can set up all your categories on one level or in a hierarchy with parent categories and subcategories. Subcategories offer an additional level of detail. It's up to you if you want to use one category called "Utilities" for all your utility transactions, or if you want to have subcategories under "Utilities" called "Cable," "Gas and Electricity," "Trash," "Water," and so on.

Or press Ctrl+C, or click the Cat List icon on the iconbar.

1   **From the Lists menu, choose Category & Transfer.**

Quicken keeps income categories at the top of the list. Expense categories follow. Transfers appear at the bottom of the list.

You can print the Category & Transfer list. Open the list, then press Ctrl+P.

These are typical expense categories in a Category & Transfer list.

Subcategories are indented under their parent categories.

Account names (enclosed in brackets) are included in this list because you can double-click an account name to create an automatic transfer between accounts. Quicken cannot categorize a transfer transaction. A transfer has the name of the source or destination account in the Category field. See "Transferring money between accounts" on page 24 for complete information about transfers between accounts.

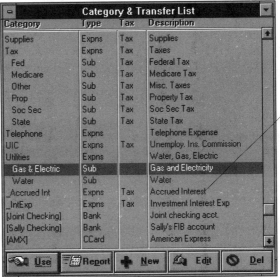

The investment income and expense categories, which all begin with an underline (for example, _DivInc, _IntExp), appear on your category list automatically (whether or not you selected standard categories) as soon as you add an investment account. See "Setting up a Quicken regular investment account" on page 165.

Or press Ctrl+N

2   **Click New.**

Quicken displays the Set Up Category window.

3 **Enter information in the Set Up Category window.**

Click a category type:

If you are setting up or editing a category, click income or expense.

If you are setting up or editing a subcategory, click Subcategory Of and enter the name of the subcategory in the Name box. Then enter the name of the parent category here. The subcategory takes on the income or expense type of its parent.

Enter a name for the new category or subcategory. You can use up to 15 characters.

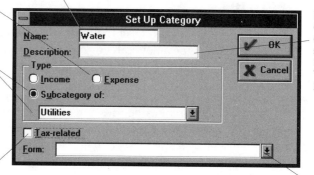

(Optional) Enter a description of the category or subcategory in the Description box. You can use up to 25 characters.

(Optional) If your category contains tax information:

Click the Tax-related checkbox if you want to use this category to track a particular type of tax information.

You may select the tax schedule now (in the Form field) to which you want the category to report (or do it later).

(Optional) If you see the Form box, from the Form drop-down list select the tax schedule line item to which you want to assign this tax category. (The Form drop-down list appears in your Set Up Category window if your preference for using tax schedules is turned on. See "Changing other register preferences" on page 42.)

4 **Click OK to add the category name to the list.**

Changing and deleting categories

When you change a category name, Quicken automatically changes all transactions categorized with the old name.

Changing categories

Or press Ctrl+C

1 **From the Lists menu, choose Category & Transfer.**

2 **Select the category you want to change.**

Or press Ctrl+E

3 **Click Edit.**

Quicken displays the Edit Categories window.

Windows tip
Replace text in a box by holding the left mouse button down and dragging the insertion point through the text to be replaced. Then enter the new text.

4 **Make any changes you want to the category information.**

5 **Click OK to record the changed category information.**

Deleting categories

Delete a category if you don't ever expect to use it.

Or press Ctrl+C

1 **From the Lists menu, choose Category & Transfer.**

2 **Select the category you want to delete.**

Or press Ctrl+D

3   **Click Del.**

4   **Click OK.**

Quicken deletes the category from the list and erases it from the Category field of any transactions to which it has been assigned. Don't delete a category name as a step in changing it. See "Moving and merging categories in the list" on this page instead.

When you delete a subcategory, Quicken deletes it from the category list and reassigns transactions currently applied to it to the parent category.

Quicken won't let you delete a category that has subcategories. You need to promote the subcategories to categories or move the subcategories under another category before you can delete the category.

Moving and merging categories in the list

After working with Quicken a while, you may want to move categories in the list. You can change a category into a subcategory, change a subcategory into a category, or move a subcategory from one category to another.

When you change the name or level of a category, Quicken automatically changes the name in each of the transactions that you've categorized with the old name.

Changing (demoting) a category into a subcategory

Or press Ctrl+C

1   **From the Lists menu, choose Category & Transfer.**

2   **Select the category you want to demote.**

Or press Ctrl+E

3   **Click Edit.**

4   **Click Subcategory Of.**

Windows tip
To pull down the list, click the underscored down arrow. Then click the Down Arrow in the scroll bar to move down the list. Click the parent category you want to use from the list.

5   **Pull down the Subcategory Of list and select the name of the parent category you want to assign the subcategory to.**

6   **Click OK to record the changed category information.**

Changing (promoting) a subcategory into a category

Or press Ctrl+C

1   **From the Lists menu, choose Category & Transfer.**

2   **Select the subcategory you want to promote.**

Or press Ctrl+E

3   Click Edit.

Quicken displays the Edit Category window with the current category information for the category you selected.

4   Click Income or Expense.

5   Click OK to record the changed category information.

Moving a subcategory from one category to another

1   From the Lists menu, choose Category & Transfer.

2   Select the subcategory you want to move.

Or press Ctrl+E

3   Click Edit.

Quicken displays the Edit Category window with the current category information for the selected subcategory.

Windows tip

To pull down the list, click the underscored Down Arrow. Then click the Down Arrow in the scroll bar to move down the list. Click the category or subcategory you want in the list.

4   Pull down the Subcategory Of list and select the name of the category or subcategory to which you want to assign the selected subcategory.

5   Click OK to record the changed category information.

Merging two categories

For example, this Category & Transfer list has categories called "Home Repair" and "Household." If you want to merge these categories into one category called "Household," first change "Home Repair" into a subcategory under "Household."

1   Change the category you don't want into a subcategory of the category you want to keep.

See the instructions for changing a category into a subcategory on page 11.

Now "Home Repair" is a subcategory of "Household."

Next, select the subcategory, click Del, and then click Yes.

2　Delete the subcategory name.

Quicken deletes the subcategory name from the category list and reassigns its transactions to the parent category.

Reporting on transactions with a specific category

You can create a QuickReport that lists all transactions, in all your accounts in the current file, using a specific category. You'll find this report useful in many ways.

For example, you can quickly list your expenses in a certain area. You can see what you have spent on car maintenance this year, or what your mortgage interest payments amount to.

Or you can check whether you're using a category at all, to help you decide whether you should delete the category.

If you want a detailed report on all your spending broken down by category, create an itemized category report instead, as described in "Creating a report" on page 236. The Category QuickReport is a small section of an itemized category report, and is quicker to create when you are interested in only one category.

Or press Ctrl+C

1　Display the Category & Transfer list (from the Lists menu, choose Category & Transfer).

2　Select the category you want to report on.

3　Click Report.

Quicken displays the report.

4　To close the report and return to the Category & Transfer list, click Close on the report button bar.

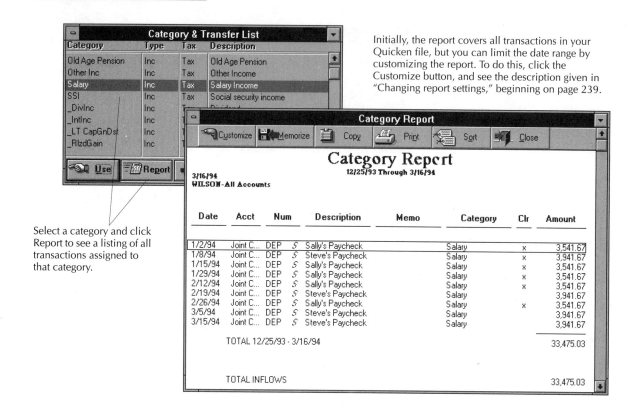

Initially, the report covers all transactions in your Quicken file, but you can limit the date range by customizing the report. To do this, click the Customize button, and see the description given in "Changing report settings," beginning on page 239.

Select a category and click Report to see a listing of all transactions assigned to that category.

About classes

You can use classes to specify where, to what, or to whom your transactions apply. Classes do not replace categories. Rather, classes complement categories by adding a second dimension to reports, graphs, and budgets.

Your use of classes can be as simple or as intricate as your finances require. You can classify transactions, categorize them, or both. You might use just one class, for example, to distinguish business transactions in a file that contains both personal and business expenses. Or you might use a number of classes; for example, if you work with a number of clients, you could set up a class for each client.

You might want to use classes in situations like these:

- If you use your personal checking account for business as well as personal expenses, you can identify business transactions with the class name Business.

- If you manage properties, you can identify transactions by property name or address. That way six different utility bills could be marked clearly as utility expenses applying to six different properties.

- If you work with multiple clients, you can identify transactions by client name. Then you could report separately on the income and expenses related to each client.

Use classes to specify	Examples
Who the transaction is for	Your clients Your salespeople (for tracking commissions) You or your spouse
Where the transaction applies	Sales regions: East vs. West Property names: Oak Street vs. North Avenue
What the transaction is for	Security names (in an asset account) Job or project names (for job costing) Business use (for tax reasons)

Using classes for business

If you have a small business, Quicken classes can help you bill expenses to clients, track actual costs versus estimates, segregate income and expenses by rental property, and track expenses by job, project, or department. If you set up and use classes for each property, client, job, department, and so forth, you can create a report showing your income and expenses for each individual class. More information about using Quicken for small business finances is in the *Quicken Business User's Guide*. To purchase this guide from Intuit, call **800-624-8742**.

It's helpful to use Quicken for a while before you begin to use classes.

Before you start using classes, think about what kind of reports you might need. As you'll discover when you begin to create reports, there may be times when you want reports based on categories, other times when you want reports based on classes, and other times when you want a report that includes both category and class information. Because people use classes in so many different ways, Quicken does not provide a preset list of classes.

Setting up classes and subclasses

You can set up class names before you enter transactions, or as you enter them. When you type a new class name in a transaction, Quicken lets you set up the class "on the fly."

Quicken displays class names in the class list, which is shared by all the accounts in the file. You cannot change a class into a category, or vice versa.

Using subclasses lets you further refine your reports. To use subclasses, simply set up a class name for each item you want to function as a subclass. Then, when you are classifying a transaction in the register, enter a colon (:) to separate the main class from the subclass.

Or press Ctrl+L

1   **From the Lists menu, choose Class List.**

If this is the first time you're setting up classes, this list is empty. Click New to set up a new class.

The property classes in this list make it possible for this family to track their rental income and expenses by property.

You can print the Class list. Open the list and then press Ctrl+P.

Or press Ctrl+N

2   **To set up a new class, click New.**

To view the information for an existing class, select it in the list and click Edit.

You can use up to 15 characters to enter a class name.

You can use up to 25 characters to enter a description.

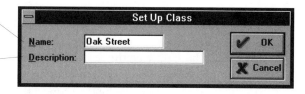

3   **Enter a name in the Class box.**

Windows tip

Place the insertion point in the Description box by clicking the box or by pressing Tab. Then start typing.

4   **(Optional) Enter a description of the class in the Description box.**

5   **Click OK to add the class name to the list.**

Reporting on transactions with a specific class

You can create a QuickReport on a specific class just as you can for a category. With the class selected in the Class list, click Report. Quicken creates a QuickReport that lists all transactions, in all accounts in the current file, that use the selected class.

Using the register

You're familiar with using a paper check register to record transactions in your checking account. Fill in Quicken's register much as you fill in a paper check register to keep a record of all activity that affects your bank account balance.

Each Quicken account has a register associated with it. This chapter describes using the check register for bank accounts. The basic steps for working in all Quicken account registers are the same.

Adding transactions to the register

When you set up a Quicken bank account for the first time, you find yourself in the Register window. Use the register to record all transactions, except checks you plan to print with Quicken.

(If you plan to print checks with Quicken, enter them at the Write Checks window, not the Register window. When you create a check in the Write Checks window, Quicken automatically adds that transaction to your register.)

Transactions are any items that affect the balance in your account. Common transactions include:

- Checks written by hand
- ATM (automatic teller machine) or debit transactions
- Deposits
- Checking account fees and interest
- Bank service charges
- Electronic transactions

1 **In the Account list, select the bank account you want to work with and click Use.**

If you are already working with the account, choose Use Register from the Activities menu, or click the Register icon on the iconbar. Quicken opens the register for the account you used last and places the insertion point in an empty transaction at the end of the register.

2 **Enter information about the new transaction into each field.**

 Press F1 or click Help if you need more help entering information in any field.

Person or institution to whom the payment is made.

Amount of the check or payment.

The Clr (Cleared) column indicates the cleared status of each transaction at the bank if you use Quicken to reconcile. Leave it blank for now.

Amount of a deposit.

Number of a printed check, handwritten check, or type of transaction.

The transaction date.

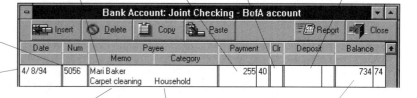

Date	Num	Payee		Payment	Clr	Deposit	Balance	
		Memo	Category					
4/ 8/94	5056	Mari Baker		255 40			734 74	
		Carpet cleaning	Household					

Enter a memo if you want to record more information than the payee or category provides.

Enter categories to track your income and expenses. See "Assigning categories to transactions" on page 22.

You cannot edit values in the Balance column. Quicken automatically calculates your new balance each time you record a transaction.

A "field" is a space for a particular item of information. "Enter" means type the information in a field and then press Tab. The insertion point moves forward to the next field. (If you prefer to press Enter instead of Tab to move from field to field, you can change your General Preferences settings. See "Changing other register preferences" on page 42.)

Quicken offers shortcuts to make it easy to enter information. The shortcuts are described on page 20.

3   When you have finished entering the transaction, click Record to record it as a permanent part of your records.

Each time you record a transaction, Quicken sorts it in the register first by date and then by check number and recalculates all subsequent balances.

The buttons in the Register window make it easy for you to enter transactions:

Click Delete to delete the selected transaction.

To copy a transaction quickly, select it, click Copy, move to the desired place in the register (or in another register), and click Paste.

Click Report to report on the register. See page 35 for details.

Click Close to close the Register window.

Click Insert to insert a new transaction above the selected one.

If you've entered postdated transactions, this bold line separates transactions dated on or before today from those that are dated after today.

Click Record when you have finished entering a transaction.

Click Restore if you make a mistake while entering or editing a transaction. The transaction reverts to the way it was before you started to change it.

Click Splits to assign more than one category to a transaction. See "Splitting transactions" on page 28.

Click 1-Line Display to see more transactions in the register. See "Condensing the register" on page 33.

Click Button Bar to hide the register's button bar if you want to display more transactions.

The Ending Balance is the balance of all entered transactions. If you postdate transactions, Quicken also displays a Current Balance, which is the balance based on all transactions entered through today only.

Bank Account: Joint Checking - BofA account

Insert   Delete   Copy   Paste   Report   Close

Date	Num	Payee / Memo	Category	Payment	Clr	Deposit	Balance
4/ 8/94	5056	Mari Baker / Carpet cleaning	Household	255 40			1,374 72
4/15/94	5058	Farah Risoen	Gifts:Birthday	35 00			1,339 72
4/16/94	5059	GMAC Financing / A/C #87239-278-2 --Splits--		587 55			752 17
4/26/94	Print	Safeco Insurance	Insurance	52 43			699 74
4/21/94	Num	Payee / Memo	Category	Payment		Deposit	

Record   Restore   Splits   ☐ 1-Line Display   ☑ Button Bar

Current Balance: 752.17
Ending Balance: 699.74

Quicken's automatic sorting keeps your records in order no matter when you enter transactions. For example, suppose the date at the end of the check register is 5/27/94 and you want to enter an ATM (automatic teller machine) withdrawal made on 5/10/94. When you enter the transaction at the end of the check register and click Record, Quicken automatically moves the transaction to where it belongs chronologically.

If you prefer, you can enter the transaction in the correct register position yourself by clicking the Insert button.

Using drop-down lists and QuickFill™ for fast entry

Quicken helps you enter a transaction as quickly as possible.

When you Tab to the Num, Payee, or Category field, a list drops down that you can select from. Just click an item from the list to enter it in the register field.

If the lists do not drop down automatically, click the drop-down button to see them. If you cannot see the drop-down button when you click in a field, or if you want to make the lists drop down automatically, go to the QuickFill Preferences window and select the Drop Down Lists Automatically checkbox. See "Changing the way QuickFill works" on page 41.

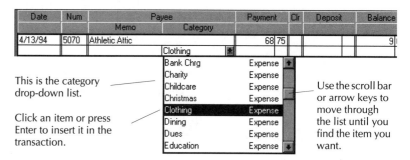

This is the category drop-down list.

Click an item or press Enter to insert it in the transaction.

Use the scroll bar or arrow keys to move through the list until you find the item you want.

Alternatively, begin typing the item's name. A feature called QuickFill fills in the entire item as you type the beginning letters, and you can just press Tab to accept it and move on to the next field.

For example, if you type ch in the Category field, Quicken fills in Charity.

4/13/94	5071	World Children		125	00					75	0
			Charity								

Begin typing the category until QuickFill completes the name. Then press Tab.

If you type a category name that isn't already in the category list, Quicken lets you set up a new category.

If the first few characters you type match the beginning of more than one category name, QuickFill enters the first category that begins with the letters you typed. Keep typing until QuickFill enters the correct category. Then press Tab to accept the entry.

QuickFill also fills in subcategory names or classes if you use these.

Typing the letter w after the colon makes QuickFill fill in the subcategory name "Water." Instead of typing additional letters, you can press Ctrl+Up Arrow or Ctrl+Down Arrow to move through the list of subcategories under Utilities.

| 4/10/94 | 223 | City Springs | | 65 | 00 | | *D* |
| | | *Memo* | Utilities:W**ater** ⬇ | | | |

In the Payee field, QuickFill does even more for you. You'll notice that the payee drop-down list contains complete transaction details. As you type the name of a payee, QuickFill offers to complete the whole transaction. (You won't see this work until you already have a few transactions in the register.) For example, if you've just eaten at the Blue Sky Cafe for the second time this month, when you start to type "Blue..." in the Payee field, Quicken selects the previous transaction in the drop-down list. Just Tab to duplicate the whole transaction, and change the amount if necessary.

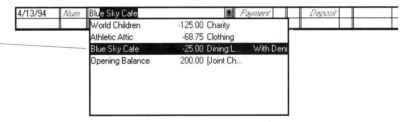

Quicken displays the details from a previous similar transaction.

Press Tab to copy the details into the new transaction.

| 4/13/94 | 5069 | Blue Sky Cafe | | 25.00 ⬇ | | *Deposit* | |
| | | With Denise | Dining:Lunch | | | | |

The payee drop-down list is composed of previous entries in the register, plus your memorized transactions. If your register contains more than one transaction for the same payee, the drop-down list contains the details from the most recently entered transaction.

You can add your own items to the Num drop-down list by clicking <NEW> in the list. To delete an item you've added, click <EDIT> and then Delete.

To change your list of categories, choose Category& Transfer from the Lists menu, as described on page 9.

If you don't want the lists to drop down automatically, you can turn the feature off. See "Changing the way QuickFill works" on page 41 if you'd like to change the way Quicken's shortcuts work.

Or press Alt+Down arrow, or click the right mouse button.

If a list isn't dropped down, you can still select an entry from the list by using the + and − keys on the numeric keypad (or use Ctrl+Up Arrow or Ctrl+Down Arrow) to move through the list entries. Or, drop down the list manually by clicking the drop-down button. (For the Num field, press Alt+Down Arrow.) Click the button a second time to make the list disappear.

The Date, Payment, and Deposit fields have special drop-down features. Just click the drop-down button to use them:

Click on the date drop-down button to display a mini-calendar. Select a date by clicking on it.

Click these arrows to display the previous or next month.

You can also press these keys to enter dates quickly:

+ next day

- previous day

t **T**oday

m beginning of the **M**onth

h end of the mont**H**

y beginning of the **Y**ear

r end of the yea**R**

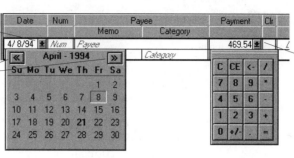

If you need to calculate an amount, click on the Payment or Deposit drop-down button to display a mini-calculator. For example, you can add up several bills this way.

Click the calculator buttons or use the numeric part of your keyboard as usual to calculate an amount.

Assigning categories to transactions

Use categories to identify exactly where your income comes from and where your expenses go. It's important to categorize your transactions so that Quicken can use the category information to create reports and graphs about your income and expenses. (See "About categories" on page 8 for an introduction to categories.)

Quicken provides standard home and business categories for you to use, but you can modify them or create your own. To create your own set of category names or to customize the standard home or business categories at any time, go to the Category & Transfer list as described in "Setting up categories and subcategories" on page 9.

You can enter a category name in the Category field by:

- Selecting it from the Category drop-down list in the register.
- Typing it in the Category field. QuickFill helps you complete the category name. If you type a category name that isn't already in the category list, Quicken lets you set up a new category.
- Choosing it from the Category &Transfer list (from the Lists menu, choose Category & Transfer, select a category, and click Use or press Enter).

| 4/25/94 | 5073 | Western Bell | | 87 | 52 |
| | | Mar/April | Telephone | | |

Always categorize your transactions to get the most use out of Quicken.

If you don't want Quicken to display a message whenever you record an uncategorized transaction, clear the Warn Before Recording Uncategorized Transactions checkbox described in "Changing other register preferences" on page 42.

To read more about customizing reports, see "Changing report settings" on page 239. To read more about QuickZoom, see "Investigating report items with Quick-Zoom" on page 248.

Quicken reminds you to enter a category whenever you attempt to record an uncategorized transaction.

If you don't categorize transactions, Quicken assigns the label "Other" to these amounts in reports and "Uncategorized" to these amounts in graphs.

To find which transactions contain uncategorized amounts, create a transaction report (listed under Other in the Reports menu or in the Create Report window) restricted to transactions with no category. (In the Customize Report window, select Categories and exclude all categories.) If you want, you can now QuickZoom™ on each transaction in turn (double-click the transaction in the report) to go to the transaction and assign a category.

If you see "Other" in a report when you have assigned categories to all transactions, it could be because you sometimes add a subcategory for a particular category and sometimes don't.

In addition to entering a category, you can use the Category field in the register for other types of entry:

You can put these items in the Category field

Categories and subcategories	With categories, you can identify transactions by type. You can categorize a transaction with multiple categories by "splitting" the transaction (see page 28).
Classes	With classes, you can define a transaction even more specifically than with a category alone. Some Quicken users benefit from using classes; others find that categories are all they need to track their finances. To decide whether classes can help you, see page 14.
Transfers	You can choose the name of another Quicken account from the Category & Transfer list to transfer money to that account. For example, you can withdraw money from your savings account and have Quicken automatically transfer the amount as a deposit to your checking account. Transfers are explained on the next page.

Entering subcategories

If you want to use subcategories to further break down the information in reports and graphs, enter the parent category, type a colon (:), and then type the subcategory. For example, Utilities:Water.

Transferring money between accounts

You can use account transfers for many types of transactions. When you set up a new account, Quicken adds the new account name to the Account list and to the Category & Transfer list so you can select the account for transfers.

Transfers can record these and other common transactions:

- Movement of funds from a checking account to a savings account
- Cash advances from your credit card account to your checking account
- Loan payments from a checking account into a liability account that tracks your loan balance

Recording a transfer transaction

To transfer money from one Quicken account to another, enter the name of the destination account in the Category field. When you record the transaction in the source account, Quicken automatically creates a parallel transaction in the destination account. If the source transaction is a payment or decrease, the destination transaction is a deposit or increase.

For example: If you record a withdrawal (payment) of $2,000 from your checking account with the name of your savings account entered in the Category field, Quicken automatically records a deposit of $2,000 in the savings account.

Here's the original transaction that you recorded in Joint Checking (the source account).

Note the square brackets around the transfer account name in the Category field.

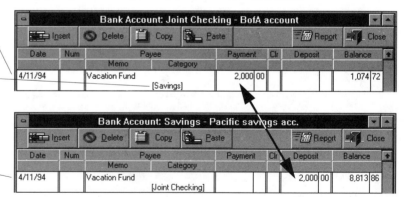

Here's the corresponding transaction that Quicken recorded in Savings (the destination account) as a result of the transfer.

Or press Ctrl+N

1. **Start a new transaction in the Register or Write Checks window.**

   Or select an existing transaction to change it into a transfer.

2. **Enter all the information for the transaction as usual, except in the Category field.**

3   **Go to the Category field. If you know the name of the account you want to transfer to, start typing the name of the account in the Category field.**

QuickFill enters the name of the account and will put brackets around it to show it's a transfer. Skip to step 4.

Or press Ctrl+C

If you're not sure of the name of the account you want to transfer to, click the drop-down button to display the list of categories. Scroll to the end of the list, where all account names are listed, and click the transfer account name to enter it in the Category field.

| 4/11/94 | | Vacation Fund | | 2,000 | 00 | | | | 1,074 | 72 |
| | | | [Savings] | | | | | | | |

[Joint Checking]	Transfer
Money Market	Transfer
[Money Market]	Transfer
Sally Checking	Transfer
[Sally Checking]	Transfer
Savings	Transfer
[Savings]	Transfer
AMX	Transfer

When you want to enter a transfer, click the name of the destination account in the drop-down list to enter it in the Category field of the transaction.

You can quickly spot account names in the list: they appear at the bottom in square brackets (after all your categories) and are marked as Transfers.

4   **Click Record to record the transfer transaction.**

Quicken records the check in your check register *and* creates a parallel transaction in the other account for that amount.

You cannot include a transfer and a category in the same Category field. A transfer is simply a movement of funds between one account and another. For example, every month you and your spouse both transfer $1,000 from your personal checking accounts to your joint checking account to cover household expenses. In the register of your personal checking account, you would enter [Joint Account] in the Category field.

To read more about entering a mortgage payment, see Chapter 23, *Tracking loans and mortgages,* beginning on page 315

You can enter a transfer for part of the total amount of a transaction by using splits. For example, in a mortgage payment, the mortgage amount of the transaction is transferred to a liability account, and the mortgage interest part of the transaction is assigned to an expense category.

You can include class information with transfer information in the Category field. For example, if you pay for an antique table from a checking account and you want to record the purchase in an asset account called "Personal Assets," you would enter [Personal Assets]/Antiques in the Category field.

Changing a transaction that includes a transfer

When you change a transaction that includes a transfer to or from another account, the transaction created by the transfer also changes in some cases:

- If you delete the transaction, Quicken deletes it from both accounts.
- If you change the date or amount of the transaction, the information changes in both accounts. But, if you change the transaction description, check number, memo, or cleared status, the information changes only in the current account.
- If you rename an account, Quicken updates every occurrence of the name in transfers.
- If a transfer was made in a split transaction, you can change it only from the original transaction. You cannot change it from the account that received the transfer.

Going to a transfer transaction

You can go directly from a transaction that includes a transfer to the parallel transaction in another account. Go To Transfer is useful when you want to see the transaction created by a transfer. Use it also when you want to make a change to a transfer that originated in a split transaction (you can change such transfers only in the split line item of the original transaction).

1   **In the Register window, select the transaction that includes the transfer information.**

(Or in the Write Checks window, display the check containing the transfer information.)

Or press Ctrl+X   2   **From the Edit menu, choose Go To Transfer.**

Quicken displays the register for the transfer account and selects the parallel transfer transaction.

If the transaction you are starting from is split and contains transfers to more than one account, you must click Splits first to open the split and click anywhere on the line containing the name of the transfer.

Assigning classes to transactions

In addition to using categories to organize your transactions, you can specify classes to further group the transactions. (See "About classes" on page 14 for an introduction to classes.)

You can enter an existing class name in the Category field by choosing it from the Class list or by typing it after a category in the Category field. (You can also assign a class to a transaction without assigning a category to the transaction.)

Choosing a class from the Class list

1 **Click after the category in the Category field of the transaction you want to classify.**

Or press Ctrl+L

2 **From the Lists menu, choose Class.**

3 **Double-click the class name in the list to paste it after a category.**

Typing a class in the Category field

1 **Click after the category in the Category field of the transaction you want to classify.**

2 **Type a forward slash (/).**

3 **Begin typing the class name in the Category field and continue until QuickFill enters the correct class.**

As soon as you type a forward slash, Quicken recognizes that you are entering a class.

In this example, the category is "Repairs" and the class is "Oak Street."

Date	Num	Payee		Payment	Clr	D
		Memo	Category			
5/11/93	5069	Tim's Carpentry Company		1,075 00		De
		Memo	Repairs/Oak Street			

Entering subclasses

If you are using subclasses to further refine the information in reports, graphs, or budgets, enter a colon (:) after the class to separate the main class from the subclass: Repairs/Oak Street:Apt1.

Changing and deleting classes

The general procedure to change or delete a class is the same as that to change or delete a category. The only difference is that you start by choosing Class from the Lists menu. See "Changing and deleting categories" on page 10.

Splitting transactions

Sometimes you need to identify more than one category for one transaction. For example, a check to a department store might cover clothing, office supplies, and home furnishings. This section describes how to "split" a transaction by categorizing it with more than one category name; you can split a transaction with multiple transfers or multiple classes in the same way.

Filling in a split transaction

When you fill in a split transaction, you enter category names and amounts to identify each line of the split. You can enter this information when you first record a transaction, or you can add it later.

1   **Select the transaction you want to split, or move to a new transaction.**

2   **Enter the total amount of the transaction in either the Payment or the Deposit field.**

    If you don't know the total amount, leave the amount fields blank. Quicken will add up the amounts for you as you fill in the splits.

Or press Ctrl+S   3   **Click Splits.**

    Quicken copies any information already entered in the Category, Payment, or Deposit field of the transaction to the first line of the split.

4   **If the first Category field of the split does not contain a category, enter a category.**

5   **(Optional) Enter a memo in the first Memo field.**

6   **In the first amount field, enter the amount to be assigned to the first category.**

    If an amount is already displayed, you can type right over it.

    Quicken subtracts the amount you entered from the total amount for the transaction and displays the remainder in the next Amount field. In this way, Quicken helps you to account for the total amount of the transaction.

    Instead of an amount, you can enter a percentage of the total amount that you entered in the register. For example, type 35% and press Tab, and Quicken calculates 35% of the total and fills in the figure for you. (This works only if you entered an amount in the register before opening the Splits window.)

7 **Continue to add categories and amounts until you have added one categorized line for each part of the transaction.**

With the Splits button bar, you can insert a line between two others, delete the selected line, or delete all lines.

Categorize each line of the split with any category you choose. As you enter amounts, Quicken prompts you to categorize any remainder by entering the remainder on the next free line.

The split transaction in this example is a mortgage payment, where part of the total is transferred to the liability account "Mortgage" and the rest is assigned to the Mortgage Interest expense category.

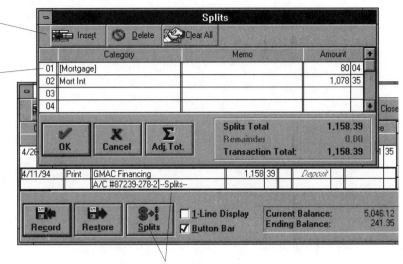

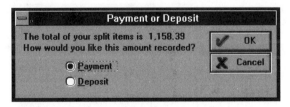

The word "Splits" in the Category field of the register indicates that more than one category is assigned to this transaction. Double-click the word "--Splits--" or click the Splits button to open the Splits window.

You can add up to 30 lines in one split transaction.

8 **Click OK to close the Splits window.**

If you didn't enter an amount in the register (in the Payment or Deposit field) before opening the Splits window, Quicken asks you if the total amount should be recorded as a payment or as a deposit.

The options depend on what type of account you are using. For example, in a credit card account you see the options Charge and Payment. In a cash account, you see Spend and Receive.

Click Payment or Deposit and click OK.

Quicken inserts the total amount in the Payment or Deposit field in the register.

9 **Click Record to record the split transaction.**

If you did enter an amount in the register before opening the Splits window, Quicken makes sure your split figures add up, as described next.

Making sure your split amounts add up

As you enter amounts in the Splits window, Quicken helps you with the arithmetic by putting the remainder on the next free line. It can sometimes happen, though, that the total of the amounts in the Splits window does not equal the figure in the register. For example, you might delete a Splits line, or change the total amount in the register. Quicken keeps a check on your figures at the bottom of the Splits window.

This is the total of the amounts you have entered in the Splits window.

If your split amounts don't add up and you would prefer Quicken to change the total amount you entered in the register, click the Adj Tot button (Adjust Totals).

This is the difference between what you have entered in the Splits window and what is entered in the register. You still have to account for this much.

The transaction total is what you entered in the register. You should enter split amounts that add up to this figure. (The figure is dimmed to show that it's a fixed amount.)

When your figures add up, the Remainder line shows 0.00.

If your split amounts don't add up to the register figure (the "transaction total") when you click OK, Quicken displays another window asking you what you want to do about it. You can have Quicken adjust the total in the register or add the remainder to the Splits window.

If you see this window, choose one of the options by clicking it and click OK.

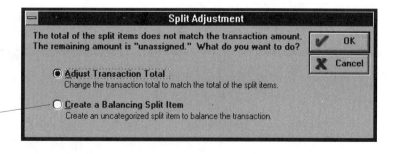

If you choose this option, you can reopen the Splits window later to categorize the extra amount.

Entering a paycheck

You can use a split transaction to enter the details of your paycheck. Although you can just enter the net pay in the register if you prefer, entering all the deductions in the Splits window gives you more accurate reports and lets you see what taxes you are paying.

1 **In a blank transaction in your register, enter "Paycheck" in the Payee field.**

2 **Click Splits.**

3 **Enter the category Salary in the first Category field and enter the gross amount of the paycheck in the Amount field.**

   The gross amount is your pay before any deductions are made.

4 **Enter the deductions from your pay on the following lines as negative amounts. Assign them to the expense categories Tax:Fed, Tax:State, and Tax:FICA.**

   Enter one deduction on each line. You may also have deductions for items such as 401(k) contributions, local withholding, medical insurance contributions, and state disability insurance. Set up new expense categories for these as needed.

   If you track your 401(k) in a separate asset or investment account, enter the account name instead of a category as shown in the example below. Quicken transfers the money to the other account, where it increases the account balance.

   When you've entered all the deductions, check the amount in the Splits Total field at the bottom of the window. It should equal the net amount of your paycheck, which is the amount you actually receive.

See also:
Chapter 12, *Tracking assets and liabilities,* beginning on page 155.
Chapter 13, *Tracking investments,* beginning on page 159

Date	Num	Payee		Payment	Clr	Deposit	Balance	
		Memo	Category					
3/31/94		Paycheck				2,062 97	3,574 34	
			--Splits--					
4/ 1/94	AT							
4/ 2/94								

Splits

Insert   Delete   Clear All

	Category	Memo	Amount	
01	Salary	Gross compensation	3,541 67	
02	Tax:Fed	Federal income tax	-885 42	
03	Tax:State	State income tax	-283 33	
04	Tax:Soc Sec	Social security tax	-177 08	
05	Insurance	Medical insurance payment	-32 87	
06	[Steve's 401k]	401(k) contribution	-100 00	
07				

	Ok	Cancel	Adj.Tot.	Splits Total	2,062.97
				Remainder	0.00
				Transaction Total:	2,062.97

If your paycheck varies from one pay period to the next, you can set up the split without amounts, then memorize the transaction (as described in "Memorizing and recalling transactions" on page 87). When you recall the transaction, open the split and fill in the amounts.

5 **Click OK to close the split, and click Record to record the transaction.**

Reviewing the register

You can review a register to find specific transactions at any time by scrolling through it. You can also condense the register to 1-Line display to view more transactions than you can see in 2-Line display.

Scrolling through the register

Use the scroll bar to move through the Register window and locate specific transactions quickly. When you drag the scroll box in the scroll bar, you'll see a date and check number appear and change as you scroll. These represent the date of the transaction, and its check number if appropriate, that will be at the top of the Register window when you release the scroll box.

Drag the scroll box in the scroll bar. The QuickScroll™ box appears and displays dates of specific transactions.

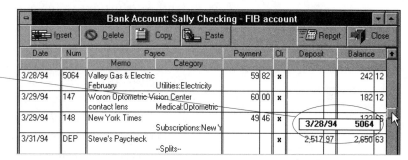

You can also use keyboard shortcuts to move through the register transaction by transaction, or page by page, or to jump directly to the first or last transaction.

Keystroke	Result
Up Arrow	Goes to the same field in the previous transaction.
Down Arrow	Goes to the same field in the next transaction.
Tab	Goes to the next field.
Shift+Tab	Goes to the previous field.
Home	Goes to the beginning of the field.
Ctrl+Home	Goes to the first transaction in the account.
Home+Home	Goes to the first field in the transaction.
End	Goes to the end of the field.
Ctrl+End	Goes to the last transaction in the account.
End+End	Goes to the last field in the transaction.
Ctrl+Page Up	Goes to the first transaction in the current month.
Ctrl+Page Down	Goes to the last transaction in the current month.
Page Up	Scrolls up one screen at a time.
Page Down	Scrolls down one screen at a time.

Condensing the register

When the register opens, it displays each transaction on two lines. You can double the number of transactions you can see at once in a window by clicking the 1-Line Display checkbox.

Use the normal 2-Line display when you're entering transactions. Then, click 1-Line Display to display and review more transactions in the same window.

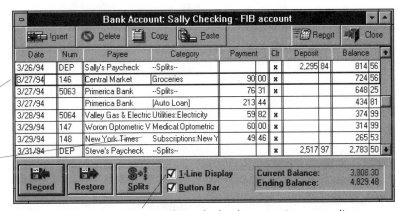

You can also enter a new transaction or edit existing transactions in 1-Line display, but the Memo field is not displayed, so you can't enter (or see) any memos.

Use 1-Line display when you want to scan many transactions quickly. Transactions in the register are condensed onto one line.

The active transaction remains selected when you switch the display.

The Memo field is not displayed, so you can't enter (or see) any memos.

Clear 1-Line Display to display the transactions on two lines

Resizing the register

You can resize, maximize, or minimize a register in the usual Windows ways.

To resize a register to see more transactions, point to any corner of the Register window to change the mouse pointer into a two-headed arrow. Then drag the corner out to make the window larger.

To maximize a register (that is, to enlarge it to the maximum size that can be displayed), click the up button (▲) in the upper right corner of the Register window. To return it to its former size, click the double arrow button (◆).

If you work with several accounts more frequently than others, you might shrink those accounts to icons positioned at the bottom of the Quicken window. Click the down button (▼) in the upper right corner of the Register window. To display the register again, all you have to do is double-click the minimized icon.

Minimize accounts instead of closing them. The register is still open but out of your way while you're working in another account.

Checking

AMX

House

Double-click minimized icons to restore the windows to their normal size.

When you quit from Quicken, if you have more than ten registers open at one time (whether or not they are minimized to icons), Quicken remembers and opens the last ten registers.

Finding a specific transaction

Quicken's Find command locates specific transactions in the Register or Write Checks window. You can find a transaction even if you don't know all the information contained in the transaction.

You might want to find a check with a specific number or payee. In an investment account register, you can search for securities and actions.

Or press Ctrl+F

Type some or all of the text or the exact amount to find here. (The text can be uppercase or lowercase and contain characters or numbers.) You can also use match characters, for example "B?A". See "Using matches to filter transactions" on page 246.

The field names in the Search drop-down list depend on the type of account you have open.

1 **From the Edit menu, choose Find.**

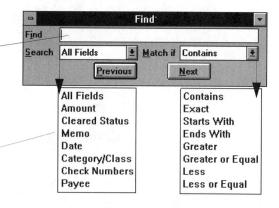

2 **Type the word, phrase, or amount you want to find in the Find box.**

3 **(Optional) Choose a field name from the Search drop-down list.**

Find can search all fields for the text or amount you want to find. But if you know which field contains the text or amount, you can speed up the search by looking only in that field.

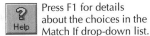 Press F1 for details about the choices in the Match If drop-down list.

4   **(Optional) Choose a search criterion from the Match If drop-down list.**

5   **Start to search.**

Click Previous to search backward for the transaction (toward the beginning of your register) or click Next to search forward for the transaction (toward the end of your register).

Quicken selects the first match it finds, or tells you that it cannot find a match.

Windows tip

Close the window by double-clicking the Control-menu box in the upper left corner of the window.

6   **If you want to continue finding items, continue to click Previous or Next.**

If you are finished with the search, close the Find window.

Searching the entire account

Quicken stops searching when it reaches the last transaction in the register (or the first transaction for backward searches) and asks whether you want to continue the search from the beginning of the register or from the end of the register. Click Yes or No.

Reporting on a payee

At the click of a button, Quicken can show you a quick listing of all transactions in your register with a specific payee. For example, you can view all payments to a car repair station. Or you can check how much your phone bills are costing this year.

1   **Select a transaction containing the payee you want to report on.**

2   **Click Report on the Register button bar.**

Quicken displays the report. The report covers the current year up to today. If you want to see transactions for past years, customize the report date range as described in "Changing report settings" on page 239. Or select a transaction from the earlier year and click Report—the report then covers the start of the selected year up to today.

(If you select a postdated transaction, the report covers transactions up to the end of the year.)

3 **To close the report and return to the register, click Close on the report button bar.**

Select any transaction with the payee to report on, and click Report.

The payee report lists all the transactions in your register containing the selected payee.

To go to a transaction listed in the report, double-click on the transaction. (This is called QuickZoom.)

The report spans the current year up to today. You can change the starting and ending dates or any other aspect of the report by customizing it. See "Changing report settings" on page 239 for details.

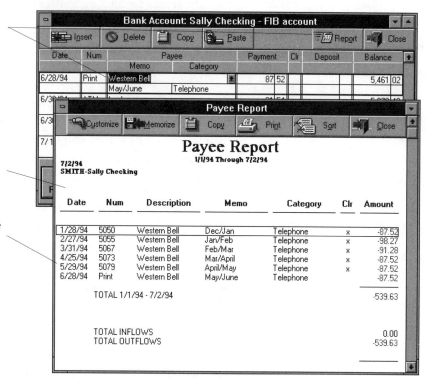

To get a report of the entire register (for all years), select the blank transaction at the end of the register and click Report.

You can also create a list of all transactions, in all your accounts, that use a specific category. To do this, select a category from the Category & Transfer list and click Report, as described in "Reporting on transactions with a specific category" on page 13.

Revising transactions

This section explains how to correct mistakes and void and delete transactions. You can edit any transaction in the register. When you finish recording changes to transactions, Quicken recalculates all subsequent balances if necessary.

Correcting mistakes

Or press Alt+Backspace

To correct a single mistake you make while you are editing a field, choose Undo from the Edit menu.

To restore an entire transaction to the way it was before you started to change it, click the Restore button at the bottom of the window.

When you leave a transaction, Quicken asks you to confirm any changes you made and then saves them. (If you prefer that Quicken save a transaction without asking you, see "Changing other register preferences" on page 42.)

The only item in the register you cannot change by normal editing is the Balance column. If you need to change the balance during reconciliation, you must do so by adding a payment or deposit as an adjustment in the register or by having Quicken adjust the difference for you. (See "Having Quicken adjust for differences" on page 80.)

Changing a reconciled transaction affects future reconciliations. Quicken lets you know if you are about to change a reconciled transaction and asks you to confirm the change.

Your ability to change transactions after they are entered or even reconciled gives you complete control of your finances. However, if you think you need to protect your data from accidental or unauthorized changes, Quicken has two kinds of passwords:

- A File password requires users to enter a password before opening a file. (See "Requiring a password to open a file" on page 344.)
- A Transaction password protects transactions prior to a specified date. (See "Requiring a password to change earlier transactions" on page 346.)

Voiding a transaction

From time to time you might need to void a transaction. By marking a printed or handwritten check as void instead of just deleting it, you'll keep an accurate record of each numbered check.

> **Caution if you use CheckFree:**
> Don't void an electronic payment. If you void an electronic payment, Quicken cannot get the confirmation number it needs to stop the payment or transmit an inquiry about its status to CheckFree. Use Quicken's Stop Payment command instead. (See "Stopping electronic payments" on page 128.)

When Quicken voids a transaction, it:

- Inserts the word *void* before the payee name
- Marks the transaction as reconciled with an **x**, so it doesn't interfere with reconciling
- Removes the dollar amount from the transaction and splits

1 **Select the check or other transaction you want to void.**

If the check was one you wrote by hand and have not yet entered in the check register, enter the date and check number in a new transaction before selecting the transaction.

Or press Ctrl+V **2** **From the Edit menu, choose Void Transaction.**

3 **Click Record to record the transaction.**

Deleting a transaction

Once you delete a transaction and confirm the deletion, Quicken can't recover it. Be sure you really want to delete a transaction before doing so. To protect previous transactions from accidental change or deletion, assign a Transaction password to them. (See "Setting up passwords" on page 344.)

1 **Select the transaction you want to delete.**

Or press Ctrl+D **2** **From the Edit menu, choose Delete Transaction, or click the Delete button on the button bar.**

Quicken asks "Delete the Current Transaction?"

3 **Click Yes to delete the transaction.**

Quicken removes the transaction from the register and recalculates all subsequent balances.

Printing the register

You can print all or some of the transactions in a register. You can specify a time period of a day, a week, a month, a year, or more so you will have a printed record of the period of time covered.

The register is printed using the same fonts as for printed reports. To change the fonts, see "Setting up your printer" on page 264.

It makes no difference to the printout whether the register is currently in 1-Line or 2-Line display.

1   **Open the register you want to print.**

Or press Ctrl+P, or click the Print icon on the iconbar.

2   **From the File menu, choose Print Register.**

3   **Enter information in the first window and click Print.**

Select this option to abbreviate each transaction to fit on one line. Quicken normally prints three lines per transaction.

Select this option to display all the lines in a split transaction.

Select this option to print in check number order instead of chronological order. When checks are sorted by number, Quicken does not print a running balance. The Balance column on your printout will be blank.

(Optional) Change the range of dates to print. The preset range is for the year to date. You can use the + or - key to increase or decrease the date in any Quicken date field.

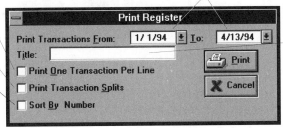

(Optional) Enter a title for the register in the Title box.

4   **Enter information in the second window and click Print.**

Select the device you want to print to:

Your printer.

A file on disk that you can read into your word processor or other program.

A tab-delimited disk file that can be read by spreadsheets.

A comma-delimited disk file that you can read into Lotus 1-2-3 and other spreadsheets.

Your screen, to see a preview of how the printout will look on paper.

Select this if you have a color printer and want negative amounts to print in red.

Select draft mode for faster but less atttractive printing.

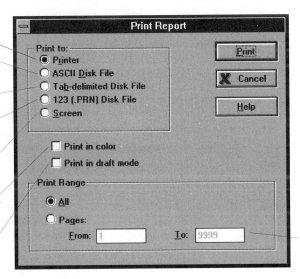

Enter a page range if you don't want to print all pages.

Changing the register colors and font

Quicken offers a wide range of colors and fonts for displaying the registers. You can change them to your liking.

Changing the colors

1 **From the Edit menu, choose Preferences.**

2 **Click the Colors icon.**

3 **Choose the color you want for each type of Quicken account.**

Each of Quicken's six types of accounts can be displayed in a different color.

Click an account type and then click a color for that account type.

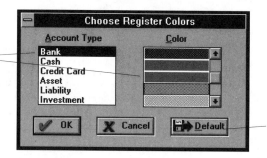

(If your registers never show any color, go to the General Preferences window as described on page 42 and click the Color Shading in Register checkbox.)

To return *all* registers to Quicken's preset color settings, click Default.

4 **Click OK.**

Changing the font

When you choose a different font, you'll see all registers and lists (for example, the Category & Transfer list) displayed in that font.

1 **From the Edit menu, choose Preferences.**

2 **Click the Fonts icon.**

3 **Choose the font you want for all Quicken registers, and click OK.**

All Quicken registers and lists are displayed in the same font.

Select a font and a type size.

You can see an example of the selected font.

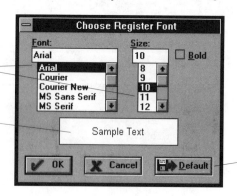

To return to Quicken's preset font setting, click Default.

Changing the way QuickFill works

Quicken's automatic entry features together are called "QuickFill." They work in the Register, Write Checks, and Splits windows. When you first install Quicken, all of the QuickFill features except Automatic Memorization of New Transactions are turned on*, but you can turn QuickFill features on or off to work the way you like.

1   From the Edit menu, choose Preferences.

2   Click the QuickFill icon.

This illustration shows the preferences that Quicken selects at installation.*

To turn on a preference, select a checkbox by clicking in it.

To turn off a preference, clear the checkbox by clicking in it.

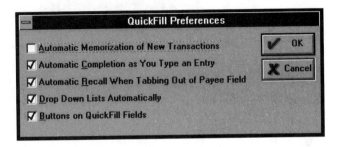

3   Click the preferences you want to change, and then click OK.

QuickFill preferences	Quicken does this if the preference is turned on
Automatic Memorization Of New Transactions	Memorizes each new transaction you enter for a new payee (except investment transactions) and adds it to the Memorized Transaction list (see page 89). Note that there is no need to turn this preference on simply to speed up transaction entry, because QuickFill automatically recalls previously entered transactions.
Automatic Completion As You Type An Entry	Fills in each field in a transaction as you type it. Works with check number (Num field in register), payee, category, subcategory, class, subclass, security names, investment action, and transfer account names.
Automatic Recall When Tabbing Out Of Payee Field	Recalls a memorized or previously entered transaction when you press Tab to leave the Payee field.
Drop Down Lists Automatically	Opens the drop-down list when you place the insertion point in a field. (If you like to see the drop-down list sometimes, but find it gets in your way when it appears in every transaction, try using "Buttons On QuickFill Fields" instead.)
Buttons On QuickFill Fields	Places buttons beside fields that QuickFill can be used in. When you click the button, the drop-down list appears.

---

*   If you have upgraded from a previous version of Quicken, the Drop Down Lists Automatically preference may also be turned off, but you can turn it on if you wish.

Changing other register preferences

You can change many of Quicken's settings from the General Preferences window.

1   **From the Edit menu, choose Preferences.**

2   **Click the General icon.**

This illustration shows the settings that are selected when Quicken is installed.

If a checkbox is selected, the preference is turned on.

If a checkbox is cleared, the preference is turned off.

Click in a checkbox to select or clear it.

🍁 **Canadian users:** click DD/MM/YY to change the date format to the usual Canadian style (day/month/year)

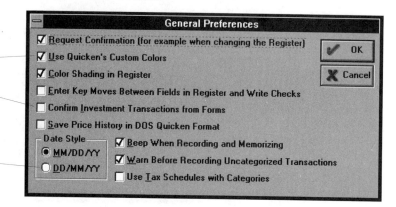

3   **Click the preferences you want to change, and then click OK.**

General preferences	Quicken does this when the preference is selected
Request Confirmation (for example, when changing the register)	Requires you to confirm any changes made to a transaction or list before going to a new transaction or a new window.
Use Quicken's Custom Colors	Overrides the background set up in your Windows Control Panel and displays Quicken's windows with a gray background to give them a three-dimensional effect. To see the new setting take effect, quit Quicken and restart it.
Color Shading in Register	Displays the Register window with color shading in each transaction. A different color is used for each account type. To change the colors, go to the Choose Register Colors window as described on page 40.
Enter Key Moves Between Fields in Register and Write Checks	Uses the Enter key as well as the Tab key to move between fields in any account register and the Write Checks window. You'll probably want to turn this option on if you are accustomed to using DOS Quicken.
Confirm Investment Transactions from Forms	(Investment registers only) When you fill in an investment form, Quicken asks you to confirm your entries before leaving the form. See page 178 for more information.
Save Price History in DOS Quicken Format	(Investments) Allows you to read your Quicken for Windows security price data in DOS Quicken. Select this option only if you update security prices in the same file from both DOS Quicken and Quicken for Windows. See page 201 for details.
Date Style	Displays dates in a MM/DD/YY (month/day/year) format. If you prefer the Canadian and European date style, select DD/MM/YY.
Beep When Recording and Memorizing	Beeps after recording, deleting, or memorizing a transaction, or memorizing a report.
Warn Before Recording Uncategorized Transactions	Prompts you to enter a category for the transaction that you are recording if you have not already entered one. This helps you remember to categorize all your transactions for complete information in your reports, graphs, and budgets.
Use Tax Schedules with Categories	Adds a Form field to the Set Up Category window to remind you to select a tax schedule form for categories you set up or edit.

Writing checks

Having Quicken prepare your checks is a great convenience. If you print checks, you avoid the duplicate work of writing checks and then recording them in Quicken. You will save hours of valuable time, avoid clerical errors, and give your checks a very professional look.

For information about how to order different kinds of Intuit checks, consult the check catalog in your Quicken package or see Appendix B, *Ordering supplies and other Intuit products*, beginning on page 363.

Filling out a check

Use the Write Checks window to enter checks that you plan to print with Quicken. Enter other transactions, such as checks that you've already written by hand, deposits, or bank fees in the check register. When you record a check in the Write Checks window, Quicken adds it automatically to the check register.

You can write checks in any Quicken bank account: checking, money market, or savings. You can write checks as bills arrive or at regular intervals: weekly, biweekly, or monthly.

You can order the check forms from Intuit. Intuit checks are accepted everywhere. See Appendix B, *Ordering supplies and other Intuit products,* beginning on page 363. Or, see the catalog included with your Quicken package.

Or press Ctrl+W, or click the Check icon on the iconbar.

1 **From the Activities menu, choose Write Checks.**

Quicken displays the Write Checks window.

Enter the payee name here (the person or organization to whom you are writing the check).

If you plan to mail the check in an Intuit window envelope, enter the payee name and mailing address. Include the payee's name, address, city, state, and zip code. You can use up to five lines (press Enter to start a new line). Press the Quote key (') to copy the payee name to the first address line.

If you want to send a message to the payee or if you want to provide additional information on the check for your own records, enter it as a memo on the check, up to 31 characters long.

The contents of the Memo line may be visible when you mail the check in an Intuit window envelope. If you need to ensure that the information is not visible from the envelope, you can display a Message box and enter information here instead of the Memo line. See "Changing check preferences" on page 48.

Enter the category, class, or transfer information in the Category field. Click Splits to split a check just as you split transactions in the register. (See page 28.)

Select the bank account from which the check is being written.

When you enter the dollar amount on the $ Amount line, Quicken automatically spells out the amount on the next line.

The date appears on the check when you print it. To change the date, enter your changes over the date shown.

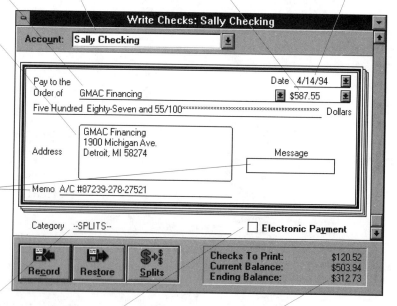

Quicken displays this option if you have set up this checking account for sending electronic payments. See "Setting up an account for electronic payments" on page 116.

The Ending Balance is the balance in the account based on all entered transactions, including any postdated transactions.

When you fill out a check, you can use all the same QuickFill features for easy entry that you can in the register. Quicken fills in the details for you if it recognizes the payee from an earlier transaction. You can use the pop-up calendar to modify the date and the pop-up field calculator to calculate the amount.

2   **Select the bank account from which payment is being made.**

3   **(Optional) Change the selected date.**

Windows tip

Enter text in a field by first clicking the insertion point in the field or by pressing Tab to place the insertion point in the field. Then enter the text.

4   **Enter the payee name as you want it to appear on the check.**

5   **Enter the amount of the check on the $ Amount line.**

When you tab from the $ Amount line, Quicken automatically spells out the amount of the check on the next line.

6   **If you plan to mail the check in an Intuit window envelope, enter the payee name and mailing address in the Address box.**

7   **(Optional) Enter a note on the Memo line or in the Message box.**

See "Changing check preferences" on page 48 to display the Message box.

8   **Enter a category on the Category line.**

Enter categories, splits, or transfers the same way that you do in the check register. If you use Intuit voucher checks, Quicken prints up to 16 lines of split information on the perforated voucher attachment. If you write a single check that covers 20 invoices, Quicken prints the first 16 invoice numbers and the amount to be applied to each invoice on the voucher attachment.

9   **If you plan to pay the check electronically with CheckFree, select the Electronic Payment checkbox.**

See "Entering electronic payments" on page 121.

10   **When you have finished writing the check, click Record to save it as a permanent part of your records.**

When you record a check, Quicken enters the information on the check into your register.

When you are ready to print the checks you have filled out, turn to Chapter 5, *Printing checks*, beginning on page 49.

The Write Checks window does not display a check number. Intuit checks are prenumbered because most banks require prenumbered checks for stop payment purposes. Quicken inserts the correct check number in the check register when it prints the check. Until the checks print, Quicken displays Print in the Num field of the check register.

Reviewing checks you've written

Once you've written and recorded your checks, you can review them before printing either by scrolling through the Write Checks window or by reviewing them in the register. After you've printed a check, you cannot review it in the Write Checks window; you must review it in the register instead.

You can add to, change, delete, or void any check in the Write Checks window exactly the same way you edit transactions in the register. When you finish changing a transaction, Quicken recalculates all subsequent balances if necessary.

Or press Ctrl+R

1 **From the Activities menu, choose Use Register.**

Or, from the Account list, select the account and click Use.

The Register window displays checks and other transactions by date, and it also shows the information written on the checks except for the Address and Message fields. Checks waiting to be printed appear in the register with Print in the Num field. After you print the check, Quicken replaces Print with the actual check number.

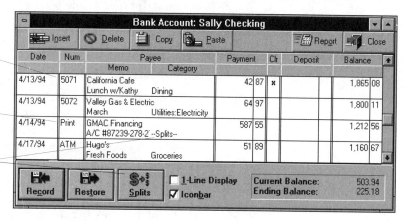

After you print a check, Quicken inserts the check number in the Num field.

Unprinted checks have Print in the Num field.

To view or edit splits (if any), select a split transaction and click the Splits button at the bottom of the register.

Windows tip
A scroll bar appears along the right side of the Register window. To scroll the register, click the Up and Down Arrows in the scroll bar.

2 **Scroll through the register.**

You can also drag the scroll box to search by date, or use the Find command to locate the transaction you want. (See "Finding a specific transaction" on page 34.)

3 **As you review checks in the check register, you can delete or change them any way you like.**

Changes you make to an unprinted check will appear on the printed check. For more information about changing transactions in the register, see "Revising transactions" on page 37.

Or press Ctrl+W

4 **Click on the Write Checks window to return to it.**

Writing postdated checks

One way of scheduling checks for future payment is to postdate them. This method helps you forecast how much money you need in the coming weeks. Later, when you print checks, you can have Quicken print checks dated through a specific date. Except for changing the date, writing postdated checks is the same as writing regular checks with Quicken. (Caution: don't mail your postdated checks!)

Also consider Quicken's scheduled transactions feature
Quicken also offers a comprehensive scheduling and forecasting feature that is easy to use through Quicken's Financial Calendar. Take a look at Chapter 8, *Scheduling with the Quicken Financial Calendar,* beginning on page 93.

---

1 **In the Write Checks window, change the current date to the date in the future when you want to print the check.**

2 **Complete the check as described on page 44.**

3 **Click Record to record the check.**

When you have postdated checks in your account, Quicken calculates a Current Balance and Ending Balance and displays them both at the bottom of the Write Checks window.

If this is a check you are printing, the Checks To Print amount shows the total amount of checks you have written, but not printed yet.

If this is a check you are sending to CheckFree, the field is labeled "Checks to Xmit" and it shows the total amount of checks you have written, but not yet transmitted.

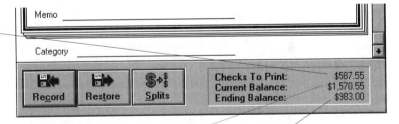

The Current Balance amount shows the balance in your account before any postdated transactions.

The Ending Balance amount shows the balance after all postdated transactions.

Quicken's Billminder and Reminder features can remind you to print postdated checks and other scheduled transactions up to 30 days before their scheduled dates. These reminders help you pay bills on time if you don't use Quicken every day. See "Using Billminder and the Quicken Reminder" on page 109.

Changing check preferences

You can change many of Quicken's settings through options in the Preferences window.

1   From the Edit menu, choose Preferences.

2   In the Preferences window, click Checks.

This illustration shows the settings that are selected when Quicken is installed.

If a button is filled in, the preference is turned on. Click another button to change the option.

If a checkbox is selected, the preference is turned on. If a checkbox is cleared, the preference is turned off. Click in a checkbox to select or clear it.

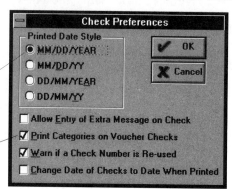

3   Click the preferences you want to change, then click OK.

Check preferences	Quicken does this when the preference is selected
Printed Date Style	Prints dates in whichever date format you select.
Allow Entry of Extra Message on Check	Adds an extra Message box on the check displayed in the Write Checks window. The message you enter in this box is not visible when you mail the check in an Intuit window envelope, so you can use it for confidential information such as a credit card number. See the illustration below. (If you use the Memo line, it may be possible to see the memo through the address opening in the envelope.) If you turn off the display of this Message box, Quicken saves any information that you may have entered into this box previously in the Write Checks window. Turn on the display of the message box to display the text again.
Print Categories on Voucher Checks	Prints categories from a split transaction on the perforated attachment to voucher checks. (See "Splitting transactions" on page 28 for more information.)
Warn if a Check Number is Re-used	Displays a warning message if you enter a check number that is already entered in the register.
Change Date of Checks to Date When Printed	Changes the date of your checks to the current date when you print them instead of the date you entered when you wrote them.

If you select the option for an extra message line, the Message box appears onscreen to the right of the Address box. You can enter up to 24 characters into the box.

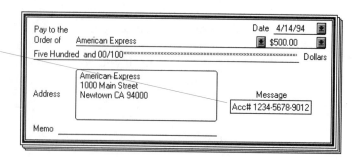

Printing checks

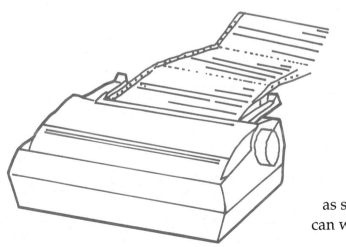

When you print checks with Quicken, you use special personalized checks from Intuit, designed to work with Quicken.

Intuit makes checks for continuous-feed printers and page-oriented printers.

You can print a batch of checks as soon as you've written them, or you can wait and print them at another time.

About printing checks

You can print checks as soon as you've written them, or you can wait and print them at another time. For example, you can enter checks in the Write Checks window at various times throughout the month, but wait and print them only once or twice each month. (If you haven't entered the check details yet, first read Chapter 4, *Writing checks*, beginning on page 43.)

To reprint checks that you have already printed, see "Reprinting checks" on page 66. You can also set your own preferences for how checks are displayed onscreen and printed. See "Changing check preferences" on page 48.

When you order personalized Intuit checks, Intuit prints your name, address, account number, bank name, check numbers, and all the information required by financial institutions on your checks. Intuit guarantees their acceptance everywhere your checks are accepted now.

Intuit checks are economical and come in a variety of styles for Windows-compatible printers. All Intuit checks fit one of the two sizes of Intuit double-window envelopes. Both your address and the payee's address appear in the windows, eliminating the need to address envelopes. See Appendix A, *Ordering supplies and other Intuit products*, beginning on page 363.

Printing checks on continuous-feed printers

This section explains how to print checks on continuous-feed (also known as tractor-feed or dot matrix) printers. If you have a laser, inkjet, postscript, or other *page-oriented* printer (including a dot matrix printer that has a paper tray), skip to page 59.

The basic steps to printing checks are:

◆ **Set up your check printer.**
  See "Setting up continuous-feed printers" on page 51.

◆ **Load the checks in your continuous-feed printer just as you would any printer paper.**

◆ **If this is the first time you've printed an Intuit check, print a sample check to make sure the alignment is correct.**

◆ **Print your checks.**
  See "Printing checks from your account" on page 56.

◆ **Examine the checks to make sure they've all printed correctly.**

Setting up continuous-feed printers

Before you print any checks from a Quicken account, you need to select the continuous-feed printer you're going to use to print the checks, and set up the form height for the style of checks you're using.

1   **From the File menu, choose Printer Setup and then choose Check Printer Setup.**

Click the underlined Down Arrow to display the Printer drop-down list.

Quicken can automatically detect whether your printer is continuous-feed or page-oriented.

There are three types of Intuit check styles:
• Standard checks
• Voucher checks
• Wallet checks.

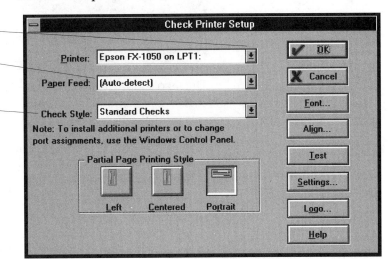

2   **Select the printer you want to use from the Printer drop-down list.**

If the printer you want to use is not listed, use the Windows Control Panel to install the printer driver for your printer. See your *Microsoft Windows User's Guide* for instructions on installing a printer.

3   **Select Auto-detect in the Paper Feed drop-down list.**

Quicken automatically detects whether your printer is continuous-feed or page-oriented. However, you can force Quicken to use one or the other by selecting that option in the Paper Feed drop-down list.

4   **Select the style of check you will be printing in the Check Style drop-down list.**

5   **(Optional) Click Font to select a different font type, style, or size for the printed type on your checks and click OK.**

6   **(Optional) Click Settings to change the paper source and click OK.**

See page 67 for more details of the settings you can choose.

7   **(Optional) Click Logo to include artwork on your printed checks.**

You can include your own logo on your checks by accessing artwork from an art file stored on disk. The artwork must be a bitmap (.BMP) file. You can create bitmaps in applications such as Paintbrush.

If you have a noncolor printer, create the artwork in black and white for best results.

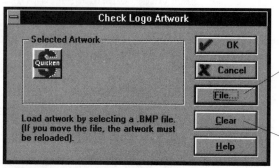

Click File to access a piece of artwork from a file. (Be careful not to change the artwork's disk location without telling Quicken.)

Click Clear to remove artwork from the Selected Artwork box.

The logo is printed in the upper left corner of each check. (You can choose whether or not to include the logo on the check each time you print checks.)

Now you are ready to print a sample check and make sure the checks are properly aligned in the printer before you print the rest of the checks. Your Quicken package includes sample checks for continuous-feed printers, and Quicken helps you line up the checks correctly in your printer.

8 **If you haven't already inserted the checks in your printer, insert them as you would any continuous-feed printer paper.**

Preventing wasted checks

You may need to use Intuit Forms Leaders to prevent wasted checks if your continuous-feed printer has a tractor head above the print head and you cannot print on the first check. See "Phone numbers" on page 372 for the Intuit Customer Service phone number to order Forms Leaders.

---

9 **Make sure your printer is turned on and online.**

10 **Click Test to print a sample check.**

Quicken prints a sample check on the printer you selected.

If you see a message that your check printer is not set up for the form size Quicken requires, click OK. You need to change your printer setup before printing any other checks. See "Changing the settings for your printer driver" on page 67.

11 **Without moving the check in the printer, look at the sample check.**

Check the horizontal alignment. Does the text appear too far to the left or right? Check the vertical alignment. If the check is aligned correctly, the type rests just above the lines on the check.

● If the sample check printed correctly, you have completed the setup. Click OK in the Check Printer Setup window to save your setup, and see "Printing checks from your account" on page 56.

OR

● If the sample check *did not* print correctly, see "Correcting the alignment of your checks" next.

Correcting the alignment of your checks

If your checks did not print correctly, you can use the Check Printer Alignment window to adjust the alignment. You can get to this window either while setting up your check printer or while printing checks.

1 **Continuous-feed printers: First make any side-to-side positioning adjustments by hand, moving the paper clamps on the printer as necessary.**

The following steps can make fine horizontal adjustments as well as vertical adjustments, but you should first make an approximate horizontal adjustment by hand.

2 **At either the Check Printer Setup window or the Print Checks window, click Align.**

The Check Printer Alignment window shows how text should be aligned on your check.

If you move the arrow cursor over the check illustrated in this window, an alignment cursor appears. The alignment cursor allows you to move the text on the screen to show Quicken how the text on your checks is actually aligned.

Your printed check may not look exactly like the check illustrated here, but you can still show Quicken how the text is actually aligned by using the name of the payee and the "Pay to the Order of" line as your guide.

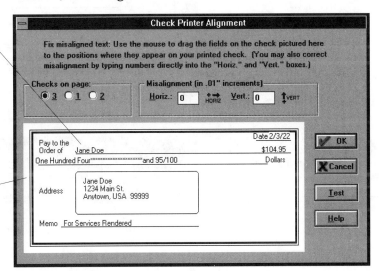

This window shows how text *should be aligned* on your check. You use the alignment cursor to show Quicken how text is *actually aligned* on your check. Quicken takes the alignment you indicate and transposes it into the correct alignment on the next sample check you print.

3   Move the arrow cursor over the check in the Check Printer Alignment window to see the alignment cursor.

The alignment cursor when it is over the check.

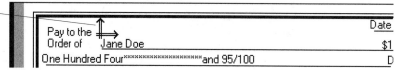

4   Show Quicken how your check is aligned incorrectly.

Using the sample check as your guide, use the text and check onscreen. There are two ways to show Quicken how your check is aligned:

- Hold down the left mouse button and move the text around until it looks the same as your printed sample check.

Use the alignment cursor to move the text in the check on the screen. In this example, the payee printed too far to the right and too low on the printed check.

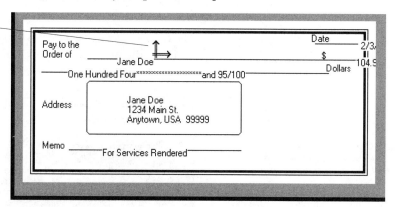

OR

- Enter numbers in the Horiz box or Vert box .

This method works well if the printing on the check needs just a small nudge to correct the horizontal or vertical alignment of the printed text.

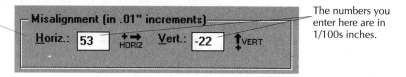

The numbers you enter here are in 1/100s inches.

Use the values from the following table to determine what to enter.

Problem	Solution
The text prints too high.	Enter a positive number in the Vertical field. For example, if the text is printing 1/4" too high, type **25** in the Vertical field to move the text down by 25/100".
The text prints too low.	Enter a negative number in the Vertical field. For example, if the text is printing 1/4" too low, type **-25** in the Vertical field to move the text up by 25/100".
The text prints too far to the left.	Enter a negative number in the Horizontal field. For example, if the text is printing 1/4" too far to the left, type **-25** in the Horizontal field to move the text 25/100" to the right.
The text prints too far to the right.	Enter a positive number in the Horizontal field. For example, if the text is printing 1/4" too far to the right, type **25** in the Horizontal field to move the text 25/100" to the left.

5   **Click Test to print another sample check with the new settings.**

Quicken aligns the check vertically or horizontally in the printer before printing the next check.

6   **Look at the second sample check.**

The alignment of the second check should be almost perfect.

- If the second check printed correctly, continue to the next step.

- If the text is misaligned by a noticeable amount, repeat the steps above until a sample check prints correctly. If the text is misaligned by a tiny amount, use the Horizontal or Vertical boxes to nudge the alignment very slightly.

7   **If you change check styles often, note the correct alignment numbers for future positioning.**

If you often alternate the style of checks you print (for example, sometimes you print voucher checks for your small business and sometimes you print standard or wallet checks for your personal finances), make a note of the numbers in the horizontal and vertical boxes in the Check Printing Alignment window.

Page-oriented printers only: Quicken saves the horizontal and vertical numbers according to the numbers of checks on a page. If you use partial pages of wallet or standard checks, you may have to adjust the alignment for each of the three options.

If you want to print a partial page of checks, you may need to change the horizontal and vertical numbers for each of these options.

Once you have determined the correct alignment for each of these conditions, Quicken remembers the correct settings until you use a different check style or select a different printer to print checks.

8 **Continuous-feed printers only: Note the correct position of the check in the printer.**

Visually line up part of your printer, such as the sprocket cover or print head, with one of the position numbers at the edge of the check. Make a note of this spot on the printer. From now on, use this spot on the printer as an alignment cue to position your checks visually each time you insert them in your printer, so you won't have to test your check alignment again by printing more sample checks.

9 **Click OK (twice) to save your check printer setup.**

You are now ready to print your checks.

Printing checks from your account

1 **If you haven't already inserted the checks in your printer, insert them as you would any continuous-feed computer paper.**

2 **Make sure your printer is turned on and is online.**

3 **Open the account you want to print checks from.**

Quicken displays a checkmark in the Chks column when you have checks to print in an account.

To open an account, select it and click Use.

4 **From the File menu, choose Print Checks.**

Enter here the number shown on the first check positioned in the printer.

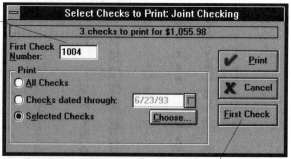

If you click the First Check button, Quicken prints only the first check in the series of checks you intend to print. You could print a First Check each time you begin printing checks. Use this option instead of Test when you're fairly sure that everything is aligned correctly and ready to print. That way, you can sign and use the printed check.

5   If the number in the First Check Number box is not the same as the number of the first check in your printer, enter the number of the first check in your printer.

6   Select the checks you want to print from the Print box:

- Click All Checks to print all unprinted checks, including postdated checks.

- Click Checks Dated Through to change the date range of the checks to be printed; usually, the date is the current date. Specify a date later than today to print postdated checks.

- Click Selected Checks and then click Choose to print only specified checks.

7   If you chose Selected Checks, mark each check you want to print, and then click OK.

Quicken lists in chronological order all the checks you've written and not yet printed.

To mark a check to be printed, select that check and press the spacebar, or click Mark, or double-click the transaction. The word "Print" appears in the column at the far right when you've selected a check to be printed. If you accidentally mark a check that you do not want to print, mark the check again.

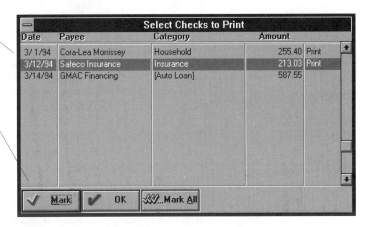

8   Click Print in the Select Checks to Print window.

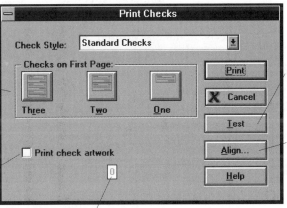

ClickTest to print a sample check so that you can make sure the checks are properly aligned.

If you need to print less than a full page of three checks, see "Printing a partial first page of checks" on page 64.

If your printed checks need alignment in the printer, click Align and see "Correcting the alignment of your checks" on page 53.

To include your logo artwork on the printed checks, select this checkbox. (Standard and voucher checks only.)

Voucher checks only: If you would like to print more than one copy of each voucher check, enter the required number of additional copies here.

9 **Make sure the correct check style is selected in the Check Style drop-down list.**

Intuit checks come in three styles: standard, voucher, and wallet.

10 **Click Print to print your checks.**

If you see a message that your check printer is not set up for the form size Quicken requires, click OK to print your checks using the preset printer font (usually Courier). This message means that your printer is not capable of printing the font you chose on the type of checks you are using.

11 **Did your checks print OK?**

If any of the checks did not print correctly, enter the check number of the first incorrectly printed check and then click OK.

If the checks printed correctly, click OK. Your check printing is finished!

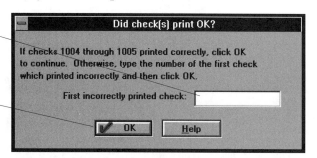

Did check(s) print OK?

If checks 1004 through 1005 printed correctly, click OK to continue. Otherwise, type the number of the first check which printed incorrectly and then click OK.

First incorrectly printed check: [   ]

[✓ OK]   [Help]

If the checks printed correctly, click OK. You are finished printing.

OR

If any of the checks did not print correctly, type the number of the first check that didn't print correctly and click OK. Quicken makes them available for printing again. Examine your printer to see if the checks jammed or the printer ran out of checks. If the text on the checks in your printer is not aligned correctly, you may need to adjust the check printing settings. See "Correcting the alignment of your checks" on page 53.

If only the first check of a series of checks did not print properly, and the rest printed properly, do not enter a number but click OK. Then reprint the check that didn't print properly—see "Reprinting checks" on page 66.

Printing checks on page-oriented printers

This section explains how to print checks on a laser, inkjet, postscript, or other *page-oriented* printer (including a dot matrix printer that has a paper tray). If you have a continuous-feed (also known as tractor-feed or dot matrix) printer, turn to page 50.

The basic steps to printing checks are:

◆ **Set up your check printer.**
See "Setting up page-oriented printers" on this page.

◆ **Load the checks in your page-oriented printer just as you would any letterhead paper.**
Refer to the manual that came with your printer for information on using letterhead with your printer. You need to know how to orient checks when you insert them in your printer. If your first page of checks is partial (has only one or two checks left on it), the instructions are a little different.

◆ **If this is the first time you've printed an Intuit check, print a sample check to make sure the alignment is correct.**

◆ **Print your checks.**
See "Printing checks from your account" on page 62.

◆ **Examine the checks to make sure they've all printed correctly.**

Setting up page-oriented printers

Before you print any checks from a Quicken account, you need to select the page-oriented printer you're going to use to print checks.

1 From the File menu, choose Printer Setup and then choose Check Printer Setup.

Click the underlined Down Arrow to display the Printer drop-down list.

Quicken can automatically detect whether your printer is continuous-feed or page-oriented.

There are three types of Intuit check styles:
• Standard checks
• Voucher checks
• Wallet checks.

These icons represent three possible orientations for when you need to print a partial page of checks. See "Printing a partial first page of checks" on page 64.

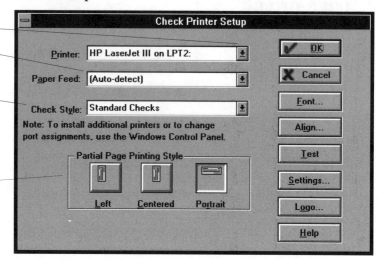

2 Select the printer you want to use from the Printer drop-down list.

If the printer you want to use is not listed, use the Windows Control Panel to install the print driver for your printer. See your *Microsoft Windows User's Guide* for instructions on installing a printer.

3 Select Auto-detect in the Paper Feed drop-down list.

Quicken automatically detects whether your printer is continuous-feed or page-oriented. (If you want, you can force Quicken to use one or the other by selecting it from the Paper Feed drop-down list.)

4 Select the style of check you will be printing in the Check Style drop-down list.

5 (Optional) Click Font to select a different font type, style, or size for the printing on your checks and click OK.

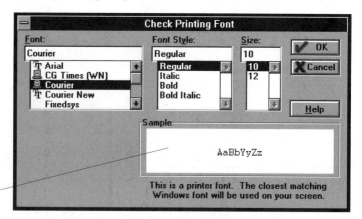

The Sample box shows the currently selected font style and size.

6 **(Optional) Click Settings to change the paper source and click OK.**

See page 67 for more details of the settings you can choose.

7 **(Optional) Click Logo to include artwork on your printed checks.**

The Check Logo Artwork window is illustrated on page 52.

You can include your own logo on your checks by specifying an art file stored on disk. The artwork must be a bitmap (.BMP) file. You can create bitmaps in applications such as Paintbrush. The logo is printed in the upper left corner of each check. (You can choose whether or not to include the logo on the check each time you print checks.)

Now you are ready to print a sample check and make sure the checks are properly aligned in the printer before you print the rest of the checks. Your Quicken package includes sample checks for continuous-feed printers. To practice printing with them in your page-oriented printer, separate the checks into pages of three checks each. Completely remove the tractor strips at the sides from each page of three checks.

8 **If you haven't already inserted the checks in your printer, insert one full page of three checks in the paper tray the same way you would insert letterhead.**

9 **Make sure your printer is turned on and is online.**

10 **Click Test to print a sample check.**

Quicken prints a sample check.

If you see a message that your check printer is not set up for the form size Quicken requires, click OK. You need to change your printer setup before printing any other checks. See "Changing the settings for your printer driver" on page 67.

11 **Look at the sample check.**

Check the horizontal alignment. Does the text appear too far to the left or right? Check the vertical alignment. If the check is aligned correctly, the type rests just above the lines on the check.

• If the sample check printed correctly, you have completed the setup. Click OK in the Check Printer Setup window to save your setup, and see "Printing checks from your account" next.

OR

• If the sample check *did not* print correctly, go to "Correcting the alignment of your checks" on page 53 before printing checks.

Saving sample check stock

If you have trouble getting your checks to print at first, don't continue to use the sample checks that came with Quicken. Instead, print sample checks on blank paper. After printing a sample check, place the paper on top of the sample checks and hold them both up to the light to see if the text printed correctly.

Printing checks from your account

1   If you haven't already inserted the checks in your printer, insert one full page of checks in the paper tray the same way you would insert letterhead.

If you need to print a partial first page of checks instead of a full page, see "Printing a partial first page of checks" on page 64.

A partial page means that the last time you printed standard or wallet checks, you may have printed only one or two checks instead of all three checks on the final page, and now you are starting to print with that leftover page. (Voucher checks only come one to a page.)

2   Make sure your printer is turned on and online.

3   Open the account you want to print checks from.

Quicken displays a checkmark in the Chks column when you have checks to print in an account.

To open an account, select it and click Use.

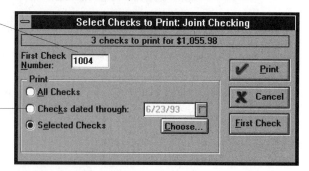

4   From the File menu, choose Print Checks.

This number should be the same as the number on the first check in the printer.

Choose this option to select checks in a different date range to be printed.

5   Make sure the number in the First Check Number box is the same as the number of the first check in your printer. Enter the correct number if necessary.

6 **Select the checks you want to print from the Print box:**

- Click All Checks to print all unprinted checks, including postdated checks.

- Click Checks Dated Through to change the date range of the checks to be printed; usually, the date is the current date. Specify a date later than today to print postdated checks.

- Click Selected Checks and then click Choose to print only specified checks.

7 **If you chose Selected Checks, mark each check you want to print, and then click OK.**

Quicken lists in chronological order all the checks you've written and not yet printed.

To mark a check to be printed, select that check and press the spacebar, or click Mark, or double-click the transaction. The word "Print" appears in the column at the far right when you've selected a check to be printed.

If you accidentally mark a check that you do not want to print, mark the check again.

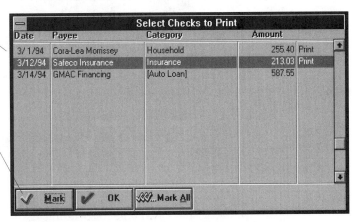

8 **Click Print in the Select Checks to Print window to print your checks.**

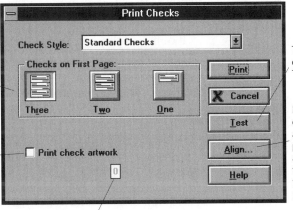

If you need to print less than a full page of three checks, see "Printing a partial first page of checks" on page 64.

To include your logo artwork on the printed checks, select this checkbox. (Standard and voucher checks only.) You must have already specified the artwork while setting up, as described earlier in this chapter.

To print a sample check first, click Test.

If your printed checks need alignment in the printer, click Align and see "Correcting the alignment of your checks" on page 53.

Voucher checks only: If you would like to print more than one copy of each voucher check, enter the required number of additional copies here.

9 **Make sure the correct check style is selected in the Check Style drop-down list.**

Intuit checks come in three styles: standard, voucher, and wallet.

10 **Show Quicken how many checks are on the first page of checks you are inserting into the printer.**

Three (a full page) is the usual setting. If your first page has only one or two of the original three checks left on it, see page 64 for information about printing a partial first page of checks. If you are printing on voucher checks, you don't need to select an icon.

11 **Click Print to print your checks.**

12 **Let Quicken know if your checks printed correctly or not.**

If any of the checks did not print correctly, enter the check number of the first incorrectly printed check and then click OK.

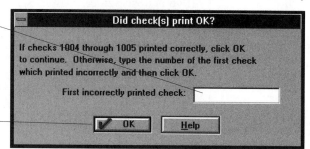

If the checks printed correctly, click OK.

If the checks printed correctly, click OK. You are finished printing.

OR

If any of the checks did not print correctly, type the number of the first check that didn't print correctly and click OK. Quicken makes them available for printing again. Examine your printer to see if the checks jammed or the printer ran out of checks. If the text on the checks in your printer is not aligned correctly, you may need to adjust the check printing settings. See "Correcting the alignment of your checks" on page 53.

If only one check in the middle of a series of checks did not print properly, and the rest printed properly, do not enter a number but click OK. Then reprint the check that didn't print properly—see "Reprinting checks" on page 66.

Printing a partial first page of checks

If you use standard or wallet checks in your page-oriented printer, you'll sometimes find that a *partial page* of one or two blank checks remains after you have finished printing. You can easily use that partial first page the next time you print checks.

You can print partial pages of standard or wallet checks, but not voucher checks, which come one to a page only.

1 **Before you start printing, turn on your printer, but don't load your checks yet.**

2   **From the File menu, choose Printer Setup and then choose Check Printer Setup.**

3   **Select one of the Partial Page Printing Style icons to show Quicken how you insert envelopes (and partial pages of checks) into your printer and click OK.**

You feed partial pages of checks into your printer the same way you feed envelopes. Consult your printer manual to find out which of these three basic positions the printer manufacturer recommends for loading envelopes in the envelope feeder or cassette.

Before you insert your checks into the envelope feeder you need to know:

- The type of envelope feeder your printer has (Left, Centered, or Portrait)

- If you should insert the check face up or face down

- If you should insert the left edge, right edge, top, or bottom of the check into the printer first.

The direction of the arrow is toward the printer.

Positioned on the left side of the envelope feeder, with the right or the left edge of the check feeding into the printer.

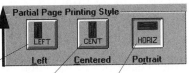

Centered in the envelope feeder, with the right or the left edge of the check feeding into the printer.

Centered in the envelope feeder, with the top or the bottom edge of the check feeding into the printer.

You feed partial pages of checks into your printer the same way you feed envelopes. Consult your printer manual to find out which of these three basic positions the printer manufacturer recommends for loading envelopes in the envelope feeder or cassette.

If your checks print upside down or on the wrong side, reverse the way you load the checks into the envelope feeder.

4   **From the File menu, choose Print Checks.**

5   **Be sure the displayed first check number is the same as the first check on your partial page of checks.**

6   **Select which checks you want to print in the Print box.**

7   **Click Print.**

8   **In the Print Checks window, choose a Checks on First Page icon:**

- Click One if your first page has one check on it.

- Click Two if your first page has two checks on it.

Three, which is initially selected, represents a complete page of three checks.

Choose the icon that represents the number of checks you will be printing. (Depending on the printer you use to print checks, the orientation of the check icons on the buttons may be vertical instead of horizontal as shown here.)

9 **Load the one or two checks in your envelope feeder or cassette as pictured in the partial-sheet icon you selected.**

If your printer requires that you load letterhead face down (as the HP LaserJet IIP printer does), load your checks that way. Look in your printer manual if you aren't sure.

Preventing wasted checks
You may need to use Intuit Forms Leaders to prevent wasted checks if your page-oriented printer does not have an envelope feeder, *and* you are using standard three-to-a page checks, *and* you want to print checks on partial pages. See "Phone numbers" on page 372 for the Intuit Customer Service phone number to order Forms Leaders.

---

10 **Click Print to start printing the checks.**

If your printer uses the Centered type of envelope feeder, Quicken asks you whether or not you have removed the tear-off strip at the side of the page. This information affects the positioning of the checks.

11 **Did your checks print OK?**

If your checks printed correctly, click OK.

OR

If the checks look as though they printed too high or low, or too far to the left or right, see "Correcting the alignment of your checks" on page 53, and then reprint your checks.

Reprinting checks

With Quicken, you can easily reprint any check at any time, for any reason. You can also fill in any number of copies in the Print Checks window to print multiple copies of checks.

1 **In the register, select the transaction for the check you want to reprint.**

2 **Select the check number and type** Print **over the check number.**

(If you have QuickFill turned on, all you have to type is P.)

Quicken replaces the check number with Print in the Num field and considers the check unprinted.

Typing Print in the Num field turns a check that has already been printed into a check that you can print again.

| 3/22/94 | Print | GMAC Financing | 587 | 55 | | |
| | | A/C #87239-278-275 --Splits-- | | | | |

3 **Click Record.**

4 **Print the check as usual, paying special attention to entering the correct first check number.**

Check printing problems and solutions

This page describes some common check printing problems and their solutions. If you continue to have problems, see your printer manual or call Intuit's technical support group. (See "Phone numbers" on page 372.)

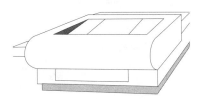

Problem Printer doesn't print.

Solution Check your equipment.

- Make sure your printer is turned on and is online.
- Make sure the cable connection between the printer and the computer is secure.
- From the File menu, choose Printer Setup and then Check Printer Setup. Make sure that the correct printer is selected.
- To check that your printer is working, try to print a Windows Write document. Look for Write in the Accessories Program Group. Open it and type a few words. Then, from Write's File menu, choose Print. If the document prints OK, the problem probably lies with your check printer setup.

Problem All text prints too high, too low, too far left, or too far right on checks.

Solution Adjust the Horizontal or Vertical setting in the Check Printer Alignment window.

- See "Correcting the alignment of your checks" on page 53.

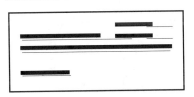

Problem Text is left-aligned correctly, but right-aligned incorrectly.

Solution If this is a wallet check, choose 10-point Courier as the font.

- See the font settings on page 60.

If you have an early version of a printer driver for your printer, you may be able to change the printer driver settings.

- See "Changing the settings for your printer driver" next.

Changing the settings for your printer driver

1 From the File menu, choose Printer Setup and then choose Check Printer Setup.

2 Make sure the printer you want to use is selected in the Printer drop-down list.

3   Click the Settings button.

Windows displays the printer driver window for your printer. The options you see on your screen may be different from the settings illustrated here, depending on the type of printer you are using.

These are the settings for the printer driver of a continuous-feed printer.

The Resolution setting does not affect check printing.

Select User Defined Size from the Paper Size drop-down list to set up the correct size for the check style you are using. If the User Defined Size option is not available, set the Paper Size at Letter 8 1/2 x 11 inches.

These are the settings for the printer driver of a page-oriented printer.

Select User Defined Size from the Paper Size drop-down list to set up the correct size for the check style you are using. If the User Defined Size option is not available, set the Paper Size at Letter 8 1/2 x 11 inches.

Set these options according to your printer's user manual.

Select a portrait orientation.

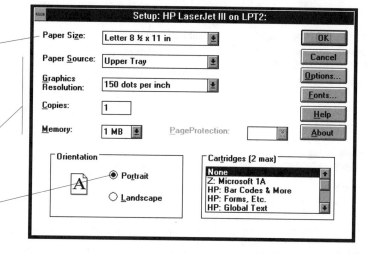

4   In the printer driver window, set the correct paper size for the style of checks you are using.

Go to the Paper Size drop-down list. Scroll in the list and select the User Defined Size option, then enter the paper size according to the following table. If there isn't a User Defined Size option in this list, select Letter 8 1/2 x 11 inches and click OK.

Check style:	Standard checks	Wallet checks	Voucher checks
Paper Size: (unit .01 inch)	Width: 850 Length: 350	Width: 850 Length: 284	Width: 850 Length: 700

5   Click OK to close the printer driver window.

Balancing your checkbook

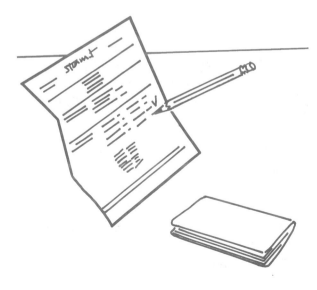

When your bank statement arrives, use Quicken to balance your checkbook, or "reconcile."

The overall goal of reconciliation is to bring your Quicken records into balance with your bank records.

Quicken allows you to reconcile to the degree of accuracy that works for you. You can track down every cent if you prefer, but Quicken does not require you to balance to the penny.

About balancing your account

When your bank statement arrives, follow the basic steps listed here to reconcile your account. Quicken reconciles one statement at a time. If you have accumulated two or more statements that need reconciling, start with the earliest statement and reconcile each one individually.

> ◆ **If this is the first time you've reconciled the bank account, check to see if you need to enter more transactions or update your opening balance.**
> See "Balancing your account for the first time" on this page.
>
> ◆ **Start reconciling by entering information from your current bank statement.**
> See "Starting reconciliation" on page 72.
>
> ◆ **Mark the transactions that have cleared your bank account in the Reconcile window.**
> See "Marking cleared transactions" on page 74.
>
> ◆ **Compare the totals of cleared items in the Reconcile window with those on your bank statement.**
> See "Completing reconciliation" on page 76.
>
> ◆ **(Optional) Create and print a reconciliation report.**
> See "Completing reconciliation" on page 76.

Balancing your account for the first time

When you set up your bank account in Quicken, you entered an opening balance in the New Account Information window. You entered this opening balance for the Quicken account from the ending balance of the bank statement.

The first time you balance your account may take some extra time. After you find the point where Quicken and the bank agree on the amount of money in your account, reconciling your account each month should be easier. Before you can reconcile your accounts accurately, you need to do two things:

1   Enter *all* uncleared transactions in your account.

For bank accounts, these are all transactions that have not cleared the bank or shown up on previous bank statements.

In most cases you'll be reminded to enter all uncleared transactions because the transactions appear on the bank statement when you're trying to reconcile. You can also enter these transactions in the register as you find them during reconciliation.

2   Update your opening balance to reflect the amount that was actually in your account when you began using Quicken with that account.

You can correct the amount of the Opening Balance transaction in your check register to match the ending balance from the last bank statement you received before you started Quicken. Or Quicken can create an opening balance adjustment at the end of your first reconciliation.

Your opening balance . . .

Suppose, for example, the ending balance on the bank statement for your checking account was $200.52 on December 31, 1993. You started using Quicken on January 12, 1994. You used the ending balance from your December bank statement as the balance for your Quicken checking account.

Then you entered transactions from your paper check register from January 1 to 12 into Quicken. From January 12 on, you entered all transactions into Quicken every few days as they occurred.

and checks that were outstanding when you started with Quicken

In February, you receive your January 31, 1994 bank statement. You see two checks (totaling $80) that you wrote in December 1993 and that had not yet cleared the bank in December. Now they have cleared the bank, so they appear on the January bank statement. You didn't enter those checks in Quicken at the time you set up the checking account because they occurred before January 1.

Even though those two checks were written before the date of the first transaction in Quicken, you need to enter them into Quicken's register. (You would not enter any other checks that you wrote in December if they had already cleared the bank in December.) If you don't enter these uncleared transactions, Quicken will create an opening balance adjustment for $80 when you have finished reconciling.

Where the balances go

Quicken uses the opening balance from the account for the opening balance in the Reconcile Bank Statement window.

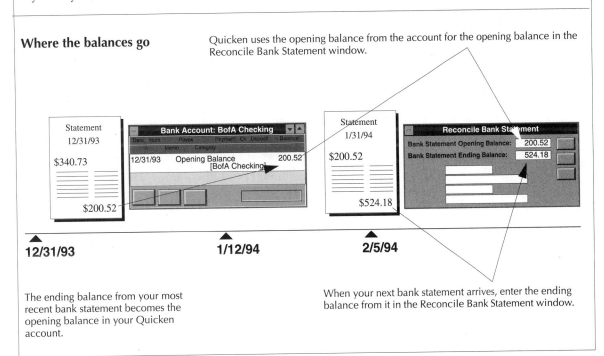

The ending balance from your most recent bank statement becomes the opening balance in your Quicken account.

When your next bank statement arrives, enter the ending balance from it in the Reconcile Bank Statement window.

Starting reconciliation

Your first step in reconciling your account is to enter some information from your bank statement.

If the balance shown on your bank statement is different from Quicken's balance for the account, do not assume that the bank balance is current. You've probably entered transactions into Quicken after the bank prepared your statement. You may also have checks or other transactions from earlier months that have not yet cleared the bank. Be sure to enter these transactions in the register now if you have not already done so.

1   Make sure the register for the account you want to reconcile is active.

2   From the Activities menu, choose Reconcile.

If this is the first time you are reconciling this account, Quicken calculates the amount in the Bank Statement Opening Balance box from the ending balance on your previous bank statement.

For example, if you started using Quicken in January and your latest bank statement was dated December 31, the ending balance amount from the December 31 statement is the same amount in the Opening Balance transaction in your Quicken check register and the same amount in the Bank Statement Opening Balance box in the Reconcile Bank Statement window.

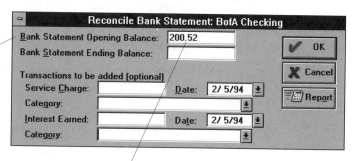

If this is not the first time you have reconciled this account, the amount in the Bank Statement Opening Balance box represents the total of all reconciled transactions in the check register. In the register, all reconciled transactions are marked with an **x** in the Clr (Cleared) column, just like your Opening Balance transaction.

3   Compare the opening balance amount shown on your bank statement with the amount shown in the Bank Statement Opening Balance box in the Reconcile Bank Statement window.

Your bank statement might call this amount the "beginning" or "previous" balance.

The amount in Quicken's Bank Statement Opening Balance box should be the same as the previous balance on your statement. If this is the first time you've reconciled your account, or if you have not reconciled in quite some time, the amounts may differ. See "Updating your previously reconciled balance" on page 81.

4   **If the amount in the Bank Statement Opening Balance box does not match the opening balance shown on your bank statement for this account, correct the Quicken amount by entering the opening balance from the bank statement.**

Quicken creates an opening balance difference that you will need to resolve later. See "Having Quicken adjust for differences" on page 80.

5   **Find the ending balance on your bank statement and enter it in the Bank Statement Ending Balance box in the Reconcile Bank Statement window.**

Your bank statement might call this amount the "current" balance.

6   **If any service charges are listed on your bank statement and you haven't already entered them in your Quicken register, enter the total amount in the Service Charge box, and then enter the date of the service charge in the Date box.**

7   **Enter a category for the Service Charge amount.**

Quicken remembers the category you use (such as Bank Chrg) and inserts it in the Category field the next time you reconcile.

8   **If your statement shows interest earned for your bank account and you haven't entered it in your Quicken register, enter the amount in the Interest Earned box, and then enter the date when the interest was earned in the Date box.**

9   **Enter a category for the Interest Earned amount.**

Quicken remembers the category you use (such as Int Inc) and inserts it in the Category field the next time you reconcile.

10   **When you've finished filling in the Reconcile Bank Statement window, click OK.**

Quicken immediately adds the Service Charge and Interest Earned transactions to the check register and displays the Reconcile Bank Account window, described in the next section. (If you click Cancel in the Reconcile Bank Account window, the Service Charge and Interest Earned transactions remain in your register. You do not need to enter them again when you return to reconciliation, unless you delete them from your register.)

Marking cleared transactions

Your next step in reconciling is to mark all cleared transactions. A cleared transaction is one that has been processed by the bank and is listed on your bank statement. The Reconcile Bank Account window contains a list of the uncleared transactions in your Quicken account, separated into payments and deposits.

1 **Compare the transactions listed on your bank statement with those listed in the Reconcile Bank Account window.**

Look for each transaction shown in the list of uncleared transactions that is also listed on your bank statement.

Verify that the transaction amount matches the amount listed on the bank statement.

2 **If you find a transaction in the Reconcile Bank Account window that matches a transaction on the bank statement, mark the transaction as cleared.**

Click the transaction to mark it. Or, to mark a group of checks, hold the left mouse button down while you drag across several transactions—Quicken marks them all. Once you've marked a transaction as cleared, a check mark appears in the Clr (Cleared) column of the Reconcile Bank Account window. To unmark a marked transaction, click the transaction again.

As you check off cleared transactions, Quicken displays their total as the cleared balance.

Quicken sorts the transactions by check number. If you'd prefer to see them sorted by date, click this checkbox.

To mark or clear a transaction:
• click it, or
• select it and click Mark or press the spacebar, or
• drag the mouse pointer across a range of transactions.

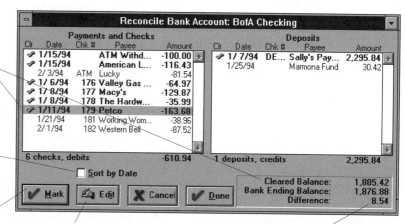

To enter a missing transaction in your check register, click Edit to go to the register.

Quicken keeps a running comparison of the total items marked cleared and the total items shown on the bank statement.

3 **If you find a transaction listed on your bank statement that is not shown in the list of uncleared transactions, enter it now in the check register.**

● Click Edit to move to the register and move to the blank transaction at the end of the register (or click Insert to insert a blank transaction).

● Enter information for the missing transaction.

● Click Record to record the transaction.

● Add any other missing transactions to the register now.

● Click back in the Reconcile Bank Account window or choose Reconcile from the Activities menu to return to the list of items you are marking.

● Mark the transaction as cleared.

4 **Similarly, if you find transactions that contain incorrect amounts or other errors, correct them now in the check register.**

● Select the transaction in the Reconcile Bank Account window.

● Click Edit to move to the transaction in the register. Quicken displays the register and selects the transaction you wish to change.

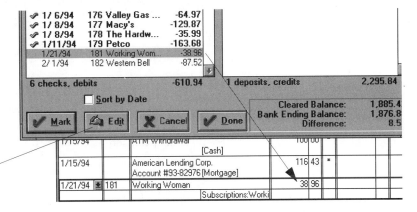

To move from a selected transaction in the Reconcile Bank Account window to the same transaction in the register, click Edit. Quicken displays the register with the transaction selected.

● Correct the error in the register.

● Click Record to record the change.

● Click back in the Reconcile Bank Account window or choose Reconcile from the Activities menu to return to the list of items you are marking.

● Mark the transaction as cleared.

5 **When you have finished marking cleared transactions, the Difference amount displayed at the bottom of the Reconcile Bank Account window should be zero.**

Completing reconciliation

When you've finished checking off cleared transactions, look at the difference amount or amounts in the Reconcile Bank Account window. Compare the amount or amounts in your Reconcile Bank Account window with the three situations described on this page and the next page.

Situation 1: If the Difference amount is zero *and* if there is no Opening Balance Difference amount displayed above the Cleared Balance, you've reconciled the current bank statement successfully.

Click Done to complete reconciliation.

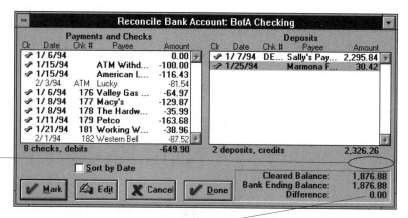

If an Opening Balance Difference amount is displayed here above the Cleared Balance, see Situation 2 on the next page.

If the Difference amount is zero and if no Opening Balance Difference amount is displayed above the Cleared Balance, you've balanced your account successfully.

Now you know that the balance in your Quicken check register is accurate as of the latest bank statement. If you examine the check register after you click Done, you'll find an x in the Clr (Cleared) field next to each reconciled transaction.

When you successfully complete balancing your account, Quicken asks if you would like to create a reconciliation report. You can create a reconciliation report at any other time too: from the Activities menu, choose Reconcile, and then click Report.

(Optional) Change the report title.

(Optional) Select All Transactions to see detail for every reconciled transaction in addition to summary information.

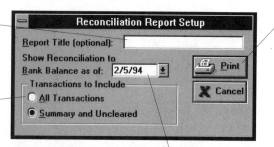

Click Print to print the report. (You see the Print Report window shown on page 266.) You can print to a printer, a file on disk, or to your screen.

(Optional) Change the date if you want the report to state your reconciled balance as of a different date than today. For example, you might want a reconciliation report that ends on the last day of your accounting period, even if your bank statements arrive mid-month.

Situation 2: If Quicken shows an Opening Balance Difference amount, you have reconciled the current bank statement successfully, but you still need to resolve the Opening Balance Difference. The Opening Balance Difference is the difference between the total of the previously reconciled items in the register and the opening balance shown in the current bank statement.

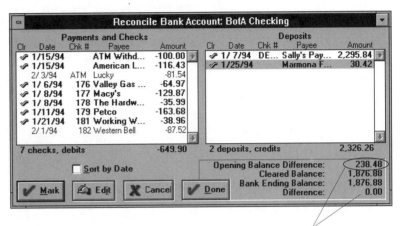

If you changed the amount in the Bank Statement Opening Balance box when you entered information in the Reconcile Bank Statement window, the difference shows up in the Reconcile window as the Opening Balance Difference.

If the Difference amount is zero, but an Opening Balance Difference amount is displayed, you need to resolve the difference.

See "Updating your previously reconciled balance" on page 81.

Situation 3: If the Difference amount is not zero, your account doesn't balance for the current bank statement period. The difference is usually due to one or both of the following reasons: incorrect number of payment or deposit items checked off as cleared, or incorrect dollar amounts on some items.

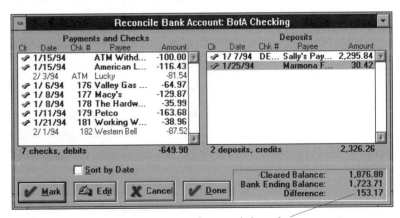

The Difference amount is a running comparison of the total items marked cleared and the total items shown on the bank statement. In this example, there's a $153.17 difference between the check register and the bank statement.

If the Difference amount is not zero, you have not balanced your account.

You have two options when your account doesn't balance:
Find the difference between your check register and the bank statement and correct it. See "Correcting differences" on page 78. **OR** Have Quicken modify your Quicken balance to agree with the bank's by recording an adjustment transaction. See "Having Quicken adjust for differences" on page 80.

Correcting differences

You can find the differences between your Quicken account and the bank statement in a systematic way.

Finding a problem with the number of items

Count the number of debit items on your bank statement and compare that number with the number of "checks, debits" items you've marked in the Reconcile Bank Account window. Count the number of credit items listed on your bank statement and compare that number with the total number of "deposits, credits" items checked off in the Reconcile Bank Account window.

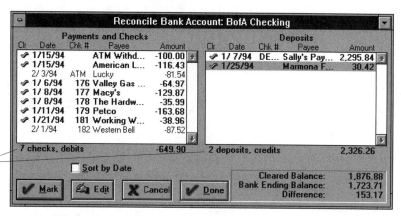

Check here for the total number and dollar amount of items that you have checked off.

Debits include checks, transfers out of the account, ATM withdrawals, service charges and fees, and automatic payments.

Credits include direct deposits, transfers into the account, ATM deposits, and interest earned.

If you know the problem is the number of debits, look only at payment transactions; if you know the problem is the number of credits, look only at deposit transactions. If the count does not agree, you may have a problem with the number of debits or credits marked as cleared. Check to see if:

- You missed recording an item in the check register.

- You missed marking an item as cleared.

- You mistakenly marked an item as cleared.

- You entered any transactions twice.

- You entered a deposit as a payment or a payment as a deposit.

Caution:
The bank may summarize transactions that you've listed separately in your register. For example, if you made several deposits on a single day, the bank might indicate the total sum of deposits for that day rather than listing each deposit separately. Similarly, you may summarize transactions in your register, such as bank charges, that the bank itemizes. Some statements count the number of credits for you; others list interest earned and ATM deposits separately. Some statements count the number of debits for you; others list service charges and ATM withdrawals separately.

Finding a problem with the dollar amount of items

If there's no problem with the number of items marked as cleared, compare the dollar amount of the "checks, debits" total in the Reconcile Bank Account window with the dollar amount of debits shown on your bank statement. If the totals do not agree, you know you have a problem with the dollar amount of debits.

Compare the dollar amount of the "deposits, credits" total in the Reconcile Bank Account window with the dollar amount of credits shown on your bank statement. If the totals do not agree, you know you have a problem with the dollar amount of credits.

If you know the problem is the dollar amount of debits, look only at payment transactions; if you know the problem is the dollar amount of credits, look only at deposit transactions.

You may have recorded all items, but typed an amount incorrectly.
Compare all amounts shown in the list of cleared transactions with the amounts shown on your statement. If you find an incorrect amount, return to the transaction in the Register window (click Edit) and correct the amount (then return to the Reconcile Bank Account window).

The bank may have made a mistake by processing a transaction for a different amount than you wrote it for. Adjust the balance by entering a transaction (or let Quicken make the adjustment for you as described in "Having Quicken adjust for differences" on page 80). Then contact your bank. The bank will make an adjustment that will appear on your next statement. Because this adjustment will appear as an already cleared item in the check register, your account will be off by the same amount at the end of the next reconciliation. Have Quicken make another adjustment when you finish reconciling the next statement.

Having Quicken adjust for differences

You might decide to ignore the difference between your check register and the bank statement. Ignoring the difference is appropriate if the amount is small and you feel it is not worth your time to track it down. Even though you decide to ignore the difference, you'll want to have Quicken enter a balance adjustment for the amount of the difference. That way you'll be starting with accurate totals the next time you reconcile your account.

1   Click Done in the Reconcile Bank Account window.

If there is an Opening Balance Difference amount to resolve, Quicken first asks "Would you like Quicken to create an adjustment of this amount to make your totals agree with the bank statement?"

- Click Yes if you want Quicken to enter an adjustment transaction and resolve the discrepancy for you.

  OR

- Click No to complete reconciliation without adjusting for the Opening Balance Difference. Do this if you want to resolve the discrepancy yourself.

  OR

- Click Cancel to return to reconciliation.

Having Quicken update your balance

If this is the first time you've reconciled and you entered a balance amount that was not the same as the ending balance from your last bank statement when you set up the account, we recommend that you let Quicken make a one-time adjustment to the previously reconciled balance in your account. You are not in danger of overdrawing your account as long as you have entered all outstanding uncleared transactions in your Quicken check register.

---

2   Adjust the balance or continue to resolve the differences.

If there is a Difference amount to resolve (resulting from transactions in the current statement period), Quicken tells you the amount of the discrepancy.

- Click Adjust Balance if you want Quicken to record an adjustment transaction in the check register equal to the difference between your cleared items and the bank statement. You can delete the adjustment transaction later if you find the error that resulted in the difference.

  OR

- Click Cancel if you want to return to the Reconcile Bank Account window and track down the difference.

Updating your previously reconciled balance

If the opening balance from your bank statement was different from the amount Quicken expected as your previously reconciled balance, you need to account for the difference so that Quicken can reconcile your account accurately.

The previously reconciled balance might differ for one of these reasons:

You are balancing your Quicken account for the first time.
Quicken uses the amount of the Opening Balance transaction in your check register as the Bank Statement Opening Balance in the Reconcile Bank Statement window (page 72). When you set up the Quicken account, you may have entered a balance that was different from the actual amount in your bank account. There are probably transactions missing from your Quicken account that affect the balance. See "Balancing your account for the first time" on page 70.

OR

You were using Quicken and reconciling your bank account, and then you started recording earlier transactions in Quicken.
For example, say it's July. You started recording transactions in May and subsequently reconciled your account for May and June. Then you went back and recorded transactions starting in January so that you could create reports based on the full year's transactions. After entering these earlier items, you noticed that the ending balance in the check register was incorrect. So you updated the date and amount of the original Opening Balance transaction that Quicken recorded in the register when you set up your account in May. In this case, see "Adding earlier transactions to Quicken" on page 83.

OR

You have started reconciling with a current bank statement, but you have not reconciled each of the previous months' statements.
You should reconcile one month at a time, starting with the earliest month. However, if you have skipped several months and don't want to balance each bank statement, see "Catching up if you skipped balancing your checkbook" on page 82.

OR

You have inadvertently changed or deleted a previously reconciled transaction.
Quicken always asks you to confirm a change to a previously reconciled transaction. If you have already ruled out other possible errors (see page 78), you probably should continue with reconciliation and have Quicken record an adjustment transaction when reconciliation is complete.

Catching up if you skipped balancing your checkbook

In some circumstances, you need to enter transactions that have already cleared the bank, or mark transactions as previously cleared. This is different from checking off transactions as cleared while you are reconciling. You can approach reconciliation in two ways: the recommended, best way and the second-best way.

If you have used Quicken for a number of months and have just decided that you want to reconcile, you might not want to go back and reconcile your Quicken account against the bank statements for each of the previous months.

For example, if you are starting to reconcile with your June bank statement after entering transactions in Quicken since January of the same year:

The best way to catch up

Balance each month separately, starting with your earliest (January) statement and continue through your most recent (June) statement. Follow the steps in "Starting reconciliation" on page 72, continue with the steps in "Marking cleared transactions" on page 74, and then in "Completing reconciliation" on page 76 for each month before starting to reconcile the statement for the next month.

The second-best way to catch up

Balance all the unreconciled bank statements at the same time. Your records may not be as accurate as they would be if you reconciled each month separately. The second best method follows.

1   **From the Activities menu, choose Reconcile.**

2   **In the Bank Statement Ending Balance box of the Reconcile Bank Statement window, enter the ending balance from the most current bank statement and click OK.**

    The ending balance from the current bank statement is June in this example.

3   **In the main Reconcile window, mark the transactions shown on all the bank statements for the period covered by your Quicken check register.**

    See "Marking cleared transactions" on page 74.

4 **Finish reconciling.**

See "Completing reconciliation" on page 76.

If there is a Difference amount, you or your bank may have made an error at an earlier date. If the difference is fairly small, you can have Quicken enter an adjustment transaction when it completes the reconciliation. Then your records will match the next time you reconcile your account. If the difference is large and you cannot account for it, you may want to ask your bank to determine which balance is accurate.

Adding earlier transactions to Quicken

If you've used Quicken to record and reconcile transactions, you may want to add earlier transactions to your Quicken bank account so you can create more comprehensive reports, graphs, and budgets. To keep the information in your account accurate, you need to follow the steps below.

In the following example, we assume that you started entering transactions in June. When you set up the Quicken bank account, you used the ending balance from your May statement as the opening balance for the Quicken account. You've already reconciled your June bank statement. Now you want to go back and add earlier transactions starting on January 1.

1 **Make a note of the ending balance in your Quicken register before you begin to enter earlier transactions.**

2 **Change the date and amount of the Opening Balance transaction in the Quicken register to reflect the opening balance on the first date for which you are about to enter transactions.**

For best results, enter the beginning balance from the first bank statement you want to reconcile.

Suppose your opening balance transaction is now dated June 1 and is in the amount of $450. Your January bank statement, which covers the period from December 14 to January 15, shows a beginning balance of $210. So, change the date of the Opening Balance transaction in the check register to December 14 and the amount to $210.

3 **Enter all the earlier transactions starting January 1 in your check register, just as you would enter any current transaction.**

Don't worry about any transactions that occurred in the period between the beginning date of the January bank statement (December 14) and the first date for which you entered transactions (January 1). You'll take care of those transactions when you update the reconciled balance in step 5.

4   When you have finished entering transactions, the ending balance in the register should be the same as it was when you started.

If the balance is not the same, you have made an error. You'll fix any errors in the next step.

5   Reconcile all the transactions that you entered for previous months (January to May).

Balance each month separately, starting with your earliest (January) statement. Follow the steps in "Starting reconciliation" on page 72, continue the steps in "Marking cleared transactions" on page 74, and then in "Completing reconciliation" on page 76 for each month before starting to reconcile the statement for the next month.

6   Now you can go on and reconcile for the current month (June).

The total of reconciled transactions in your register now includes all the transactions that appeared on your bank statements from January to June.

Memorizing special transactions

In addition to using QuickFill to save time with repetitive typing, you may like to save some special transactions separately. For example, you can memorize more than one type of paycheck from your employer, and then recall the correct transaction whenever you need to enter it again.

When to memorize transactions

You can memorize any transaction you think you may need to enter again in the future. You won't need to do this very often, because Quicken offers other time-saving features to handle transactions that recur frequently:

- As you type the name of a payee in the register, QuickFill instantly recalls the details of a previous transaction to the same payee. You can accept the details or change them before recording the transaction. See "Using drop-down lists and QuickFill™ for fast entry" on page 20.

- For transactions that recur regularly, such as bills, paycheck deposits, and mortgage payments, you can set up a recurring scheduled transaction. Quicken enters the transaction for you on the dates and at the frequency you specify. See "Scheduling a transaction on the Financial Calendar" on page 104.

Nevertheless, there are occasions when you may want to memorize a transaction to recall for entry later. For example:

- If you often write more than one type of transaction to the same payee, you can memorize several transactions with the same payee but with different payment details.

- You can memorize a transaction with the amount split according to percentages, so that, for example, several roommates contribute the same relative amounts to a bill.

- If you want to set up transaction groups for fast entry of several transactions, as described in "Setting up groups of transactions" on page 99, you need to memorize the transactions first.

- You can put icons for your most frequently used transactions and transaction groups on the iconbar to make this task more convenient. For example, if you withdraw cash from an ATM regularly, you might want to set up an icon on the iconbar for that transaction. Then you can click the icon and Quicken instantly opens the account you specify, inserts the ATM cash withdrawal for the amount you specified, fills out the rest of the transaction, and waits for you to click Record. See "Entering a specific transaction" on page 362. You must memorize the transaction before you can set up an icon for it.

Memorizing and recalling transactions

You can follow the next procedures to have Quicken memorize any transaction in the Register or Write Checks windows. *

QuickFill will recall any memorized transaction automatically, as soon as you type the first letters of the payee's name. (QuickFill looks for the payee in the Memorized Transaction list first, before searching through the register for a previous transaction to that payee.)

If you turn off automatic recall in your QuickFill preferences (see page 41), you can still recall a memorized transaction in the Register or Write Checks window by selecting it from the Memorized Transaction list as described on page 90.

Memorizing an existing transaction

1 **If the transaction has already been entered in the register, select it in the register (or scroll to the transaction in the Write Checks window).**

Or press Ctrl+M

2 **From the Edit menu, choose Memorize Transaction.**

Quicken tells you the transaction is about to be memorized.

(If you haven't yet entered an amount in the register for the transaction, Quicken memorizes the transaction as a Payment type.)

3 **Click OK.**

Quicken memorizes all the information in the transaction except the date and the check number.

Memorizing a new transaction

Or press Ctrl+T

1 **To set up a new memorized transaction, from the Lists menu, choose Memorized Transaction. ***

Quicken displays the Memorized Transaction list.

Or press Ctrl+N

2 **Click New.**

---

* Memorizing an investment transaction is just like memorizing any other transaction except that Quicken keeps a separate list for these.

** To set up a new memorized investment transaction, choose Memorized Investment Trans.

3 In the Type box, select the type of transaction you want to memorize.

Select Check if this is a check transaction you intend to print in Quicken. Select Payment if this is a check you intend to write manually, or if it is some other type of withdrawal from the register. Select Deposit if this transaction adds money to your account. Select E-Payment if you will be paying this through CheckFree.

Enter information you want the memorized transaction to contain in each of these boxes.

Leave this new transaction uncleared.

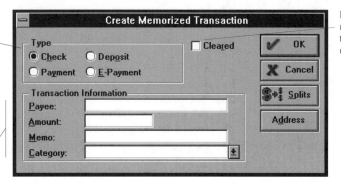

Windows tip

To move to the next box in a window, click in the box or press Tab.

4 Enter transaction information in each box as if you were entering the transaction in the register.

5 (Optional) Click Splits to fill out a split transaction.

6 (Optional) Click Address if this is a check to be printed, and enter the address.

7 Click OK to add the new memorized transaction to the list.

Looking at your Memorized Transaction list

1 From the Lists menu, choose Memorized Transaction.

After you've memorized a few transactions, your Memorized Transaction list may look like this.

You can group memorized transactions together for easier recall. See "Setting up groups of transactions" on page 99.

In the Spl column, "A" means that the transaction is amortized. (See "Setting up a loan" on page 316.) "S" means that the transaction is split. (See "Splitting transactions" on page 28.)

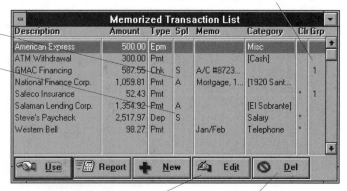

You can print the Memorized Transaction list. Open the list. From the File menu, choose Print List (or press Ctrl+P).

To change the details of a memorized transaction, select the transaction and click Edit.

To remove a memorized transaction from the list, select the transaction and click Del.

2   **(Optional) To report on all entries of a memorized transaction in all accounts in the current file, select the transaction in the list and click Report.**

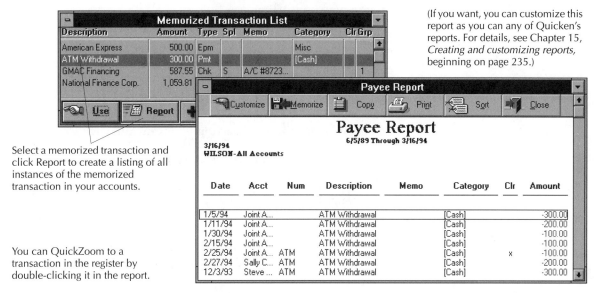

(If you want, you can customize this report as you can any of Quicken's reports. For details, see Chapter 15, *Creating and customizing reports,* beginning on page 235.)

Select a memorized transaction and click Report to create a listing of all instances of the memorized transaction in your accounts.

You can QuickZoom to a transaction in the register by double-clicking it in the report.

Click Close to close the report.

Automatically memorizing transactions

You can have Quicken automatically memorize each new transaction you enter (except investment transactions). To do this, turn on the Automatic Memorization Of New Transactions setting in your QuickFill preferences. See "Changing the way QuickFill works" on page 41.

When you enter a new payee (who is not already in the Memorized Transaction list), Quicken adds the payee to the list when you record the transaction.

After you have entered transactions for several months with automatic memorization turned on, you may want to turn off this feature. Most of your monthly transactions will be memorized by then.

The Memorized Transaction list can hold about 2,000 transactions. If the Memorized Transaction list becomes half-full, Quicken tells you it is turning off automatic memorization. Your list fills up like this only if you don't usually make payments to the same payee more than once or twice. If this is the case, automatic memorization is not much of a benefit to you anyway, so you should consider turning it off.

Recalling a memorized transaction manually

1 **Scroll to the bottom of the Register or Write Checks window to select a new transaction.**

   Or, in the register. click Insert to open a new transaction.

   (If you do not select a new transaction, Quicken overwrites the currently selected transaction.)

Or press Ctrl+T 2 **From the Lists menu, choose Memorized Transaction.***

3 **Select the memorized transaction you want and click Use.**

4 **(Optional) Review the transaction and make any changes or additions you want.**

   Any changes you make do not affect the transaction in the Memorized Transaction list unless you rememorize the transaction in the register.

5 **Click Record to record the transaction as usual.**

Changing a memorized transaction

There are two ways of changing the details of a memorized transaction:

- Through the Memorized Transaction list. From the Lists menu, choose Memorized Transaction (or press Ctrl+T). Select the transaction you want to change and click Edit (or press Ctrl+E). Quicken displays the Edit Memorized Transaction window.

  If the transaction is an amortized payment that you memorized when setting up a loan, you see the Set Up Loan Payment window instead. See "Setting up a loan," beginning on page 316, for details of what to enter in that window.

- In the register. Recall the memorized transaction into the register, make the changes you want, and then press Ctrl+M to rememorize the transaction in the list.

Deleting a memorized transaction

From the Lists menu, choose Memorized Transaction. Select the transaction you want to delete and click Del (or press Ctrl+D).

---

* For investment transactions, choose Memorized Investment Trans.

Using percentages in a split transaction

Quicken offers two ways to split amounts according to percentages. For example, two people may have agreed always to split their phone bill 60%/40%.

The first way is simply to type, for example, 60% in the Amount field on the first line of the Splits window, as described on page 28, and then type 40% on the second line. (Be sure you entered the total amount in the register before opening the split.)

The second way is to memorize a split transaction, but with the different amounts saved as percentages of the total. The next time you recall the transaction, you enter the total amount and Quicken calculates how much each person owes.

Setting up a split transaction using percentages

Whenever you memorize a split transaction, you can memorize the split amounts either as dollars or as percentages of the total.

If you already have an existing transaction in your register that has the split amounts entered in the correct proportion, select it and go to step 5. Otherwise, set up the first such transaction as follows.

1   **In the Register or the Write Checks window, enter the payee name and then enter the total transaction amount in the Payment or Deposit field.**

2   **Click Splits.**

3   **In the Splits window, enter the amounts for this first transaction.**

You can let Quicken calculate the dollar amounts if you want. For example, in the Amount field on the first line type 60% to have Quicken calculate 60% of the total. On the second line, type 40%.

In this example, $75 was entered in the register as the the total amount of the bill.

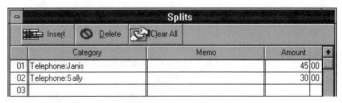

4   **Click OK to close the split.**

Or press Ctrl+M   5   **From the Edit menu, choose Memorize Transaction.**

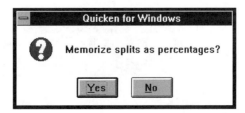

6 Click Yes.

7 Click OK to memorize the transaction.

8 Click Record to record the transaction.

In the memorized transaction list, Quicken shows %SPLIT in the Amount column, rather than a dollar amount.

Recalling a memorized transaction with percentages

1 Start with a blank transaction in the register or display a blank check in the Write Checks window.

2 Start typing the payee name in the transaction and press Tab to recall the transaction from the list.

Or press Ctrl+T

If QuickFill is not turned on or you want to recall the transaction manually, choose Memorized Transaction from the Lists menu, select the transaction, and click Use.

Use QuickFill to recall the transaction. ——

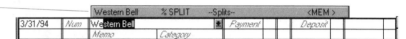

Quicken asks you to enter the total transaction amount.

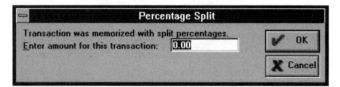

3 Enter the total dollar amount you want Quicken to divide into the percentages stored in the split transaction, and click OK.

Quicken enters a transaction for the amount you specify, with the dollar amount split according to the percentages stored in the memorized transaction.

In this Splits window, Quicken calculates the dollar amounts on the basis of the percentages stored in the memorized transaction.

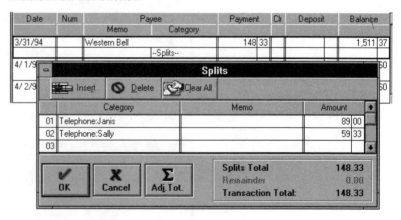

4 Click Record to record the transaction.

Scheduling with the Quicken Financial Calendar™

Instead of scribbling on your wall calendar, use Quicken's Financial Calendar. Enter payments and deposits that are coming up, and let Quicken record them in your register as they become due. You can schedule single transactions, or recurring transactions like your mortgage payment.

Now you can see exactly what lies ahead, remind yourself of upcoming bills, and plan your spending more efficiently.

How Quicken helps you schedule

Think of the expenses and deposits coming up that you already know about. You may know that you will be paid every two weeks, that you have to pay rent once a month, that the car needs a service soon. You know there's a trip you need to plan for, although it's still a couple of months off.

Quicken has a month-by-month Financial Calendar you can use to keep track of all these known transactions. It looks just like the calendar on your wall. On Quicken's Financial Calendar, you can mark one-time transactions such as the car service or vacation, and you can also mark recurring transactions like your rent and paycheck.

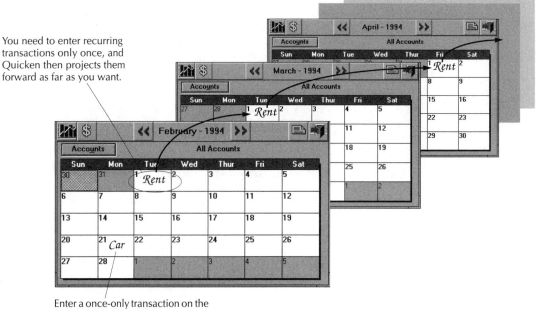

You need to enter recurring transactions only once, and Quicken then projects them forward as far as you want.

Enter a once-only transaction on the day you think it will happen.

Quicken's Financial Calendar shows you your upcoming bills, and enters them into your registers as they become due. For one-time bills, this serves as a useful reminder. For recurring bills, you've put your bill-paying on autopilot.

Use Quicken's Financial Calendar as an integral part of entering transactions into your registers.

Scheduling transactions

(Note: if you use automatic drafting to make amortized payments for a loan or mortgage, set these up through the View Loans window instead—see "Setting up a loan," beginning on page 316.)

Instead of waiting until you pay a bill or receive a check before turning to Quicken, you can *schedule* any transaction that you know is coming up. On the day the transaction becomes due, Quicken enters it for you in your register. It can prompt you first, if you wish.

If you define a scheduled transaction to be a recurring transaction, Quicken will regularly enter it in your register on the scheduled days, saving you time and, if it's a bill, giving you a reminder that it needs to be paid. You can set up automatic drafting transactions in this way.

There are two ways to schedule a transaction. Once you get used to Quicken's Financial Calendar, you may find it faster to schedule transactions directly on the Financial Calendar—that method is described on page 104. But you can also schedule a transaction through the Scheduled Transaction list as described next.

Setting up a scheduled transaction

1 **From the Lists menu, choose Schedule Transaction.**

2 **Click New.**

You see the Set Up Scheduled Transaction window, in which you enter all the details of the future transaction. When you've finished making entries, your window may look something like the one shown below, which shows a recurring transaction to pay the rent.

Payment (Pmt), Deposit (Dep), Check to write (Chk), or CheckFree payment (Epmt). If you want to record a deposit into your account, select Dep (for example, for paychecks).

For more information on each field, press F1 at this window.

The top part of the window contains the same fields as a transaction in your register. Whatever you enter here will be written into your register on the next payment date.

For recurring transactions, Quicken updates this date as it records each payment.

For a one-time transaction, select Only Once.

Quicken can enter the transaction in your register with or without asking you to confirm first. (See page 97 for more details.)

Select the account into which the transaction should be entered.

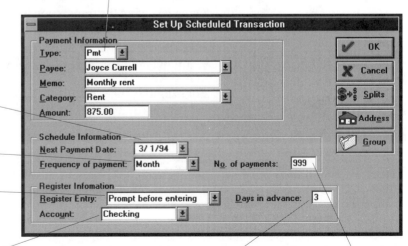

Quicken can record the payments in your register ahead of time if you want. (Otherwise, enter 0 here.)

Leave this as 999 if you want Quicken to record transactions indefinitely.

3   **Fill in the fields of the Set Up Scheduled Transaction window.**

If you want to break down the transaction into several parts, click Splits to open a split transaction, just as you do in the register.

If you're setting up a check payment (the Type is Chk), click Address to enter the payee's address.

4   **Click OK to set up the scheduled transaction, and confirm the information message that is displayed.**

The transaction is added to the Scheduled Transaction list. You can change the details of any scheduled transaction at any time by selecting that transaction in the list and clicking Edit. Remember that Quicken does not enter the transaction in the register until it becomes due. (However, you can pay a scheduled transaction ahead of time if you wish—see "Paying scheduled transactions ahead of time" on page 98.)

When a scheduled transaction becomes due

Quicken enters the scheduled transaction for you in the register of the selected account. This normally happens as soon as you start Quicken on or following the Next Payment Date. (If the Next Payment Date is today, you need to exit Quicken and restart it to see the transaction entered.)

However, you might find it useful to have Quicken enter transactions for bills a few days in advance, to remind you and give you time to send the bills off. To do this, when you set up a scheduled transaction, enter a number in the field "Days in advance"—Quicken enters the transaction in the register that many days before the Next Payment Date. The transaction is then entered as a postdated transaction. Its transaction date does not change as a result of being entered in advance.

For example, the scheduled transaction example shown on page 95 creates this transaction. Quicken enters it in the register on February 26:

Date	Num	Payee		Payment	Clr	Deposit	Balance	
		Memo	Category					
3/ 1/94	Sched	Joyce Currell		875 00			401 74	
		Monthly rent	Rent					

Depending on what you entered in the Register Entry field at the Set Up Scheduled Transaction window, Quicken may ask you to confirm first that it should enter the transaction.

If you entered this in the Register Entry field:	Quicken does this:
Enter w/o prompting	When you start Quicken (or open the Quicken file), Quicken enters and records the scheduled transaction automatically, without notifying you. If you go into the register, you will see it there.
Prompt before entering	When you start Quicken (or open the Quicken file), Quicken displays the details of the transaction and asks you to confirm that Quicken should enter it in the register. You can change the details before Quicken enters it in the register.
For planning only	Quicken does nothing. The transaction is never entered into your register. This option allows you to set up scheduled transactions for planning purposes only, to see their effect on the financial planning graph in "what-if" scenarios. (See Chapter 22, *Projecting the future,* beginning on page 301, to read how to use the financial planning graph.)

If you aren't sure which Register Entry option to choose when you schedule transactions, choose Prompt Before Entering. This option allows you to check the details of the transaction and change them if necessary before Quicken records the transaction in your register.

With Prompt Before Entering, you see this window when you start Quicken:

You can change any of the details, including the transaction date, before entering the transaction.

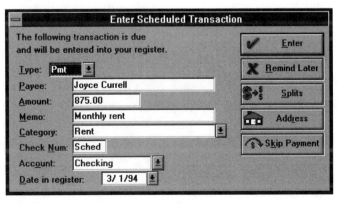

- Click Enter to record the transaction in your register. If the transaction was set up as Only Once, Quicken removes it from the Scheduled Transaction list.

OR

- Click Remind Later to postpone the entry of the transaction; Quicken will prompt you again the next time you start Quicken

OR

- Click Skip Payment to skip the transaction entry completely. If the transaction was set up as Only Once, Quicken deletes the transaction from your Scheduled Transaction list without recording anything in your register. If the transaction is set up to recur at regular intervals, Quicken skips this one entry and resets the Next Payment Date for the following due date.

Viewing your Scheduled Transaction list

1 **From the Lists menu, choose Scheduled Transaction.**

Your Scheduled Transaction list will eventually show all the future payments and deposits you have defined, as shown below.

To pay a scheduled transaction before it becomes due:
Select the scheduled transaction and click Pay Now.

To change information:
Select the scheduled transaction and click Edit.

To delete an entry:
Select the scheduled transaction and click Del.

To print the Scheduled Transaction list:
Press Ctrl+P. The printed list includes the number of payments yet to be made for each item.

Scheduled Transaction List				
Description	Amount	Pmts	Frequency	Next Date
GMAC Financing	-587.55	54	Monthly	6/11/94 (Saturday)
Joyce Currell	-875.00		Monthly	4/ 1/94 (Friday)
PlayTime	-400.00	5	Monthly	3/ 3/94 (Thursday)
Salaman Lending Corp.	-1,533.91	1	Only Once	5/13/94 (Friday)
Sally's Paycheck	1,442.25		Every two weeks	3/12/94 (Saturday)

Pay Now   New   Edit   Del

If you left the number of payments as 999, this field is blank, meaning Quicken will continue entering transactions until you edit the scheduled transaction to stop it.

This column shows the next payment date for each scheduled transaction.

Remember that you don't need to delete an item from the Scheduled Transaction list just to deactivate it. If you think you might need the scheduled transaction again, edit the scheduled transaction and enter 0 in the No. of payments box. Quicken will not record any more transactions in your register until you enter a new number in this box, though the item remains in your Scheduled Transaction list.

Paying scheduled transactions ahead of time

You may sometimes want to record a scheduled transaction earlier than the date you originally scheduled. For example, you planned to have your car serviced next week but did it today instead. Use Quicken's Pay Now function to enter the transaction immediately.

On page 107 you can read how to pay scheduled transactions ahead of time using the Financial Calendar.

1   **Display the Scheduled Transaction list. (From the Lists menu, choose Scheduled Transaction.)**

2   **Select the scheduled transaction and click Pay Now.**

3   **If you set up the transaction to prompt you before being entered, you now see the Enter Scheduled Transaction window. Check the details and click Enter to record the transaction.**

Quicken enters the transaction in your register immediately, though with the original Next Payment Date unless you changed the date to today. For an Only Once transaction, Quicken removes the transaction from the Scheduled Transaction list.

If you set up the scheduled transaction as a check to write in Quicken, you can go now print the check immediately.

When you become familiar with the Financial Calendar, described later in this chapter, you may prefer to use the Pay Now function through the Financial Calendar instead.

Setting up groups of transactions

You may find that you are paying a group of bills regularly at the same time. For example, at the start of each month you pay your phone bill, electric bill, and car payment. Instead of setting up each payment separately as a recurring scheduled transaction, you can group them together into a recurring *transaction group*. This cleans up your Scheduled Transaction list, as the group appears as just one item in the list.

If you have used an earlier version of Quicken:
You can still use any transaction groups you set up in your earlier version of Quicken. In this version, transaction groups are even easier to set up and use.

Transaction groups behave just the same as single scheduled transactions. When a group is due to be recorded, Quicken enters each transaction in the group into your register. If necessary, you can then go into the register and edit each transaction separately.

A transaction must be memorized before you can include it in a group for automatic entry. (See "Memorizing an existing transaction" on page 87.)

Setting up a transaction group

You set up a transaction group from the Scheduled Transaction list by assigning memorized transactions to it. You can have up to twelve transaction groups.

1   **From the Lists menu, choose Scheduled Transaction.**

2   **Click New.**

3   **Go to the Account field at the bottom of the window and enter the name of the account into which the group transactions should be entered.**

All transactions in the group will be entered into the same account register.

4   **Click Group.**

5   **In the Set Up Transaction Group window, enter a group name.**

The group name can be a descriptive name such as "Utility bills" or "Monthly payments."

6   **Select whether this will be a group of regular or investment transactions.**

Unless all the transactions in the group were memorized in an investment account, select "Regular."

7   **Fill in the schedule and register information as you would for a single scheduled transaction.**

Your completed window may look like this:

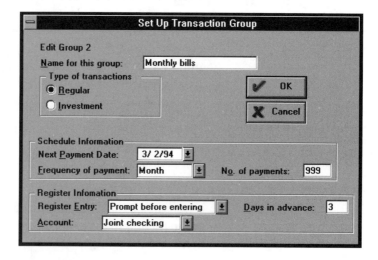

8   **Click OK.**

Quicken displays the Assign Transactions to Group window. This window lists all your memorized transactions. Now you need to mark the transactions you want to include in this group.

Each transaction in this list can belong to only one group.

Assign Transactions to Group 1: Monthly bills

Description	Amount	Type	Spl	Memo	Category	Clr	Grp
American Express	500.00	Epm			Misc		
ATM Withdrawal	300.00	Pmt			[Cash]		
Central Market	47.89	Pmt			Groceries	*	
GMAC Financing	587.55	Chk	S	A/C #8723...			1
Primerica Bank	289.75	Pmt	S	Account #9...	Interest Paid	*	1
Safeco Insurance	52.43	Pmt				*	1
Salaman Lending Corp.	1,354.92	Pmt	A		[El Sobrante]		
Service Charge	8.00	Pmt				*	
Steve's Paycheck	2,517.97	Dep	S		Salary	*	
Transfer to savings	1,500.00	Pmt			[Savings]		
Western Bell	98.27	Pmt		Jan/Feb	Telephone	*	

√ **Mark**   √ **Done**   ✗ **Cancel**

The number in the Grp column tells you to which group the transaction has already been assigned.

"A" in the Spl column indicates this is an amortized transaction.

"S" in the Spl column indicates this is a split transaction.

9 **Select the memorized transactions you want to include in the group.**

To include a transaction in the list, double-click it, or select it and press the spacebar, or select it and click Mark.

If you want to create printable checks by recalling a transaction group, be sure that Chk appears in the Type column for those memorized transactions when you are assigning them to a transaction group. Quicken reads Chk as "printable check." Printable checks appear in the register with Print in the Num field. To change the type of a memorized transaction, edit the transaction in the Memorized Transaction list. (See "Changing a memorized transaction" on page 90.)

10 **When you have finished assigning transactions to the group, click Done.**

The group is listed as a single item in your Scheduled Transaction list. The amount is not shown, because there are several transactions in the group with different amounts.

To enter a group of transactions ahead of the scheduled time, select the group in the Scheduled Transaction list and click Pay Now.

Changing and deleting transaction groups

You can edit a transaction group at any time (by clicking Edit at the Scheduled Transaction list), to change the schedule details, assign new transactions, or unassign transactions from the group. You can also display the Memorized Transaction list and edit a memorized transaction at any time, even if it belongs to a transaction group.

Caution:

If you delete a memorized transaction from the Memorized Transaction list, Quicken automatically removes it from the transaction group.

If you delete a transaction group (by clicking Delete at the Scheduled Transaction list), the memorized transactions included in the group remain in the Memorized Transaction list.

Viewing your Financial Calendar

Quicken's Financial Calendar is a visual planning tool that shows you what lies ahead.

1   From the Activities menu, choose Financial Calendar, or click the Calendar icon on Quicken's iconbar.

The Financial Calendar shows your scheduled transactions for one month. To see other months, click Prev or Next, or click the date to enter a new date.

The Financial Calendar shows all transactions for the accounts named. Click Accounts to select other accounts.

Transactions you previously entered in your register are listed in black. *

Today's date is shown in a different color (or shade).

The future transactions you have scheduled appear in blue on the date they are scheduled to be recorded in your register.

To see more information about the transactions, double-click on the date box.

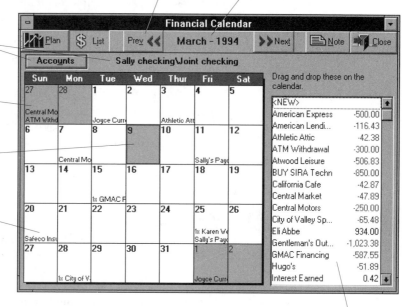

To schedule a transaction, drag it from this list to a day in the Financial Calendar. If the transaction isn't listed, drag <NEW> to the day to set up a new transaction.

(To hide this list and expand the Financial Calendar, click List on the button bar.)

---

*   Font display: Quicken displays transactions in the font Small Fonts, which is a Windows default font. (If you have deleted this font, Quicken chooses a similar font—install Small Fonts again to use that font in the Financial Calendar.) If you prefer a larger font, open the file QUICKEN.INI in your WINDOWS directory and add the line CalendarFont=1 in the [Quicken] section. Then the usual register font is used instead in the Financial Calendar. Or add CalendarFont=−1 to get a smaller font.

The Financial Calendar displays all transactions for the selected accounts, which may be:

- All past transactions already in your registers

- Single scheduled transactions you know are coming up soon (these are marked with "1x")

- Recurring scheduled transactions like your rent

You can enter scheduled transactions through the Scheduled Transaction list, as described previously in this chapter, or directly on the Financial Calendar, as described next. Enter one-time transactions as a reminder of upcoming bills. Also schedule all your recurring transactions (paycheck, rent, car payments, insurance, and so on) to save time entering transactions in your register.

Please note that transactions scheduled on your Financial Calendar ahead of today *are not yet entered in your register.* You can view them *only on the Financial Calendar* or in the Scheduled Transaction list. As they become due, Quicken enters them for you in the register and removes them from the Financial Calendar.

However, if you have entered any future transactions directly into your register as postdated transactions, these also show up on the Financial Calendar, marked in black.

Entering recurring transactions also helps with the projections described in Chapter 22, *Projecting the future,* beginning on page 301.

Selecting accounts to view

You can select which accounts you want to view. The Financial Calendar shows only transactions (both past and scheduled) for the selected accounts, and the drag and drop list contains only transactions from the selected accounts, plus all your memorized transactions. If you don't see a transaction in the drag and drop list to the right of the Financial Calendar that you know is in your register, it's because you need to select the right account first.

1   **Click the Accounts button above the Financial Calendar.**

2   **Mark the accounts to include.**
    To mark or unmark an account, either double-click it in the list, or select it and click Mark or press the spacebar.

3   **Click OK.**

Scheduling a transaction on the Financial Calendar

To the right of the Financial Calendar is a list of transactions you may want to schedule for the future. This list is made up of transactions currently in your selected registers plus your memorized transactions. (It's similar to the payee drop-down list you see when entering transactions in the register.)

1   Make sure the right month is displayed.

Click the Prev or Next buttons to change the month.

2   Move the mouse pointer over the list of transactions on the right.

The pointer changes shape to show you are ready to pick up a transaction.

3   Click on the transaction you want to schedule and hold the button down as you move the pointer to the scheduling day on the Financial Calendar.

To create a new transaction that isn't listed, click on <NEW> and drag that to the scheduling day instead. (Or double-click on the day and click New, as described in the next section.)

The pointer changes shape again to show that you can drop the transaction into a day.

4   With the pointer over the day, release the mouse button.

5   If you dragged <NEW> to the Financial Calendar, fill in the Set Up Scheduled Transaction window as described on page 95.

For more information on how to fill in each field, press F1.

6   For a previously entered transaction, confirm the transaction details.

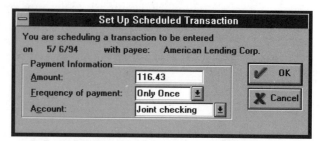

For example, you may want to set up this transaction as a recurring transaction by changing the frequency of payment.

7　**Make any changes to the transaction details and click OK.**

Quicken drops the transaction into the day you selected.

An Only Once payment is marked by a red 1x.
An Only Once deposit is marked by a green 1x.

Fri	Sat	Drag and drop these on the calendar.	
6	7	<NEW>	
		American Express	-500.00
1x America		American Lendi..	-116.43
13	14	Athletic Attic	-42.38
		ATM Withdrawal	-300.00

Recording past transactions

Although the Financial Calendar is most useful for scheduling your upcoming transactions, you can also drag and drop transactions into the past. So, if you like, you can use it as your primary data entry method, instead of using the registers.

When you drop a transaction into a past date on the Financial Calendar, Quicken immediately enters the transaction into your register as well as displaying it on the Financial Calendar.

The pointer changes to a register icon for past dates, because Quicken inserts the transaction straight into your register.

Fri	Sat	Drag and drop these on the calendar.	
4	5	<NEW>	
		American Express	-500.00
		ATM Withdrawal	-300.00
11	12	Central Market	-47.89
		Central Motors	-250.00

Quicken asks you to confirm all the details of the transaction before entering it.

Important: Check that the correct account is shown. Unless you select a different account, Quicken uses the same account as this transaction was last entered into.

Click OK to record the transaction.

Edit Register Transaction

Enter this transaction into your Register

Date: 2/ 4/94

Account: Sally checking

✓ OK

✗ Cancel

$→$ Splits

Register Transaction

◉ Payment　○ Deposit

Payee: ATM Withdrawal

Memo:

Category: [Wallet]

Amount: 300.00

Num Field: ATM

Checking or changing your scheduled transactions

As your Financial Calendar begins to fill up with transactions you've scheduled, you can see at a glance how many transactions are planned for the weeks ahead. But the date box isn't big enough to show all the payment details for each transaction. Also, each date box cannot show more than about four transactions at a time. It's easy, though, to see more information or to change the details.

1   To check on the transactions for a particular day, double-click on that day (or click the right mouse button).

Quicken displays a list of all the transactions scheduled for that day.

The list window shows the transactions for the day you double-click.

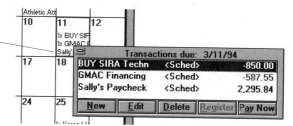

If you double-click on a day in the past, the Register button takes you directly to the transaction in the register.

This list window gives you complete control over your scheduled transactions:

- To set up a new scheduled transaction for this day, click New.

- To check on the details of a scheduled transaction, select the transaction and click Edit. At the Edit Scheduled Transaction window, you can change any of the details. To reschedule a transaction for a different date, for example, change the Next Payment Date. (See the Set Up Scheduled Transaction window shown on page 95.)

  If you are investigating past transactions already in your register, you see the Edit Register Transaction window instead, which lets you edit the transaction details just as you would edit the transaction in the register.

- To delete a scheduled transaction, select the transaction and click Delete. The transaction is removed from your Financial Calendar. If the transaction was a recurring one, all future transactions are removed also.

- If you are investigating past transactions already in your register, you can click the Register button to go to the transaction in the register. In this way, you might like to use your Financial Calendar as a kind of "home base" for viewing and editing your registers.

- To pay the transaction immediately, click Pay Now (see page 107).

When scheduled transactions become due

Quicken organizes your bill-paying.

Each time you start Quicken, Quicken checks your Financial Calendar and finds any transactions that are due. (This may be ahead of the actual scheduled date if you entered a number in the Days In Advance field.) For each transaction that is due, Quicken records the transaction in your register and removes it from the Financial Calendar. If you specified Prompt Before Entering for the transaction, Quicken first displays the details of the transaction and asks you to confirm that it should record the transaction. (See page 96 for more information.)

If you set up the transaction as a check to write in Quicken, you can now print the check.

> As you can see, by using Quicken to schedule your bills in this way, you'll never forget to pay another bill. Quicken's Financial Calendar is a reminder tool and a bill-writer combined.

Often, the transaction you scheduled on your Financial Calendar will contain only an estimate of the amount involved. You may schedule estimated amounts to remind yourself of bills to pay, or to help you plan your finances ahead of time. In these cases, you should set up the transaction to Prompt Before Entering, so that you have a chance to enter the correct amount before the transaction is recorded in your register.

Paying scheduled transactions ahead of time

You may sometimes want to record a scheduled transaction earlier than the date you originally scheduled. For example, you're going away for two weeks. You look at your Financial Calendar and see there are some bills coming up in the next two weeks that you had better pay now, before you leave. To do this, use Quicken's Pay Now function.

1   **Look through the days ahead on your Financial Calendar to see which bills you want to pay now.**

Or click the right mouse button.

2   **For each bill you find, double-click the date box to list the transactions scheduled for that day.**

3   **Select the bill transaction and click Pay Now.**

4   **If you set up the transaction to prompt you before being entered, you now see the Enter Scheduled Transaction window. Check the details and click Enter to record the transaction.**

Quicken enters the transaction in your register immediately, with the transaction date you originally entered unless you changed the date. For an Only Once transaction, Quicken removes the transaction from the Scheduled Transaction list.

If you set up the scheduled transaction as a check to write in Quicken, you can now print the check.

Adding notes to your Financial Calendar

In addition to scheduling transactions on your Financial Calendar, you can add information notes. Just as you might write "Visit Granny" or "Check price of Pepsi stock" on the calendar on your wall, you can stick notes on your Quicken Financial Calendar too. You can color-code the notes for extra usefulness.

1   **Select a day on your Financial Calendar by clicking the date box.**

2   **Click Note on the Financial Calendar button bar.**

Quicken opens a notepad for you to write any text you want.

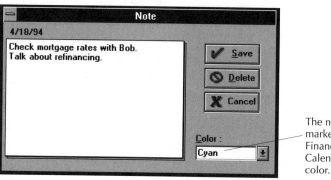

The note will be marked on your Financial Calendar in this color.

3   **Write your note.**

4   **Choose a display color from the drop-down list.**

5   **Click Save.**

The note is marked on your Financial Calendar by a little colored square in the date box.

This square tells you you've added a note to the Financial Calendar for this day.

To read the note, simply click on the little square.

To delete the note, click on the little square and click Delete.

A date box can hold only one note at a time.

You can use the colors to code your notes for importance, business subjects, financial vs. social, or any other system you want to use.

Using Billminder and the Quicken Reminder

The Financial Calendar gives you useful reminders to pay your bills when you start Quicken (and, if you have more than one Quicken file, open the appropriate file). Billminder™ and Reminder are two other features that can remind you even earlier—when you start your computer, when you start Windows, or when you start Quicken.

Billminder and Reminder keep you informed about upcoming bills, scheduled transaction groups, investment reminders, and, if you use CheckFree, electronic payments to transmit.

If you chose to run Billminder "From DOS At Boot Time" when you installed Quicken, Billminder displays DOS messages like this one when you start your computer.

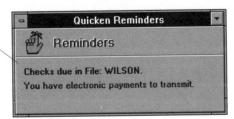

If you chose to run Billminder "At Windows Startup" when you installed Quicken, Billminder displays messages when you run Windows and open the Billminder icon.

Quicken Billminder

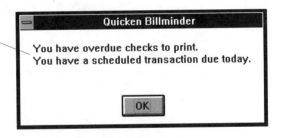

When you start Quicken, Reminder displays messages like this one.

If you have any checks to print, scheduled transaction groups that are due, investment reminders, or electronic payments to transmit, you'll see the Quicken Reminders window whether or not you are running Billminder.

For Billminder to work, you must have selected the option to Install Billminder when you installed Quicken. (If you used Express Installation, Billminder is already installed to appear whenever you start Windows.) If you didn't install Billminder and want to install it now, you can insert these commands to run Billminder in your AUTOEXEC.BAT or your WIN.INI file:

- To see Billminder when you start your computer:
  In AUTOEXEC.BAT, enter PATHNAME\BILLMNDW.EXE PATHNAME /P
  (For example, c:\quickenw\billmndw.exe c:\quickenw /p)

  When you include the /P at the end of the command, Billminder messages remain displayed on the screen until you press Enter, before executing any other items in your AUTOEXEC.BAT file.

OR

- To see Billminder when you run Windows:
  In WIN.INI, enter LOAD=PATHNAME\BILLMNDW.EXE
  (For example, load=c:\quickenw\billmndw.exe)

Once installed into your system, Billminder automatically checks all your Quicken files for upcoming bills each time you start your computer. If Billminder finds checks to print, scheduled transaction groups due, investment reminders due, or payments to transmit, it displays a window.

Changing Billminder Preferences

1   **From the Edit menu, choose Preferences and click Billminder.**

2   **Select Billminder if it is not already turned on.**

To turn off Billminder, clear this checkbox.

Enter a number of business days between 0-30.

To turn off the Reminder, clear this checkbox.

> **Billminder Preferences**
>
> ☑ **Turn on Billminder**
>
> How many days in advance do you want to be reminded of postdated checks, scheduled transaction groups, and investment reminders (0-30)?   `3`
>
> ☑ **Reminder Messages on Startup**
>
> ✓ OK
> ✗ Cancel

3   **Enter the number of business days in advance that you want Quicken to remind you of upcoming bills.**

If you use Quicken:	Set business days in advance to:
Daily (except weekends)	0 days
At least every other day	1 day
At least once every three days	2 days
At least weekly	5 days
At least once every two weeks	10 days
At least once a month	30 days

4   **Select whether you would like Reminder to remind you of upcoming bills when you first start Quicken.**

5   **Click OK.**

Paying bills electronically

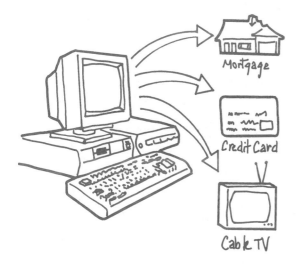

With CheckFree, you can pay bills electronically, using your personal computer and a modem. This service is offered by the Checkfree Corporation of Columbus, Ohio, the nation's leading provider of electronic payment services.

You enter your bills directly into Quicken and then tell Quicken to send the information to CheckFree.

How CheckFree works

The CheckFree bill payment service* provides convenience and security. It's convenient because you don't need stamps or envelopes and you don't have to print and sign checks. It's secure because you have a CheckFree "Personal Security Code" and you control access to this number. You enter all data offline and your financial records reside only in your computer.

Many small businesses use CheckFree; however, it is not specifically designed for business use. (For example, it can't pass invoice numbers through to merchants.) CheckFree works for any house-hold with a computer, modem, and Quicken. If you are undecided about the benefits of paying bills through CheckFree, give it a try. The first month is free. See the information booklet and sign-up form included in your Quicken package.

When you use Quicken to pay bills through CheckFree, you start a series of events.

1   **You enter an "electronic payment" transaction in Quicken, much as you enter transactions in the register or in the Write Checks window.**

Your transaction includes the payment date (the date the payee receives payment from CheckFree).

2   **Using your modem and the communications options in Quicken, you transmit your payment instructions to CheckFree before the payment date.**

See page 123 for payment scheduling guidelines.

3   **Quicken dials the CheckFree Processing Center and transmits your instructions.**

Quicken tells you that the transmission was successful and updates your check register as soon as transmission is complete. The Check-Free Processing Center returns a confirmation number for each transmission, which Quicken stores in the register.

4   **The CheckFree Processing Center makes the payment.**

Some payees are set up to receive electronic payments, and others receive a printed check. See the table on page 125 for details.

5   **You receive verification of the payment both in your bank state-ment and in the statement you receive from the payee (if the payee usually sends statements).**

---

*   You can use CheckFree for payments in the United States regardless of where you transmit from. The bank account used for CheckFree must also be in the United States. CheckFree is an independently owned company.

If you've never used CheckFree before

Check off these preliminary steps before you follow the rest of the instructions in this chapter.

1   Set up service with CheckFree.

You can't send electronic payments until CheckFree has processed your signed CheckFree Service Form and voided check. Service begins immediately after CheckFree processes your sign-up form and enters you as a subscriber to the service. As of the date of this manual, the monthly fee for the service is $9.95, with added charges for more than 20 monthly transactions (see the information booklet). The first month of service is free.

2   Get the CheckFree confirmation package and have it handy.

CheckFree sends you a package to confirm that you are set up for service. The confirmation package also contains information that you will need when you set up Quicken for electronic payments, as well as additional information about CheckFree services and rates.

3   Equip your computer with a Hayes-compatible modem.

You can use any Hayes-compatible modem that works at 300, 1200, 2400, or 9600* baud. (Baud is a unit of speed.) Note which communication port you (or your dealer) attached your modem to. Consult your computer dealer or the modem user manual for help with these tasks.

If you need a modem, CheckFree sells one for $99.00, plus $4.00 shipping. To order a modem, call CheckFree at 800-882-5280.

If you're already using CheckFree to pay bills

If you've been using CheckFree with either DOS Quicken or a previous version of Quicken for Windows, continue using Quicken and CheckFree as always. All the information and data you have entered are retained as you begin using Quicken 3 for Windows. Plus, you can now set up fixed payments in Quicken (see page 118.)

If you've been using any other CheckFree-capable software, follow these important preliminary steps:

1   Back up your CheckFree data.

2   Use your current CheckFree-capable software to print the list of merchants you have set up. Then delete every one of the

---

*   If you will be using a modem at 9600 baud, refer to your confirmation letter for the number to call to obtain an alternative access number.

merchants. Be sure to transmit these deletions to the CheckFree Processing Center.

If you do not delete these merchants, the CheckFree Processing Center may make errors in processing your payments. Note that any pending payments scheduled for the next few business days are already in process at CheckFree and will *not* be stopped by your deletions. Any payments dated in the future are deleted, so you must reschedule them with Quicken.

3   **If necessary, update your Quicken register by importing the historical data from your CheckFree register. You can use Quicken to import transactions (but not merchant names) from CheckFree software.**

Instructions for importing historical data from CheckFree into Quicken are in Help. (Press F1 and then click Contents. Click "Paying bills electronically," and then click "How to..." Click "Importing data from CheckFree.") Quicken for Windows imports only CheckFree version 3.0 files.

After you use Quicken even once to make payments, the Checkfree Corporation will no longer permit you to process payments using another CheckFree-capable product. Other CheckFree-capable products and Quicken are not designed to be used alternately or concurrently. For recurring bills, set up fixed payments in Quicken. (See page 118.) You'll learn how to record the monthly CheckFree service charge next.

4   **Copy the information from the CheckFree-capable software setup screens to the appropriate Quicken electronic payment setup screens as you follow the instructions on page 115.**

Handling the CheckFree service charge

You pay a monthly service charge to use CheckFree, which the Checkfree Corporation automatically charges to your bank account. You will see this charge on your bank statement.

Do not use electronic payments to pay Checkfree Corporation directly for the service charge.

To keep your Quicken register up to date for this charge, set up the fee as a recurring scheduled transaction so that Quicken automatically enters it into your register once a month. See "Scheduling a transaction on the Financial Calendar" on page 104.

Alternatively, add the CheckFree charge to the Service Charge field in the Reconcile Bank Statement window each time you reconcile your account.

Setting up your modem to transmit electronic payments

With Quicken, you can send electronic payment instructions directly to CheckFree. When you install Quicken, the electronic payment option is not turned on, but you can set up your modem and turn on electronic payment capability for your file at any time.

1 **From the Edit menu, choose Preferences and then click Modem.**

2400 baud is the most common modem speed, but many older modems support only 1200 baud.

Enter the telephone number CheckFree gives you. (If you've already been using IntelliCharge to update your credit card account automatically, you don't need to change the number that you've already entered here.) Omit the area code if the number is a local phone call.

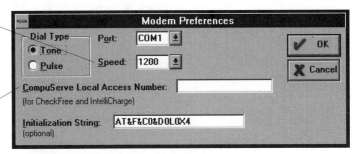

2 **Select Tone for a touch-tone (pushbutton) phone or Pulse for a rotary dial phone.**

Most telephone lines are touch-tone lines.

3 **From the Port drop-down list, select the number for your modem port.**

If you are unsure which port to select, ask your computer dealer which port your modem is attached to, or try COM1 first. If you have a mouse that uses COM1, try COM2 for your modem.

4 **From the Speed drop-down list, select the number that corresponds to the modem speed (baud rate) required by CheckFree and by your modem.**

5 **In the CompuServe Local Access Number box, enter the telephone number you received from CheckFree in your confirmation package.**

(See also the instructions on page 142.)

Omit the area code if the number is local (that is, it contains the same area code as the number you are calling from).

6 **In the Initialization String box, enter any special letters, digits, and other characters to be sent to the modem.**

For more information, look in the modem user's guide. (Most modem commands must begin with the prefix AT.)

7 **Click OK and then click Done.**

Now you can enable electronic payments for a bank account.

Setting up an account for electronic payments

After you have set up your modem, you can set up electronic payment for the bank account you specified when you filled out the CheckFree Service Form. CheckFree allows you to use one bank account with one CheckFree account. You can have as many as five CheckFree bank accounts in a single Quicken file. If you need to use more than one bank account with CheckFree, contact CheckFree Customer Service at 614-899-7500 for instructions.

1   **From the Activities menu, choose CheckFree and then Setup.**

The Electronic Payment Setup window lists all of your bank accounts.

2   **Choose the bank account you want to set up from the list and click Setup. (This must be the account you specified on the service form.)**

Quicken displays the Electronic Payment Account Settings window.

The Enable Electronic Payments checkbox should already be selected and the bank account you want to set up is displayed.

Enter your telephone number, beginning with the area code. You don't have to type punctuation characters such as hyphens or parentheses.

Enter the CheckFree Account Number that you provided in your sign-up form. (In most cases, this number is your Social Security number.)

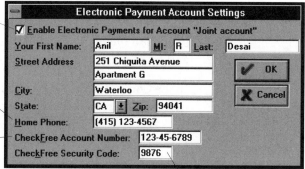

Enter the four-digit Personal Security Code you selected when you signed up for CheckFree.

If you decide later you will no longer make electronic payments, select the account again (steps 1 and 2) and clear the Enable Electronic Payments checkbox. Then notify CheckFree Corporation in writing that you are canceling service.

3   **Ensure that the Enable Electronic Payments checkbox is selected and the bank account you want to set up is displayed.**

4   **Enter information in the Electronic Payment Account Settings window.**

For more information about any field, press F1.

5   **When you have finished entering information, click OK.**

Quicken returns to the Electronic Payment Setup window. Note that the word "Enabled" and a lightning bolt appear in the Electronic Pmts field beside the bank account you are setting up for electronic payments.

6   **Click Close to close the Electronic Payment Setup window.**

7   **Open the Account list to see the account.**

From now on, when you see a list of accounts, you'll see this lightning bolt beside "Bank" in the Type field for this account. This account is set up for electronic payments.

Account	Type	Description	Trans	Balance	Chks
Joint account	Bank⚡		84	3,189.49	✓
Money Market	Bank	Money market	1	321.55	
Sally Checking	Bank		12	786.80	
Savings	Bank	Pacific savings acc.	3	3,814.86	

You are ready to set up electronic payees by adding them to the Electronic Payee list.

Setting up electronic payees

For Quicken to record an electronic payment, you must first add the payee to the Electronic Payee list. You can also authorize CheckFree to make a series of fixed, recurring payments from your bank account to an electronic payee. (CheckFree calls electronic payees "merchants," but you can send an electronic payment to any business or individual.)

You have to add a payee to the Electronic Payee list only once; all accounts in a Quicken file share the same list. You can add payees before you begin writing electronic payments or as you write payments. (Quicken transmits changes you've made to the Electronic Payee list to CheckFree the next time you make payments, or transmit for some other reason.)

Setting up payees for normal electronic payments

1   **From the Activities menu, choose CheckFree and then choose Electronic Payee List.**

If Electronic Payee List is dimmed on the CheckFree menu, none of your accounts has been set up for electronic payments. See "Setting up an account for electronic payments" on page 116.

Your list is initially empty until you set up your electronic payees. When you have set up electronic payees, you can edit information about a payee here by selecting the payee and clicking Edit, or you can delete the payee from the list by selecting the payee and clicking Del.

Payee	Type	Account Number
Montgomery Ward	FIXED	20394
State Farm		HO-8888

Once you've set up electronic payees, you can use the list to print a mailing list of payees (addresses and phone numbers of vendors). To print the Electronic Payee List window, press Ctrl+P while the list is displayed.

2   **Click New.**

Quicken displays the Choose Type of Electronic Payee window.

3   **Select Normal Payee and click OK.**

A normal payee is one to which you intend to transmit individual payments, because the amount varies each time (such as the phone company or a department store).

A fixed payee is one you set up once and intend to have CheckFree automatically send regular, recurring payments to after that (such as your rent, mortgage, or car payment).

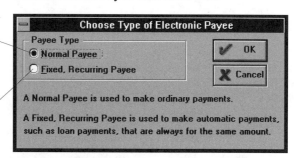

4   **Enter information in the Set Up Electronic Payee window.**

Enter the electronic payee's address, phone number, and account number accurately. CheckFree uses all the information in this window to ensure that your payment is routed correctly

Enter a number the electronic payee uses to identify you (account number, policy number, or loan number). If you don't know the number, enter your last name. The electronic payee needs the account number to credit your account for the payment.

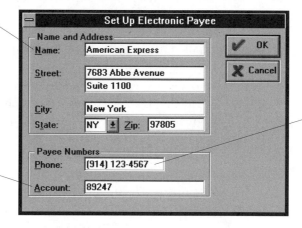

Enter the phone number you would call if you had a billing question, beginning with the area code. CheckFree must have the correct phone number to route your payments correctly.

The payee address, phone number, and account number must be accurate. CheckFree may need the address to mail your payment to the payee. In addition, CheckFree uses the phone number as a reference to identify and route your payment to the proper payee.

5   **Click OK to record the information.**

You can set up more electronic payees or begin entering payments. See "Entering electronic payments" on page 121.

Setting up payees for fixed payments

You can authorize CheckFree to make a series of fixed, recurring payments from your bank account to an electronic payee. You specify payment frequency and other details, and Quicken sets up as many payments as you need.

Future CheckFree fixed payments show up in your Financial Calendar too. (The Financial Calendar is described starting on page 102.)

You set up this payment once, and then CheckFree takes care of paying all the bills at the frequency you specify, and Quicken automatically enters the transactions in your account register. (For example, you might want to schedule 36 months of car payments, to be paid on the third day of each month, starting 1/3/94.)

You cannot change a normal payee into a fixed payee and you cannot change a fixed payee into a normal payee. If you want to make fixed payments to a payee you have already set up as a normal payee, you need to delete the normal payee from the Electronic Payee list, transmit the deletion to CheckFree, and then set up the payee as a fixed payee.

1   From the Activities menu, choose CheckFree and then choose Electronic Payee List.

2   Click New.

Quicken displays the Choose Type of Electronic Payee window.

3   Select Fixed, Recurring Payee and click OK.

4   Enter information in the Set Up Electronic Payee window.

If you have one account set up for electronic payments, Quicken automatically displays the account from which electronic payments will be drawn. If you have more than one electronic payment account, choose the account from a drop-down list here.

Enter information here as you would to set up normal electronic payees. See step 4 on page 118.

Enter the amount of the fixed payment.

Enter the length of time you expect the fixed payments to continue.

Enter the payment date of the first fixed payment.

From the drop-down list, choose how often CheckFree should make the payments.

5   Click Categories.

Enter a category here. Click Splits if you want the fixed payment transaction to cover more than one category or class.

6   **Enter a category and memo for the payment and click OK.**

7   **Click OK to authorize CheckFree to make the fixed payments you specified.**

CheckFree does not know about a fixed payment until you transmit it. If you are ready to send the information to CheckFree, see "Transmitting electronic payments" on page 125.

Setting up more than one account for a payee

If you have multiple accounts with one payee, you may want to set up that payee more than once. You can set up multiple accounts with one payee, but the account numbers you enter must be different. (For example, use a homeowner's insurance policy number and life insurance policy number from the same insurance company.) If you set up more than one account for the same payee, Quicken also asks you to add extra characters to the name to make the name unique.

Here's how the Electronic Payee list looks with two entries for the same insurance company. You can edit an existing payee by adding characters in braces at the end. In this example, this family could add {homeowner} to the first entry for State Farm Insurance.

Quicken does not transmit the characters within the braces ({Life}) to CheckFree. The braces help you to distinguish the two accounts in the Electronic Payee list and in Quicken reports.

If you change an electronic transaction to a paper check transaction and then print checks, Quicken will not print the characters after the first brace or the brace itself. You might find this feature useful for paper checks as well as for electronic payments.

Amortizing a fixed payment

If your fixed payment is for an amortized loan, such as a mortgage, you can set up the loan details in Quicken's View Loans window. Then, Quicken automatically calculates the split between principal, interest, and any impound items, and enters the details in a split transaction in your register with each payment. You have all the advantages of being able to analyze your loan amortization in the View Loans window. For full details of Quicken's loan handling features, see Chapter 23, *Tracking loans and mortgages,* beginning on page 315.

To amortize a CheckFree fixed payment, follow these two steps in this order:

- Set up the payee for the fixed payment as described on page 118.
- Set up the loan in the View Loans window, as described in "Setting up a loan," beginning on page 316.

    In step 8 on page 320, click Method of Pmt and select CheckFree Fixed Payment. Select the payee from the drop-down Fixed Payee list and click OK to return to the Set Up Loan Payment window.

Quicken uses the total amount from your loan in the fixed payment transaction it sends to CheckFree. If you change the total payment amount in the View Loans window (for example, if the rate changes for an adjustable rate mortgage), Quicken sets up a change transaction to transmit to CheckFree, giving instruction to alter the payment amount. Remember that CheckFree won't change the payment amount until you actually transmit the change transaction.

If you delete the loan from the View Loans window, Quicken does not delete the payee from the Electronic Payee list, nor does it create a stop payment transaction. If you want to stop the payment, you must do it as a separate action: see "Stopping fixed payments" on page 129.

Entering electronic payments

Entering normal electronic payments in the register or Write Checks window is very similar to entering any other kind of payment. See "Entering normal electronic payments in Write Checks" on page 122 or "Entering normal electronic payments in the register" on page 123.

Entering fixed electronic payments

If you set up fixed payments, you don't need to enter transactions in the Write Checks window or the register. All you need to do is transmit the first fixed payment to CheckFree. See "Transmitting electronic payments" on page 125.

After that, CheckFree sends the payments to the payees at the intervals you've specified, and Quicken enters the transactions into your register automatically. In the check register, Quicken inserts the word FIXED in the Num field of any fixed payment transaction. Five days before the payment date, Quicken replaces FIXED with E-PMT and enters the next FIXED payment to that payee.

Entering normal electronic payments in Write Checks

After you have set up a normal payee, each time you want to send a payment to that payee, enter the payment in your Quicken account. This is how you enter the payment in the Write Checks window.

Or click the Check icon on the iconbar.

1   **From the Activities menu, choose Write Checks.**

2   **Make sure the correct account is selected in the Account box.**

3   **Select the Electronic Payment checkbox to display the screen in electronic payment format.**

Quicken automatically postdates any electronic payment by five business days from today. You can change the date to postdate this check even further. See "Scheduling electronic payments" on page 123.

Enter a payee name or choose it from the Electronic Payee list.

When you have electronic payment set up for an account, and select the Electronic Payment checkbox, Quicken clearly labels the window.

You can clear the Electronic Payment checkbox if you want to write and print a paper check next.

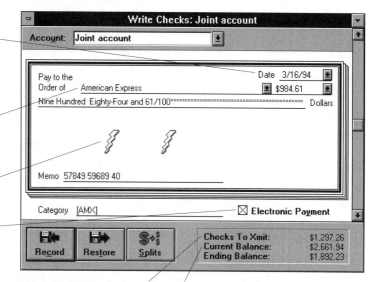

Checks To Xmit tracks the total amount of electronic payments you have written and have yet to transmit.

The Current Balance does not include postdated transactions; the Ending Balance does. (All electronic payments must be postdated by at least five business days.)

4   **In the Date field, enter the payment date.**

Quicken automatically postdates any electronic payment by five business days from today. You can change the date to postdate this check even further (but not earlier). See "Scheduling electronic payments" on page 123.

5   **In the Payee field, enter the payee name.**

If you type the name of a payee who is not in the Electronic Payee list, Quicken lets you select from the list or set up a new payee.

6   **Fill in the $ Amount, Memo, and Category fields as usual.**

(Quicken does not transmit the contents of the Memo field to CheckFree. The information in the Memo field is for your records.)

7   **Click Record to record the payment.**

Quicken records the payment in the check register with XMIT in the Num field. Quicken does not transmit the payment until you tell it to. (See "Transmitting electronic payments" on page 125.)

Entering normal electronic payments in the register

You can enter electronic payments in the register instead of in the Write Checks window. Open the register and enter the transaction using the information in steps 4 through 6 above. Type XMIT in the Num field (or choose it from the drop-down list) to indicate to Quicken that this is an untransmitted electronic payment. Record the payment as usual.

Type XMIT in the Num field of a transaction to tell Quicken that this transaction is an electronic payment.

XMIT indicates that the transaction *will be* transmitted.

Bank Account: Joint account						
Insert	Delete	Copy	Paste		Report	Close

Date	Num	Payee		Payment	Clr	Deposit	Balance
		Memo	Category				
3/17/94	XMIT	American Express		984 61			1,169 85
		57849 59689 40	[AMX]				

Making duplicate electronic payments

CheckFree will not process a payment that appears to be a duplicate of a previous payment (a payment that has the same payee, amount, and payment date). Although you will receive a confirmation number for the duplicate payment, only the previous payment will be processed. If you need to send a second payment to the same payee, you must vary the amount or payment date slightly.

Scheduling electronic payments

Using CheckFree does not mean you can pay your bills at the last moment. Quicken and CheckFree require lead time between the date you transmit your payment instructions and the date your payment is due. The first time you make a payment to each payee, use this table to determine how to schedule the payment.

Quicken and CheckFree require that you transmit the payment at least five business days before the payment date.

In addition to the five business days between the transmission date and the payment date, Intuit advises you to schedule the payment date to each *new electronic payee* five business days in advance of the due date. The additional five days allow you to see how promptly the payee was able to process the payment.

Date	Definition	Calculation
Transmission date	Date you send payment instructions from Quicken to CheckFree	Five business days before the payment date, ten business days before the due date
Payment date	Date that you've entered in the Date field in Quicken; it's the date the payee receives payment from CheckFree	Five business days before the due date
Due date	Due date on the statement from the payee	

For example, suppose you have a bill due on November 15. *If this is the first electronic payment to the payee*, you would transmit the payment on November 1, ten business days before the due date.

November

The transmission date is November 1, five business days before the payment date.

The payee receives payment from CheckFree on the payment date, November 8, five business days before the due date.

The due date of the bill is November 15.

Shaded areas on this calendar are nonbusiness days.

If a payment is due on or after a holiday like Thanksgiving, be sure you still allow a minimum of five business days between the transmission date and the payment date.

To decide how to schedule your future payments, examine the next statement from the payee to see how promptly the payee was able to process the payment. If you need to adjust the schedule for your next payment, see the guidelines below. The latest possible date you can transmit a payment from Quicken to CheckFree is five business days before the bill is due.

Guidelines to avoid late payments

Enter the correct telephone number, account number, and address for the payee when you set up an electronic payee in Quicken.

After you have made several payments to an electronic payee, use the table below to determine when to transmit the payment to CheckFree.

After you have made several payments to the electronic payee and you determine how quickly the payee can process a CheckFree payment, you may want to decrease the length of time between the payment date and the due date. You might even treat the payment date and the due date as the same date if you know that a particular payee always processes the payment from CheckFree immediately.

You cannot decrease the length of time required between the transmission date and the payment date (five business days).

Date	Definition	Calculation
Transmission date	Date you send payment instructions to CheckFree	Five business days before the payment date (can be no less than five business days, but may be more)
Payment date	Date that you've entered in the Date field in Quicken; it's the date the payee receives payment from CheckFree	Five business days before the due date (if the payee always processes the payment immediately, the payment date may be the same day as the due date)
Due date	Due date on the statement from the payee	

Transmitting electronic payments

The transactions you transmit to CheckFree can include payments, changes to the Electronic Payee list (payees that are edited, added, or deleted), stop payments, payment inquiries, and E-mail messages to the CheckFree Processing Center.

You should view a summary of payment and payment-related transactions before you transmit them. Then transmit payments to CheckFree at least five business days before bills are due.

The way the CheckFree Processing Center makes the payment depends on the payee you're paying.

Payment method	Description
Electronic-to-check	CheckFree mails a check on your behalf to the payee and then receives funds electronically from your bank on the payment date you specified. Your bank statement will list the payee name, payment amount, and date for this type of transaction, instead of attaching a canceled check as a receipt.
Laser-printed draft	CheckFree mails a check drawn on your bank account to the payee. The check contains information such as your account number and address. If your checks are returned with your bank statement, this laser-printed check from CheckFree will be returned like any other paper check.
All electronic	If the payee is set up to receive electronic payments via one of CheckFree's payment networks, CheckFree initiates an electronic payment directly from your bank account to the payee's bank account. Your bank statement will list the payee name, payment amount, and date for this type of transaction, instead of attaching a canceled check as a receipt.

Previewing and transmitting transactions

1   **Start in the Write Checks window or in the register.**

   If you have more than one account enabled for use with CheckFree, make sure you are in the right account register, or that the right account is selected in the Write Checks window.

2   **From the Activities menu, choose CheckFree and then choose Transmit.**

   Quicken tells you how many payments are ready to be transmitted.

3   **Click Preview to preview the transmission.**

Quicken places electronic payments to be transmitted at the top of the window in the payment date order. All electronic payments are indicated by the abbreviation "Pmt" or "Fxd."

These are updates you have made to the Electronic Payee list since the last time you transmitted payments to CheckFree. Whenever you add a payee, delete a payee, edit a payee, or set up a fixed payment, the action appears in this list. CheckFree uses all the changes you make in Quicken to update your records at the CheckFree Processing Center.

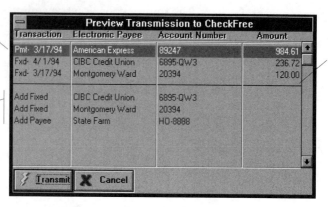

Payments to be transmitted appear above this line.

Changes to the Electronic Payee list appear below the line. (Fixed payments appear in both places.)

4   **If you need to modify transactions to be transmitted, click Cancel to return to the register or the Write Checks window, where you can make changes.**

You can send some of the payments that appear in the Preview window without sending them all to CheckFree. See "Deferring the transmission of an electronic payment" on page 127.

5   **If you need to modify electronic payees, go to the Electronic Payee list to make the changes.**

Quicken transmits updates to the Electronic Payee list along with the payments you send; you cannot modify these updates in the Preview Transmission to CheckFree window.

6   **If the transactions are correct, click Transmit.**

Quicken initializes the modem and dials the CheckFree Processing Center. As it transmits, Quicken displays messages indicating progress. If you see an error message, try the procedure again. See "CheckFree problems and solutions" on page 132.

Unposted payments

You should allow at least 10 business days from the payment date for a payee to post your payment. If a payee does not post your payment within this period, you should:

- Call the merchant directly. In most cases, the payment will be posted by the time you call and any questions can be cleared up easily. If this is not the case, follow the next step.

- Contact CheckFree Customer Service (see page 372 for the phone number). Provide a contact name and phone number for the payee, and CheckFree will provide proof of payment remittance to the payee. If the posting problem is due to a CheckFree error, CheckFree will resolve the situation directly with the payee (including paying any late fees up to a maximum of $50).

Deferring the transmission of an electronic payment

To defer the transmission of a recorded transaction to CheckFree, you can temporarily change the status of the transaction.

1 **In the register, select the transaction that you don't want to send right now.**

2 **In the Num field, type** Print **over** XMIT.

E-PMT marks an electronic payment, either fixed or normal, that has already been transmitted.

XMIT marks an electronic payment that has been entered but not transmitted yet.

FIXED marks the next fixed payment in a series of recurring payments.

Don't void or delete an E-PMT transaction. See "Stopping normal electronic payments" on page 128. If you want to cancel a FIXED payment transaction, see "Stopping fixed payments" on page 129.

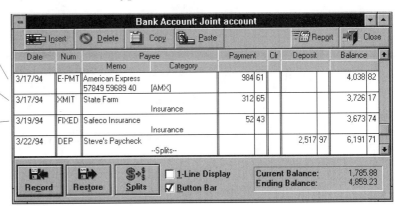

3 **Click Record to record the transaction.**

When you want to transmit the transaction, delete Print and type XMIT in the Num field.

Getting a confirmation number

CheckFree sends a confirmation number back to Quicken for each transmission. Quicken stores this confirmation number and automatically uses it if you send an inquiry or a stop payment request regarding the transaction.

1 **Select the transaction in the check register.**

2 **From the Activities menu, choose CheckFree and then choose Electronic Payment Info.**

You'll see the transmission date of the transaction, the payment date of the transaction, the transmission status, and the confirmation number.

Stopping electronic payments

After Quicken transmits an electronic payment, you can stop payment on the transaction if you don't wait too long. On the basis of the five days it can take CheckFree to make a scheduled payment, Quicken determines whether you are likely to be able to stop the payment and tells you if it's clearly too late.

Caution:

Don't void an electronic payment. If you delete or void an electronic payment, Quicken cannot get the confirmation number needed to stop the payment or transmit a status inquiry to CheckFree. Use the Stop Payment command instead.

Stopping normal electronic payments

1 **Select the transaction in the check register.**

2 **From the Activities menu, choose CheckFree and then choose Stop Payment.**

Quicken tells you when the payment is scheduled to be made. If it is possible to stop payment, Quicken asks if you want to do so. If it's too late to stop the payment or the payment has not yet been transmitted, Quicken lets you know.

Timing is critical: Quicken determines whether you can still stop a payment, taking into account the usual five business days between the transmission date and the payment date. The Checkfree Corporation does not assess a charge for stop payments performed in this manner. If Quicken tells you that it is too late to transmit the stop payment, you can contact CheckFree by telephone—they may be able to stop the payment manually. CheckFree does assess an additional fee to stop payments manually. See the "How to Get the Most from CheckFree" booklet enclosed in the CheckFree confirmation package for details.

3 **Click OK if it's still possible to stop the payment.**

Quicken immediately transmits your request to CheckFree. Messages inform you of the progress of the transmission. If the transmission is successful, Quicken marks the payment VOID in the register and records the stop payment confirmation number received from CheckFree in the Memo field of the transaction.

Stopping fixed payments

There are two ways to stop fixed payments. Either way, if you stop one payment, you stop them all:

- If you use the stop payment command described in "Stopping normal electronic payments" on page 128, Quicken stops all future fixed payments and saves all the information you entered for the payee.

FIXED payees become INACTIVE payees when you either finish paying all the fixed payments or stop the fixed payments before you finish the payments. Keep inactive payees in the Electronic Payee list if you think you may need access to any of the payee or payment information in the future.

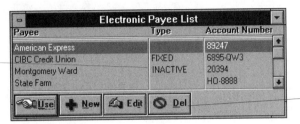

Click Del to delete a payee from the list.

- If you delete the fixed payee from the Electronic Payee list and transmit the deletion to CheckFree, Quicken stops all future fixed payments and deletes all information you entered for the payee and any confirmation number history it has for the payee.

Editing or deleting a payee

You can edit or delete a payee in the Electronic Payee list as long as you do not have an untransmitted payment for that payee.

You can edit payees even if there are payments pending (transmitted but not yet paid.) However, if you edit payee information or delete a payee from the Electronic Payee list, Quicken waits to send the changes to CheckFree until the next time you transmit payments.

Action	Normal Payments Untransmitted	Normal Payments Pending	Fixed Payments
Can you edit payee information?	No	Yes	Yes
Can you delete the payee from the Electronic Payee list?	No	Yes	Yes

Changing or deleting payees

1. **Select the name in the Electronic Payee list.**

2. **Click Edit to edit the payee or click Del to delete the payee.**

   Deleting a payee also deletes any confirmation number history for that payee.

3. **If you're editing the payee, enter the changes you want and click OK.**

   Quicken transmits the edit or deletion the next time you transmit a payment.

Changing or deleting a normal payee with pending payments

If you have pending (transmitted but not paid) payments to a normal payee, Quicken waits to transmit the change until Check-Free has processed all pending payments to that payee.

1 Set up a new payee with the correct information.

Set up a new electronic payee.

Quicken keeps the electronic payee you want to delete or edit in the Electronic Payee list until after CheckFree pays the pending transaction to the payee.

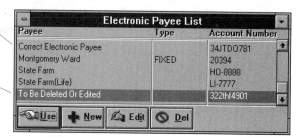

2 Select the pending payment in the check register and choose the new payee name from the Electronic Payee list (select it and click Use).

Repeat if there are multiple untransmitted payments to this payee.

Quicken transmits the payee changes the next time you transmit a payment.

3 After CheckFree pays the pending transaction, delete the incorrect payee from the Electronic Payee list.

Communicating with CheckFree

You can send electronic messages directly to CheckFree, to make a payment inquiry or to send electronic mail. If you want to speak with a CheckFree customer service representative, see the telephone number on page 372.

Inquiring about electronic payments

CheckFree knows nothing about a payment until you transmit it to them. To get information about an untransmitted payment, you can view it in the check register or preview it as part of the transmission procedure.

You can find out the status of a transaction that you've already transmitted to CheckFree.

1 In the Quicken register, select the payment transaction.

2 From the Activities menu, choose CheckFree and then choose Inquiry.

Quicken displays a window showing the date the transaction was transmitted, the payment date, the account number, and the confirmation number, and then asks if you want to transmit an inquiry to CheckFree regarding this transaction.

3   **Check to make sure this transaction is the one you want to inquire about. If it is, click OK to send an inquiry.**

Quicken displays the Transmit Payment Inquiry to CheckFree window.

4   **Enter information in the fields.**

After the date, the reference to the payee, and the salutation, you can type three lines of text. Quicken supplies the signature line.

5   **Click Transmit to send the inquiry to CheckFree.**

CheckFree responds to your message by electronic mail (CheckFree E-Mail) or by U.S. mail. To view your electronic mailbox in Quicken, see "Sending or receiving electronic mail" next.

Sending or receiving electronic mail

You can send CheckFree a message that is not specific to a payment. CheckFree replies to your message with E-Mail that you can read in Quicken or by U.S.mail.

1   **From the Activities menu, choose CheckFree and then choose E-Mail.**

2   **Choose either to send or to read a message.**

- Click Create to send a message. Quicken displays the Transmit Message to CheckFree window. Type your message in the text area and Click Transmit to transmit the message. Quicken transmits the message to CheckFree immediately.

   OR

- Click Retrieve to read a message from CheckFree. Quicken connects to the CheckFree Processing Center and looks for new messages that are addressed to you. Quicken displays all the messages you've already received from CheckFree in chronological order. (It also displays messages you've sent to CheckFree.) If there is a new message from CheckFree, it will be at the top of the list. Select the message you want to read. The text of the message appears in the Message window.

CheckFree problems and solutions

If you have trouble transmitting to CheckFree, wait a minute or two and try transmitting again. The CheckFree system may simply have been busy when you first tried to transmit. If that doesn't work, try the troubleshooting steps in this section one by one. After each step, try transmitting until you transmit successfully.

Do this	Here's how
Check that you've set up your modem correctly.	See "Setting up your modem to transmit electronic payments" on page 115.
Check all hardware connections at both ends.	Check the modular phone plugs, RS-232-C cable, and power cords to be sure they are securely plugged in and the power is on.
Check the modem switch settings, if any.	Your modem manual describes the function of each switch on the modem. With the modem turned off, set the switches to originate a call (not to answer), to respond to DTR ("data terminal ready"), and to recognize commands.
Dial the service number yourself.	Your service number is supplied by CheckFree for your particular modem speed and geographic location. Dial the number that the modem dials to be sure that you're getting a dial tone and that when you dial the access number, the CheckFree Processing Center answers with a high-pitched tone.

Code to turn off call waiting / Digit for a long-distance call (1)

*70, 1, 800 555 1111

Pauses (commas) / Area code and (fictional) telephone number

Do you have to wait to get an outside line or do you have to add extra digits? Write down the sequence of digits, characters, and pauses you dialed. An example of a character is an asterisk (*), which many phone systems use as a signal for a special phone feature.

Translate what you've written down into the sequence of numbers, commas, and characters you need to enter in CompuServe Local Access Number box in the Modem Settings window. (Use a comma for each pause, or several commas for longer pauses. For example, if you need to dial 9 to get an outside line and then need to wait a second to hear a dial tone, enter 9 and then enter a comma in this field.)

Do this	Here's how
Change one of the settings in the Modem Settings window.	See "Setting up your modem to transmit electronic payments" on page 115. Change the **Dial Type** setting for tone or pulse dialing. Try this step only if you are getting no response at all from your modem: change the serial port from its current setting, typically COM1, to COM2, to see if you've been using the wrong port. Change the setting for the modem speed and check that the access number is correct for the modem speed. If possible, change to a slower speed. In the Initialization String box, you may need to include a different sequence of commands for Quicken to send to the modem before dialing the access number. Enter any special letters, digits, and other characters to be sent to the modem. To find out what codes you need, look in the modem user's manual. (Most modem commands must begin with the prefix AT.)
Ask your computer dealer if your serial port is wired DCE.	If it is, you may need a "null modem" cable. This type of cable switches the connections of two wires.
Ask your dealer if your serial card or your modem has nonstandard connectors.	If either is nonstandard, install a cable with appropriate connectors.
Change a setting on your computer.	If your computer can run at a slower speed, try setting it at the slowest speed. Remove any memory-resident programs.
If your modem appears to be operating correctly, but the CheckFree Processing Center does not respond.	Call CheckFree Customer Service at **614-899-7500** from 8:00 am to 8:00 pm Eastern time. Do **not** call Intuit with these questions; we have no control or knowledge in these areas. Be sure to note any error messages exactly as they are displayed.

Tracking credit card transactions

Credit card expenses are often an integral part of personal and business finances. With Quicken, you can handle your credit cards by using either a Quicken bank account or a separate Quicken credit card account.

You can also automate entering transactions into a credit card register with a special Quicken credit card and IntelliCharge™. Each month, you either receive an electronic statement disk in the mail or download your statement by modem. IntelliCharge updates your register in seconds (even assigning categories to transactions) and writes a check for the credit card bill.

When to use Quicken credit card accounts

Credit card accounts are useful if you want detailed records of your credit card transactions or if you pay your credit card charges over time. Use the following information to determine the best way to use Quicken to track your credit card transactions and payments.

Credit habits	Account to use	Actions to take
You usually pay your credit card bills in full, and you want to keep records of only a few individual credit card transactions.	Bank account	Record the check that pays the bill in your Quicken bank account. Split the transaction if you want to categorize particular credit card charges or groups of charges. See "Tracking credit card transactions in Quicken bank accounts" on this page. This is the fastest way to handle credit cards. However, this method doesn't track your outstanding credit card balance.
You pay your credit card bills over time, and you want to keep records of some (but not all) credit card transactions.	Credit card account	In each credit card account, enter only those transactions you want to keep a record of. (You can use your charge slips, or work from your monthly credit card statement.) Create one transaction covering all the charges you don't want to take the time to enter. This method lets you keep detailed records of selected transactions without taking the time to enter every credit card transaction.
You want to keep a record of every credit card transaction *and* know your outstanding credit card balance at all times.	Credit card account	Enter each credit card transaction in the account from your charge slips as you make purchases throughout the month. The credit card register shows your card balance and the available credit remaining on the card. Use Quicken to update your credit card statement and pay your bill. See "Reconciling credit card accounts" on page 137.
You want to keep a record of every credit card transaction, but you don't want to take the time to enter transactions in the account. You don't need to know what your outstanding credit card balance is more often than once a month.	Credit card account with IntelliCharge	Use IntelliCharge to update your credit card account *automatically* every month. See "Using IntelliCharge" on page 140.

There are two methods for entering transactions into Quicken's credit card accounts. In regular credit card accounts (for VISA, MasterCard, and so on), you enter some or all of the transactions. In a credit card account with IntelliCharge, IntelliCharge adds the transactions, updates your credit card account, and pays your bill automatically. See "Using IntelliCharge" on page 140.

Tracking credit card transactions in Quicken bank accounts

The next example shows you how to track credit card expenses in your Quicken bank account. With this method, you keep track of some or all of your credit card purchases by entering multiple categories in a split transaction when you write a check to pay your bill.

Suppose your credit card statement shows seven new transactions: five are clothing and two are gifts. You also need to pay a finance charge.

1 **Enter the payment as usual in either the Write Checks or Register window.**

Fill in everything but the category information.

2 **Click Splits.**

The total amount of the check appears in the first line of the split.

See also:
"Assigning categories to transactions" on page 22.

3 **Categorize the first line with the category Gifts and type the amount you spent on gifts over the amount in the first line.**

4 **Categorize the second line with the category Clothing and enter the amount you spent on clothing in the Amount field on the second line.**

5 **Categorize the third line as Finance Charges and enter the amount.**

You may need to set up the category Finance charges.

Quicken includes the expenses for gifts, clothing, and finance charges when you create any report or graph based on categories.

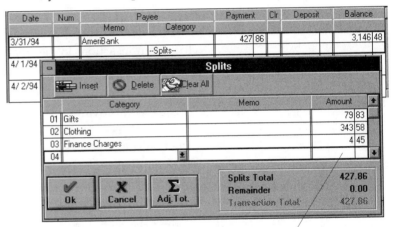

If your figures add up correctly, there should be no remainder.

You can classify credit card transactions with classes as well as categorize them with income and expense categories. For example, if you use a credit card for both business and personal expenses, you might want to use a class called Business to identify business-related charges.

6 **Click OK to close the split transaction.**

7 **Click Record to record the transaction.**

Using regular credit card accounts

A Quicken credit card account is very similar to a Quicken bank account. If you've used a Quicken bank account, you already know most of what you'll need to use a credit card account.

◆ **Set up the account.**
See "Setting up additional Quicken accounts" on page 2 to set up a credit card account for each card you use.

◆ **Save your transaction slips when you charge an item, and enter the transactions as they occur throughout the month.**
See "Entering credit card transactions" on this page.

◆ **Update your account with the credit card statement.**
See "Updating regular credit card accounts" on page 137.

◆ **Pay your credit card bill.**
See "Paying credit card bills" on page 139.

Entering credit card transactions

To enter transactions in the credit card register you can:

● Save your transaction slips when you charge an item and enter the transactions as they occur throughout the month.

This method provides you with your current credit card balance at all times. It also lets you double-check your charges against those listed on your credit card statement.

● Wait until you receive your monthly statement and enter the transactions from the statement.

If you don't need to know your balance throughout the month, this method is easy to use. You can also enter some or all of the transactions.

● Create transfers between the credit card account and other Quicken accounts. You use transfers to track the movement of money from your bank account to your credit card account (bill payments, for example), or from your credit card account to your bank account (overdraft protection through your credit card account, for example).

If you want to keep a record of every credit card transaction, but you don't want to take the time to enter transactions in the account and you don't need to know what your outstanding credit card balance is more often than once a month, consider using IntelliCharge. IntelliCharge updates your credit card account *automatically* every month. See "Using IntelliCharge" on page 140.

To open the register for a credit card account, open the Account list and choose the account name.

The credit card register has no Num column, but it does have a Ref column that you may use to track transaction numbers, if desired.

The Clr (Cleared) column displays an x for transactions you have already reconciled with previous credit card statements.

This type of transfer payment is recorded automatically with Quicken's bill-paying feature. The account name tells you in what account Quicken recorded the check. To pay the credit card bill, see page 139.

Instead of the Payment and Deposit columns of the check register, the credit card register has Charge and Payment columns. Use the Charge column for amounts you have charged, finance charges, and other fees. Use the Payment column to record bill payments or a credit to your account.

Date	Ref	Payee	Charge	Clr	Payment	Balance
		Memo Category				
2/28/94		Tilenius Records	18 56	x		-878 63
		Compact Discs				
3/ 1/94		Designs by Rick	32 95	x		-911 58
		Flowers Gifts				
3/ 2/94		Linda Cassel Appliances	325 98			-1,237 56
		New Microwave Household				
3/10/94		Village Bookstore	35 82			-1,273 38
		Swim With Sharks Books				
3/11/94		Quicken Visa			1,000 00	-273 38
		[Sally Checking]				
3/12/94		Duke of Edinburgh Pub	62 58			-335 96
		Dining				

Credit Card: Visa

Insert   Delete   Copy   Paste   Report   Close

Record   Restore   Splits   □ 1-Line Display   ✓ Iconbar

Credit Remaining: 4,436.48
Ending Balance: 563.52

Categorize your credit card charges. That way, you'll see credit card expenses categorized in income and expense reports and graphs.

The credit limit for this account is $5,000. Credit Remaining is your credit limit for the account less the balance of the account. Ending Balance is your outstanding balance.

Updating regular credit card accounts

You update your Quicken credit card statement much as you reconcile your Quicken bank account against your bank statement. You mark transactions as cleared, and enter any missing transactions you want to keep a record of. Reconcile one monthly statement at a time, the oldest statement first. Then pay your bill.

Reconciling credit card accounts

To make sure that your credit card account contains accurate information, you should reconcile it each month with your credit card statement. Such reconciliation also allows you to take advantage of the following Quicken features:

- You don't have to enter every credit card charge. Instead, Quicken can record a single adjustment transaction that covers all the charges that you choose not to record individually.

- Quicken automatically records a transaction for any finance charges to your credit card account.

- If you have a bank account, Quicken automatically records any credit card payment.

1   Open the credit card account.

2   From the Activities menu, choose Pay Credit Card Bill.

3   In the Charges, Cash Advances box, enter the total amount of charges and advances shown on your statement.

Don't include interest or service charges.

4   In the Payments, Credits box and New Balance box, enter the total amount of payments and credits and the new balance for your card, as shown on your statement.

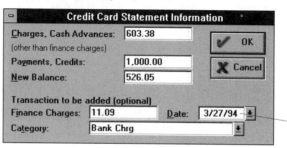

Quicken uses this information to create a transaction in your account for finance charges. You can also select a different category to assign to the transaction.

Quicken uses the current date unless you change it.

5   In the Finance Charges box, enter any finance charges shown on your statement.

Quicken will add a Finance Charges transaction to your credit card register.

6   Click OK.

7   Reconcile your credit card statement in the same way that you reconcile a bank statement for a Quicken bank account.

Click the transaction or select it and click Mark or press the spacebar to mark each transaction listed on your credit card statement with a check mark.

You can select a range of transactions by dragging the mouse pointer down them.

When the Difference amount is zero, you've marked every item that appears on the statement.

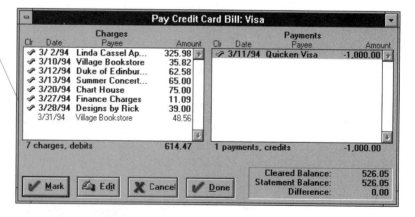

8   If you find transactions listed on your statement that are missing from the list of uncleared items, you can enter them now in the register.

Click Edit to go to the register and enter the missing transactions. (Or, if you prefer, Quicken can lump these new charges into a single adjustment transaction when you finish reconciling your statement.)

9 **When you have finished marking items as cleared, check the Difference amount.**

If the Difference amount is zero, click Done and make the credit card payment. See "Paying credit card bills" on this page.

If the Difference amount is not zero, see "Completing reconciliation" on page 76.

Paying credit card bills

As the final step in reconciling your credit card statement, Quicken can write a check to print with Quicken or record a handwritten check in the check register.

Select the account name. Quicken records the payment in the checking account as a transfer to the credit card account.

Select Hand Written if you want Quicken to enter the payment in the Register window instead of the Write Checks window.

Select Electronic if you plan to transmit the check electronically.

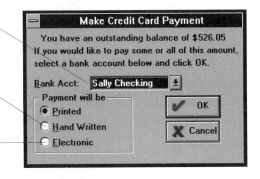

1 **Select the name of the checking account you plan to write the check from.**

2 **Specify whether you are planning to print the check with Quicken, write it manually, or send it electronically.**

3 **Click OK to enter the payment and the transfer information in the Write Checks or Register window.**

After Quicken records the payment, it selects the payment transaction in the Write Checks window or the check register.

4 **Complete the transaction and click Record.**

Quicken remembers the payment information and uses it the next time you make a payment on this credit card.

Using IntelliCharge

There are two methods for entering transactions into Quicken's credit card accounts. In regular credit card accounts (for VISA, MasterCard, and so on), you enter some or all of the transactions. In credit card accounts with IntelliCharge, IntelliCharge adds the transactions, updates your credit card account, and pays your bill automatically.

IntelliCharge reads transactions from an electronic credit card statement (which Intuit sends you), enters the transactions that you have charged and paid, and categorizes the transactions automatically. IntelliCharge enters the transactions, so you don't have to. You receive the electronic credit card statement by floppy disk or modem.

To use an IntelliCharge account, you must have a Quicken credit card. If you would like to apply for a Quicken credit card, see the application included in your Quicken package. (Call Intuit Customer Service at the phone number listed on page 372 if you have misplaced the application.)

♦ **Set up the account to use IntelliCharge.**
See "Setting up a credit card account to use IntelliCharge" on this page.

♦ **Let IntelliCharge update your account.**
See "Updating credit card accounts with IntelliCharge" on page 143.

♦ **Let IntelliCharge pay your bill.**
See "Paying credit card bills with IntelliCharge" on page 146.

Setting up a credit card account to use IntelliCharge

To set up a new credit card account with IntelliCharge, follow these steps.

1 **From the Activities menu, choose Create New Account.**
Quicken displays the Select Account Type window.

2 **Choose Credit Card Account and click OK.**
Quicken displays the New Account Information window.

3   Enter information in the New Account Information window, and then click OK.

Enter the name of the credit card. To use an IntelliCharge account, you must have a Quicken credit card.

Enter 0 for the starting balance.

Select the IntelliCharge checkbox by clicking it. When you click the checkbox, the Description box becomes the Credit Card Number box.

Enter the Quicken credit card account number.

(Optional) Enter the credit limit for the Quicken credit card.

4   Enter information in the IntelliCharge Account Information window, and then click OK.

If you will receive your IntelliCharge statement by modem, select this checkbox.

If you will receive your IntelliCharge statement by modem, enter your Social Security Number.

Quicken requires a password when you download your electronic statement by modem. Enter a password to prevent unauthorized access to your statement file, and click OK. The password you enter here can be anything you like, but it must be from four to eight (non-blank) alphanumeric characters long.

- If you selected the Statement Delivery On Modem checkbox, you still need to set up your modem. See "Setting up your modem to use IntelliCharge" on page 142.

- If you will receive your electronic statement on a floppy disk, you are finished setting up the credit card account.

From now on, when you see the Account list, you'll see this lightning bolt beside "CCrd" in the Type column. This account is set up to use IntelliCharge.

Once you have set up your account, you need to wait until it is time to receive the statement disk in the mail. See "Updating credit card accounts with IntelliCharge" on page 143 when you receive the disk.

Setting up your modem to use IntelliCharge

1 **From the Edit menu, choose Preferences and click the Modem icon.**

2 **Enter information in the Modem Preferences window.**

Select the correct Dial Type and COM port.

Select the correct speed for your modem. 2400 baud is the most common modem speed, but many older modems support only 1200 baud.

If you use CheckFree to pay your bills electronically, you may have already entered the correct port and speed settings for your modem.

```
┌─────────────────────────────────────────────────┐
│ ▬                 Modem Preferences              │
│ ┌─Dial Type─┐  Port:  ┌─COM1─┬─┐                │
│ │ ● Tone    │         └──────┴─┘     ✓  OK      │
│ │ ○ Pulse   │  Speed: ┌─1200─┬─┐                │
│ └───────────┘         └──────┴─┘     ✗  Cancel  │
│ CompuServe Local Access Number: ┌──────────────┐│
│ (for CheckFree and IntelliCharge) └────────────┘│
│ Initialization String: ┌─AT&F&C0&D0L0X4───────┐ │
│ (optional)             └──────────────────────┘ │
└─────────────────────────────────────────────────┘
```

You can customize Quicken's modem settings to handle special requirements of your modem. To find out what codes you need, look in the manual that came with your modem for the correct configuration codes to enter in the Initialization String box.

Enter the local access number for CompuServe. (If you've already been using CheckFree to pay your bills electronically, you don't need to change the number that you've already entered here.) Call 800-848-8980 to get the local access number.

You do not need a CompuServe membership to use IntelliCharge. Just follow this step to get the access number.

If the local access number contains the same area code as the phone number you are calling from, do not enter the area code.
(For example, if your phone number is (415) 555-1234 and CompuServe gives you the local access number (415) 555-6789, you would enter 555-6789 in the CompuServe Local Access Number box.)

3 **Enter a telephone number in the CompuServe Local Access Number box.**

To get the local access number for CompuServe, from where Quicken downloads your personal statement information, call **800-848-8980**. At the prompt, press 2.

The system first asks for the phone number *you will be calling from*, and then for the speed of your modem. It then gives you the access number nearest to you.

You are not charged for this call or the time you are connected to the CompuServe network. Your local telephone company charges you for the phone call when you download your statement if the number is outside your local calling area.

If you have problems with your modem, try troubleshooting with the tips in "CheckFree problems and solutions" on page 132. Even if you do not use CheckFree to pay your bills electronically, the tips in that section may help you to set up and use your modem correctly.

4 **Click OK.**

After you have set up your account, you need to wait until it is time to download your IntelliCharge statement. See "Updating credit card accounts with IntelliCharge" on page 143 when it is time to receive your IntelliCharge statement.

Entering data in your credit card account

You don't need to enter credit card transactions into Quicken manually as you used to before you started using IntelliCharge. IntelliCharge enters transactions automatically when you update your account. (If you still decide to enter transactions manually, see "Entering transactions manually" on page 146.)

Updating credit card accounts with IntelliCharge

Each month, Intuit either mails you an IntelliCharge statement disk or makes an electronic statement available for you to download by modem. The disk or file contains all the transactions for your credit card that occurred in the current statement period. These transactions include credit card purchases, finance and cash advance charges, credits from merchants, and payments.

You will not be sent an electronic statement if your Quicken credit card account is closed or if there was no activity during the billing period. (If the bank sends you a paper statement, Intuit sends you a disk or file; if the bank sends no statement, neither does Intuit.)

Caution:
Get your IntelliCharge statement either from a disk or by modem only once a month. Do not update your account more than once with the same statement or you'll end up with duplicate transactions in your register.

Getting your IntelliCharge statement from a disk

1 **Open the credit card account.**

2 **From the Activities menu, choose Get IntelliCharge Data.**

3 **Insert your IntelliCharge statement disk in your floppy drive and type the letter of that drive (for example, A or B).**

The number shown here is the account number you entered when you set up the IntelliCharge account in Quicken.

Insert your IntelliCharge statement disk in your computer's floppy drive.

4 **Click OK.**

See "Checking transactions in the IntelliCharge Statement window" on page 144 to continue.

Getting your IntelliCharge statement by modem

If you choose to download your electronic statement by modem, it will be available for you to download at approximately the same time you receive your paper statement in the mail. Billminder and the Quicken Reminder let you know when the information should be ready for you to download.

Receiving your statement by modem takes a few minutes longer the first time you receive it.

The first time you try to download your electronic statement, wait until the paper statement arrives to save yourself repeated modem calls.

1 **Be sure your modem is turned on (if it is external) and the phone line is plugged in.**

2 **Open the credit card account.**

3 **From the Activities menu, choose Get IntelliCharge Data.**

Quicken displays the Get IntelliCharge Data window, which tells you to prepare your modem.

4 **Click OK to download your data.**

Quicken dials the phone number you entered and downloads your statement file.

Checking transactions in the IntelliCharge Statement window

IntelliCharge reads the statement it has just received by modem or from a floppy disk and checks your file's category list. If it reads a transaction whose category is not in the list, it asks you whether you want to set up a new category or select a different one. Click Set Up to add the new category to the list. Click Select to select an existing category from the list.

In this example, IntelliCharge tells you that the category "Dining" is not set up in the current Quicken file. You can add this new category to Quicken's Category & Transfer list or pick an existing category instead.

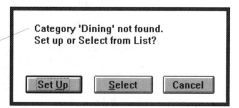

After reading your statement, IntelliCharge displays your transactions in the IntelliCharge Statement window as it has read them from the statement disk or from the file it just downloaded by modem.

The IntelliCharge Statement window contains information about your account and lists all the transactions from your IntelliCharge statement. This transaction-by-transaction display is for you to review and accept into the credit card register. You can always change or edit your transactions after they are recorded in the register.

1   **Review the transactions in the IntelliCharge Statement window.**

This onscreen statement is just like the paper statement you receive from a bank.

Mark a transaction for further review by pressing the spacebar. See "Handling credit card disputes with IntelliCharge" on page 147.

A credit or a payment appears as a negative number in the Amount column. These transactions decrease the balance due on your Quicken credit card.

Note that IntelliCharge has automatically categorized your credit card transactions. See "How IntelliCharge categorizes your transactions" on page 148 for more information.

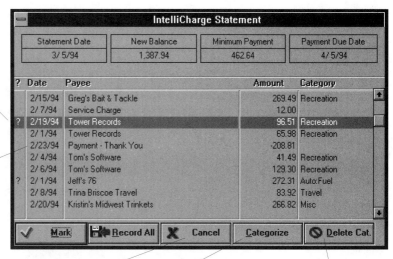

	IntelliCharge Statement		
Statement Date	New Balance	Minimum Payment	Payment Due Date
3/ 5/94	1,387.94	462.64	4/ 5/94

?	Date	Payee	Amount	Category
	2/15/94	Greg's Bait & Tackle	269.49	Recreation
	2/ 7/94	Service Charge	12.00	
?	2/19/94	Tower Records	96.51	Recreation
	2/ 1/94	Tower Records	65.98	Recreation
	2/23/94	Payment - Thank You	-208.81	
	2/ 4/94	Tom's Software	41.49	Recreation
	2/ 6/94	Tom's Software	129.30	Recreation
?	2/ 1/94	Jeff's 76	272.31	Auto:Fuel
	2/ 8/94	Trina Briscoe Travel	83.92	Travel
	2/20/94	Kristin's Midwest Trinkets	266.82	Misc

✓ Mark   Record All   ✗ Cancel   Categorize   ⊘ Delete Cat.

To cancel the IntelliCharge update without recording any transactions, click Cancel.

To enter or change the category assigned to a transaction, click Categorize and choose a category from the list.

To delete the category assigned to a transaction, select the transaction and click Delete Cat.

2   **(Optional) Change the categorization of any transaction.**

IntelliCharge searches for previous transactions with the same payee and categorizes your new transactions the same way. If IntelliCharge finds no previous transaction with the same payee, it uses Quicken's standard category list to categorize the new transactions. See "How IntelliCharge categorizes your transactions" on page 148 for more information.

3   **(Optional) Select any transaction and click Mark (or press the spacebar) to mark it for special attention.**

Here are some reasons to mark a transaction in the IntelliCharge Statement window for further review:

- To check or change the payee information
- To split the transaction
- To add text in the Memo field of the transaction
- To compare a transaction with your credit card receipt or charge slip and possibly dispute it

For each transaction you mark, IntelliCharge places a single question mark in the left column of the IntelliCharge Statement window. It also puts five question marks (?????) in the Ref field of the register, so you can find a marked transaction easily after IntelliCharge has recorded all the transactions from the IntelliCharge Statement window in the credit card account register.

4 Click Record All to record the new transactions in the register.

IntelliCharge records the transactions and displays the Make Credit Card Payment window.

Paying credit card bills with IntelliCharge

1 Enter information in the Make Credit Card Payment window.

If you don't want to pay your bill at this time, click Cancel.

Enter the name of the bank account from which you will pay the credit card bill.

Indicate whether you will pay your bill with a check you print from Quicken, a handwritten check (a register entry), or an electronic payment.

Quicken displays the option for electronic payment only if you have already set up a bank account as an electronic payment account.

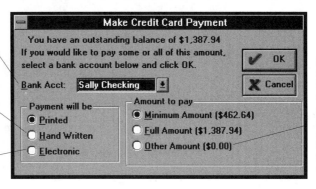

If you click Other Amount (for example, if you pay $200 every month), IntelliCharge remembers the amount the next time you pay your bill.

2 Click OK.

The Register window appears if you are paying with a manually written check.

The Write Checks window appears if you are paying with a check printed with Quicken or through CheckFree. For a printed check, Quicken inserts the name and address of the bank.

If you pay your bill electronically with CheckFree, the payment date is the due date from the statement or five days from today, whichever is later.

3 (Optional) Make any necessary changes to the transaction in the register or the Write Checks window and click Record.

Entering transactions manually

When IntelliCharge updates your account, it records all the transactions in the IntelliCharge Statement window that are not already in the current register. If you have recorded any transactions in the register manually, IntelliCharge attempts to match the amount of the transaction with a transaction from the electronic statement. If it is successful, IntelliCharge marks the transaction with an x in the Clr (Cleared) column in the credit card register. (An x in your Intelli-Charge register means that the transaction appeared on your credit card statement.) Otherwise IntelliCharge does not change the transaction in the register, since the matching transaction may appear on a future electronic statement.

> **Caution:**
> If you enter a transaction manually but the amount differs from what is on the electronic statement, IntelliCharge will not match the transaction and your balance will not be correct. Because of this possibility, we strongly recommend that you *not* enter transactions manually. Let IntelliCharge enter the transactions.

Handling credit card disputes with IntelliCharge

Your paper and electronic statements should always match. However, if there is ever any discrepancy between the information in your electronic statement and the information on the paper statement you receive from the bank, the bank always considers the paper statement to be correct.

You can use IntelliCharge to help single out a charge that you don't recognize or an amount that does not match the charge amount on your credit card receipt.

1 **Mark the disputed item with a question mark in the IntelliCharge Statement window.**

2 **Click Record All in the IntelliCharge Statement window to let IntelliCharge record the disputed item and all the other transactions in the register.**

3 **Locate each disputed transaction in the register so you can review it.**

   Do not delete the disputed transaction! Whatever the reason the charge has appeared on your credit card statement, you must notify the bank and follow the bank's instructions to dispute the charge. If the charge was an error, a credit will appear on a subsequent statement disk to correct the balance of your account.

   To look for transactions with 5 question marks (?????) in the Ref field:

Or press Ctrl+F

*   From the Edit menu, choose Find.
*   Type ????? (five question marks) in the Find box.
*   Click Next or Previous to search forward or backward in the register.

4 **Call the bank immediately about the disputed charge.**

   Check the Revolving Loan Agreement and Disclosure Statement that you received from the bank, or consult the back of your paper credit card statement to find out how the bank advises you to handle a disputed transaction. The bank's telephone number is on page 372.

5   **Notify the bank, *in writing*, of the disputed item.**

How IntelliCharge categorizes your transactions

The first time that IntelliCharge updates your register with transactions from your electronic statement, it categorizes the transactions according to Quicken's standard category list.

After your first IntelliCharge update, you can change the categories assigned to particular transactions at any time. When you make changes, you automatically teach IntelliCharge how you would like transactions categorized in the future.

IntelliCharge *learns* how you want to categorize transactions with a particular payee, so the next time it records a transaction with the same payee, it uses the same category.

IntelliCharge uses the payees in your transactions to learn how to categorize them. When categorizing a new transaction from the electronic statement, IntelliCharge first searches your Quicken credit card account register for a matching payee.

If IntelliCharge finds this:	It does this:
No matching payee	Assigns a category to the new transaction from its own list of credit card categories. Your IntelliCharge statement contains a list of standard credit card industry code numbers for payees that it maps to Quicken category names. For example, IntelliCharge assigns the Quicken category "Medical" to a credit card transaction you charged to "Dr. Leeron Karash."
A transaction with a matching payee	Copies the category information from the most recent transaction with a matching payee.
A split transaction with a matching payee	Copies the category information from the first line of the Splits window.

Keep IntelliCharge in mind when you make changes to past transactions. If you change the information in the Payee field after IntelliCharge records the transactions in your register, it will not be able to match payees and categories correctly the next time you update your register.*

---

*   IntelliCharge's use of payee information may also affect your decision whether to use Quicken's Start New Year option. This option removes the previous year's transactions from your accounts (including payee information). When payee information is removed, IntelliCharge may not be able to match payees and categories correctly the next time you update your register.

Tracking cash transactions

You can record cash transactions in two different ways in Quicken. You can set up a separate Quicken cash account, or you can categorize your cash spending right in your Quicken bank account.

Both methods allow you to categorize your cash expenses so that you can include them in reports, graphs, and budgets. The method you choose depends on how much detail you want about your cash spending.

When to use Quicken cash accounts

Cash accounts are useful if you want to keep detailed records of most cash transactions you make. If you prefer to use cash instead of checks or credit cards, you'll find setting up a separate cash account lets you easily track what you spend. Just save your cash receipts and enter them in the register for your cash account. You'll also find cash accounts useful if you are often paid in cash. Businesses can use cash accounts to track petty cash.

On the other hand, many people want to track only a few cash transactions, treating the rest as miscellaneous expenses. If that's true for you, don't set up a separate cash account. Instead, enter the information in the register for your bank account, as explained in the next section. Neither method requires you to account for every penny.

Handling cash in your checking account

If you want to track only a few cash expenditures, you don't need to set up a separate cash account. Instead, record cash withdrawals (checks or ATM) in your Quicken bank account as usual. Categorize these transactions with a category such as Cash Withdrawal. Then when you have important cash purchases that you want to record, split one of those cash transactions.

Categorizing insignificant cash expenses

Let's say you have a $500 bonus check and you want to deposit $400 of it in your checking account and keep $100 in cash. You don't want to track how you spend the $100.

1 **Open your checking account.**

2 **Go to a blank transaction.**

Or press Ctrl+N

3 **In the Deposit column, enter $400.**

4 **Click Splits.**

5 **Categorize the first line with the income category Bonus.**

(See "Assigning categories to transactions" on page 22.)

6 **Type the bonus amount ($500) over the amount in the first line ($400).**

7 **Press Tab to move to the next line.**

Quicken shows you the remainder ($100) at the bottom of the window.

8 **Categorize the second line as a cash withdrawal expense and enter the remainder amount (negative) in the Amount field.**

Make sure there is no remainder (lower right corner of the Splits window) after you have entered your split lines.

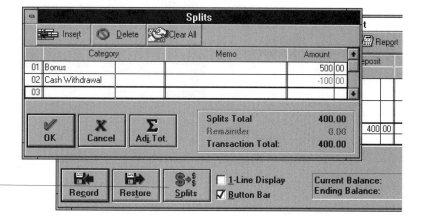

In the register, click Splits to open, view, and edit split transactions.

9 **Click OK to close the Splits window.**

10 **Click Record to record the transaction.**

Categorizing important cash expenses

When you categorize cash expenses in your bank account, Quicken includes them whenever you create summary and budget reports and graphs.

Suppose you give $100 in cash to a charity, and spend $45 in cash for dinner in a restaurant. You want to categorize the first amount as "Charity" and the second as "Dining."

1 **Select a payment in your checking account register that gives you enough cash to cover the cash expenses that you want to record.**

Pick any one dated on or around the date of the cash expenses.

2 **Click Splits.**

3 **Categorize the first line of the split transaction as Charity and type 100 over the transaction total indicated on the first line.**

4 **Categorize the second line as Dining and enter 45 in the Amount field.**

5 Categorize the third line as Cash Withdrawal or whatever category you use for miscellaneous cash expenses, and enter the remainder amount.

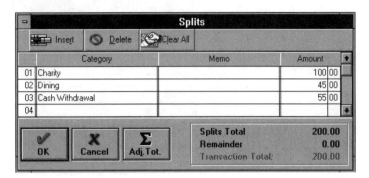

6 Click OK to close the Splits window.

7 Click Record to record the transaction.

Setting up and using cash accounts

Use a cash account if you want to keep records of most or all of the cash transactions you make. If you need to keep records of only a few cash expenditures, see "Handling cash in your checking account" on page 150.

◆ **Set up a cash account.**
See "Setting up additional Quicken accounts" on page 2 to set up a new account.

◆ **Open the account.**
Select the account from the Account list.

◆ **Enter transactions in the cash account.**
See "Entering transactions in a cash account" next.

◆ **From time to time, update the value of the account.**
By updating, you can keep this account accurate even if you do not enter every single cash transaction. See "Updating your cash balance" on page 154.

Entering transactions in a cash account

Save the cash receipts and other records of your cash transactions and enter each one as a separate transaction. If one receipt covers several items that you want to keep track of individually, you can split the transaction. Also enter transactions for cash received when you're paid in cash or given cash, or when you cash a check without depositing it in another account.

To review entering transactions in a register, see page 18. The basic steps for entering transactions are the same for all account types.

If you enter transactions for most or all of the cash you spend, you can add icons to the iconbar to make recording your most common transactions more convenient. See "Entering a specific transaction" on page 362.

Create transfer transactions when you withdraw cash or make a deposit less cash from a bank account. (See "Transferring money between accounts" on page 24 for information about creating transfers between accounts.)

You don't have to enter transactions for all the cash you've spent. However, you should have transactions that show all the cash you've received, either directly or by recording transfer transactions for cash withdrawals or advances from your other accounts.

The cash account register has no Num column, but it does have a Ref column, which you can use to track ATM transaction codes, for example.

Instead of the Payment and Deposit columns of the check register, the cash account register has Spend and Receive columns. Use the Spend column for purchases made with cash; use the Receive column to record increases in the amount of cash on hand.

Categorize all cash transactions so they'll be included in income and expense reports and graphs.

Here the Payee field specifies the store where the cash purchase was made.

The cash account received cash as a transfer when an ATM withdrawal was recorded in a checking account. The name of the checking account is in the Category field.

Updating your cash balance

You don't need to reconcile your cash accounts in the same way you do the register for your bank account or accounts. The main purpose of the Update Account Balance window for cash accounts is to save you from having to enter every cash transaction. You enter only those cash transactions you want to track in the register.

When you update your cash balance, Quicken handles all the other expenditures for you by entering one adjustment transaction for the remaining amount of miscellaneous cash expenses.

1   **If the cash account is not already open, open it by choosing the account name from the Account list.**

2   **From the Activities menu, choose Update Balances and then choose Update Cash Balance.**

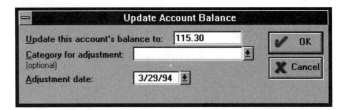

3   **Enter the amount of cash you currently have on hand.**

Quicken compares this amount with the current balance in the account. Note that you are not entering the amount of the adjustment here, but rather the ending balance of your cash account.

4   **Enter a category if you want Quicken to categorize the adjustment transaction.**

5   **Click OK.**

Quicken creates the balance adjustment transaction in the register.

Tracking assets and liabilities

With Quicken's asset and liability accounts, you can track such things as loan balances, lines of credit, capital equipment, 401(k) retirement plans, and the tax basis of your home. Quicken then provides a home net worth report and a business balance sheet that each combine the balances from all your accounts for a complete financial picture.

If you have a small business, you can use a Quicken asset account to track accounts receivable and a liability account to track accounts payable. More information about using Quicken for small business finances is in the *Quicken Business User's Guide*. To purchase this guide from Intuit, call **800-624-8742**.

When to use asset and liability accounts

Assets show what you own; *liabilities* show what you owe. The difference between your assets and your liabilities is your *net worth*. The balances in your bank and cash accounts represent part of your assets. The balances due on your credit cards represent part of your liabilities. But they may not give a total picture of your finances.

Use Quicken's investment accounts to track assets such as stocks, mutual funds, and Individual Retirement Accounts (IRAs).

Type of asset	Sample uses for asset accounts
Home tax basis	You can set up an asset account to track your home improvements over the years. Use your purchase price as the opening balance and record each improvement in the register as you make it. When you sell your home, accurate records will allow you to justify a higher tax basis and reduce your taxes.
Capital equipment	Businesses can set up an asset account that tracks the value of all capital equipment as it is acquired and depreciation as it occurs.
Accounts receivable	Businesses can keep up-to-date A/R records in an asset account.

Type of liability	Sample uses for liability accounts
Loan balances	You can use liability accounts to keep track of loans, such as car loans and lines of credit. When you write a check to make a loan payment, transfer the amount of the principal payment to your loan liability account, so you can see your up-to-date loan balance at any time. If you use Quicken's amortization feature to track your mortgage, Quicken automatically tracks your remaining principal in a liability account.
Accrued liabilities	Businesses can use liability accounts for accrued liabilities, such as payroll taxes and income taxes payable. When you do your company's payroll, as part of the split transaction detail, transfer the payroll taxes portion of each check to a payroll liability account. This technique makes it easy for you to keep track of how much is due for payroll taxes.
Accounts payable	Businesses can keep up-to-date A/P records in a liability account.

Setting up and using asset and liability accounts

Quicken asset and liability accounts are very similar to Quicken bank accounts. If you've used a Quicken bank account, you already know most of what you need to use an asset or liability account.

◆ **Set up an asset or liability account.**
See "Setting up additional Quicken accounts" on page 2.

◆ **Enter transactions in the asset or liability account.**
See the facing page.

◆ **From time to time, close inactive items in the account or update the value of the account.**
See "Updating the value of asset and liability accounts" on page 158.

Using the liability account register

The Opening Balance shows the balance of the loan at the time you set up the liability account.

These transactions show monthly car payments recorded in a checking account as transfers to the loan account. The amounts appear in the Decrease column because they decrease the total amount owed.

The Ending Balance amount is the outstanding balance of the loan (principal only).

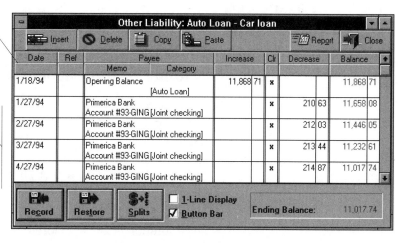

This example shows a liability account set up for one car loan. If you set up a single liability account for a group of related liabilities, you should use classes to identify specific items. Then you can track both transfers and classes in the Category field. For example, if you have one liability account for tracking three loans, you could set up a class name for each loan: Car Loan, Boat Loan, and Equity Loan. When you use classes in this way, you can create summary reports subtotaled by class to get detail about each of the loans. (See "Summary" on page 231.)

Using the asset account register

These purchases of new capital equipment were recorded in a checking account as transfers to the Cap Equipment asset account. The amounts appear in the Increase column because they increase the total value of the account. You set up a single asset account for a group of related assets.

Instead of the Payment and Deposit columns of the check register, the asset account register has Decrease and Increase columns. Use the Decrease column to record amounts that decrease the value of your asset; use the Increase column to record amounts that increase the value of your asset.

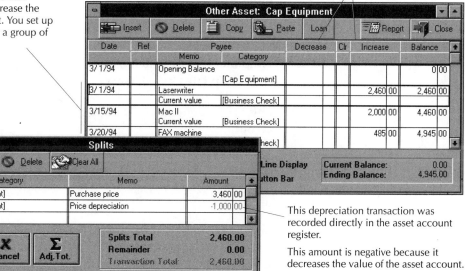

This depreciation transaction was recorded directly in the asset account register.

This amount is negative because it decreases the value of the asset account.

Updating the value of asset and liability accounts

In asset and liability accounts, you don't have to reconcile the account in the same way you reconcile a checking account. Instead, you can mark transactions that are closed or update the values of those that are still open.

Closing assets or liabilities

Closed items are those that are no longer active as assets or liabilities. For example, if you sell an asset listed in an asset account, such as an antique, or you pay off a loan listed in a liability account, those items are no longer part of your net worth. You won't want to include them in most reports; however, you don't want to delete them from your account, either. (In the event of an audit, you might want to produce a report that includes them.)

The solution is to mark closed items as cleared. Then you can filter your report to uncleared items only. Open the asset or liability account and mark as cleared both the transaction for the purchase and for the sale of an item. Click in the Clr (Cleared) column of a transaction and type x to clear it. Use Find to locate related transactions.

Updating the account balance

You can have Quicken make an adjustment to the balance in the account to update the current value of the account. For example, if you have an asset account for some real estate you own, you can tell Quicken to enter a transaction to update the current value of the property.

1   **Open the account.**

2   **From the Activities menu, choose Update Balances and then choose Update Cash Balance.**

3   **Enter the amount and date that represent the true balance of the account.**

    For example, if you know that your property is worth $15,000, enter that amount. Quicken compares this amount with the current balance in the account and creates an adjustment transaction for the difference.

4   **Enter a category name for the adjustment transaction.**

5   **Click Record to record the balance adjustment transaction in the register.**

13

Tracking investments

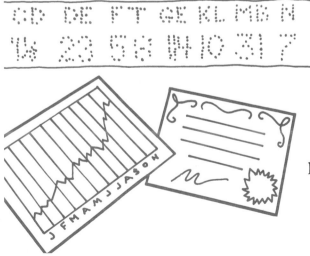

This chapter describes how to use Quicken to track your investments in stocks, bonds, mutual funds, and other investments that fluctuate in price.

Quicken shows you whether you are making or losing money on each investment and lets you compare the performances of your investments. At tax time, you can create reports of investment income and capital gains for the year to use when filling out income tax Schedules B and D.

How Quicken helps you with investments

We designed investment accounts for investors who want to track their investment transactions, see the performance of investments, update current market values, and create tax reports.

A Quicken investment account has a register just like any other account in which you record your transactions, such as buying and selling shares, reinvesting dividends, recording interest income and capital gains distributions, and so on.

In addition, the investment portfolio views show you snapshots of your portfolio, displaying the current market value, return on investment, price changes, and other essential data.

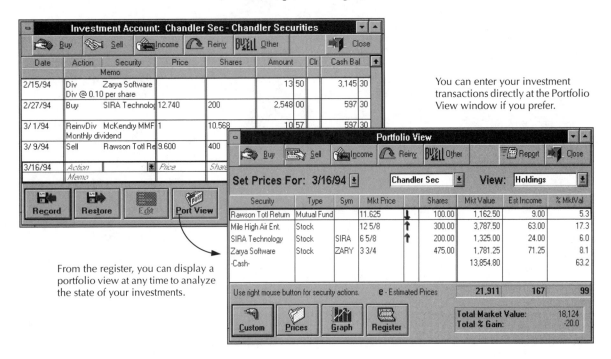

You can enter your investment transactions directly at the Portfolio View window if you prefer.

From the register, you can display a portfolio view at any time to analyze the state of your investments.

Quicken investment reports and graphs complete the information you need to analyze your investment portfolio. Quicken's reports distinguish between taxable investment income and tax-deferred accounts such as an IRA or a 401(k) account.

You can update security prices very simply at the Portfolio View window. But if you're a keen follower of the stock market, you may be interested in a companion program called Quicken Quotes, with which you can instantly retrieve the latest prices via modem. It's part of the Quicken Companion package. Call the Customer Assistance phone number on page 372 to order the product. You can read a description of the product on page 367.

Please be aware that, while Quicken provides tax reports, it doesn't keep track of changes in tax laws. Also, Quicken doesn't track aspects of sophisticated transactions such as commodities trading, strike prices of options, or expiration dates.

When to use an investment account

The table below suggests what type of Quicken account to use with different types of investments. It's simpler to use an asset account if an investment has a constant share price or no share price and is not in a brokerage account with investments that do fluctuate. (See Chapter 12, *Tracking assets and liabilities,* beginning on page 155.) However, you may want to use an investment account to take advantage of Quicken's ability to calculate return on investment.

To track an investment in an investment account, you must know the share price and dollar amount for each purchase or sale transaction. If you don't have this information (retirement plans often don't provide these details), use an asset account instead of an investment account.

If you invest in:	Use this type of account:
One or more securities (stocks, bonds, or mutual funds) for which you want to track a cash balance in addition to the securities (for example, a collection of investments in a brokerage account)	Investment
A single mutual fund account that has no cash balance	Investment (mutual fund type)
Real estate investment trusts (REITs) or partnerships	Investment
Unit trusts	Investment
IRA or Keogh accounts	Investment
Variable annuities	Investment
Cash management accounts (CMAs)	Bank for checking part of account Investment for everything else (use transfers for purchases, dividends, and so on)
Money market funds	Bank if you write checks Investment (mutual fund type) if you are interested in tracking rate of return
CDs or Treasury bills	Investment or asset
Fixed annuities	Investment or asset
Collectibles and precious metals	Investment or asset
Real estate	Asset
Employer retirement plans (401(k), 403(b), pension)	Investment or asset

How to arrange your investment accounts

Quicken has two types of investment accounts: the regular investment account and the mutual fund investment account. When you set up an investment account, you designate the type.

Type	Description
Regular investment account	Designed for one or more than one security.
	May have either a cash balance, as in a brokerage account, or no cash balance.
	Its register displays the cash balance after every transaction and the current market value of the account. It does not display the share balance (total number of shares) of individual securities within the account. (Quicken displays share balances of individual securities in the Portfolio View window, which you access directly from the register.)
	The advantage of the regular investment account is its flexibility. You can change the securities in it and leave cash in it.
Mutual fund investment account	Designed for a single mutual fund.
	Restricted to only one security. (You should not have two or more mutual funds in the same mutual fund account.)
	It has no cash in it, only shares of the security.
	Its register displays the share balance (total number of shares) of the single security and the current market value of the security.
	The name of the security and the most recent price, if you enter no new price, appear automatically in the register when you enter a new transaction.
	The advantage of the mutual fund investment account is that certain procedures are streamlined. For example, when you write a check from your Quicken checking account to the mutual fund account, the transaction automatically appears in the investment register as a purchase of shares.

Regular investment accounts and mutual fund investment accounts give you the same information about your investments. The main difference is that a cash balance appears in the register for a regular account, and a share balance appears for the mutual fund account. Quicken allows you to track income, capital gains, and performance of individual securities in either type of account.

If you wish, you can track several mutual funds in one regular investment account.

Once a regular account, always a regular account
Once you have set up an account as a regular investment account, you cannot change it to be a mutual fund account. However, you can change a mutual fund account to make it a regular investment account if you need to.

Arranging your securities within accounts

Here are some recommendations about how to group your securities within one or more Quicken investment accounts.

Security type	Recommendation
Brokerage accounts	Use a separate, regular investment account for each actual brokerage account or other managed account you have.
	If you have a cash management account (CMA) with a broker, set up the checking part as a Quicken bank account. (You'll be able to print checks, track check numbers, and reconcile easily.) Set up a regular investment account for the rest of the investments in the brokerage account. You transfer money between the two Quicken accounts when you buy and sell investments or receive investment income.
IRAs	Use separate (regular) investment accounts for your IRA and for your spouse's IRA. (Even if you do not now have securities with fluctuating prices in your IRA, it's a good idea to set up your IRA as an investment account, as you may want to change the investments later.) This advice applies to other retirement plans that you manage directly, such as a Keogh plan.
	If you have more than one security in your IRA, put them in the same (regular) investment account, even if the securities are managed by, say, different mutual fund managers. If you transfer an IRA security from one manager to another, Quicken can still track the performance of your IRA as a whole.
Securities you hold directly	If you have a few individual securities you hold directly, you may wish to set each one up as a separate (regular) investment account. Then you can easily reconcile each account with its statement.
	On the other hand, you may prefer to lump the securities in a single (regular) investment account, especially if you have other investment accounts. Then you can subtotal these securities by account on reports and track them as a group.

Choosing how much detail to set up

When you set up a new investment account, you have three options for creating your opening balance, depending on how much historical data you want to include, as shown on the next page. We recommend the first option.

Options	Advantages	Disadvantages
Option 1: Enter all historical data. For each security in the account, enter the initial purchase and all subsequent transactions: • Name and type of security • Date, amount invested, and number of shares bought (or price per share) for initial purchase • All subsequent acquisitions (including reinvestments), sales and gifts, stock splits, and return of capital • All dividends, interest, and capital gains distributions for the current year • (Optional) All nonreinvested dividends, interest, and capital gains distributions from prior years (This data gives you a more complete value for the performance of your security for past years but does not affect Quicken's value for the cost basis.) • Price per share at the end of last year (and prior years, if available) and today	All Quicken reports are complete and accurate. If you sell a security, the capital gains report displays the purchase dates, amounts invested, and the realized gain, so you can use this report to prepare Schedule D tax information. All your investment records are in one convenient place, making it easier for you to analyze your investments and produce data for tax and other purposes.	You have to locate data for transactions that occurred in the past. You must spend time entering all prior transactions.
Option 2: Set up for this year. Enter your investment holdings as of the end of last year. Then enter all investment transactions for each security since the beginning of this year. For each security in the account, enter: • Name and type of security • Number of shares owned at the end of last year • Price per share at the end of last year and today • All transactions (purchases, sales, dividends, reinvestments, and so on) for the current year	The information you need to gather goes back only to the end of last year and is probably easy for you to find. Data for the year is complete, so you can use the investment income report to prepare Schedule B tax information. Quicken produces accurate reports on performance, income, and changes in unrealized gain for time periods starting with the beginning of this year.	Because you are starting as of the end of last year, Quicken cannot give you an accurate value for all quantities that depend on cost basis for a security: average cost per share, percent gain, total unrealized gain. If you sell the security, the capital gains report does not display an accurate purchase date. Also, because the cost basis dates back only to the beginning of the year, the "realized gain" is not accurate.
Option 3: Set up fast. Enter your current investment holdings. For each security in the account, enter: • Name and type of security • Number of shares you now own • Current price per share	You can get started with the minimum amount of information to gather. You can start using the account right away to see whether you think it's worthwhile to gather and enter more information. (If you set up quickly using this option, you can go back later and enter historical data, as described in "Entering prior history for investments" on page 205.) Quicken produces accurate reports on performance, income, and changes in unrealized gain for time periods starting now.	Data for this year is incomplete, so you can't use the investment income report to prepare Schedule B tax information. You may have to wait a few months before your investment data is in the range where Quicken can display a valid investment performance report. Because you are starting from today, Quicken cannot give you an accurate value for all quantities that depend on cost basis: average cost per share, percent gain, total unrealized gain. If you sell the security, the capital gains report does not display an accurate purchase date. Also, the realized gain is not accurate.

Setting up a regular investment account

To set up a mutual fund investment account, skip to page 173.

A regular investment account is designed to track more than one security. To set up a regular investment account in Quicken, you need to do three things:

- ◆ Set up the Quicken regular investment account (below).

- ◆ Set up all the securities in the account (page 166).

- ◆ Set up the opening share balance (the number and value of shares you own) for each security in the account (page 169).

Setting up a Quicken regular investment account

1 **From the Activities menu, choose Create New Account.**

Quicken displays the Select Account Type window (shown on page 2).

2 **Choose Investment Account at the bottom of the list and click OK.**

Make sure this checkbox is clear.

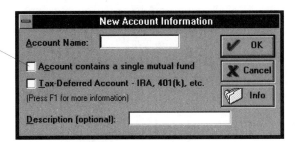

3 **Enter a name for the investment account in the Account Name box.**

You may want to use the broker's name or a descriptive name such as "Sally's IRA" or "CD rollover." You may use up to 15 letters, numbers, or spaces.

4 **Make sure the "Account contains a single mutual fund" checkbox is clear.**

You may track a variety of securities, including mutual funds, in a regular account. You may also have a cash balance.

(Note that, after setting up a regular investment account, you cannot later change it to be a mutual fund account.)

5 **If the earnings from this account are free from taxation until you take possession of them, select the Tax-Deferred Account checkbox.**

Some examples of tax-deferred accounts are IRAs, 401(k) plans and 403(k) plans, annuities, and Series EE and HH U.S. Savings Bonds.

When generating a tax summary or tax schedule report, Quicken excludes transactions from tax-deferred accounts. (If you want, you can specifically include them by customizing the reports.) Although a tax schedule report does not normally include transfers between accounts, this report will include transfers between a tax-deferred investment account and another account.

6   **(Optional) Enter a description of the account.**

You may use up to 21 letters, numbers, or spaces.

7   **(Optional) Click Info to enter additional information about the account for your own benefit.**

8   **Click OK to set up the account.**

If this is the first investment account you have set up, Quicken asks you if you would like to add an icon to the iconbar to give more direct access to the Portfolio View window. If you click Yes, you can always delete the icon later if you want. Or you can click No and add the icon later. (See Appendix A, *Customizing the iconbar,* beginning on page 357.)

The investment categories, which all begin with an underline (for example, _DivInc, _IntInc), appear on your category list automatically, whether or not you selected standard categories, as soon as you add an investment account. You cannot delete these categories nor edit their names while you have investment accounts in your Quicken file. (You *can* change their descriptions. If you'd like reports to show the categories' descriptions instead of the names, see "Changing report preferences" on page 250.)

You're ready to set up each security in the account, as described next.

Setting up securities for a regular investment account

Before you can enter transactions for your securities, you must set up the securities to give Quicken some information about them. You can set up new securities at any time, either in advance or "on the fly" as you enter transactions for them. All investment accounts in the same Quicken file share the same Security list, so the same security can appear in more than one account.

Or press Ctrl+Y

1   From the Lists menu, choose Security.

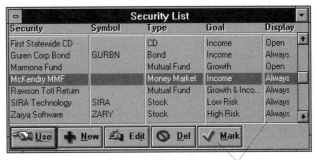

To edit or delete an existing security, select the security and click Edit or Delete. You can delete a security only if you have no transactions for it.

The Display column indicates the display status for the security in the Portfolio View window. (See "Customizing your portfolio views" on page 194.) Click Mark to change the security display status.

Or press Ctrl+N

2   Click New to create a new security.

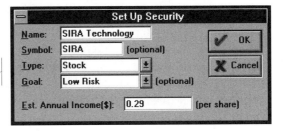

Select a Type and Goal from the drop-down lists. If none is appropriate, you can set up new ones. (However, you cannot set them up "on the fly." See steps 5 and 6 below.)

3   Enter the name of the security in the Name box.

4   (Optional) Enter a symbol in the Symbol box if you plan to export or import price data from a file.

For more information about using symbols, see "Importing prices" on page 207.

5   In the Type drop-down list, select the type appropriate for your security.

Quicken displays the securities in the Portfolio View window alphabetically within security type, making it convenient for you to enter prices from the newspaper. You can also use types for sorting and subtotaling in investment reports and graphs.

The preset list of security types is:

Bond
CD
Mutual Fund
Stock

If the preset list of types doesn't serve your needs, you can customize it. For example, you may wish to add Money Fund, T-Bill, Tax-Free Bond, Option, REIT, Unit Trust, NYSE, NASDAQ, or AMEX. To customize the Security Type List:

- Click Cancel to temporarily leave the Set Up Security window.
- From the Lists menu, choose Security Type.

Or press Ctrl+N

- To set up a new security type (up to a maximum of 15), click New.
- After customizing the Security Type list, return to this procedure to set up your securities.

At the Edit Security Type window, you can specify whether prices for that security type should be displayed in decimals or fractions (multiples of 1/16).

6 **(Optional) In the Goal drop-down list, select the goal appropriate for your security.**

Investment goals give you an idea of what you hope the investment will achieve for you. When you create reports, you can sort and subtotal by investment goal. Using goals allows you to group investments within the same account or within different accounts.

The preset list of investment goals is:

College Fund
Growth
High Risk
Income
Low Risk

As for security types, you can customize the Investment Goal list by adding new goals up to a total of 16, deleting unused goals, or modifying existing goals. You may wish to add Retirement, Down Payment, Remodeling, Growth & Income, or Medium Risk to this list of goals. Or you may use goals to label investments for your children or grandchildren, or to distinguish taxable income from tax-free income within the same account, or to distinguish different industry groups, such as energy, computer, environmental, and so on. To customize the Investment Goal List:

- Click Cancel to temporarily leave the Set Up Security window.
- From the Lists menu, choose Investment Goal.

Or press Ctrl+N

- To set up a new goal (up to a maximum of 16), click New.
- After customizing the Investment Goal list, return to this procedure to set up your securities.

7 **(Optional) Enter the estimated annual income per share for this security.**

Often, when you buy a security you will be provided with this information. Entering the figure into Quicken can help give you a more complete picture. (It's used for calculating yield.)

8 **Click OK to record the new security.**

9 **Repeat steps 1 through 8 to set up each security in the account.**

You are now ready to enter transaction information about your securities in your new investment account, as described next.

Setting up the opening balance of each security

If you don't remember which option you decided to use for first-time setup, see "Choosing how much detail to set up" on page 163. We recommend that you record a complete transaction history for each security in the account, starting with your initial purchase or acquisition of the security. If you don't enter a complete transaction history, Quicken cannot report accurate unrealized or realized gains. (This is discussed in more detail on page 205.)

As with any investment transactions, you can enter the security opening balances in either the investment Register window or in the Portfolio View window. In the following steps, we refer to the register, but you can follow the same procedure in the Portfolio View window if you prefer.

The Register window and the Portfolio View window have the same button bar for entering investment transactions.

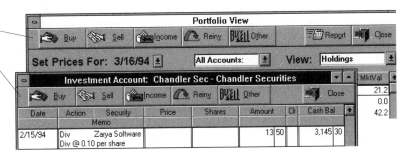

1   **Open the register for your new investment account (select it in the account list and click Use) and go to a new transaction.**

You can type information directly into the register fields if you want (as with earlier versions of Quicken), but the following steps describe Quicken's investment forms that make transaction entry much easier.

2   **Click the Other button in the button bar (with the Buy/Sell graphic) and then click Add Shares to Acct.**

If your investments date back to before you started using Quicken, you need to record an Add Shares transaction for each security in the account. Add Shares has two functions:

- It allows you to add shares you already own to a Quicken account.

- It also allows you to enter a purchase of shares for a date prior to when you started using Quicken, without deducting the money from a Quicken account.

    (Alternatively, if you opened your real-world investment account AFTER you started using Quicken, you might want to start by transferring money from your Quicken bank account to your Quicken investment account. Use the Transfer Cash In form (from the Other forms drop-down menu) to record the opening cash balance of the investment account as a transfer from your bank account. Then, use the Buy form instead of the Add Shares form to record the initial

purchase of a security. For specific information about filling in any of the fields of these forms, press F1.)

Quicken displays the Add Shares To Account investment form. How you fill in the form depends on which of the three setup options described on page 164 you chose. We recommend that you use option 1 to enter a complete transaction history for each of your securities.

3 **Enter the date appropriate for the setup option you have chosen.**

For option 1: Enter the date of your initial purchase or acquisition of the security.

For option 2: Enter 12/31 of last year.

For option 3: Enter today's date.

4 **Enter the name of the security.**

If you have not yet set up this security, you can do so now (see the description on page 167).

5 **Enter the number of shares (up to four decimal places) you owned on the date you entered in the Date box.**

Security type	Number of shares to enter
Stock or mutual fund	Actual number of shares
Bonds	Ten times the actual number of bonds (to match the way prices are quoted). Equivalently, enter one hundredth of the total face value of the bonds. For example, if you have two bonds with a total face value of $2,000, enter 20 in the Shares field.
Money market fund or CD	The total value
Collectible	One (1)
Precious metal	The number of ounces

6 **In the Price per Share box, enter a share price in fractions or decimals.**

- For option 1, enter your actual initial cost per share (including commission, fees, and load) or (if you prefer to enter the total cost) leave the Price field blank.

- For options 2 and 3, enter the cost per share (including commission, fees, and load) if you purchased the security all at one time, or leave the Price field blank.

Security type	Price to enter
Stock or mutual fund	Actual price per share
Bonds	One-tenth of the actual market value of each bond (to match the way prices are quoted)
Money market fund or CD	One dollar
Collectible	Total value
Precious metal	Price per ounce

To enter a share price as a whole number plus a fraction, leave a space after the whole dollar amount, and use a slash (/) between the numerator and denominator. For example, enter 36 3/8. If a price for a stock or bond is not an exact multiple of 1/16, Quicken displays it as a decimal.

If you leave the Price per Share box blank but fill in the Total Cost Basis, Quicken calculates and fills in the price per share.

7   **In the Total Cost Basis field, enter a dollar amount, including commission, fees, and load, if you did not enter a price per share.**

8   **(Optional) In the Memo field, enter a memo.**

9   **Click OK to record the transaction.**

10 **Repeat steps 2 through 9 for each security in the account.**

   Now that you have set up the opening balances for your securities, you are ready to bring your investment account up to date. If you chose setup option 3, it is already up to date—skip to step 12.

11 **For options 1 and 2, use the buttons in the button bar to enter all subsequent transactions for each security (purchases, sales, dividends, reinvestments, and so on).**

   See "Recording your investment transactions" on page 177 for details about entering the most common transactions. Temporarily ignore amounts that appear in the Cash Bal field.

Quicken normally displays prices
for stocks and bonds as whole
numbers plus fractions (multiples of
1/16) and all other prices in
decimals. You can change this
format by editing the Security Type.

Investment Account: Steinman							
Buy	Sell	Income	Reinv	Buy/Sell	Other		Close

Date	Action	Security Memo	Price	Shares	Amount	Clr	Cash Bal
6/13/90	ShrsIn	SIRA Technology	5.670	100	567 00		0 00
6/13/90	ShrsIn	Zarya Software	4.135	1,375	5,685 62		0 00
12/1/90	ShrsIn	Mile High Air Ent.	4.870	2,000	9,740 00		0 00
12/31/91	ReinvDiv	SIRA Technology	6 1/8	9.2149	56 44		0 00
5/12/93	SelX	Zarya Software [Joint checking	3 3/4	400 1,500.00	1,500 00		0 00

Record	Restore	Edit	Port View	Ending Cash Bal:	0.00
				Market Value:	15,614.45

12 When you have finished entering historical transactions for all the securities in this account, determine whether or not the ending cash balance in this account is correct.

In the Register window, look at the Ending Cash Balance at the lower right corner. In the Portfolio View window, the cash balance is shown on the last line (but make sure first that the correct account is selected in the account box).

• If the final amount displayed for the cash balance in this account is correct, your investment account is now set up. See "Updating the prices of your securities" on page 199 to continue.

• If the final amount displayed for the cash balance in this account is not correct, continue below.

Entering the beginning cash balance for a regular investment account

You might have a cash balance in your regular investment account if, for example, you have transferred some funds from a bank account, sold some securities, or received a cash dividend or interest.

1 From the Activities menu, choose Update Balances and then choose Update Cash Balance.

Quicken displays the Adjust Cash Balance window. (From the Portfolio View window, you must select a single account before you can choose the Update Balances option.)

2 Enter the current cash balance and date for this account.

Quicken adds a balance adjustment that makes your cash balance correct.

Your regular investment account is now set up. Quicken displays the market value of your account in the lower right corner of the investment register, based on the latest prices you have supplied.

For a regular investment account, this column displays the cash balance for the account. When you record a transaction, Quicken calculates the correct cash balance. If you have no cash in the account, the column displays zeros.

If Quicken displays a row of asterisks (*****) in a register column, the number is too large for Quicken to display. Quicken displays dollar amounts between -$999,999.99 and $9,999,999.99. Outside of that range, Quicken keeps track of the amount but doesn't display it.

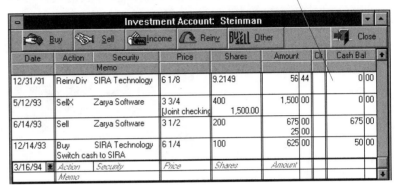

3 **Update the security prices in the Portfolio View window.**

See "Updating the prices of your securities" on page 199.

- For options 1 or 2, you need to enter prices for the end of last year as well as for today. Then you can track unrealized (paper) gains or losses and performance for the current year.

- For option 3, you need to enter current prices for your securities.

Setting up a mutual fund investment account

A mutual fund investment account is designed to track a single mutual fund with no cash balance. To set up a mutual fund investment account in Quicken, you need to do two things:

◆ Set up the account.

◆ Set up the opening share balance—the number and value of shares you own.

Setting up a Quicken mutual fund investment account

1 **From the Activities menu, choose Create New Account.**

2 In the Select Account Type window (shown on page 2), choose Investment Account at the bottom of the list and click OK.

3 Enter a name for the mutual fund account in the Account Name box.

You probably want to use the name of the mutual fund. You may use up to 15 letters, numbers, or spaces.

4 Make sure the "Account contains a single mutual fund" checkbox is selected.

Make sure this checkbox is selected.

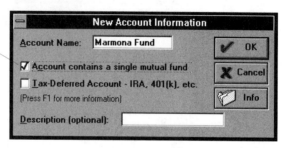

Changing the account type
If you set up a mutual fund account and then decide you'd like to be able to include another security or a cash balance, you can edit the account information and clear the "Account contains a single mutual fund" checkbox to change to a regular investment account. (But you cannot then change the account back to be a mutual fund account!)

5 If the earnings from this account are free from taxation until you take possession of them, select the Tax-Deferred Account checkbox.

Some examples of tax-deferred accounts are IRAs, 401(k) plans and 403(k) plans, annuities, and Series EE and HH U.S. Savings Bonds.

When generating a tax summary or tax schedule report, Quicken excludes transactions from tax-deferred accounts. (You can specifically include them if you want by customizing the reports.) Although a tax schedule report does not normally include transfers between accounts, this report will include transfers between a tax-deferred investment account and another account.

6 (Optional) Enter a description of the account.

You may use up to 21 letters, numbers, or spaces.

7 (Optional) Click Info to enter additional information about the account for your own benefit.

8   Click OK.

Quicken now displays the Set Up Mutual Fund Security window. In mutual fund investment accounts, you set up the single security in the account when you first set up the account.

Although the name for the security is filled in with the account name, you can change it. The security name doesn't need to be the same as the account name.

(Optional) Enter a symbol in the Symbol box if you plan to export or import price data from a file.

For more information about using symbols, see "Importing prices" on page 207.

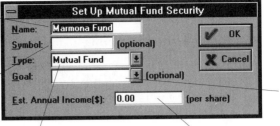

Press F1 for more information on what to enter in each field.

(Optional) Select a goal for this investment, for example Low Risk.

Unless you decide to customize the Security Type list to your own needs, leave the type as Mutual Fund.

(Optional) If you know the estimated annual income per share, enter it here.

9   Enter information in the Set Up Mutual Fund Security window and click OK to set up the investment account.

Quicken adds the account to your Account list. The investment categories, which all begin with an underline (for example, _DivInc, _IntInc), appear on your category list automatically (whether or not you selected standard categories) as soon as you add an investment account. You cannot delete these categories nor edit their names. (You *can* change their descriptions. If you'd like reports to show the categories' descriptions instead of the names, see "Changing report preferences" on page 250).

10   Open the new mutual fund account (select it in the account list and click Use).

Quicken displays the Create Opening Share Balance window.

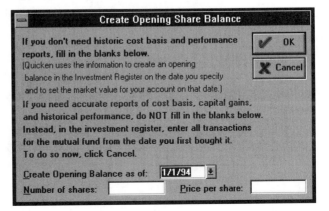

If you don't remember which option you decided to use for first-time setup, see "Choosing how much detail to set up" on page 163. We recommend that you record a complete transaction history for the mutual fund, starting with your initial purchase or acquisition. If you don't enter a complete transaction history, Quicken cannot report accurate unrealized or realized gains. See page 205.

11   **If you're entering historical data under option 1, click Cancel now and continue with "Setting up the opening balance of each security" on page 169.**

If you're setting up for today or for this year under option 2 or 3, fill in the information requested.

- For option 2, enter the date 12/31 of last year, the number of shares you owned then, and the price per share. Click OK.

- For option 3, enter today's date, the number of shares you now own, and today's price per share. Click OK.

After you click OK, Quicken displays the investment register with your opening balance filled in. In the Action field, ShrsIn (an abbreviation for "shares in") indicates that you added existing shares to this new Quicken account. Quicken also recorded the price per share and used this price to display the market value in the lower right corner of the register.

In a mutual fund account, this column displays the number of shares you hold (to two decimal places, although Quicken calculates to four decimal palces). When you record a transaction, Quicken automatically calculates the correct total number of shares of the security you hold in the account.

If Quicken displays a row of asterisks (*****) in a register column, the number is too large for Quicken to display. Quicken displays dollar amounts between -$999,999.99 and $9,999,999.99. Outside of that range, Quicken keeps track of the amount but doesn't display it.

	Investment Account: Marmona Fund						
	Buy	Sell	Income	Reinv	Buy/Sell Other		Close
Date	Action	Security	Price	Shares	Amount	Clr	Share Bal
		Memo					
1/ 1/94	ShrsIn	Marmona Fund	22.310	265.376	5,920 54	*	265 37
	Opening Balance						
3/ 3/94	BuyX	Marmona Fund	25.460	39.2773	1,000 00		304 65
	Buy additional shares			[Joint checking	1,000.00		
3/25/94	DivX	Marmona Fund			30 42		304 65
	Qtrly div @ 0.10 per share			[Joint checking			
6/25/94	CGLongX	Marmona Fund			152 11		304 65
				[Joint checking			
6/25/94	DivX	Marmona Fund			30 42		304 65
	Qtrly div @ 0.10 per share			[Joint checking			

Record	Restore	Edit	Port View	Ending Share Bal: 304.65
				Market Value: 6,988.14

The market value of the account.

12   **For option 3, your mutual fund account is now set up.**

13   **For option 2, enter transactions for this year.**

See "Entering investment transactions" on page 177.

14   **For option 2, update the market value of your account to reflect today's share price.**

See "Updating the prices of your securities" on page 199. (You may want to read through the description of the Portfolio View window first, to gain an understanding of the window— it begins on page 191.)

Recording your investment transactions

When you have set up your Quicken investment account or accounts, you can begin entering transactions. Record a transaction any time a security or money enters or leaves one of your accounts, for example when you buy or sell shares, reinvest a dividend, receive interest, or transfer money into a broker account.

Only changes in the prices of your securities do not constitute transactions. Record price changes as described in "Updating the values of your investments," beginning on page 199.

Before you can enter investment transactions, you must set up your investment account or accounts. See "Setting up a regular investment account," beginning on page 165, or "Setting up a mutual fund investment account," beginning on page 173.

Entering investment transactions

You can enter investment transactions either in the register of your investment account or in the Portfolio View window. Each of these windows has an investment button bar near the top that you use to enter transactions.

Use the investment button bars to enter transactions in either window.

(If you prefer to enter the details directly in a blank transaction in the register, you can—see page 180.)

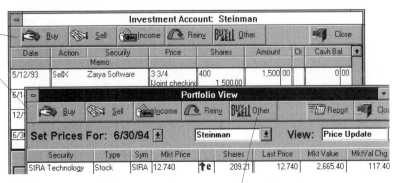

When you click the Other button, Quicken lets you choose from a menu of transactions that are used less frequently.

1 Click a button on the investment button bar.

Quicken displays an easy-entry investment form in which you enter the details of the transaction. For example:

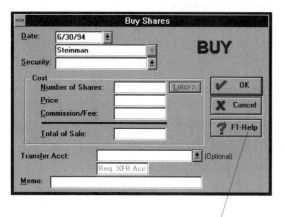

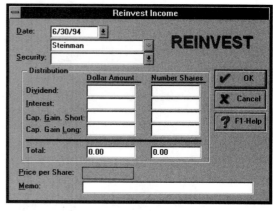

Click Help for more information on how to fill in a form.

Quicken displays a different form for each type of transaction.

2 Fill in the form and click OK. *

Quicken writes your entries into a transaction in the investment register. (Quicken may create more than one transaction if you entered several transactions in the same form.)

If you're entering transactions in the Portfolio View window, click Register to see the transactions listed.

The header bar tells you what information is in each field.

The Action field tells you what type of transaction this is. To see an alphabetic listing of Action codes with descriptions, click the drop-down button when the cursor is in the Action field.

To change a transaction's details, either click Edit to display the investment form or edit the entries directly in the register.

---

* With standard behavior, Quicken leaves the form when you click OK. If you would prefer Quicken to ask you to confirm your entries before leaving the form, to avoid errors, choose Preferences from the Edit menu, click General, and select the option Confirm Investment Transactions from Forms. (See page 42.)

The next table summarizes the types of transactions you can enter. Continue reading this section for more details on how to enter transactions.

To enter this type of transaction:	Click this button:
Buy a security, or shares in a security (see page 181). (For example, buy shares, bonds, or a CD.)	**Buy**
Sell a security, or shares in a security (page 181).	**Sell**
Receive money from dividends, interest, or capital gains distributions (page 184). Also any miscellaneous income.	**Income**
Reinvest earnings from dividends, interest, or capital gains distributions (page 184). (Also stock dividends, page 186).	**Reinv**
Increase the balance of shares in the account without a monetary transaction. (Use this to set up the opening share balance, as described on page 169.)	**Other** ➤ Add shares to account
Adjust the share balance downwards, with no money involved (see also page 207).	**Other** ➤ Remove shares from account
Pay interest on a margin loan (page 187).	**Other** ➤ Margin interest expense *
Any type of expense associated with a security, for example, portfolio management fees.	**Other** ➤ Miscellaneous expense *
A reminder note to yourself (page 191).	**Other** ➤ Reminder transaction
Return of capital or principal (page 189).	**Other** ➤ Return of capital *
Receive additional shares from a stock split (page 186).	**Other** ➤ Stock split
Transfer cash into the investment account from another account (page 185). (For example, transfer cash into your broker account.)	**Other** ➤ Transfer cash in *
Transfer cash out of your investment account (page 185).	**Other** ➤ Transfer cash out *

* This option is not available for mutual fund investment accounts, as it adds cash to or removes cash from the account.

Understanding what each transaction does

The key to each transaction in the register is the *action*. Quicken enters this in the Action field according to what you entered in the investment form. The action identifies the type of transaction.

So that Quicken can create investment reports and graphs, each action has a category associated with it, though the category isn't displayed in the register. If you generate, for example, an itemized category report, you'll see your investment transactions sorted by category.

The following table matches actions to categories, and shows what effect each investment transaction has on your portfolio. (Skip this table if it doesn't interest you; Quicken takes care of all these details for you.) The cost basis is the total cost of all shares of a security.

Transaction	Action *	Category	Number of shares	Cost basis
Buy	Buy or BuyX	—	Increases	Increases
Sell	Sell or SellX	_RlzdGain	Decreases	Decreases
Receive income from:				
dividend	Div or DivX	_DivInc	—	—
interest	IntInc	_IntInc	—	—
short-term capital gains distributions	CGShort or CGShortX	_ST CapGnDst	—	—
long-term capital gains distributions	CGLong or CGLongX	_LT CapGnDst	—	—
miscellaneous income	MiscInc	choose from list	—	—
Reinvest earnings from:				
dividend	ReinvDiv	_DivInc	Increases	Increases
interest	ReinvInt	_IntInc	Increases	Increases
short-term capital gains distributions	ReinvSh	_ST CapGnDst	Increases	Increases
long-term capital gains distributions	ReinvLg	_LT CapGnDst	Increases	Increases
Add shares to account	ShrsIn	—	Increases	Increases
Remove shares from account	ShrsOut	—	Decreases	Decreases
Margin interest expense	MargInt	_IntExp	—	—
Miscellaneous expense	MiscExp	choose from list	—	—
Reminder	Reminder	—	—	—
Return of capital	RtrnCap	—	—	Decreases
Stock split	StkSplit	—	Increases (usually)	—
Transfer cash in	XIn	(account name)	—	—
Transfer cash out	XOut	(account name)	—	—

* An X in the action name (for example, BuyX) indicates that the money for or from the transaction is transferred from or to another Quicken account, and so does not affect the cash balance of the investment account.

Entering transactions directly in the register

You don't have to use the investment forms for entering transactions. If you prefer, you can fill in the fields of the register directly, just as you can with other Quicken registers. (If you are upgrading from a previous version of Quicken, you may find this method more familiar.)

Quicken is set up so that when you QuickZoom from an investment report you are taken to an investment form to edit the transaction. If you would prefer to be taken to the register transaction, choose Preferences from the Edit menu (or click the Prefs icon on the Quicken iconbar), then click Reports, and then clear the QuickZoom to Investment Forms checkbox (illustrated on page 251).

Or press Ctrl+M

You can memorize a recurring transaction (such as a quarterly dividend) and recall it for quick entry. Memorizing investment transactions is just like memorizing any other kind of transaction. See "Memorizing and recalling transactions" on page 87.

Entering numbers in investment transactions

Quicken knows that share price, number of shares, and dollar amount are related. If you fill in only two of the three quantities, it will calculate the third quantity from the relationship:

Number of Shares $\times$ Price = Total Amount

Rounding of these amounts varies by field.

Field	Rounding rules
Shares	Quicken displays the number of shares to four decimal places. It displays exact integers without decimals. It does not display zeros after the decimal point unless they are followed by nonzero digits. If there are more than four decimal places, Quicken cuts off the additional places. For example, Quicken truncates the number of shares 8.21678 to 8.2167.
Price	Quicken keeps internal track of decimal prices to the nearest 0.0005 and normally displays them to the nearest 0.001. It displays exact integers without decimals. If the fourth decimal place is a 5, Quicken displays it; otherwise it rounds to three decimal places. For example, Quicken displays 8.2175 but rounds the price 8.2177 upward to 8.218.
Total Amount	Quicken displays total amounts in dollars and whole cents. When it calculates the amount from the price and number of shares, it rounds to the nearest cent. For example, if you enter 40.3 shares at $8.26, Quicken rounds the total amount upward to $332.88.

At the end of each year, you may wish to adjust for the effects of rounding, to make the register match your statements. You can adjust the cash balance or the share balances of individual securities. See "Adjusting the cash or share balance" on page 207.

Buying securities

Click the Buy button.

When you buy a security with money you already have, you pay for it either with cash in the same account (for example, cash in your broker account) or with cash you transfer in from another account, such as your checking account.

- If you're buying with cash in the same account, Quicken subtracts the purchase amount from the cash balance in the account.
- If you're buying with cash you transfer in from another account, enter the source account in the Transfer Acct box in the investment form. (Quicken will enter BuyX in the Action field.) Quicken automatically subtracts the purchase amount from the cash balance

in the source account. See also "Transferring money to and from other accounts" on page 185. It describes situations in which it may be more convenient to record the transaction from the source account.

Commissions and fees. If an explicit commission or fee is added to the purchase, enter it in the Commission/Fee field. (If the Total of Sale amount doesn't equal the price times the number of shares, Quicken enters the difference in the Commission/Fee field.)

Loads. A "load" (sometimes called a "front-end load") is a commission built into the purchase price of a mutual fund or other security. A load fund has two share prices: a "Buy" or "Offer" price, and a "Sell" or net asset value (NAV) price. Enter the purchase of a load fund at the "Buy" price with no additional commission.

The true market value of your investment is based on the Sell or NAV price. If you want to correct the market value, update the price of the fund (see "Updating the values of your investments" on page 199) using the NAV price. The difference between the market value and what you paid is the load.

A "back-end load" is a commission built into the selling price. Funds with these loads have a net asset value (share price) greater than the selling price. Enter the sale of such a fund using the actual selling price.

Accrued Interest. When you buy a bond after its original date of issue, you usually have to pay "accrued interest" to the previous owner. Accrued interest is interest the bond has already earned but not yet paid out.

Use the Buy form to enter the bond purchase transaction without including accrued interest.

Enter the payment of accrued interest as a separate transaction. Click Other and choose Miscellaneous expense. Enter the security name in the Security box, the dollar amount, and the expense category _Accrued Int in the Category box. (Quicken adds this category at the end of your expense categories when you set up your first investment account.)

If you paid the accrued interest out of another Quicken account, enter a third transaction to show a cash transfer equal to the accrued interest. Click Other and choose Transfer cash in. Enter the other account name in the Transfer Acct box.

Selling securities

Click the Sell button.

When you sell a security, you can leave the cash in the account or transfer it out:

- If you're keeping cash from a sale in the same account, Quicken adds the sale proceeds to the cash balance in the account.

- If you're transferring cash from a sale to another account, enter the destination account in the Transfer Acct box. Quicken automatically adds the sale proceeds to the cash balance in the receiving account.

Commissions and fees. If an explicit commission or fee is subtracted from the sale proceeds, enter it in the Commission/Fee field. (If the Total of Sale amount doesn't equal the price times the number of shares, Quicken enters the difference in the Commission/Fee field.)

Specifying which lot you're selling. If you have bought shares in the same security more than once, and now want to sell only a portion of your shares, you can specify which shares you're selling. If you don't specify which shares you're selling, Quicken assumes you're selling the ones you bought first (a rule known as First In, First Out, or FIFO).

In the Sell form, enter the name of the security and the number of shares to sell. Then click Lots.

Your previous purchases of the security are listed as different lots.

As you select all or part of a particular lot, Quicken keeps a count of the total number of shares selected. This must match the total number of shares to sell that you entered.

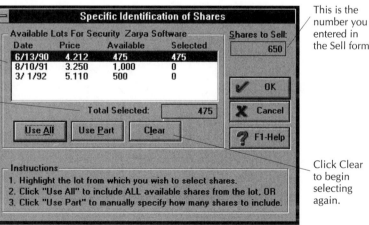

This is the number you entered in the Sell form.

Click Clear to begin selecting again.

To sell all the shares in a particular lot (up to the total number you are selling), select the lot and click Use All. To sell just some of the shares, select the lot and click Use Part, and then specify the number to sell from that lot. When you have finished, the Total Selected should equal the Shares to Sell. Click OK.

Entering income (dividends, interest, and capital gains distributions)

Click Income to enter the receipt of cash from dividends, interest, or capital gains distributions.

If the cash is being transferred out of the investment account, enter the receiving account's name in the Destination of Funds box. Quicken automatically adds the income to the cash balance in the receiving account.

- For dividend income from a money market fund that is the cash balance of a brokerage account, enter the name of the money market fund as the security name.

- An "income distribution" is money a mutual fund pays you as a result of dividends and interest it receives from the securities within the fund. Treat it like dividends in Quicken.

- A "capital gains distribution" is money paid to you by a mutual fund as a result of capital gains the fund earns by selling securities within the fund. The fund usually informs you whether the distribution is for "short-term" or "long-term" capital gains. (You may receive both at the same time. If the fund doesn't tell you whether a capital gains distribution is short-term or long-term, assume it's long-term.) Under U.S. tax law at the time of this printing, short-term capital gains distributions are treated the same as dividends.

For reinvested dividends, interest, or capital gains distributions, including interest that stays in a CD or dividends that stay in a money market fund, click Reinv instead of Income—see "Entering reinvestments" next.

Entering reinvestments

A "reinvestment" is the purchase of additional shares of a security with money paid to you by that security as dividend or interest income or capital gains distribution. (For a CD or money market fund, you are buying new shares at a share price of one dollar.)

Reinvestments work like an Income and a Buy transaction combined. Reinvestments increase your cost basis and your Return On Investment (ROI).

Click Reinv. Enter the dollar amount (in the appropriate box) and the number of new shares you are receiving. Quicken calculates the price per share. If a mutual fund doesn't tell you whether a capital gains distribution is short-term or long-term, assume it's long-term.

Redeeming shares for IRA custodial fees

In a mutual fund account set up as an IRA or other retirement account, the fund custodian may redeem shares as a custodial fee.

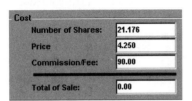

For redemption of shares as a custodial fee, click Sell. Enter the share price and the Total amount, so that Quicken calculates the number of shares. Now enter the same dollar amount of the fee in the Commission/Fee box, to make the net amount of the transaction zero. Enter the name of the investment account itself in the Transfer Acct box.

Transferring money to and from other accounts

If you have never created a transfer before, see "Transferring money between accounts" on page 24.

When you fill in the Transfer Acct box in an investment form, for example when buying shares, Quicken creates a cash transfer between the investment account and the other account. For regular investment accounts, the transfer amount need not be the same as the total transaction amount—the difference is added to or subtracted from the cash balance of the investment account. (For mutual fund accounts, you cannot do this because the account does not have a cash balance.)

Examples of when you would use a transfer:

- If you write checks by hand to pay for a security in a regular investment account, fill in a Buy form in the investment account, and afterwards fill in the check number on the bank account side of the transfer.

- If you're buying a security in a mutual fund account, Quicken knows that you have only one security. When you write a check or enter the transaction in your checking account register, Quicken records the transaction in the investment register with the security name, and fills in the number of shares on the basis of the most recent price known to Quicken. Thus, you'll probably choose to record the transaction from your checking account.

- If you record a check at the Write Checks window or in the check register to pay for a security in a *regular* investment account, enter the transaction as a cash transfer to the investment account that contains the security you're buying. The action for the transaction in the investment register is XIn. Now you must go to the investment register, change the XIn action to BuyX, click Edit, and fill in the Buy form.

- If you're transferring cash out of an investment account, start at the investment register. You can enter more information about the transaction in this register.

The action for any investment transaction involving a transfer has an X in the name, for example, BuyX or DivX.

Giving and receiving securities

When you give or receive shares of a security, without using cash, Quicken treats the transaction differently than it treats a purchase or sale.

- If you're giving shares that are now in a Quicken account, click Other and choose Remove shares from account. Enter the number of shares. Quicken reduces your number of shares and records a sale with a capital gain of zero, without adding cash to any account.

If you're transferring the shares to another Quicken account, enter a separate transaction for receipt of the shares in the register of the second account. In the second account, click Other and choose Add shares to account.

- If you're receiving shares, click Other and choose Add shares to account. This form increases your number of shares without subtracting cash from any account. Enter the number of shares received and the actual initial cost per share (including commission, fees, and load). The way you figure the cost depends on whether you're receiving the shares as a gift or as an inheritance:

Inherited shares. The cost basis of inherited shares is generally the value of the shares on the date that the deceased died or alternative valuation date. When you receive the inherited shares, record the cost per share on that date.

Gift shares. The cost basis of shares you received as a gift depends on the value of the shares on the date of the gift and the price that the giver paid for the shares, as well as your sale price if you sell the shares. When you receive the gift shares, record the cost per share when the giver originally purchased the shares.

Consult your tax advisor about any additional rules that may apply to determining your gain or loss.

Entering stock splits and stock dividends

Stock splits. When a security declares a "stock split," you are given additional shares. Each share is now worth less than it was before the split, but the total market value of all your shares is unchanged. (In a "reverse split," you receive fewer shares than you have now.)

For a stock split, click Other and choose Stock split. In the New Shares and Old Shares boxes, use numerals to enter the ratio of new shares to old. For example, if you receive one additional share for every three old shares, you now have four for every three you had before, so enter 4 in the New Shares field and 3 in the Old Shares field. Also enter the new price per share, after the split.

If you have more than one transaction for the security on the same day, Quicken places the stock split ahead of the other transactions. For example, if you had 100 shares before a two-for-one split, and you sell 100 shares on the day of the split, Quicken knows you still have 100 shares remaining.

When you record a stock split, Quicken recalculates your average cost per share. (Quicken doesn't change any transactions previously recorded in the register.)

Stock dividends. A "stock dividend," which is rare, is a dividend in the form of additional shares *instead of cash*. Most stock dividends are nontaxable. The company issuing the stock dividend will inform you whether it is taxable.

A stock dividend is *not* the same as a cash (normal) dividend issued by a company nor is it the same as a reinvested cash dividend.

- Enter a nontaxable stock dividend as a stock split (click Other and choose Stock split). For the ratio of new shares to old shares, add 1 to the number of dividend shares given per existing share. For example, if you receive 0.05 share per existing share, enter 1.05 to 1 as the ratio of new shares to old shares.

- Enter a taxable stock dividend as a reinvested dividend (click Reinv).

Buying on margin

A "margin loan" is money you borrow from a broker to pay for a security you're buying.

You don't have to tell Quicken you have a margin loan. (If you buy a security and don't have enough cash for it in your account, Quicken displays a negative cash balance.) Alternatively, you may want to set up a liability account for the loan.

- To record interest you pay on the margin loan, click Other and choose Margin interest expense.

- If you have set up a liability account for the loan, click Other and choose Transfer cash in. Enter the amount you are borrowing and the name of the liability account in the Transfer Acct box. (Click Other and choose Transfer cash out when you pay off the loan.)

Buying and redeeming U.S. Savings Bonds

The U.S. government issues Series EE bonds in various face value denominations. You buy a Series EE bond at a discount from its face value. Interest is paid only when a bond is redeemed. The interest from a Series EE bond is exempt from state and local taxes, and no federal tax is due until the bond is redeemed.

- When you buy a Series EE bond, use this format:

In this example, the buyer purchased one Series EE bond with a face value of $1,000.

(To match the way bond prices are quoted, divide the price by 10 and multiply the number of shares by 10.)

The purchase price was $500 because it was purchased at half face value. The security name is

US $1000 6% 1/23

This means "face value $1000, Series EE Bond, maturity date 1/2023."

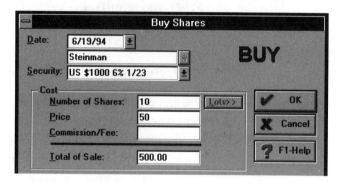

- When you redeem the savings bond (at or before maturity), enter the purchase price as the sales price in the Sell transaction. The difference between the purchase price and the redemption price is taxable interest. Use the Record Income form to record the remainder of the proceeds as interest income.

If you use the cash method of accounting, as most individual taxpayers do, you generally report the interest on U. S. savings bonds when you receive it. If you use the accrual method of accounting, you must report interest on U. S. savings bonds each year as it accrues. To record the annual accrual of interest, use the method described for recording taxable interest in "Recording zero-coupon bonds" on page 189.

Redeeming Treasury bills (T-bills)

When you buy a T-Bill, you buy it at a discount from its face value. When you sell it, part of the sale proceeds is interest you've earned while you've held the bill or bond.

- To record interest received when you sell, use the Record Income form.

- Subtract the interest received from the total you receive. Enter the difference as the dollar amount for the sale transaction (using the Sell form).

Entering a return of capital or principal

A "return of capital" is money paid to you as total or partial repayment of the money you invested. Return of capital differs from a sale in that you are not the one who initiates the return of capital. For example, a mortgage-backed security (such as a Ginnie Mae) returns capital when the underlying mortgages pay off principal, which is passed on to you. A unit trust returns capital as it sells the bonds within the trust. Note that return of capital, which is not a taxable event, is different from capital gains distribution.

- For a return of capital or principal, click Other and choose Return of capital.

  Quicken reduces the cost basis of the security by the amount of the return of capital. If you have purchased shares of the security on different dates, Quicken reduces the cost basis of each set of shares in proportion to the number of shares in each set. If you enter a *negative* amount in the Return Of Capital form, you *raise* the cost basis and decrease the cash balance in your account.

Recording zero-coupon bonds

You buy a zero-coupon bond at a discount. While you hold it, its value increases because of the interest it earns. Even though you don't receive this interest (until you sell), it is reported to you every year on a Form 1099-OID as taxable interest.

- To record interest shown on a Form 1099-OID, click Income and fill in the Interest box.

- To record the subsequent increase in value of the bond, use the Return Of Capital form to record a second transaction. Enter a dollar amount equal to the *negative* of the interest. (The negative return of capital increases your cost basis. It thus reduces unrealized gain if you sell the bond or update to the current market price of the bond.) Your cash balance is increased by the interest income and then decreased by the return of capital. It should be unchanged after the two transactions.

Handling tax-free bond income

If you have a tax-free bond for which you want to record income, set up a new "TaxFree Int" category. When you receive a nontaxable dividend, use the Income form and record the dividend amount in the Other box. Assign the TaxFree Int category to the transaction to separate your tax-free income from regular interest income.

Selling short

A "short sale" is the sale of a security you don't own. You deliver to the purchaser shares you borrow from your broker. You hope to buy the security later at a lower price to pay back your broker.

- For a short sale, click Sell and enter the details of the sale. Before it records the transaction, Quicken warns you that this transaction is a short sale, in case you have entered it in error.

- When you buy the security later, use the Buy form. Quicken calculates your gain or loss on the entire process at that time. The gains from short sales do not appear on Quicken capital gains reports. Use the investment income report to see your gains on short sales.

When you buy a security, Quicken always closes a short sale before opening a new position on the security. For example, if you sell 100 shares short, then later buy 150 shares, Quicken closes the short sale and records a purchase of 50 new shares.

If you ever record two short sales in the same security before buying the security, when you buy the security you can specify which lot you are closing. (See the description of specifying lots on page 183.)

In investment performance reports, the average annual total return for short sales is displayed as a negative value.

(If you have a short sale that you want to appear in a capital gains report, you need to close out the short sale with a Buy at the original sales amount. Then enter a Buy at your actual purchase price and enter a second Sell transaction at the original sales amount.)

Entering options (puts and calls)

Treat an option as a security but give it a distinctive name (such as "XYZ put Aug 40"). For example, you might buy a $40 call for $5 (use the Buy form). When you exercise the call, close your position with a Sell transaction for the amount of the call ($5, in this case). When entering the purchase of the underlying security, include the cost of the call as a fee paid (to correct the cost basis). In this case, you would enter a purchase (Buy) of $40 plus $5 commission.

If you sell an option you don't already own, Quicken treats it like a short sale. If an option you bought or sold expires worthless, enter the opposite transaction (Sell or Buy) for the option at a price of zero to close your position. Quicken then records a realized gain or loss.

Using reminder memos

You can enter a reminder memo in the investment register. For example, you may want to remind yourself that a CD is maturing next month. If you have installed Quicken's Billminder program, every time you turn on your computer or start running Windows, you see a message that you have a reminder (until you turn off the reminder memo).

Click Other and choose Reminder Transaction. Enter the wording of your reminder memo in the Description and Memo boxes. Enter a date for which you are reminding yourself to do something. (You'll see the reminder message anyway, whatever date you enter here.)

To turn off a reminder memo, double-click the Clr (Cleared) field of the transaction in the register.

If you have not installed Quicken's Billminder, see "Using Billminder and the Quicken Reminder" on page 109.

Viewing your portfolio

Quicken's Portfolio View window shows you a complete picture of your investments. The window lists your securities alphabetically and gives you analytical information about each security, such as the number of shares you own, the current price, market value, and return on investment.

(Definitions of all the terms used in the Portfolio View window are listed on page 197.)

In addition to seeing how your investments are doing, in this window, you can:

- Update security prices (see page 199 for details)
- Record all your investment transactions, such as buying and selling securities, receiving interest, reinvesting dividend income, and so on
- Create reports listing all transactions involving a security
- Create graphs showing a security's price and value history

From the Activities menu, choose Portfolio View OR click the Port View button in the investment Register window.

You can see the state of your investments on any particular day by changing the date here.

The Portfolio View window can actually display up to six different "views" of your investments. Click the drop-down button to select a different view.

Use the button bar to enter your investment transactions (see "Recording your investment transactions" on page 177).

The portfolio view lists all the securities in the selected account (in this example, All Accounts has been selected). The window gives information about each security.

To print the portfolio view, choose Print View from the File menu, or press Ctrl+P.

Portfolio View

Set Prices For: 3/15/94   All Accounts: View: Holdings

Security	Type	Sym	Mkt Price		Shares	Mkt Value	Est Income	% MktVal
First Statewide CD	CD		1		10,224.65	10,224.65	0.00	19.8
McKendry MMF	Money Mark		1		5,392.54	5,392.54	269.62	10.5
Marmona Fund	Mutual Fund		25.625	↓	512.03	13,120.70	0.00	25.5
Rawson Totl Return	Mutual Fund		13.250	↑	352.33	4,668.35	31.70	9.1
SIRA Technology	Stock	SIRA	12.740	↑e	200.00	2,548.00	24.00	4.9
Zarya Software	Stock	ZARY	3 1/2	e	1,975.00	6,912.50	296.25	13.4
-Cash-						8,649.80		16.8

Use right mouse button for security actions.   **e** - Estimated Prices   51,516   621   100

Custom   Prices   Graph   Register

Total Market Value: 51,517
Total % Gain: -3.2

Customize the view (see page 194).

List the security's price changes (see page 200).

Graph the security's price and value changes (see page 201).

Go to the register (only when a single account is selected).

The window summarizes your portfolio by showing totals.

Here are some of the ways in which you can control the view:

Set Prices For: 1/25/94

Change the viewing date: The portfolio view shows the state of your securities on a certain date (like a snapshot). To change the viewing date, click the button next to the date and select a date in the pop-up calendar, or click the date itself to enter a new date. Quicken ignores any transactions that happened after the viewing date. Also, if you sold all your shares in a security on a date before the viewing date, you won't see the security any more in the Portfolio View window. (If you want, you can change this to display securities you don't hold any more—see page 195.)

Chandler Sec

Select one or several accounts: The portfolio view normally lists only those securities that are currently held in the account shown near the top of the window. To list the securities of a different account, click the button and select an account from the drop-down list. Or select All Accounts or Selected Accounts.

Edit the securities: You can edit or delete securities, or set up new ones, directly from the portfolio view. Move the mouse pointer over one of the securities and in the left part of the window (for example, in the Security column) until the cursor changes to a QuickZoom magnifying glass (). Now click the right mouse button to display a small menu of options for editing that security. (The QuickReport option is described on page 193.) You cannot delete a security if you have transactions for it in any of your accounts.

Go to the register: To go to the register of the selected investment account, click the Register button at the bottom of the window. You can click this button only when a single account is selected.

Shortcut icons: You can put a Portfolio View icon on the iconbar to take you straight to the Portfolio View window. See "Adding an icon to the iconbar" on page 359. You can also add a Use Account icon to open a specific investment account with the Portfolio View window displayed—you may find this icon useful if you frequently update security prices for a certain account. See "Opening a specific account" on page 360.

Reporting on a security's transactions

If you want to see the transactions behind the figures in your Portfolio View window, create a QuickReport.

1   **To report on a security's transactions, select the security and click the Report button on the Portfolio View button bar.**

The security report lists all transactions in the selected account(s) involving the one security.

You can QuickZoom to the investment form to edit any transaction by double-clicking the transaction in this report.

(If you would prefer to QuickZoom to the transaction in the register, select Preferences from the Edit menu, then click Reports and clear the checkbox QuickZoom to Investment Forms.)

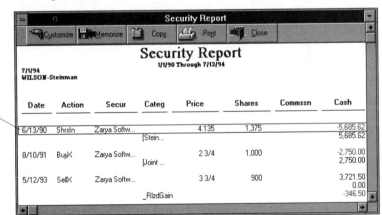

Changing the view

The Portfolio View window can actually show you up to six different "views" of your investments, each view containing different information about your securities. The three right-most columns in the window change according to the view you choose.

For example, the Holdings view tells you the current market value of your securities, whereas the Performance view shows you the return on your investment (ROI). Here is what each view shows you:

View	When to select it	What it shows you
Holdings	Select Holdings when you want to assess the total value of your investments, and to see their relative values (as a percentage of the total market value of all investments).	Mkt Value Est Income % MktVal
Performance	Select Performance to compare how well each of your investments is performing, shown by the ROI (Return on investment) percentage.	$ Invested $ Return ROI
Valuation	Select Valuation to see how much an investment is worth compared to how much it has cost you.	$ Invested $ Return Mkt Value
Price Update	Select Price Update to enter current prices for your securities and to see the price trends. See "Updating the prices of your securities" on page 199 for details.	Last Price Mkt Value MktVal Chg
Custom1 and 2	You can compose your own custom views to give other facts about your investments. See page 194 for details.	

For a detailed explanation of what the column headings in each view mean, see the table on page 197.

1   To change the view, click the button next to the View box and select a view from the drop-down list.

Customizing your portfolio views

Just as you can customize Quicken reports to change the layout and settings, you can also change the layout and settings of the portfolio views.

1   To customize the portfolio view, click Custom.

The Customize Portfolio Summary window works the same as the Customize Reports window. Select an area to customize and then click the options on the right.

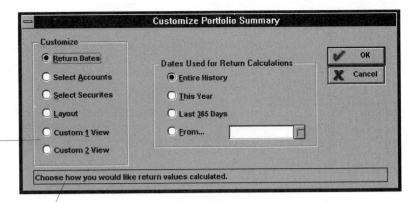

You can set up your own arrangements of column headings in the Custom Views. See "Setting up your own portfolio views" on page 196 for details.

A one-line Help message describes each of the areas you can customize.

2   **Click the area you want to customize (in the left-hand part of the Customize Portfolio Summary window).**

3   **Modify the settings in the right-hand part of the window, and click OK.**

   The next table describes the customize options.

Customize area	What you can change	Options	Results
Return Dates	Choose the period over which Quicken should calculate the returns on investments. All options calculate returns up to and including the date displayed in the Portfolio View window ("Set Prices For:").	Entire History	Use all transactions entered in Quicken.
		This Year	Calculate returns from this year only.
		Last 365 Days	Calculate returns over the preceding year.
		From (specify date)	Calculate returns since the entered date.
Select Accounts	Define which accounts should be included when you choose Selected Accounts in the Portfolio View window. (All other accounts are still offered for selection in the Portfolio View window.)	Select Accounts to Include	When you click Selected accounts in the account drop-down list in the Portfolio View window, the window shows only the securities from the accounts you selected.
Select Securities	Select which securities should be displayed. Initially, all securities will be displayed so long as they are currently held in the selected account(s); you can deselect securities to hide them from the Portfolio View window.	Select Securities to Include	Selected securities are displayed *if* they are currently held in the account(s) selected in the Portfolio View window (but see below).
		Only show securities with open positions *	Clear this checkbox if you want all securities to be displayed at all times in the Portfolio View window (regardless of which account is selected). When the checkbox is cleared, it works in conjunction with the Display field in the Security List (see page 167). Quicken displays all securities marked Always in the Display field, plus any Open securities in the selected accounts.

Customize area	What you can change	Options	Results
Layout	Normally, the Portfolio View window lists each security's name, security type, and symbol. You can hide the type and symbol columns if you want, to give more space to the other columns.	Name/Type/Symbol Name/Type Name/Symbol Name Only	If you hide the security type or symbol column, or both, they are removed from all views.
		Copy price updates to all matching symbols	You may want to separate two different trades in the same security. For example, you and your spouse invest in the same security but want to keep your transactions separate. You can do this by using two slightly different security names but the same symbol. When this checkbox is selected, if you change the price of one security, Quicken copies the price to the other security with the same symbol.
Custom 1 View Custom 2 View	You can set up your own arrangements of column headings in the Custom Views. See "Setting up your own portfolio views" next for details.		

* "Open" means to hold the security or to have a short position in it as of the date shown at the top of the Portfolio View window.

Setting up your own portfolio views

Quicken comes with four preset portfolio views: Holdings, Performance, Valuation, and Price Update. If these do not give you the information you want in the best grouping, you can set up your own views with different column headings.

1   **At the Portfolio View window, click Custom.**

2   **Click Custom 1 View (or Custom 2 View).**

3   **Click Column 1 and select a column heading from the drop-down list.**

Quicken offers some column headings not included in the four preset views. Scroll through to see which might interest you.

The column headings are explained in detail in the following table.

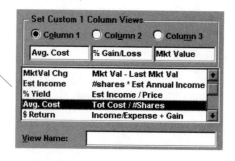

4   **Repeat for Column 2 and Column 3.**

5   **In the View Name box, type a name for your view.**

6   Click OK.

Now you can select your custom view in the View drop-down list in the Portfolio View window. Instead of "Custom 1" or "Custom 2," it has the name you gave it.

This table shows what the column headings mean.

Column heading	Description
Avg. Cost	(Average cost) The average cost of each share of the security. This is equal to the total cost of all currently-held shares of a security (the cost basis) divided by the number of shares currently held.
Cost basis	The total cost of all currently-held shares of a security, including income reinvested in the security.
Est Income	The estimated annual income from each security's interest, dividends, and distributions. This is the per share estimate you entered when setting up the security multiplied by the number of shares.
Gain/Loss	The gain or loss (in $) of all currently-held shares of the security. This is the market value of the shares minus the cost basis.
Inv. Yield	The yield on investment is the estimated income (as you specified when setting up the security) divided by the dollar amount invested (see $ Invested in this table).
Last Price	The market price before the most recent price was entered.
Mkt Price	The most recent price entered for this security. (If today's price has not been entered, Quicken puts an "e" for Estimated next to the price.)
Mkt Value	The market value of your holdings in each security, equal to the market price per share multiplied by the number of shares you hold.
MktVal Chg	The increase or decrease in the market value as a result of the latest price change.
ROI	Return on investment, defined as $ Return divided by $ Invested. This is an indication of how well a security has performed. It is the total profit you could make from a security if you sold your shares in it today, expressed as a percentage of the amount you invested in the security. ROI takes account of the current market price, and includes previous sales of the security and income received from the security. For example, let's say you bought shares for $100, have received $5 in dividends, and today the shares are worth $120. The $ Invested is $100, and the $ Return is $25 ($5 dividends plus the increase in market value). The ROI is $25/100 = 0.25$, displayed as 25%.
	ROI is a *guide* to performance and not a precise analysis. For example, it does not take timing of purchases and sales into account. To see a more exact calculation of performance, generate an investment performance report to find the average annual total return, or IRR (see page 202).
Sym	The security's symbol, which is used for importing prices. (See "Importing prices" on page 207.)
Total Market Value	The total market value of all the securities you hold in the selected account(s).
Total % Gain	The percentage increase in the total market value of the selected account(s). To be specific, this is the current market value less the cost basis of all currently-held securities, divided by the cost basis. A negative value indicates a loss.
Type	The security type, as you specified when setting up the security.
% Gain/Loss	The gain or loss of all currently-held shares of the security (the market value minus the cost basis) divided by the cost basis.[*]

Column heading	Description
% Income	The total dollar amount received from income from a security (interest, dividends, capital gains distributions, not including reinvested income) divided by the cost basis.
% Invested	The amount you have invested in a security (excluding reinvestments) expressed as a percentage of what you have invested in all securities.
% MktVal	The market value of a security expressed as a percentage of the total market value of all your securities.
% Yield	The estimated income per share divided by the current market price per share.
$ Income	The total income received from a security (including reinvested income), in dollars.
$ Invested	The actual dollar amount that you have invested in a security to date, including any expenses for that security (but *excluding* reinvestments). Note that, when you change the period over which Quicken calculates returns (see page 195), Quicken calculates $ Invested to be the market value of the security at the starting date plus the dollar amount you have invested in the security since that date (excluding reinvestments). In this way, $ Invested indicates the total cost of the security to you since the starting date.
$ Return	The total return (or profit) from a security since you invested in it. This is the current market value plus the income taken out as cash plus cash received from sales of shares, minus the amount invested. For example, let's say you bought 100 shares for $5 each ($500 total). You later sold 50 shares for $6 each ($300 total), and now the market price of your 50 remaining shares is $7 each ($350 total). The $ Return is $350 (current market value) plus $300 (sales), minus the $500 you invested = $150 total return. (Note that reinvestments are not explicitly added to $ Return, because they contribute to the market value, which is a part of $ Return.)

Choosing which securities to display

The Portfolio View window normally displays only those securities with open positions in the selected account(s). "Open" means to hold the security or to have a short position in it as of the date shown at the top of the Portfolio View window.

If you want to see all securities with open positions in all accounts, select All Accounts in the Account box near the top of the window.

If you want to see all securities in the Portfolio View window at all times, whether they are open or not, click Custom, then click Select Securities, and clear the checkbox "Only show securities with open positions."

If you want to hide a constant-price security such as a CD or money market fund from the window, click Custom, then click Select Securities, and clear any securities you don't want to display.

Updating the values of your investments

Quicken makes it easy for you to update the prices of your securities from the newspaper. In the Portfolio View window, Quicken lists your securities alphabetically within each security type, just as the newspaper does. Quicken uses the prices you enter in the window to recalculate the market value of each investment account.

Updating the prices of your securities

Or press Ctrl+U

1   **From the Activities menu, choose Portfolio View.**

If you often update prices for a specific account, add a Use Account icon to the iconbar. Specify the account's name, and that it should be opened directly at the Portfolio View window. See "Opening a specific account" on page 360 for more details.

2   **In the View box, choose Price Update.**

You can update the prices at any of the portfolio views, but the Price Update view gives the most relevant information. The market prices are the only values you can edit directly in this window.

3   **Make sure the window is displaying the investment account or accounts you want to deal with (shown in the Account box).**

Select an account, or all accounts, by clicking the drop-down button and choosing an account from the list.

The window lists only the securities in the account shown here.

See "Viewing your portfolio" on page 191 for a detailed explanation of this window.

Make sure the date displayed is the date for which your price updates are valid. Quicken displays today's date. But if, for example, you are entering prices from last week's newspaper, you might want to change the date for greater correctness.

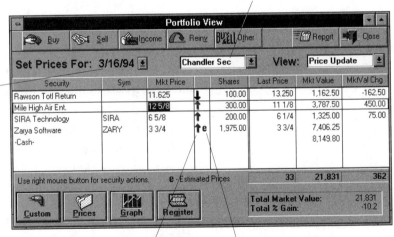

An up arrow (↑) means the price has gone up since the previous price entered. A down arrow (↓) means it has gone down.

"e" is for "estimated," meaning this is not today's price, but the most recently entered price.

4   **Use the Up Arrow or Down Arrow key to select a security, and enter the latest market price.**

For more about entering prices of different kinds of securities, see page 171.

Use this key	To do this
+ or −	Change the price to the next 1/8 (or 0.125).
* (Asterisk)	When a price is unchanged, press the asterisk key (*) to indicate that the price is correct for the current date. (The "e" now displayed disappears.)
	If you make a mistake changing a price and want to return to the estimated price previously displayed, press the asterisk key (*).

5 Repeat for each security.

Quicken records the price as soon as you leave the Market Price field. (You don't need to click a Record button or confirm the price change.)

Quicken recalculates the market value as you change the price, and shows you the change in market value.

Or press Ctrl+P

6 (Optional) From the File menu, choose Print Summary to print the contents of the window.

Entering security market prices for other dates

If you want to build up a price history for a security, see "Listing a security's price history" next. If you want to enter prices for just one date, follow these steps.

1 At the Portfolio View window, click on the button next to the date and click a date in the pop-up calendar.

Select the date for which you wish to enter market prices.

Or press Ctrl+G

Or click the date itself in the Portfolio View window and then, in the Go To Date window, enter a date and click OK.

Quicken displays the market prices and market values for that date (or the most recent prices you have entered before that date).

2 Enter correct prices for the chosen date just as you would a current price.

Listing a security's price history

Quicken stores a price history for each security as you update the prices at the Portfolio View window. Also, whenever you enter a buy or sell transaction, Quicken adds the new security price to the price history (and updates the calculations in the Portfolio View window).*

Or press Ctrl+E

1 **To view the price history in the form of a list, select the security and click Prices.**

The most recent prices are at the top of the list.

Price History for: Zarya Software	
Date	**Price**
3/15/94	3 3/4
3/ 1/94	3 5/8
6/14/93	3 1/2
5/12/93	3 3/4
3/ 1/92	5.110
8/10/91	2 3/4
6/14/90	3 1/2
6/13/90	4.135

Print | New | Edit | Del

To print the price history, click Print.

You can add new prices to the price history by clicking New.

To change or delete an existing price in the price history, click Edit or Del.

Graphing a security's price and value history

1 **To display a graph of a security's price history, select the security and click the Graph icon.**

The line shows the change in price over time for this security.

The bars show the value of your investment in this security (that is, the price multiplied by the number of shares you own).

The graph plots the prices over the previous 24 months. To cover an earlier or later period, change the viewing date first, as described on page 200.

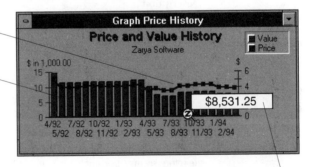

As with all Quicken graphs, whenever you see the QuickZoom magnifying glass you can hold down the right mouse button to show the actual price or value in the graph.

Use QuickZoom to see a Price and Value History report for the security. Just double-click the graph bar for the final month you want to include in the report. The report shows all transactions up to that date affecting the market value of your holding, plus all price changes.

* If you use both DOS Quicken and Quicken for Windows, you can update security prices for the same file in either program. Your price updates in DOS Quicken are visible in Quicken for Windows. However, the reverse is not normally true. If you want to see Quicken for Windows price updates in DOS Quicken, choose Preferences from the Edit menu, click General, and select the checkbox Save Price History in DOS Quicken Format. (Also see page 42.)

Creating reports and graphs

Quicken's investment registers and portfolio views show you almost everything you need to know about your investments. But creating investment reports and graphs can summarize the information more clearly and help you analyze your portfolio.

- Quicken offers five types of preset investment reports. For examples, see "Investment reports," beginning on page 218. Full details of how to create reports are given in Chapter 15, *Creating and customizing reports*, beginning on page 235.

  In addition, you can create transaction reports on each security from the Portfolio View window (see page 193) and price and value history reports from the price history graph (see page 201).

- You can create two types of investment graphs. The investment performance graph, described on page 262, shows your portfolio value and the average annual total return of your investments. In addition, you can create a price history graph to show the price trend of any security, as shown on page 201.

Here are explanations of some of the terms used in Quicken's reports and in this *User's Guide*.

Term	Description
Average annual total return (or IRR, internal rate of return)	The "average annual total return" is a percentage equal to the interest rate on a bank account that would give you the same total return on your investment. It takes into account money earned by the investment (interest, dividends, capital gains distributions) as well as changes in share price. Since it's an annual rate, it acts like a bank interest rate that compounds annually.
	• For example, if you invest $10,000 and get an average annual total return of 12.0% over two years, you'd have $12,544 (an increase of $2,544, or 25.4%) at the end of the two years.
	Average annual total return depends on the date range you have set for the report. If the return seems surprisingly high, it could be because you have set a short date range.
	Average annual total return is not the same as percent unrealized gain or loss. First, average annual total return includes money earned by the investment (for example, dividends received). Secondly, average annual total return depends on the amount of time it takes for the investment to grow to its value at the end of the time period. An investment that earns no income and that doubles in five years has a higher average annual total return than one that doubles in ten years. The percent gain, on the other hand, is 100% in both cases.
	Quicken displays the average annual total return in the investment performance report. A negative value indicates a loss, which can be either paper or real.

Term	Description
Average cost per share	The average cost per share of a security equals the cost basis divided by the number of shares. $$\text{avg. cost per share} = \frac{\text{cost basis}}{\text{number of shares}}$$ (This value will not be accurate unless you entered all historical purchases and sales of this security. See "Entering prior history for investments" on page 205 if you want to give Quicken data to calculate the correct average cost per share.)
Cost basis	The cost basis is the total cost of all shares of a security.
Market value	The market value for each security equals the market price times the number of shares. $$\text{market value} = \text{market price per share} \times \text{number of shares}$$ Quicken cannot display a market value greater than $9,999,999. Quicken displays a row of asterisks (******) when the market value is greater than that amount.
Realized gain/loss	The realized gain or loss is the difference between the selling price of a security and the cost basis. If you sell it for more than you paid, there is a (real) gain; if you sell it for less, there is a (real) loss. Quicken displays realized gains or losses in the capital gains report.
Unrealized gain/loss	The unrealized gain or loss is the difference between the current market value of a security and the cost basis. If the current market value is greater, there is a (paper) gain; if the cost basis is greater, there is a (paper) loss. • For example, if your 525 shares have a cost basis of $1,250 but they're now worth $2,100, you have an unrealized (paper) gain of $850. Quicken displays unrealized gain or loss in the portfolio value report under the heading Gain/Loss. A negative value indicates a (paper) loss. If Quicken doesn't have the data to calculate the average cost per share, it displays "NA" (not available) in reports for the gain.
%Gain/loss	The percent unrealized (paper) gain (or loss) equals the market price per share minus the average cost per share, divided by the average cost per share, expressed in percent. $$\% \text{ gain} = \frac{\text{market price per share} - \text{avg. cost per share}}{\text{avg. cost per share}} \times 100\%$$ A negative value is a (paper) loss.

Tracking indexes and securities you don't own

You may want one or more of the popular stock indexes, such as the Dow Jones Industrial Average or Standard & Poor's 500-stock index, to appear in the Portfolio View window. Or, perhaps you'd like to follow the price of a security you don't own. By creating a special account to hold the security or index (treated as a security), you can track its price and performance.

1 **Set up a new regular investment account.**

   You can call the account "Index" or "Other Securities." See "Setting up a Quicken regular investment account" on page 165 for full details of setting up an investment account.

   You can track mutual funds in a regular investment account too.

2 **Add the index or security to your Securities list.**

   See "Setting up securities for a regular investment account," beginning on page 166. For an index, you may wish to set up a security type called "Index."

   You can set up as many securities or indexes as you want to track, and track them all in the one account.

3 **In the new investment register, click Other and choose Add Shares To Account.**

4 **Enter the date from which you are beginning to track.**

5 **Enter the name of the index or unowned security in the Security box.**

6 **Enter 1 in the Number of Shares box.**

7 **Enter the index value or security price in the Price per Share box and record the transaction.**

   In the Portfolio View window, choose the Index or Other Securities account to track the price and performance.

   If you watch the price of a mutual fund you don't own, be aware that the price may drop because of income or capital gains distributions. When a fund makes a distribution, the share price is reduced by an equal amount (in addition to any changes caused by changes in market value of the underlying securities in the fund).

Entering prior history for investments

The more information you give Quicken about your investments, the more complete and accurate your reports and summaries will be. You may have set up a new investment account by entering a rough estimate of what you paid for the securities. You may have omitted dividends or capital gains distributions that you received since buying the securities.

To get:	Tell Quicken:
Accurate market values for a specified date	• Price and number of shares of securities owned on that date
Accurate average annual total return for a specified time period	• Price and number of shares on *day before* beginning of period and on last day of period • All transactions during the period
Accurate capital gains summary (realized short-term and long-term gain or loss) for a specified time period	• Number of shares and cost basis on date at least one year before beginning of period for all securities you have sold • All purchases and sales (including stock splits, reinvestments, and return of capital) from that date to end of period
Accurate income and expense summary for a specified time period	• All transactions during the period • Number of shares owned and price per share at beginning and end of period (if you're including unrealized gains)

If you decide to go back and enter a complete transaction history for your securities, the first step is to revise the Add Shares To Account transactions that you first entered for each security.

Revising the initial ShrsIn transaction for a security

1 **In the investment register, select the initial transaction for the security (look for ShrsIn in the Action field), and click Edit.**
   Quicken displays the Add Shares To Account form.

2 **(Optional) Revise the date to the initial date of acquisition.**

3 **Revise the number of shares.**

4 **Erase the price in the Price field to leave it blank.**

5 **Revise the total cost basis.**
   Enter the amount paid, including commission, fees, and load, or, if you acquired the shares from someone, your cost basis for the shares.

6 **Click Record to record the revised transaction.**

The revised transaction appears in the register in the correct sequence for the new date.

Entering transactions for dates in the past

Enter additional transactions as described in "Recording your investment transactions," beginning on page 177. Make sure you enter the correct date for each transaction. Each transaction moves up and appears in the register chronologically.

If a transaction involves a transfer of cash out of the account (for example, a dividend paid directly to you), enter the name of the investment account itself in the Destination of Funds box. Use this procedure for both types of investment accounts. It has no effect on the cash balance in a regular account.

After you've entered the transactions from the past, your cash balance for the whole account or your share balance for any security may be incorrect. Adjust it by choosing Update Balance from the Activities menu. See "Adjusting the cash or share balance" on page 207.

Reconciling the investment register

When you get a statement from your broker or other financial adviser, you can reconcile your account with the statement.

Reconciling an investment account is similar to reconciling other Quicken accounts. If you've been reconciling your other Quicken accounts, follow the same procedures. See "Starting reconciliation" on page 72 for more information.

You reconcile regular investment and mutual fund investment accounts the same way, except that you reconcile a cash balance in one and a share balance in the other.

- After you've reconciled the cash balance for a regular investment account, Quicken can take you to the Portfolio View window. If you haven't already entered the share prices from the statement, you have a chance to do so now.

- After you've reconciled the share balance for a mutual fund account, Quicken displays your new market value in the Share Balance Reconciled window. Quicken automatically adds the latest price to the price history for the security.

Adjusting the cash or share balance

If you don't want to use the Reconcile command, you can still adjust the cash or share balance to match what appears on your statement. Start in the investment register.

1   **From the Activities menu, choose Update Balances and then choose Update Cash Balance or Update Share Balance.**

2   **Enter the date for the adjustment, the correct value for the balance, and the security name (if requested).**

In the Security to Adjust box, you can press Ctrl+Y to view and choose from the Security list.

The adjustment appears in the register with the action MiscExp or MiscInc for cash balance adjustments, and with the action ShrsIn or ShrsOut for share balance adjustments. The memo for the adjustment is "Balance Adjustment."

Importing prices

Instead of updating security prices manually, you can save time by importing prices electronically. By far the easiest way of doing this is to use Quicken Quotes, part of the Quicken Companion product.

Note that Quicken matches up the prices it imports based on the *symbol*, not the *name*, of the security. To import prices, you may need to add symbols to the securities on your security list. (From the Lists menu, choose Security, select the security name, and click Edit.)

Using Quicken Quotes

Quicken Quotes uses your modem to retrieve today's prices. Quicken Quotes is tightly linked to Quicken. You open it from the Quicken iconbar, and click a button to send prices back to Quicken.

Updating prices with Quicken Quotes is as simple as clicking three buttons:

1 Get Symbols From Quicken, to read in the ticker symbols from your Quicken investment accounts

2 Retrieve Stock Prices, to call out for the latest prices

3 Send Prices to Quicken, to instantly add the new prices to the Quicken portfolio view.

Quicken Quotes is part of the Quicken Companion product. For more information about Quicken Companion, see page 367. To order the product, call our Customer Assistance number for software products, listed on page 372.

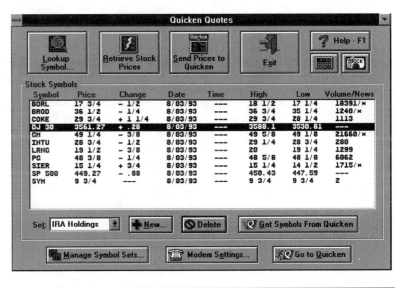

Using Quicken Quotes is free for most CompuServe members, or $1 per minute using the Quotes Hotline (a 900 number).

Importing prices from an ASCII file

These import formats are all acceptable:

ABC, 123.456

ABC, 123.456, 12/31/93

ABC 123.456 12/31/93

"ABC", 123.456, "12/31/93"

"ABC", "123.456", "12/31/93"

If your import file does not include quotation marks, it must have double spaces between items.

If you don't have Quicken Quotes, you can import security price data from an ASCII file. For example, the Prodigy Quote Track feature can export stock prices to a Quicken-compatible ASCII file (see below). The data to import must be in standard ASCII format with one symbol/price/date per line, delimited by either commas or double spaces (using only one type of delimiter per line).

1 **From the Activities menu, choose Portfolio View.**

2 **From the File menu, choose Import Prices.**

3 **Enter the name of the ASCII file that contains the price data.**

Specify the full DOS path for the location of the file to be imported (for example, C:\PRODIGY\QTRACK00.CSV).

4 **Change the date in the window, if necessary.**

Saving security prices from Prodigy's Quote Track feature to a file that Quicken can import

Follow these steps before you start Quicken.

For more information about using Prodigy quotes, open the Prodigy ABOUT menu and select the appropriate topic.

1 **In Prodigy, [Jump]: QUOTE TRACK and follow the onscreen instructions for creating or viewing a Quote Track list.**

2 **From the FILE menu, choose REPORT SET UP.**

3 **Set your report options:**

Destination:	File (You can use the file name QTRACK00.CSV or change it.)
Range:	Entire List
Type:	Closing
Format:	Comma Delimited
Headings:	No

4 **Select COMPLETE to save your options, and then select PRINT to save your changes to the file you specified.**

If the file already exists, Prodigy asks whether you want to write over it or add these quotes to it.

5 **If you have more Quote Track lists, you can view them and print them to the same file without resetting your print options.**

Sample reports

Once you've entered transactions, Quicken can automatically create reports based on transactions in one or more of your accounts. These reports help you examine your finances in detail.

Look through this chapter for examples of Quicken's home, investment, and business reports. The next chapter (beginning on page 235) explains how to create and customize them.

Home reports

This section briefly describes each of Quicken's home reports. To see what home reports are available, click the Reports icon on the iconbar and select the Home report family.

The basic procedure to create a report is in "Creating a report" on page 236.

Cash Flow	Summarize income and expense by category
Monthly Budget	Compare actual income/expense to budget
Itemized Categories	List transactions and subtotal by category
Tax Summary	List tax-related transactions
Net Worth	Calculate net worth based on account balances
Tax Schedule	List transactions and subtotal by tax line item
Missing Checks	List transactions in order and highlight missing checks
Comparison	Compare two transaction periods by category (or other item)

Cash flow

A cash flow report summarizes income and expenses by category.

Quicken groups income categories with any transfers *from* accounts not included in the report.

Quicken groups expense categories with any transfers *to* accounts not included in the report.

Initial settings for this report (a type of summary report)

Row headings:	Category
Column headings:	Don't subtotal
Organization:	Cash flow basis
Accounts to report on:	Bank, cash, credit card
Transfers:	Exclude internal

These are transfers to asset, liability, and investment accounts from bank, cash, and credit card accounts.

```
                         Cash Flow Report
                      1/1/94 Through 3/31/94
  3/31/94
  WILSON-Bank,Cash,CC Accounts                                 Page 1
                                              1/1/94-
               Category Description           3/31/94
          ------------------------    -----------------------
          INFLOWS
            Salary                                 42,291.69
            FROM Mutual Fund                           30.42
                                               -----------
          TOTAL INFLOWS                             42,322.11

          OUTFLOWS
            Auto:
              Fuel                   191.00
              Loan                   580.49
              Repairs                165.98
                                   -----------
            Total Auto                                937.47
            Clothing                               1,588.10
            Dining                                   988.61
            Entertain                              1,214.63
            Gifts                                    228.40
            Groceries                              1,040.44
            Household                                769.64
            Insurance                                530.32
            Mort Int                               3,242.30
            Tax:
              Fed                 10,047.94
              Soc Sec              2,114.56
              State                3,383.31
                                   -----------
            Total Tax                              15,545.81
            Telephone                                277.07
            Utilities:
              Garbage                130.00
              Gas & Electric         187.14
                                   -----------
            Total Utilities                          317.14
            TO Auto Loan Balance                   1,182.16
            TO Brokerage Account                   1,850.00
            TO Mortgage Balance                      232.87
            TO Mutual Fund                           700.00
                                               -----------
          TOTAL OUTFLOWS                            30,644.96

                                               -----------
          OVERALL TOTAL                             11,677.15
                                               ===========
```

A cash flow report initially excludes transfer transactions that occur between the accounts included in the report (that is, between bank, cash, and credit card accounts). For example, Quicken does not include a transfer of funds from checking to savings.

Monthly budget

The monthly budget report compares actual income and expenses against budgeted income and expenses by month. Before creating a budget report, you must set up budget amounts for each category, as described in "Setting up a budget" on page 290.

The Actual column contains the amounts for categories used in transactions that fall within the date range for the report column.

The Budget column contains the amounts you entered in the Set Up Budgets window.

The Diff column is the difference between what you budgeted and what you actually spent or received.

A negative value means your Actual amount was less than your Budget amount.

A monthly budget report is organized like a cash flow report. Income categories are shown at the top under INFLOWS and expense categories are shown below them under OUTFLOWS.

Initial settings for this report (a type of budget report)

Column headings:	Month
Organization:	Cash flow basis
Accounts to report on:	Bank, cash, credit card
Include unrealized gains:	No
Transfers:	Exclude internal
Categories:	Budgeted categories only

These are transfers to asset, liability, and investment accounts from bank, cash, and credit card accounts.

The OVERALL TOTAL at the bottom of the Actual column is your net savings for the month. If the number is positive, you earned more than you spent. If the number is negative, you spent more than you earned.

```
                           Monthly Budget Report
                          1/1/94 Through 1/31/94
1/31/94
WILSON-Bank,Cash,CC Accounts                                     Page 1
                                  1/1/94       -       1/31/94
     Category Description         Actual     Budget      Diff
-------------------------    ----------- ----------- -----------
  INFLOWS
    Div Income                      0.00       16.15      -16.15
    Invest Inc                      0.00       75.00      -75.00
    _RlzdGain                       0.00        0.00        0.00
    Salary                     18,125.01   18,125.01        0.00
    FROM Auto Loan Balance          0.00        0.00        0.00
    FROM Family House               0.00        0.00        0.00
    FROM Mortgage Balance           0.00        0.00        0.00
    FROM Sally's 401(k)             0.00        0.00        0.00
                             ----------- ----------- -----------
  TOTAL INFLOWS               18,125.01   18,216.16      -91.15

  OUTFLOWS
    Auto:
      Fuel                         60.00       60.00        0.00
      Loan                        198.52      198.52        0.00
      Repairs                      35.00        0.00       35.00
      Auto - Other                  0.00        0.00        0.00
                             ----------- ----------- -----------
    Total Auto                    293.52      258.52       35.00
    Clothing                    1,065.76      300.00      765.76
    Dining                        375.54      300.00       75.54
    Entertain                     586.93      300.00      286.93
    Gifts                           0.00        0.00        0.00
    Groceries                     439.54      400.00       39.54
    Household                      75.99       75.99        0.00
    Insurance                     227.28      227.28        0.00
    Mort Int                    1,081.36    1,081.36        0.00
    Tax:
      Fed                       4,306.26    4,306.26        0.00
      Soc Sec                     906.24      906.24        0.00
      State                     1,449.99    1,449.99        0.00
      Tax - Other                   0.00        0.00        0.00
                             ----------- ----------- -----------
    Total Tax                   6,662.49    6,662.49        0.00
    Telephone                      87.52       90.00       -2.48
    Utilities:
      Garbage                      65.00       65.00        0.00
      Gas & Electric               64.97       60.00        4.97
      Utilities - Other             0.00        0.00        0.00
                             ----------- ----------- -----------
    Total Utilities               129.97      125.00        4.97
    TO Auto Loan Balance          389.03      389.00        0.03
    TO Family House                 0.00        0.00        0.00
    TO Mortgage Balance            77.03       77.00        0.03
    TO Sally's 401(k)             300.00      300.00        0.00
                             ----------- ----------- -----------
  TOTAL OUTFLOWS               11,791.96   10,586.64    1,205.32

                             ----------- ----------- -----------
  OVERALL TOTAL                6,333.05    7,629.52   -1,296.47
                             =========== =========== ===========
```

Itemized categories

An itemized category report lists transactions from all your accounts, grouped and subtotaled by category.

Quicken lists income transactions first, unless no income transactions occurred during the report date range.

Quicken lists expense transactions after income transactions, followed by transfers between accounts and balances forward.

Initial settings for this report (a type of transaction report)	
Subtotal by:	Category
Sort transactions by:	None
Organization:	Income and expense
Accounts to report on:	All accounts
Include unrealized gains:	No
Transfers:	Include all

```
                         Itemized Category Report
                          2/15/94 Through 2/22/94
2/22/94
All Accounts                                                        Page 1

   Date   Acct    Num    Description     Memo     Category    Clr  Amount
 -------- ------ ------- ------------- ----------- ----------- --- --------

          INCOME/EXPENSE
            EXPENSES
             Auto:

              Fuel
2/20/94  Quicke         Central Motor  Jack, Oil  Auto:Fuel    x    -50.00
                        Total Fuel                                 ---------
                                                                   -50.00
              Loan
2/15/94  Checki 5012 S  GMAC Financin            Auto:Loan Int x   -193.50
                        Total Loan                                 ---------
                                                                  -193.50
                        Total Auto                                ---------
                                                                  -243.50
              Mort Int
2/15/94  Checki 5013 S  American Lend            Mort Int      x -1,080.77
                        Total Mort Int                            ---------
                                                                -1,080.77
                        TOTAL EXPENSES                            ---------
                                                                -1,324.27

                        TOTAL INCOME/EXPENSE                     ---------
                                                                -1,324.27

          TRANSFERS
            Auto Loan
2/15/94  Checki 5012 S  GMAC Financin            [Auto Loan]   x   -394.05
                        Total TO Auto Loan                        ---------
                                                                  -394.05
            Cash
2/15/94  Checki         ATM Withdrawa            [Cash]        x   -100.00
                        Total TO Cash                             ---------
                                                                  -100.00
            Mortgage
2/15/94  Checki 5013 S  American Lend            [Mortgage]    x    -77.62
                        Total TO Mortgage                         ---------
                                                                   -77.62
            Checking
2/15/94  Cash           ATM Withdrawa            [Checking]         100.00
2/15/94  Auto L         GMAC Financin A/C #87239-2 [Checking]       394.05
2/15/94  Mortga         American Lend A/C #871-348 [Checking]        77.62
                        Total FROM Checking                       ---------
                                                                   571.67
                        TOTAL TRANSFERS                           ---------
                                                                     0.00

                        OVERALL TOTAL                             ---------
                                                                -1,324.27
                                                                =========
```

Tax summary

A tax summary report lists tax-related transactions from all your accounts except tax-deferred investment accounts (such as IRAs or 401(k) accounts), grouped and subtotaled by category.

If you set up a file with Quicken's standard home category list, tax-related categories are already marked for you in the list. If you have set up your own categories, you need to mark the ones that are related to the tax forms you want to fill out. See "Setting up categories and subcategories" on page 9 for instructions.

Quicken lists expense transactions after income transactions, followed by transfers between accounts and balances forward.

```
                              Tax Summary Report
                            1/1/94 Through 1/31/94
      1/31/94
      All Accounts                                                    Page 1

       Date    Acct    Num   Description   Memo      Category    Clr   Amount
      -------- ------ ------- ----------- ----------- ----------- --- ----------

               INCOME/EXPENSE
                 INCOME
                   _IntInc

      1/10/94  Sally' IntInc  Guren      Semiannual i _IntInc          75.00
                                                                   -----------
                      Total _IntInc                                    75.00

                 Salary

      1/1/94   Checki    S  Paycheck               Salary       x   2,500.00
      1/1/94   Checki    S  Paycheck               Salary       x   3,541.67
      1/15/94  Checki    S  Paycheck               Salary       x   3,541.67
      1/15/94  Checki    S  Paycheck               Salary       x   2,500.00
      1/29/94  Checki    S  Paycheck               Salary       x   3,541.67
      1/29/94  Checki    S  Paycheck               Salary           2,500.00
                                                                   -----------
                     Total Salary                                  18,125.01
                                                                   -----------
                   TOTAL INCOME                                    18,200.01

                 EXPENSES
                   Mort Int

      1/15/94  Checki 5004 S  American Len         Mort Int     x  -1,081.36
                                                                   -----------
                     Total Mort Int                                -1,081.36

                   Tax:

                     Fed

      1/1/94   Checki    S  Paycheck               Tax:Fed      x    -550.00
      1/1/94   Checki    S  Paycheck               Tax:Fed      x    -885.42
      1/15/94  Checki    S  Paycheck               Tax:Fed      x    -885.42
      1/15/94  Checki    S  Paycheck               Tax:Fed      x    -550.00
      1/29/94  Checki    S  Paycheck               Tax:Fed      x    -885.42
      1/29/94  Checki    S  Paycheck               Tax:Fed           -550.00
                                                                   -----------
                     Total Fed                                     -4,306.26

                     State

      1/1/94   Checki    S  Paycheck               Tax:State    x    -200.00
      1/1/94   Checki    S  Paycheck               Tax:State    x    -283.33
      1/15/94  Checki    S  Paycheck               Tax:State    x    -283.33
      1/15/94  Checki    S  Paycheck               Tax:State    x    -200.00
      1/29/94  Checki    S  Paycheck               Tax:State    x    -283.33
      1/29/94  Checki    S  Paycheck               Tax:State         -200.00
                                                                   -----------
                     Total State                                   -1,449.99
                                                                   -----------
                   Total Tax                                       -5,756.25
                                                                   -----------

                 TOTAL EXPENSES                                    -6,837.61

                                                                   -----------
                 TOTAL INCOME/EXPENSE                              11,362.40
                                                                   ===========
```

Initial settings for this report (a type of transaction report)

Subtotal by:	Category
Sort transactions by:	None
Organization:	Income and expense
Accounts to report on:	All accounts except tax-deferred investment accounts
Include unrealized gains:	No
Tax-related transactions only:	Yes
Transfers:	Include all

Net worth

A net worth report calculates your net worth on the basis of all accounts in the current Quicken file. Net worth is the difference between your assets and your liabilities.

Initial settings for this report (a type of account balances report)

Report at intervals of:	None
Organization:	Net worth format
Accounts to report on:	All accounts
Include unrealized gains:	Yes
Tax-related transactions only:	No

```
                          Net Worth Report
                           As of 3/31/94
3/31/94
All Accounts                                                     Page 1
                                               3/31/94
                        Acct                   Balance
          ------------------------------------ ---------------
          ASSETS
          Cash and Bank Accounts
            Cash                                        39.00
            Checking
              Ending Balance            1,244.82
              plus: Checks Payable        100.00
                                       ------------
              Total Checking                         1,344.82
            Savings                                 13,500.00
                                                   ------------
            Total Cash and Bank Accounts           14,883.82

          Other Assets
            Family House                            152,879.50
            Sally's 401(k)                            5,431.11
                                                   ------------
            Total Other Assets                      158,310.61

          Investments
            Assorted Mutual Funds                    13,034.08
            Brokerage Account                         4,416.07
            Chandler Brokerage                       11,861.12
            Mutual Fund                               8,930.86
                                                   ------------
            Total Investments                        38,242.13

                                                   ------------
          TOTAL ASSETS                              211,436.56

          LIABILITIES
            Checks Payable                              100.00

          Credit Cards
            1111-2222-3333-4444                          48.56
            American Express                            235.00
                                                   ------------
            Total Credit Cards                          283.56

          Other Liabilities
            Auto Loan Balance                        17,396.23
            Mortgage Balance                        132,664.41
                                                   ------------
            Total Other Liabilities                 150,060.64

                                                   ------------
          TOTAL LIABILITIES                         150,444.20

                                                   ------------
          OVERALL TOTAL                              60,992.36
                                                   ============
```

If your bank accounts include any unprinted or postdated checks, Quicken adds them to your bank balance and also lists them as a liability.

The OVERALL TOTAL shows your net worth.

If you have set up investment accounts, the net worth report shows the market value of your investments based on the most recent prices you entered prior to the report date.

Tax schedule

A tax schedule report lists those transactions with categories assigned to tax schedule line items, grouped and subtotaled by tax form name and line item. The initial report excludes tax-deferred investment accounts (you can customize the report to include them).

See "Setting up categories with tax time in mind" on page 270 for information about assigning categories to a tax form and line item. Before you can assign categories to tax forms, you must turn on the option. From the Edit menu, choose Preferences and click the General icon. Then select the checkbox Use Tax Schedules With Categories.

You can define an investment account to be tax-deferred when setting up the account. See "Setting up a regular investment account," beginning on page 165, or "Setting up a mutual fund investment account," beginning on page 173.

Initial settings for this report (a type of transaction report)

Subtotal by:	Tax schedule
Sort transactions by:	None
Organization:	Income and expense
Accounts to report on:	All accounts except tax-deferred investment accounts
Include unrealized gains:	No
Tax-related transactions only	No
Transfers:	Include all

After creating this report, you can export the report to a file to use in tax preparation software. See "Creating tax schedule reports" on page 271.

```
                        Tax Schedule Report
                      3/1/94 Through 3/31/94
 3/31/94
 All Accounts                                                      Page 1

    Date    Acct    Num    Description    Memo    Category    Clr    Amount
 --------  ------  -------  ------------  -----------  ------------  ---  ----------


            Schedule A

            Home mortgage interest

 3/15/94  Checki 5029 S  American Len             Mort Int    x   -1,080.17
                                                                 -----------
            Total Home mortgage interest                         -1,080.17


            W-2

            Salary

 3/12/94  Checki       S  Paycheck                Salary            2,500.00
 3/15/94  Checki DEP   S  Paycheck                Salary       x    3,541.67
 3/26/94  Checki       S  Paycheck                Salary            2,500.00
 3/31/94  Checki DEP   S  Paycheck                Salary       x    3,541.67
                                                                 -----------
            Total Salary                                          12,083.34

            Federal Withholding

 3/12/94  Checki       S  Paycheck                Tax:Fed            -550.00
 3/15/94  Checki DEP   S  Paycheck                Tax:Fed       x    -885.42
 3/26/94  Checki       S  Paycheck                Tax:Fed            -550.00
 3/31/94  Checki DEP   S  Paycheck                Tax:Fed       x    -885.42
                                                                 -----------
            Total Federal Withholding                            -2,870.84

            FICA

 3/12/94  Checki       S  Paycheck                Tax:FICA           -125.00
 3/15/94  Checki DEP   S  Paycheck                Tax:FICA      x    -177.08
 3/26/94  Checki       S  Paycheck                Tax:FICA           -125.00
 3/31/94  Checki DEP   S  Paycheck                Tax:FICA      x    -177.08
                                                                 -----------
            TOTAL FICA                                             -604.16

            State Withholding

 3/12/94  Checki       S  Paycheck                Tax:State          -200.00
 3/15/94  Checki DEP   S  Paycheck                Tax:State     x    -283.33
 3/26/94  Checki       S  Paycheck                Tax:State          -200.00
 3/31/94  Checki DEP   S  Paycheck                Tax:State     x    -283.33
                                                                 -----------
            Total State Withholding                               -966.66
```

Missing checks

The missing checks report lists payments in the current account by check number, and highlights any breaks in the check number sequence. It shows you both missing and duplicate check numbers. This report is based on the transaction report (see page 229).

**Initial settings for this report
(a type of transaction report)**

Organization:	Income and expense
Accounts to report on:	Current account
Transfers:	Include all

```
                              Missing Check Report
                            3/ 1/94 Through 3/31/94
   4/ 9/94
   MURPHY-Joint Account                                              Page 1

   Date    Num     Description        Memo          Category    Clr Amount
   ------- ------  ----------------   -----------   ----------- --- --------

           Joint Account
           -------------
   3/ 3/94 5018    Marmona Fund       Buy additional [Marmona Fund]  x -1,000.00
   3/ 2/94 5019    County of Santa Cor 909 Exmoor Way Tax:Prop       x   -750.00

              *** Missing Check(s) 5020  ***

   3/ 8/94 5021    City of Valley Spri Services     Utilities:Garbage x   -65.00
   3/14/94 5022    San Francisco Opera Fall Season  Entertain        x  -250.00
   3/15/94 5023 S  American Lending Co A/C #871-34824 --SPLIT--       x -1,158.39
   3/15/94 5024 S  GMAC Financing      A/C #87239-278 --SPLIT--       x  -587.55
   3/28/94 5025    Valley Gas & Electr February    Utilities:Gas     x   -59.82

              *** Duplicate Check 5025  ***

   3/31/94 5025    Cabinet Supply Ware Kitchen Cabine [House]         x -2,002.00
   3/31/94 5026    National Wildlife C              Charity          x  -100.00
   3/31/94 5027    Western Bell        Feb/Mar      Utilities:Phone   x   -91.28
                                                                     ---------
           Total Joint Account                                       -6,064.04
                                                                     =========
```

If a check number is duplicated in the sequence, Quicken lists it as a "Duplicate Check" item.

If a check number is missing in the sequence, Quicken lists it as a "Missing Check" item.

Comparison

With a comparison report, you can compare your income and spending for two different periods. For example, you can see if, and in which areas, you are spending more or earning more than a year ago. The report shows you a breakdown of your finances by category, and lets you define two different periods to display side by side.

You can display the difference between the two periods in dollars, or as a percentage of the first figure, or both.

Initial settings for this report (a type of summary report)

Comparison dates:	Last year and year-to-date
Row headings:	Category
Subtotal by:	Don't subtotal
Organization:	Cash flow basis
Show difference as %:	No
Show difference in $:	Yes
Accounts to report on:	Bank, cash, credit card
Transfers:	Exclude internal

The figures in the difference column are the second column amounts minus the first column amounts. They normally show how much more you are earning or spending in each category compared with an earlier period. A negative amount means you are earning or spending less now than before.

As an option if you customize the report, you can display another column which shows the percentage change from the first period to the second. (If you see INF in the % Difference column, meaning Infinity, it's because the first amount is zero.)

The overall difference shown in the lower right corner of the report indicates that this person has saved $407.25 less this year than in the same period last year.

```
                              Comparison Report
                            1/1/93 Through 3/31/94
           3/31/94
           WILSON-Bank,Cash,CC Accounts                        Page 1

                                   1/1/1993-      1/1/1994-          $
               Category Description 3/31/1993      3/31/1994      Difference
           --------------------- ----------  --------------  -------------

           INFLOWS
             Bonus                      0.00        3,000.00       3,000.00
             Interest Income            0.42            0.42           0.00
             Salary                18,508.35       11,025.01      -7,483.34
             Inflows - Other          162.19            0.00        -162.19
                                 --------------  ------------  ------------
           TOTAL INFLOWS           18,670.96       14,025.43      -4,645.53

           OUTFLOWS
             Auto:
               Fuel                   190.31          150.00         -40.31
               Maintenance            262.00            0.00        -262.00
                                   ----------      ----------      ----------
             Total Auto               452.31          150.00        -302.31
             Books, Music               0.00          129.76         129.76
             Childcare                400.00          400.00           0.00
             Clothing               1,226.63          189.69      -1,036.94
             Computer                 145.01            0.00        -145.01
             Entertain                276.50          290.91          14.41
             Groceries                319.54          449.43         129.89
             Int Exp                   79.12           77.72          -1.40
             Mort Int               1,417.48            0.00      -1,417.48
             Recreation:
               Hiking                 319.51            0.00        -319.51
               Skiing                 506.83            0.00        -506.83
                                   ----------      ----------      ----------
             Total Recreation         826.34            0.00        -826.34
             Taxes:
               Fed                  4,127.10        2,456.26      -1,670.84
               FICA                 1,097.90          637.49        -460.41
               SDI                     65.74           32.87         -32.87
               State                1,204.15          743.74        -460.41
                                   ----------      ----------      ----------
             Total Taxes            6,494.89        3,870.36      -2,624.53
             Telephone                187.52          198.27          10.75
             Utilities:
               Electricity            64.97           62.35          -2.62
               Garbage                 0.00           15.50          15.50
               Water                   0.00           28.75          28.75
                                   ----------      ----------      ----------
             Total Utilities          64.97          127.83          62.86
             Vacation                  0.00        1,332.31        1332.31
             Outflows - Other        177.97          515.85         337.88
             TO Auto Loan          1,210.63        1,212.03           1.40
             TO Mortgage           5,116.43        5,312.90         196.47
             TO Steve's IRA          100.00            0.00        -100.00
                                 --------------  ------------  ------------
           TOTAL OUTFLOWS          18,495.34       14,257.06      -4,238.28

                                 --------------  ------------  ------------
           OVERALL TOTAL             175.62         -231.63        -407.25
```

Investment reports

This section briefly describes each of Quicken's investment reports. To see what investment reports are available, click the Reports icon on the iconbar and select the Investment report family.

You cannot run investment reports unless you have set up investment accounts. See Chapter 13, *Tracking investments,* beginning on page 159. The basic procedure to create a report is in "Creating a report" on page 236.

Portfolio Value	Calculate value of securities in investment accounts
Investment Performance	Calculate investment returns (internal rate of return)
Capital Gains	List realized gains on securities sold
Investment Income	Summarize investment income and expenses by category
Investment Transactions	List investment transactions

Portfolio value

A portfolio value report shows the value of each of your securities on a specified date. The portfolio value report shows unrealized gain in dollars (instead of as a percentage), and has options for subtotaling by account, security type, or investment goal.

Most recent price per share. Quicken marks estimated prices with an asterisk (*). (Quicken estimates the price if you haven't updated the price for the date of the report.)

Your cost basis for the security. Quicken displays 0.00 if you did not enter the cost basis of the security.

Unrealized (paper) gain or loss in dollars.

Market value on the date of the report.

Number of shares (to the nearest 0.01).

Initial settings for this report (a type of account balances report)

Subtotal by:	Don't subtotal
Investment accounts to report on:	Current
Tax-related transactions only	No
Select to include	All securities, security types, and investment goals

```
                                    Portfolio Value Report
                                         As of 3/31/94
3/31/94
WILSON-Chandler Sec                                                              Page 1
                                         * Estimated Prices

     Security            Shares     Curr Price     Cost Basis  Gain/Loss   Balance
------------------    ----------   ----------    ----------  ----------  ----------
First Statewide CD    10,224.65        1.000  *    10,224.65       0.00   10,224.65
Marmona Fund             472.75       24.940  *    10,549.23   1,241.16   11,790.39
McKendry MMF           4,052.53        1.000        4,052.53       0.01    4,052.54
Rawson Totl Return       252.32       26.170  *     5,992.79     610.63    6,603.42
-Cash-                 2,819.58        1.000        2,819.58       0.00    2,819.58
                                                  ----------  ----------  ----------
Total Investments                                 33,638.78   1,851.80   35,490.58
                                                  ==========  ==========  ==========
```

Investment performance

The investment performance report shows the average annual total return of your securities during a specified time period. This return takes into account dividends, interest, and other payment you receive as well as increases and decreases in the market value of your securities. Generally, if the average annual return on an investment is 10%, that investment is performing as well as a bank account that pays 10% interest.

When the average annual total return is greater than 10,000% or less than -99.9%, or when the timing of cash flows prevents Quicken from calculating a figure, Quicken displays a message that one or more calculations appear as N/A (not available).

The average annual total return is the internal rate of return (IRR) for your investment. Technically, it equals the discount rate at which all the cash flows associated with the investment have a net present value of zero. (See page 202 for more details.)

Initial settings for this report	
Subtotal by:	Don't subtotal
Cash flow detail:	Yes
Investment accounts to report on:	Current
Tax-related transactions only:	No
Select to include	All securities, security types, and investment goals

```
                       Investment Performance Report
                          7/6/93 Through 7/6/94
   7/6/94                                                    Page 1
   WILSON-Chandler Sec

                                                         Avg. Annual
   Date   Action  Description      Investments    Returns  Tot. Return
   -----  ------- ------------   -------------- ----------- ------------

                  7/6/93 - 7/6/94
                  ---------------

   7/5/1993       Beg Mkt Value      15,257.82
   7/6/1994       End Mkt Value                   16,989.65
                                  -------------- ----------- ------------
          TOTAL 7/6/93 - 7/6/94     15,257.82    16,989.65       11.3%
```

Capital gains

A capital gains report shows long-term and short-term capital gains for securities sold during a specified time period. (For capital gains distributions from a mutual fund, use the investment income report.)

To get an accurate capital gains report, you must tell Quicken the date or dates you bought the shares you sold, and the actual cost basis of those shares. If you haven't already done so, you can enter this information in the investment register after you make the sale. See "Entering prior history for investments" on page 205. Quicken warns you if you report on the sale of a security with a zero cost basis that you should enter more information.

If you sold only part of your shares of a security in one account, Quicken assumes that the shares you sold are the ones you've held the longest, unless you specifically identified some other lot for selling. (See "Selling securities" on page 183.)

Quicken does not distinguish "wash sales" from other sales. (A "wash sale" is a sale at a loss within 30 days of acquiring the same security. Special tax rules apply.)

Initial settings for this report	
Subtotal by:	Short- vs Long-term
Maximum short-term gain holding period:	365 days
Organization:	Income and expense
Investment accounts to report on:	Current
Include unrealized gains:	No
Tax-related transactions only:	No
Select to include	All securities, security types, and investment goals

```
                           Capital Gains Report
                          1/1/94 Through 5/31/94
5/31/94
WILSON-Chandler Sec                                              Page 1

Security   Shares   Bought    Sold    Sales Price Cost Basis  Gain/Loss
--------- -------- -------- -------- ----------- ----------- ----------
           LONG TERM

SIRA Tech    400    7/6/92  3/31/94    3,840.00    3,148.00     692.00
Zary Soft  1,000   2/20/92   4/6/94    4,450.00    3,750.00     700.00

                                     ----------- ----------- ----------
          TOTAL LONG TERM              8,290.00    6,898.00   1,392.00
                                     =========== =========== ==========
```

After creating this report, you can export the report to a file to use in tax preparation software. See "Creating tax schedule reports" on page 271.

To use this report for Schedule D (after you've entered all prior history for any security you've sold), subtotal by short-term vs. long-term gain. Select only those accounts that have taxable capital gains (for example, exclude IRAs).

Investment income

The investment income report shows dividend income (taxable and tax-exempt), interest income (taxable and tax-exempt), capital gains distributions, realized gain or loss, unrealized gain or loss (as an option), and margin interest and other investment expenses during a specified time period.

If you want to use this report to gather information for Schedule B, be sure you've entered all investment transactions for the year. Select only those accounts for which you must report income (for example, exclude IRAs). Subtotal by security. Create one report for all your reportable income, both taxable and tax-exempt. Then create a second report, selecting only securities that generate reportable but tax-exempt income. Again, subtotal by security. Do not select the option to include unrealized gains.

Initial settings for this report (a type of summary report)

Subtotal by:	Don't subtotal
Organization:	Income and expense
Investment accounts to report on:	Current
Include unrealized gains:	No
Tax-related transactions only:	No
Transfers:	Include all

```
                        Investment Income Report
                        1/1/94 Through 3/31/94
   3/31/94
   WILSON-Chandler Sec                                        Page 1
                                              1/1/94-
                    Category Description       3/31/94
                    ----------------------- -----------
   INCOME/EXPENSE
     INCOME
       _DivInc                                   39.24
       _RlzdGain                                400.00
                                            -----------
     TOTAL INCOME                              439.24

     EXPENSES
       Expenses - Other                           0.00
                                            -----------
     TOTAL EXPENSES                              0.00

                                            -----------
     TOTAL INCOME/EXPENSE                       439.24

   TRANSFERS
     FROM Checking                            1,600.00
                                            -----------
   TOTAL TRANSFERS                            1,600.00

   Balance Forward
     Broker                                   2,376.83
                                            -----------
   Total Balance Forward                      2,376.83

                                            -----------
   OVERALL TOTAL                              4,416.07
                                            ===========
```

Investment transactions

The investment transactions report shows you how transactions during a specified time period have affected either the market value or the cost basis of your investments and the cash balance in your investment accounts.

If you do not include unrealized (paper) gains, the report shows the change in cost basis of your investments between the beginning and the end of the period. On the other hand, if you select the option of including unrealized gains, the report shows the change in the market value of your investments between the beginning and the end of the period.

You may subtotal the report by period, account, category, security, security type, or investment goal.

Initial settings for this report (a type of transaction report)	
Subtotal by:	Don't subtotal
Organization:	Income and expense
Investment accounts to report on:	Current
Include unrealized gains:	No
Tax-related transactions only:	No
Transfers:	Include all

A reinvested dividend shows up as a buy transaction on one line, followed by an income transaction on the next line. In general, complex transactions appear on several lines, with one line for each component of the transaction.

The Cash column shows the change in the cash balance of your account or accounts as a result of each transaction.

For each transaction, the Invest. Value column shows the change in cost basis of the security if unrealized gains are not included, or the change in market value if unrealized gains are included. The balance is the current cost basis or market value of all the securities.

For each transaction, the Cash + Invest. column shows the sum of the amounts in the Cash and Invest. Value columns.

```
                          Investment Transactions Report
                             1/1/94 Through 3/31/94
      3/31/94
      WILSON-Chandler Sec                                                        Page 1

                                                                      Invest.     Cash +
       Date   Action   Secur    Categ    Price     Shares   Commssn    Cash      Value      Invest.
      ------- -------- --------- ------ ---------- --------- ---------- --------- --------- ----------

              BALANCE 12/31/92                                           0.00      0.00      0.00

       1/1    ShrsIn   McKendry M         1.000   2,376.826          -2,376.83  2,376.83
                                [Chandl                               2,376.83             2,376.83

       1/31   ReinvDiv McKendry M         1.000      9.903              -9.90      9.90
                                _DivInc-Dividend                         9.90                 9.90

       2/12   BuyX     SIRA Techn         8.000      200             -1,600.00  1,600.00
                                [Checki                              1,600.00             1,600.00

       2/15   Div      Zarya Soft _DivInc-Dividend                      10.00                10.00
       2/20   Buy      McKendry M         1.000       10               -10.00     10.00

       2/28   ReinvDiv McKendry M         1.000      8.774              -8.77      8.77
                                _DivInc-Dividend                         8.77                 8.77

       3/31   Sell     SIRA Techn        10.000      200              1,600.00 -1,600.00
                                _RlzdGain-Realized Gain/Loss             400.00               400.00

       3/31   ReinvDiv McKendry M         1.000     10.568             -10.57     10.57
                                _DivInc-Dividend                        10.57                10.57

                                                                     --------- --------- ----------
              TOTAL 1/1/94 - 3/31/94                                  2,000.00  2,416.07  4,416.07

              BALANCE 3/31/94                                         2,000.00  2,416.07  4,416.07
```

Business reports

This section briefly describes each of Quicken's business reports. To see which business reports are available, click the Reports icon on the iconbar and select the Business report family.

The basic procedure to create a report is in "Creating a report" on page 236.

More information about creating Quicken reports for your small business finances is in the *Quicken Business User's Guide*. To purchase this guide from Intuit, call **800-624-8742**.

P&L Statement	Summarize profit and loss by category
Cash Flow	Summarize income and expense by category
A/P by Vendor	Summarize bills-to-pay, by creditor
A/R by Customer	Summarize payments due, by customer
Job/Project	Summarize income and expense by class
Payroll	Summarize payroll income and expenses by employee
Balance Sheet	Calculate equity based on assets and liabilities
Missing Checks	List transactions in order and highlight missing checks
Comparison	Compare two transaction periods by category (or other ite

P & L statement

A profit and loss (P & L) statement summarizes the revenue and expenses of a business by category (first income, then expenses).

Initial settings for this report (a type of summary report)

Row headings:	Category
Column headings:	Don't subtotal
Organization:	Income and expense
Accounts to report on:	All accounts
Transfers:	Exclude all

If you run your business using cash-basis accounting, you want your income to show up when you receive it, not when you issue invoices. Use a cash flow report instead of a P & L statement for income and expense reporting.

```
                         Profit & Loss Statement
                          1/1/94 Through 3/31/94
    3/31/94
    DESIGN-All Accounts                                          Page 1
                                                   1/1/94-
                 Category Description              3/31/94
    ------------------------------------------    --------------

    INCOME/EXPENSE
      INCOME
        Design                                        31,627.75
        Interest Inc                                     383.66
        Production                                     17,628.83
                                                  ------------
      TOTAL INCOME                                     49,640.24

      EXPENSES
        Ads                                             1,005.87
        Auto:
          Gas                         279.81
          Insurance                   301.73
          Leasing                     417.12
          Service                      59.95
          Tickets                      23.00
                                  ------------
          Total Auto                                    1,081.61
        Computer                                          458.69
        Depreciation                                      950.00
        Fed Ex                                            580.07
        Insurance                                         559.05
        L&P Fees                                          348.25
        Mailing Lists                                     658.00
        Meals & Enter                                     271.02
        Mech Prep                                       1,479.25
        Office                                            240.20
        Paper                                           1,456.89
        Payroll:
          Comp FICA                 1,117.76
          Comp FUTA                   280.00
          Comp MCARE                  261.45
          Comp SUI                    140.00
          Gross                    18,027.59
                                  ------------
          Total Payroll                                 19,826.80
        Photocopying                                       607.06
        Photostats                                         341.70
        Postage                                            424.32
        Printing                                         5,075.66
        Ref. Materials                                     132.16
        Rent Paid                                        1,600.00
        Telephone                                          347.73
                                                  ------------
      TOTAL EXPENSES                                    37,444.33

                                                  ------------
      TOTAL INCOME/EXPENSE                              12,195.91
                                                  ============
```

Cash flow

This report is identical to the home cash flow report (see page 210). Remember that cash flow reporting and cash-basis accounting are different ideas: you do not have to use cash-basis accounting to create a cash flow report.

A/P by vendor

An accounts payable (or A/P) report summarizes the dollar amount of all the unprinted checks in your bank accounts by payee name.

If you are not using Quicken to print checks, the A/P report still works if you enter all your payables as printable checks. When you pay the bill, go back to the register and record the actual check number in the Num field (just type right over the word "Print").

<table>
<tr><td>Initial settings for this report
(a type of summary report)</td><td></td></tr>
<tr><td>Row headings:</td><td>Payee</td></tr>
<tr><td>Column headings:</td><td>Month</td></tr>
<tr><td>Organization:</td><td>Income and expense</td></tr>
<tr><td>Accounts to report on:</td><td>Bank, cash, credit card</td></tr>
<tr><td>Transaction types:</td><td>Unprinted checks only</td></tr>
<tr><td>Transfers:</td><td>Include all</td></tr>
</table>

```
                    A/P (Unprinted Chks) by Vendor
                        3/1/94 Through 4/30/94
    4/30/94
    DESIGN-Bank,Cash,CC Accounts                              Page 1
                                                             OVERALL
                  Payee              3/94        4/94         TOTAL
    ----------------------------- ----------- ----------- -----------
    Chris Jacobson                     0.00     -961.15     -961.15
    First Statewide Bank               0.00   -4,950.00   -4,950.00
    Richard Long                       0.00   -1,058.20   -1,058.20
    State Board of Equalization        0.00   -3,265.28   -3,265.28
    Valley Real Estate                 0.00     -400.00     -400.00
                                  ----------- ----------- -----------
    OVERALL TOTAL                      0.00  -10,634.63  -10,634.63
                                  =========== =========== ===========
```

A/R by customer

The accounts receivable (or A/R) report summarizes uncleared transactions in all your Quicken asset accounts by payee. You might want to restrict the report to the asset account for receivables. (See "Selecting accounts to include" on page 243 to learn how to restrict a report to a single account.)

<table>
<tr><td>Initial settings for this report
(a type of summary report)</td><td></td></tr>
<tr><td>Row headings:</td><td>Payee</td></tr>
<tr><td>Column headings:</td><td>Month</td></tr>
<tr><td>Organization:</td><td>Income and expense</td></tr>
<tr><td>Accounts to report on:</td><td>Asset accounts only</td></tr>
<tr><td>Transaction types:</td><td>All</td></tr>
<tr><td>Transaction status:</td><td>Blank cleared status only</td></tr>
<tr><td>Transfers:</td><td>Include all</td></tr>
</table>

```
                        A/R by Customer
                    3/1/94 Through 4/30/94
    4/30/94
    DESIGN-Selected Accounts                              Page 1

                                                         OVERALL
              Payee              3/94        4/94         TOTAL
    -------------------- ----------- ----------- -----------
    Ace Computer Sales      438.70    1,959.10    2,397.80
    Balloon Adventures        0.00    1,426.85    1,426.85
    Blaine Associates     1,417.75    1,037.90    2,455.65
    Computer Waves          843.16    1,926.00    2,769.16
    Engineering Control       0.00      920.20      920.20
    Osborne Studios         736.70    2,874.02    3,610.72
    Reynolds Markets      2,316.55        0.00    2,316.55
    Robinson Shoes        1,257.25    2,889.00    4,146.25
    Tower Concerts        1,653.15        0.00    1,653.15
                        ----------- ----------- -----------
    OVERALL TOTAL         8,663.26   13,033.07   21,696.33
                        =========== =========== ===========
```

If you use the balance forward method of recording payments, the accounts receivable report includes *all* transactions in your report: unpaid invoices, paid invoices, and payments.

Job/project

A job/project report summarizes your income and expenses for each job, property, client, project, department, or other Quicken class. The report shown here summarizes income and expenses for two projects. To get a report like this, you must set up each project name as a class; then categorize each project-related transaction with an income or expense category and identify it with a project name as the class. (See "Setting up classes and subclasses" on page 16 for information about setting up classes.)

If you manage properties and have set up properties as class names, you can use this report to report on income and expenses by property.

Initial settings for this report (a type of summary report)	
Row headings:	Category
Column headings:	Class
Organization:	Income and expense
Accounts to report on:	All accounts
Transfers:	Include all

```
                              Job/Project Report
                            1/1/94 Through 3/31/94
3/31/94
DESIGN-All Accounts                                                  Page 1

                                                             OVERALL
      Category Description    Ace Computer Co Blaine Associat    TOTAL
----------------------------- --------------- --------------- ---------------
INCOME/EXPENSE
  INCOME
    Design                           3,602.00        3,917.50        7,519.50
    Production                       1,234.85        2,483.97        3,718.82
                                ---------------  ---------------  ---------------
  TOTAL INCOME                       4,836.85        6,401.47       11,238.32

  EXPENSES
    Ads                                  0.00           89.97           89.97
    Contractor                           0.00          140.00          140.00
    Fed Ex                              77.54          111.40          188.94
    Mech Prep                           17.00          124.75          141.75
    Paper                              109.41          200.00          309.41
    Photocopying                        57.44            0.00           57.44
    Photostats                          13.90           65.00           78.90
    Printing                            63.00            0.00           63.00
                                ---------------  ---------------  ---------------
  TOTAL EXPENSES                       338.29          731.12        1,069.41


                                ---------------  ---------------  ---------------
TOTAL INCOME/EXPENSE                 4,498.56        5,670.35       10,168.91
                                ===============  ===============  ===============
```

Payroll

The payroll report summarizes income and expenses by category and has a separate column for each payee. The report is restricted to transactions categorized with payroll categories and transfers to payroll liability accounts. (The report is set up to be limited to transactions with category or transfer account names that start with the word "Payroll.")

In the payroll report, the TRANSFERS TO columns show decreases in your accrued payroll liabilities. For example, each time you record a FICA payment in your checking account, Quicken automatically transfers the amount to the Payroll-FICA account, where it decreases the balance you owe.

In the payroll report, the TRANSFERS FROM columns show increases in your accrued payroll liabilities. For example, each time you record a paycheck, Quicken automatically transfers the FICA contribution amount from your checking account to the Payroll-FICA account, where it increases the balance you owe. In the same way, the report can track your liability for items like FUTA, SUI, Federal Withholding, and so on.

Initial settings for this report (a type of summary report)	
Row headings:	Category
Column headings:	Payee
Organization:	Income and expense
Accounts to report on:	All accounts
Transfers:	Include all
Matching:	Categories and transfer accounts that start with "payroll"

If you have employees to pay as part of your business, you need to do payroll tasks such as make calculations, write checks with numerous deductions, track data for payroll taxes, and fill out payroll tax forms. The easiest way to do payroll tasks is to use the program QuickPay™ together with Quicken. QuickPay is an add-on utility specifically designed to run inside Quicken. (See page 368 for a description.) However, if you want to use Quicken without QuickPay to track payroll, you can read how best to accomplish this in the *Quicken Business User's Guide*, which you can purchase from Intuit by calling **800-624-8742**.

This row shows gross wages.

This column shows the total increase in your accrued payroll liabilities.

```
                              Payroll Report
                         1/1/94 Through 4/15/94
    4/15/94
    DESIGN-Selected Accounts                                           Page 1
                                                                      OVERALL
      Category Description  Chris Jacobson  First Statewide  Richard Long    TOTAL
    ------------------------  --------------  ---------------  ------------  ---------------
    INCOME/EXPENSE
      EXPENSES
        Payroll:
          Comp FICA           610.48           0.00           666.96        1,277.44
          Comp FUTA           160.00           0.00           160.00          320.00
          Comp MCARE          142.80           0.00           156.00          298.80
          Comp SUI             80.00           0.00            80.00          160.00
          Gross             9,846.16           0.00        10,756.80       20,602.96
                          -----------      -----------      -----------     -----------
        Total Payroll      10,839.44           0.00        11,819.76       22,659.20
                          -----------      -----------      -----------     -----------
      TOTAL EXPENSES       10,839.44           0.00        11,819.76       22,659.20

                          -----------      -----------      -----------     -----------
      TOTAL INCOME/EXPENSE -10,839.44           0.00       -11,819.76      -22,659.20

    TRANSFERS
      TO Payroll-FICA           0.00       -1,500.00            0.00       -1,500.00
      TO Payroll-FUTA           0.00         -300.00            0.00         -300.00
      TO Payroll-FWH            0.00       -2,500.00            0.00       -2,500.00
      TO Payroll-MCARE          0.00         -300.00            0.00         -300.00
      TO Payroll-SUI            0.00         -150.00            0.00         -150.00
      TO Payroll-SWHCA          0.00         -200.00            0.00         -200.00
      FROM Payroll-FICA     1,220.96           0.00         1,333.92        2,554.88
      FROM Payroll-FUTA       160.00           0.00           160.00          320.00
      FROM Payroll-FWH      1,304.32           0.00         1,337.28        2,641.60
      FROM Payroll-MCARE      285.60           0.00           312.00          597.60
      FROM Payroll-SUI         80.00           0.00            80.00          160.00
      FROM Payroll-SWHCA       99.36           0.00           130.96          230.32
                          -----------      -----------      -----------     -----------
      TOTAL TRANSFERS       3,150.24       -4,950.00         3,354.16        1,554.40

                          -----------      -----------      -----------     -----------
      OVERALL TOTAL        -7,689.20       -4,950.00        -8,465.60      -21,104.80
                          ===========      ===========      ===========     ===========
```

How transfers show up in payroll reports

Amount of income tax withheld from employee paycheck. Decreases amount of paycheck.

Other side of tax withholding transfer increases liability.

This report item represents an increase in cash on hand because you withheld tax from the paycheck.

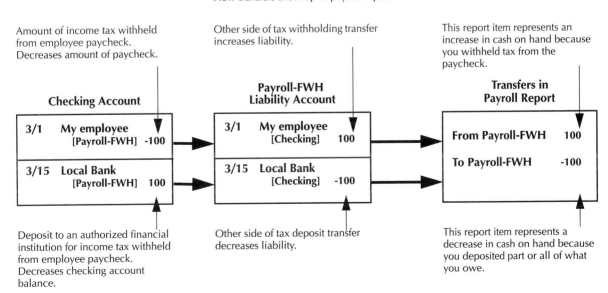

Deposit to an authorized financial institution for income tax withheld from employee paycheck. Decreases checking account balance.

Other side of tax deposit transfer decreases liability.

This report item represents a decrease in cash on hand because you deposited part or all of what you owe.

Balance sheet

A balance sheet is a snapshot of the assets, liabilities, and equity (or capital) of a business as of a specific date.

```
                              Balance Sheet
                        (Includes unrealized gains)
                            As of 4/15/94
4/15/94
DESIGN-All Accounts                                              Page 1
                                                    4/15/94
                          Acct                      Balance
        -------------------------------------   -----------------------
        ASSETS

          Cash and Bank Accounts
            First Statewide
              Ending Balance                     11,978.01
              plus: Checks Payable               10,634.63
                                                 -----------
              Total First Statewide                           22,612.64
                                                              -----------
          Total Cash and Bank Accounts                        22,612.64

          Other Assets
            AR                                                 21,696.31
            Cap Equip                                          9,960.00
                                                              -----------
          Total Other Assets                                  31,656.31

          Investments
            Mutual Fund                                        3,600.00
                                                              -----------
          Total Investments                                   3,600.00

                                                              -----------
        TOTAL ASSETS                                          57,868.95
                                                              ===========
        LIABILITIES & EQUITY

          LIABILITIES
            Checks Payable                                    10,634.63

            Credit Cards
              Amer Express                                    0.00
                                                              -----------
            Total Credit Cards                                0.00

            Other Liabilities
              AP                                              2,582.34
              Payroll-FICA                                    1,054.88
              Payroll-FUTA                                    20.00
              Payroll-FWH                                     141.60
              Payroll-MCARE                                   297.60
              Payroll-SUI                                     10.00
              Payroll-SWHCA                                   30.32
              Sales Tax                                       853.57
                                                              -----------
            Total Other Liabilities                           4,990.31

                                                              -----------
          TOTAL LIABILITIES                                   15,624.94

          EQUITY                                              42,244.01
                                                              -----------
        TOTAL LIABILITIES & EQUITY                            57,868.95
                                                              ===========
```

If your bank accounts include any unprinted or postdated checks, Quicken adds them to your bank balance and also lists them as a liability.

Quicken calculates equity as the difference between your total assets and liabilities.

Missing checks

This report shows you missing and duplicate check numbers. It is identical to the home missing checks report described on page 216.

Comparison

With this report, you can compare your income and spending for two different periods. It is identical to the home comparison report described on page 217.

Standard reports ("Other")

This section briefly describes each of Quicken's standard reports. All other Quicken reports are based on one of these five standard reports. If none of Quicken's preset home, investment, or business reports shows you the information you need in the best format, try creating one of these standard reports and customizing it to your liking (change the layout or other settings). The basic procedure to create any report is described in "Creating a report" on page 236. The section "Changing report settings," beginning on page 239, describes how to customize any report.

To see what standard reports are available, click the Reports icon on the iconbar and select the Other report family.

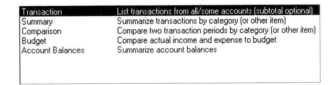

Transaction	List transactions from all/some accounts (subtotal optional)
Summary	Summarize transactions by category (or other item)
Comparison	Compare two transaction periods by category (or other item)
Budget	Compare actual income and expense to budget
Account Balances	Summarize account balances

Examples of standard reports are shown, starting on the next page.

Transaction

A transaction report lists transactions from one or more registers. Unlike a summary report, it shows individual transactions.

Initial settings for this report	
Subtotal by:	Don't subtotal
Sort by:	None
Organization:	Income and expense
Accounts to report on:	Current
Include unrealized gains:	No
Transfers:	Include all
Subcategory display:	Show all

```
                           Transaction Report
                        1/1/94 Through 1/31/94
  3/31/94
  WILSON-Checking                                                       Page 1

    Date     Num    Description        Memo          Category     Clr   Amount
  --------  ------  -----------------  ------------- -------------- --- ---------

            BALANCE 12/31/93                                              0.00

  1/1/94            Opening Balance                  [Checking]     x   2,230.00
  1/1/94      S     Paycheck           Sally's       --SPLIT--      x   1,482.11
  1/1/94      S     Paycheck           Steve         --SPLIT--      x   2,162.97
  1/2/94   582      Gentleman's Outfi  New Suits     Clothing       x  -1,023.38
  1/4/94            Transfer                         [Savings]      x  -4,000.00
  1/5/94            ATM Withdrawal                   [Cash]         x    -100.00
  1/8/94   5002     City of Valley     Services      Utilities:Garba x    -65.00
  1/11/94  583      Central Market                   Groceries      x    -102.92
  1/11/94           ATM Withdrawal                   [Cash]         x    -200.00
  1/15/94  5003 S   GMAC Financing     A/C #87239-278 --SPLIT--     x    -587.55
  1/15/94  5004 S   American Lending   A/C #871-34824 --SPLIT--     x  -1,158.39
  1/15/94      S    Paycheck           Steve         --SPLIT--      x   2,162.97
  1/15/94      S    Paycheck           Sally's       --SPLIT--      x   1,482.11
  1/16/94  584  S   Costco             BBQ Supplies  --SPLIT--      x    -167.42
  1/16/94  585      California Cafe    Lunch w/Kathy Dining         x     -42.87
  1/17/94  585      Hugo's             Fresh Foods   Groceries      x     -51.89
  1/19/94  586      The Outdoorsman    New Rossies!  Entertain      x    -319.51
  1/23/94  587      Athletic Attic     New Nikes     Clothing       x     -42.38
  1/23/94           ATM Withdrawal                   [Cash]             -200.00
  1/25/94  588      Central Market                   Groceries      x     -94.73
  1/25/94           ATM Withdrawal                   [Cash]             -100.00
  1/28/94  5005     Western Bell       Dec/Jan       Telephone      x     -87.52
  1/28/94  5006     Valley Gas & Elec  December      Utilities:Gas & x    -64.97
  1/29/94      S    Paycheck           Sally's       --SPLIT--          1,482.11
  1/29/94      S    Paycheck           Steve         --SPLIT--      x   2,162.97
  1/30/94           ATM Withdrawal                   [Cash]         x    -100.00
  1/31/94           Transfer to savin                [Savings]         -2,500.00
  1/31/94  5007     Quicken Visa                     [Quicken Visa]    -1,577.88
  1/31/94  5008     American Express                 [AMX]             -172.67
                                                                    -----------
            TOTAL 1/1/94 - 1/31/94                                      406.16

            BALANCE 1/31/94                                             406.16

            TOTAL INFLOWS                                            13,165.24
            TOTAL OUTFLOWS                                          -12,759.08
                                                                    -----------
            NET TOTAL                                                   406.16
                                                                    ===========
```

Summary

A summary report summarizes transactions from your accounts by category or whatever else you choose for the row headings. Unlike a transaction report, it does not show individual transactions.

A summary report groups income and expense items in separate sections, followed by transfers and balances forward, unless you select the cash flow report organization option (see "Changing report settings," beginning on page 239).

Initial settings for this report	
Row headings:	Category
Column headings:	Don't subtotal
Organization:	Income and expense
Accounts to report on:	Current
Transfers:	Include all

Quicken groups all transfers to and from the current account.

If an included account has an Opening Balance during the period, Quicken calls it a "balance forward" because you brought an existing balance into Quicken.

```
                           Summary Report
                       1/1/94 Through 3/31/94
  3/31/94
  WILSON-Checking                                          Page 1

                                            1/1/94-
      Category Description                   3/31/94
  --------------------------     --------------------------
  INCOME/EXPENSE
    INCOME
      Salary                                42,291.69
                                            -----------
    TOTAL INCOME                            42,291.69

    EXPENSES
      Auto:
        Loan                      580.49
                                -----------
        Total Auto                            580.49
      Clothing                              1,493.28
      Dining                                   42.87
      Entertain                              731.93
      Groceries                              710.44
      Insurance                              530.32
      Mort Int                             3,242.30
      Tax:
        Fed                     10,047.94
        Soc Sec                  2,114.56
        State                    3,383.31
                                -----------
        Total Tax                          15,545.81
      Telephone                              277.07
      Utilities:
        Garbage                   195.00
        Gas & Electric            187.14
                                -----------
        Total Utilities                      382.14
                                            -----------
    TOTAL EXPENSES                          23,536.65

                                            -----------
    TOTAL INCOME/EXPENSE                    18,755.04

  TRANSFERS
    TO 1111-2222-3333-4444                  -2,720.80
    TO American Express                       -534.81
    TO Auto Loan Balance                    -1,182.16
    TO Brokerage Account                    -1,600.00
    TO Cash                                 -1,200.00
    TO Mortgage Balance                       -232.87
    TO Mutual Fund                          -1,000.00
    TO Sally's 401(k)                         -700.00
    TO Savings                             -10,500.00
    FROM Mutual Fund                            30.42
                                            -----------
  TOTAL TRANSFERS                          -19,640.22

  Balance Forward
    Checking                                2,230.00
                                            -----------
  Total Balance Forward                     2,230.00

                                            -----------
  OVERALL TOTAL                             1,344.82
                                            ===========
```

A summary report usually displays category or class names rather than category or class descriptions, but you can change the report to display descriptions; see "Changing report preferences" on page 250. (Then, if a category or class has no description, Quicken displays the category or class name.)

Comparison

A comparison report lets you compare your income and spending for two different periods. For example, you can see if, and in which areas, you are spending more or earning more than a year ago. The report shows you a breakdown of your finances by category, and lets you define two different periods to display side by side.

You can display the difference between the two periods in dollars, or as a percentage of the first figure, or both.

Initial settings for this report (a type of summary report)	
Comparison dates:	Last year and year-to-date
Row headings:	Category
Subtotal by:	Don't subtotal
Organization:	Cash flow basis
Show difference as %:	No
Show difference in $:	Yes
Accounts to report on:	Current
Transfers:	Exclude internal

The preset comparison report listed in the Other report family differs from the ones in the Home and Business families in that it reports on the current account only, whereas the preset home and business versions report on all your bank, cash, and credit card accounts. You can, of course, select different accounts by customizing the report (see page 243).

The figures in the difference column are the second column amounts minus the first column amounts. They normally show how much more you are earning or spending in each category compared with an earlier period. A negative amount means you are earning or spending less now than before.

The overall difference shown in the lower right corner of the report indicates that this person has saved $407.25 less this year than in the same period last year.

```
                          Comparison Report
                        1/1/93 Through 3/31/94
        3/31/94
        WILSON-Joint checking                               Page 1

                              1/1/1993-      1/1/1994-          $
          Category Description 3/31/1993      3/31/1994     Difference
        -------------------- ----------   --------------  -------------

        INFLOWS
          Bonus                    0.00       3,000.00       3,000.00
          Int Inc                  0.42           0.42           0.00
          Salary              18,508.35      11,025.01      -7,483.34
          Inflows - Other        162.19           0.00        -162.19
                              ------------   -----------    ------------
        TOTAL INFLOWS          18,670.96      14,025.43      -4,645.53

        OUTFLOWS
          Auto:
            Fuel                 190.31         150.00         -40.31
            Maintenance          262.00           0.00        -262.00
                              ----------     ---------      ---------
          Total Auto             452.31         150.00        -302.31
          Books, Music             0.00         129.76         129.76
          Childcare              400.00         400.00           0.00
          Clothing             1,226.63         189.69      -1,036.94
          Computer               145.01           0.00        -145.01
          Entertain              276.50         290.91          14.41
          Groceries              319.54         449.43         129.89
          Interest Paid           79.12          77.72          -1.40
          Mort Int             1,417.48           0.00      -1,417.48
          Recreation:
            Hiking               319.51           0.00        -319.51
            Skiing               506.83           0.00        -506.83
                              ----------     ---------      ---------
          Total Recreation       826.34           0.00        -826.34
          Taxes:
            Fed                4,127.10       2,456.26      -1,670.84
            FICA               1,097.90         637.49        -460.41
            SDI                   65.74          32.87         -32.87
            State              1,204.15         743.74        -460.41
                              ----------     ---------      ---------
          Total Taxes          6,494.89       3,870.36      -2,624.53
          Telephone              187.52         198.27          10.75
          Utilities:
            Electricity           64.97          62.35          -2.62
            Garbage                0.00          15.50          15.50
            Water                  0.00          28.75          28.75
                              ----------     ---------      ---------
          Total Utilities         64.97         127.83          62.86
          Vacation                 0.00        1332.31        1332.31
          Outflows - Other       177.97         515.85         337.88
          TO Auto Loan          1210.63        1212.03           1.40
          TO Mortgage           5,116.43       5,312.90         196.47
          TO Steve's IRA         100.00           0.00        -100.00
                              ------------   -----------    ------------
        TOTAL OUTFLOWS         18,495.34      14,257.06      -4,238.28

                              ------------   -----------    ------------
        OVERALL TOTAL            175.62        -231.63        -407.25
```

Budget

The budget report compares your actual expenses with your
budgeted expenses for each category. Before creating a budget
report, you must set up budget amounts for each category, as
described in "Setting up a budget" on page 290.

Initial settings for this report	
Column headings:	None
Organization:	Income and expense
Accounts to report on:	All accounts
Include unrealized gains:	No
Transfers:	Include all
Categories:	Budgeted categories only

A positive value means that you spent
more than you budgeted for.

A negative value means that you spent
less than you budgeted for.

See "Monthly budget" on page 211 for
an explanation of what the Actual
column, Budget column, and Diff
column contain in a budget report.

```
                          Budget Report
                      1/1/94 Through 3/31/94
3/31/94
WILSON-All Accounts                                        Page 1
                                1/1/94   -    3/31/94
           Category Description   Actual     Budget      Diff
---------------------------   ------------------------------------
INCOME/EXPENSE
  INCOME
    Div Income                  78.09       78.09        0.00
    Invest Inc                  75.00       75.00        0.00
    _RlzdGain                  400.00        0.00      400.00
    Salary                  42,291.69   42,291.69        0.00
                           ----------  ----------  ----------
  TOTAL INCOME             42,844.78   42,444.78      400.00

  EXPENSES
    Auto:
      Fuel                    191.00      180.00       11.00
      Loan                    580.49      580.49        0.00
      Repairs                 165.98      100.00       65.98
      Auto - Other              0.00        0.00        0.00
                           ----------  ----------  ----------
    Total Auto                937.47      860.49       76.98
    Clothing                1,588.10      900.00      688.10
    Dining                    988.61      900.00       88.61
    Entertain               1,214.63      900.00      314.63
    Gifts                     228.40      228.40        0.00
    Groceries               1,040.44    1,200.00     -159.56
    Household                 769.64      875.99     -106.35
    Insurance                 530.32      530.32        0.00
    Mort Int                3,242.30    3,242.30        0.00
    Tax:
      Fed                  10,047.94   10,047.94        0.00
      Soc Sec               2,114.56    2,114.56        0.00
      State                 3,383.31    3,383.31        0.00
      Tax - Other              0.00        0.00        0.00
                           ----------  ----------  ----------
    Total Tax              15,545.81   15,545.81        0.00
    Telephone                 277.07      270.00        7.07
    Utilities:
      Garbage                 195.00      195.00        0.00
      Gas & Electric          187.14      180.00        7.14
      Utilities - Other         0.00        0.00        0.00
                           ----------  ----------  ----------
    Total Utilities           382.14      375.00        7.14
                           ----------  ----------  ----------
  TOTAL EXPENSES           26,744.93   25,828.31      916.62

                           ----------  ----------  ----------
  TOTAL INCOME/EXPENSE     16,099.85   16,616.47     -516.62

TRANSFERS
  TO American Express         -534.81     -600.00       65.19
  TO Auto Loan Balance      -1,182.16   -1,167.00      -15.16
  TO Family House               0.00        0.00        0.00
  TO Mortgage Balance        -232.87     -231.00       -1.87
  TO Sally's 401(k)          -700.00     -700.00        0.00
  TO Savings              -10,500.00   -9,000.00   -1,500.00
  FROM American Express         0.00        0.00        0.00
  FROM Auto Loan Balance        0.00        0.00        0.00
  FROM Family House             0.00        0.00        0.00
  FROM Mortgage Balance         0.00        0.00        0.00
  FROM Sally's 401(k)           0.00        0.00        0.00
  FROM Savings                  0.00        0.00        0.00
                           ----------  ----------  ----------
  TOTAL TRANSFERS         -13,149.84  -11,698.00   -1,451.84

                           ----------  ----------  ----------
OVERALL TOTAL               2,950.01    4,918.47   -1,968.46
                           ==========  ==========  ==========
```

Account balances

An account balances report lists and totals the balances for all accounts in the current file. If you have investment accounts, the balances for those accounts include unrealized gains. The result shows the net worth of your Quicken accounts.

If you want Quicken to include "Checks Payable" (unprinted checks) under "ASSETS" and "LIABILITIES" in an account balances report, be sure to enter an ending date for the report that is later than any of your postdated checks in the register.

Initial settings for this report	
Report at intervals of:	None
Organization:	Net worth format
Accounts to report on:	All accounts
Include unrealized gains:	Yes

```
                    Account Balances Report
                   (Includes unrealized gains)
                        As of 3/31/94
        3/31/94
        WILSON-All Accounts                        Page 1

                                                   3/31/94
                            Acct                   Balance
        ------------------------------------   ------------
        ASSETS
          Cash and Bank Accounts
            Cash                                      39.00
            Checking                               1,344.82
            Savings                               13,500.00
                                                ------------
            Total Cash and Bank Accounts          14,883.82

          Other Assets
            Family House                         152,879.50
            Sally's 401(k)                         5,431.11
                                                ------------
          Total Other Assets                     158,310.61

          Investments
            Assorted Mutual Funds                 13,034.08
            Brokerage Account                      4,416.07
            Chandler Brokerage                    11,861.12
            Mutual Fund                            8,930.86
                                                ------------
          Total Investments                       38,242.13

                                                ------------
        TOTAL ASSETS                             211,436.56

        LIABILITIES
          Credit Cards
            1111-2222-3333-4444                       48.56
            American Express                         235.00
                                                ------------
          Total Credit Cards                         283.56

          Other Liabilities
            Auto Loan Balance                      17,396.23
            Mortgage Balance                      132,664.41
                                                ------------
          Total Other Liabilities                 150,060.64

                                                ------------
        TOTAL LIABILITIES                         150,344.20

                                                ------------
        OVERALL TOTAL                              61,092.36
                                                ============
```

15

Creating and customizing reports

Quicken makes it easy for you to create reports and then change them to your liking. You can customize any report by changing the start and end dates, the layout, the accounts included, and many other settings.

This chapter explains how to create and customize reports, how to memorize a customized report setup for repeated use, and how to investigate the transactions that are listed in the report.

Creating a report

Your usual starting point for creating reports is the Create Report window. Follow these same simple steps to create any Quicken report.

1 **Click the Reports icon on the iconbar.**

(If you prefer, you can also access the Create Report window through Quicken's menus, as described on page 238.)

Select a date range for the report to cover.

Select the type of report you want to see:

First select the report family.

Then select the report type.

Quicken shows you an example of the type of report you've selected. (This is not your real data.)

Create Report

Report Dates

Year to date   from: 1/ 1/94   to: 5/19/94

OK
Cancel
Customize

Report Family

- ● Home
- ○ Investment
- ● Business
- ○ Other
- ○ Memorized

Cash Flow	Summarize income and expense by category
Monthly Budget	Compare actual income/expense to budget
Itemized Categories	List transactions and subtotal by category
Tax Summary	List tax-related transactions
Net Worth	Calculate net worth based on account balances
Tax Schedule	List transactions and subtotal by tax line item
Missing Checks	List transactions in order and highlight missing checks
Comparison	Compare two transaction periods by category (or other item)

Itemized Categories Report

Date	Num	Description	Memo	Category	Clr	Amount
1/1/94	582	Vypur Records	CDs	Music	x	-65.00
1/4/94	583	Fanatic Windsurfing		Recreation	x	-477.29
1/7/94	600	Tim's Fiat Service	Exhaust	Auto:Service	x	-140.00

---

2 **If necessary, in the Create Report window, change the report date range for the transactions to be included in the report.**

Unless you change the dates, the report runs from the first day of this year to today. If the report is an "as of" report (for example, a net worth report), the closing date is today. For comparison reports, enter two date ranges for comparison.

Either:

If you regularly need a date range that isn't shown in Quicken's preset list, you can customize the preset date range that appears when you first open this window—see "Changing report preferences" on page 250.

- Select a preset date range from the drop-down list by the left field, or
- Enter dates in the From and To fields (month/day/year). You can use the pop-up calendar to help you select dates by clicking the drop-down buttons by the date fields.

You can select a preset date range and then modify the start or end date.

3 **Select the type of report to create by clicking the report name.**

If necessary, click on a different report family first (Home, Investment, and so on) to display the reports in that family.

When you select a report, Quicken displays an example at the bottom of the window of what the report will look like. This example does not contain your own data.

Most of Quicken's home, investment, and business reports are based on standard reports listed under "Other." If the preset reports don't give you what you want, start with one of the standard reports and customize it.

You can customize any report by changing its layout, the accounts covered, the type of transactions it includes, and various other aspects. You can do that now, before creating the report, or after it is displayed on your screen.

For examples of all Quicken's reports, see Chapter 14, *Sample reports,* beginning on page 209

4   **(Optional) Click Customize to change the report settings before creating the report.**

For full details of customizing a report, see "Changing report settings," beginning on page 239.

5   **Click OK to create the report.**

Quicken searches the current file for transactions within the date range and displays the report on the screen. The search may take several seconds, depending on the size of your accounts.

With the report displayed, you can click the buttons at the top of the report (the Report button bar) to change your report or save it in some way.

Change the report to your liking. See "Changing report settings," beginning on page 239.

Save your report settings. See "Memorizing and recalling reports" on page 249.

Print the report or save it to a file. See "Printing reports" on page 266.

Sort the transactions in a different order. (See page 241 for details.) The Sort button appears only for transaction reports.

Close the Report window.

Copy the report to the clipboard. This is an easy way of transferring your Quicken data to other programs, such as a spreadsheet program. For details, see "Transferring report data to other programs" on page 253.

(The tax schedule report has an additional Export button for transferring tax data to other tax preparation software. See page 273 for details.)

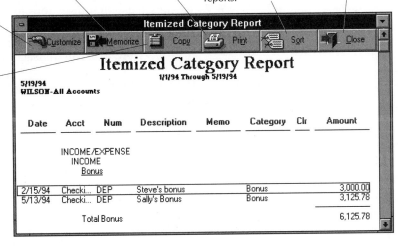

Date	Acct	Num	Description	Memo	Category	Clr	Amount
	INCOME/EXPENSE						
	INCOME						
	Bonus						
2/15/94	Checki...	DEP	Steve's bonus		Bonus		3,000.00
5/13/94	Checki...	DEP	Sally's Bonus		Bonus		3,125.78
			Total Bonus				6,125.78

Itemized Category Report
1/1/94 Through 5/19/94
5/19/94
WILSON-All Accounts

Selecting a report from the menu bar

Instead of clicking the Reports icon in the iconbar, you can select a report on the Quicken menu bar.

1   **From the Reports menu, choose Home, Investment, Business, Other, or Memorized and then choose the type of report you want to produce.**

Quicken takes you to the Create Report window with the chosen report already selected. You can change the date range or click Customize to change other report settings (see page 239), and then click OK to create the report.

If you prefer, you can make Quicken skip the Create Report window altogether, so that when you select a report from the menu bar, Quicken displays the report immediately. To set Quicken up in this way, go to the Report Preferences window as described on page 250 and select the option Skip Create Report Prompt.

Creating QuickReports

Although the Create Report window is your usual starting place for creating a report, in some Quicken windows you'll see a Report button that gives you an instant transaction listing (a QuickReport) relevant to that window. For example, with the Category & Transfer list displayed, select a category and click the Report button for a quick listing of all transactions (in all accounts) with that category. You can display QuickReports for the:

- Category & Transfer list (see page 13 for details)
- Class list (see page 16)
- register, to list all transactions for a certain payee (see page 35)
- Memorized Transaction list (a payee report, see page 89)
- Portfolio View, to list all transactions for a certain security (page 193)

These QuickReports are actually standard transaction reports that have been filtered to include only the transactions you're interested in. With the report displayed, you can change the report settings as you can for any Quicken report.

Changing report settings

Quicken gives you great flexibility in creating your reports. You can change the layout, the date range, which accounts to include, and various other settings. You can also filter the report, for example to include only certain payees or categories. After customizing a report in this way, you can save the settings for future use by *memorizing* the report.

You can customize a report either while creating it or when it is already displayed on your screen.

1   **Select a report and a date range as described in "Creating a report" on page 236.**

2   **Either click Customize in the Create Report window OR click OK to create the report and then click the Customize button on the report button bar.**

You can change many different settings for the report.

First click the area you want to customize.

Then set up the detailed settings as you want them.

Quicken tells you what changing each area does.

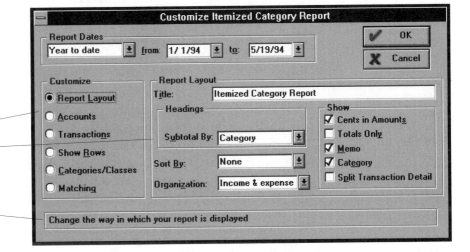

3   **(Optional) Change the date range.**

See page 236, step 2, for instructions on how to choose a date range.

4   **In the Customize section, click on the area of the report you want to change, for example Report Layout, Accounts, and so on.**

Note the Help information displayed at the bottom of the window.

5   **Change the settings for that area in the right-hand part of the window.**

The rest of this section gives you complete details of all the options. The options available depend on what type of report you are customizing.

6 **When you are satisfied with the settings, click OK to display the report.**

Quicken immediately applies your new settings to the report.

Quicken also offers you a shortcut to changing the title, date range, or accounts to report on. With the report displayed on your screen, move the mouse pointer over the title and heading information at the top of the report. Notice the pointer change to a hand as you position it over the title, dates, or account information. Now double-click on the item. Quicken takes you directly to the part of the Customize Report window where you can change that item.

Double-click on the title to change the title, or on the dates to change the date range.

Double-click the accounts label to select other accounts.

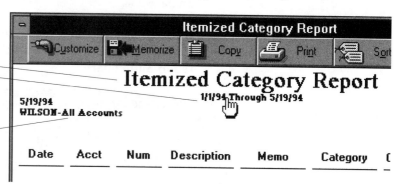

Changing the report layout

Click Report Layout at the Customize Report window.

In the right-hand part of the window, you can rename the report, rearrange the report with different row and column headings, or change the accounting organization.

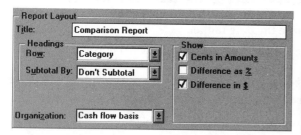 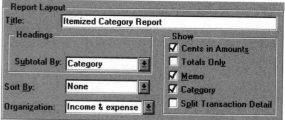

What you see in the Report Layout area depends on the type of report you are customizing. Not all options may be offered.

The next table shows all the report layout settings in Quicken reports. The settings available vary for each report type.

Name of setting	Choice	Results
Title	(Your choice)	Quicken displays and prints the report with the title you enter.
Row headings (summary reports)	Category Class Payee Account	Creates a row for each category, class, payee, or account.
Column headings (summary, budget, and account balances reports)	Don't subtotal (Various periods) Category Class Payee Account	Creates a column for each week, two weeks, half month, month, quarter, half year, year, category, class, payee, or account. (See "How Quicken defines report periods" on page 242.) If you choose Don't Subtotal, Quicken creates a report with a single column.
Subtotal by (transaction reports)	Don't subtotal (Various periods) Category Class Payee Account Tax schedule	Groups and totals transactions by week, two weeks, half month, month, quarter, half year, year, category, class, payee, account, or tax schedule. (See "How Quicken defines report periods" on page 242.) If you choose Don't Subtotal, Quicken doesn't subtotal amounts in the report.
Interval (account balances reports)	None	Includes one total for account balances based on the ending date you enter at the top of the window.
	(Various periods)	Creates a column and totals account balances for each week, two weeks, half month, month, quarter, half year, or year.
Sort by (transaction reports)	None	Sorts transactions first by account type, then by account name, and then by date.
	Date/Acct	Sorts transactions first by date, then by account type, and then by account name.
	Acct/Chk #	Sorts transactions first by account type, then by account name, and then by check number.
	Amount	Sorts transactions from smallest to largest amount.
	Payee	Sorts transactions alphabetically by payee name.
	Category	Sorts transactions alphabetically by category.
Max short-term gain holding period (investment capital gains reports)	Enter a number	This number defines how many days you must have held a security before selling it for the resulting capital gain to qualify as a long-term gain.
Organization	Income and expense	Totals income, expense, and transfer transactions in separate sections of your report.
	Cash flow basis	Groups and totals inflows and outflows (including expenses and transfers out of the account). For example, if you have an asset account called "House," and you treat home improvement transactions as transfers to that account, choosing cash flow basis lets you treat those transfers as spending, giving you a more accurate picture of your total expenditures.
	Net worth format	(Account balances reports) Prints your net worth as the last item.
	Balance sheet format	(Account balances reports) Prints net worth as a liability ("equity") with total liabilities and equity last.

Name of setting	Choice	Results
Show Cents in Amounts	☐	Displays amounts in dollars (Quicken rounds to the nearest dollar).
	☑	Displays amounts in dollars and cents.
Amount as % (summary reports)	☐	Show amounts only as dollars (and cents).
	☑	Also show amounts in relative terms, as percentages of the total.
Difference as % (comparison reports)	☐	Do not show the percentage differences.
	☑	Show the percentage increase or decrease from the first column amount to the second.
Difference in $ (comparison reports)	☐	Do not show the dollar differences.
	☑	Show the dollar differences between the first column amount and the second.
Show Totals Only (transaction reports)	☐	Lists all the transactions that meet the criteria you've specified.
	☑	Displays only the total dollar amount of transactions that meet the criteria you've specified.
Show Memo (transaction reports)	☐	Does not show memos in the report
	☑	Includes a column for memos.
Show Category (transaction reports)	☐	Does not show categories in the report
	☑	Includes a column for categories.
Show Split Transaction Detail (transaction reports)	☐	Does not include the detail from the Splits window in the report.
	☑	Includes the detail from the Splits window.
Show Cash Flow Detail (investment performance reports)	☐	Show only the Average Annual Total Return figure.
	☑	Show all transactions that contribute to the Average Annual Total Return figure.

How Quicken defines report periods

You can subtotal certain reports by period. You can use the following periods (next page) as row headings for transaction reports and as column headings for summary, transaction, and budget reports.

These definitions are for whole periods. Your report will include a partial period if your starting or ending date doesn't fall on the first or last day of a period as defined here.

Period	Quicken definition
Week	Starts on Sunday, runs through Saturday
Two weeks	Starts on Sunday, runs for 14 days (ends on Saturday)
Half month	Runs from the 1st through the 15th or from the 16th through the last day of the month
Month	Starts on the 1st of the month, ends on the last day of the month
Quarter	Includes three consecutive calendar months, starting with January 1, April 1, July 1, or October 1
Half year	Starts on the starting date and ends on the last day of the month five months later; for example, January 2 through June 30
Year	Starts on the starting date, runs for 365 days (366 days for leap years)

Selecting accounts to include

Click Accounts at the Customize Report window.

In the right-hand part of the window, you can select which accounts to include in the report. Simply click on an account to select it.

Depending on what type of report you have displayed, certain accounts may be preselected. For example, a cash flow report preselects all your bank, cash, and credit card accounts. Standard transaction and summary reports include only the current account.

Click Mark All to select or deselect all accounts at once.

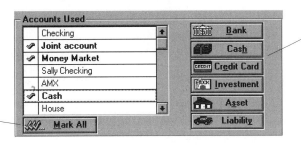

Click an account type button to quickly select all the accounts of that type.

Selecting transactions to include

Click Transactions at the Customize Report window.

The right part of the window lets you select only certain transactions for the report by filtering on the transaction amount or type. For example, you can have Quicken report only on payments from your accounts or only on deposits. Or you can create a report limited to transactions assigned to tax-related categories.

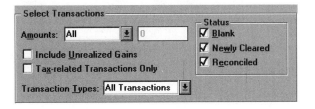

Name of setting	Choice	Results
Amounts	All	Includes all transaction amounts.
	less than	Includes amounts less than the amount you enter.
	equal to	Includes amounts equal to the amount you enter.
	greater than	Includes amounts greater than the amount you enter.
Include Unrealized Gains	☐	Determines whether Quicken generates additional transactions (in transaction reports) or income/inflow lines (in summary reports) to represent the impact of price increases and decreases for securities. Appears only if you have set up investment accounts. If the checkbox is cleared, Quicken does not include unrealized gains.
	☑	Includes unrealized gains.
Tax-related Transactions Only	☐	Includes both tax-related and nontax-related transactions.
	☑	Includes only transactions that have been categorized with tax-related categories.
Transaction Types	Payments	Includes payments only (including checks). For nonbank accounts, payments are decreases to cash and other asset accounts, and increases to credit card and other liability accounts.
	Deposits	Includes deposits only.
	Unprinted Checks	Includes unprinted checks only.
	All Transactions	Includes all transactions.
Status	Blank Newly cleared Reconciled	Refers to a transaction's entry in the Clr (Cleared) field. Quicken reports include all transactions, regardless of cleared status, unless you change this filter. Do not change or clear any of the checkboxes for these choices unless you are creating a report specifically to show which of your transactions are cleared or uncleared.

Showing row information

Click Show Rows at the Customize Report window.

In the right-hand part of the window, you can show or hide transfer and category information in the row heading.

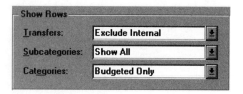

Name of setting	Choice	Results
Transfers	Include All	Includes all transfers in the report.
	Exclude All	Excludes all transfers in the report. Use for a report showing income and expenses without transfers (similar to Quicken's business profit and loss statement).
	Exclude Internal	Excludes transfers between accounts that are included in the report. Essentially, these are transfers that cancel each other out in the report.
Subcategories	Show All	Displays subcategories and subclasses grouped under their main categories.
	Hide All	Does not display subcategory or subclass information.
	Show Reversed	Displays subcategories with the main categories grouped under them. For example, if you have transactions assigned to Car Repairs:Honda and to Insurance:Honda, you can use the reversed option to generate a report totaling expenses for Honda.
Categories (budget reports only)	Include All	Includes all categories from the current list, regardless of whether you've used them yet in a transaction.
	Non-Zero Actual/ Budgeted	Includes any categories that you have already used in transactions, and also all categories to which you have assigned budget amounts in the Set Up Budgets window.
	Budgeted Only	Includes only the categories to which you have assigned budget amounts in the Set Up Budgets window.

Selecting categories, transfers, and classes to include

Click Categories/Classes at the Customize Report window. (For investment reports, this is renamed Select to Include.)

In the right-hand part of the window, you can select which categories and classes to include in the report. For investments reports, you can select actions, categories, securities, security types, and investment goals. Click on a category or class (or investment item) to select or deselect it.

Click on an item to select or deselect it.

(Select Not Categorized to include only transactions with no category assigned.)

Click Mark All to select or deselect all items at once.

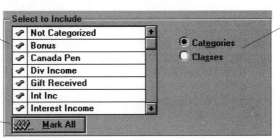

Click Categories or Classes (or the investment item) to display the list to select from.

(To match investment actions and categories to transaction types, see the table on page 180.)

The list of categories also includes, at the bottom of the list, the names of all your accounts. By selecting or deselecting these names, you can include or exclude transfers between specific accounts and the accounts you're reporting on. (See also the Transfers option listed on page 245.)

If you use classes, you may find it useful to create a report with only certain classes selected, to report on the finances for particular jobs or projects.

Using matches to filter transactions

Click Matching at the Customize Report window.

In the right-hand part of the window, you can further define or limit the transactions to be included in your reports, depending on the details of each transaction. You can tell Quicken what must be true about a transaction for it to be included in a report. For example, you can tell Quicken to include only transactions with a specific payee. Just type the payee's name in the Payee Contains box.

You can enter:

The exact name, using QuickFill or the drop-down lists to help you, or

A partial name, using two periods (..) to represent characters you're not sure of.

Case (capitals or non-capitals) doesn't matter, and Quicken ignores any spaces before or after the phrase you type.)

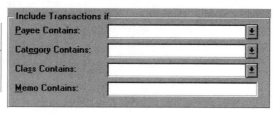

For investment reports, you can filter your reports by the security or the memo contents.

In the Category Contains box, you can type a category name or an account name to report on transfers to a specific account. For a category or class match, Quicken also searches through entries in the Splits window.

In addition to typing an entire payee, category, class, memo, or security name, you can use special *match characters* to limit a report.

Match character	Type of match
= (equal sign)	An exact match (include only transactions that match the text you type exactly)
.. (two periods)	A match that contains unspecified characters where you type .. (at the beginning, in the middle, or at the end of the text you type)
? (question mark)	A match with one unspecified character
~ (tilde)	The report excludes all matches for the text that follows

If you type ~.. (a tilde and two periods), Quicken excludes all transactions except those that are empty in the specified field. For example, if you type ~.. in the Category Contains box, Quicken includes only those transactions that are uncategorized. Uncategorized transactions show up as "Other" in reports.

For an investment report, if you type ~.. in the Security Contains box, the report includes only cash transactions, which do not have a security. If you type .. in the box, the report will exclude all cash transactions.

The following chart shows some examples of what your report can include with and without using special match characters.

Example	The report includes	The report does not include
=tax	tax, Tax, TAX	taxable, tax deduction, Tax:State, surtax, new tax loss, rent, utilities
tax	tax, Tax, TAX, taxable, tax deduction, Tax:State, surtax, new tax loss	rent, utilities
tax..	tax, Tax, TAX, taxable, tax deduction, Tax:State	surtax, new tax loss, rent, utilities
..tax	tax, Tax, TAX, surtax, property tax	taxable, tax deduction, Tax:State, new tax loss, rent, utilities
~=tax	taxable, tax deduction, Tax:State, surtax, new tax loss, rent, utilities	tax, Tax, TAX
~tax	rent, utilities	tax, Tax, TAX, taxable, tax deduction, Tax:State, surtax, new tax loss
t..x	trix, tx, tkx, t——x, tax, Tax, TAX	taxable, tax deduction, Tax:State, surtax, new tax loss, rent, utilities
=t?x	tkx, tax, Tax, TAX	trix, tx, t——x, taxable, tax deduction, Tax:State, surtax, new tax loss, rent, utilities
..	tax, rent, utilities, and so on	*blank*
~..	*blank*	tax, rent, utilities, and so on
.. in the Security Contains field	All transactions for which the Security column is filled in	All cash transactions and totals that are not associated with a security

You can use QuickZoom to examine the transaction detail in most Quicken reports (in summary, transaction, budget, comparison, investment income, and investment transactions reports). For example, if you are curious about the individual transactions that are represented by an "Actual" amount in a budget report or an uncategorized "Other" amount in a summary report, you can double-click the amount to see a list of the transactions that make up that amount.

Or press Ctrl+Z

1 **Select an amount in the report and double-click it.**

You can QuickZoom an item when the arrow cursor turns into a magnifying glass: 🔍

Quicken displays a QuickZoom report, which is a list of the transactions that make up that amount. (Or, if you use QuickZoom in a transaction report, Quicken displays the register.)

Click Print on the Report button bar or press Ctrl+P to print the list of transactions.

You can sort the transactions in a QuickZoom report by clicking the Sort button.

If you want to examine or change a transaction, double-click it to go to the account register with that transaction selected.

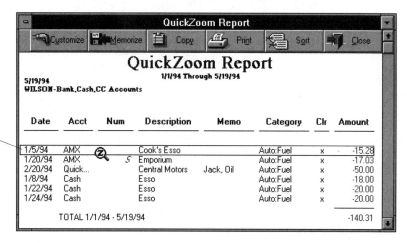

Or press Ctrl+Z again

2 **(Optional) To examine a transaction in the register or make any changes, double-click the report line.**

Quicken displays the register and selects the transaction.

If you need to modify a large number of transactions in the register, it's best to close or minimize (to an icon) the Report window to avoid the delay that would be caused by recalculation. (This recommendation also applies when you are changing budget amounts while a budget report is open.) When you're ready to see your changes, double-click on the report icon to open and update your report.

Windows tip

To shrink a window to an icon, click the minimize button in the upper right corner. The window appears as an icon on the Windows desktop. To restore a minimized icon, double-click it.

3 **To return to the QuickZoom report from the register, close or minimize the register, or click in the QuickZoom report window.**

If you used QuickZoom to move directly from a transaction report to the register, Quicken returns you to the transaction report when you close or minimize the register.

Memorizing and recalling reports

Once you change the settings or sort criteria for a report, you can memorize the changes so you can recall the report using the same report instructions time after time. This feature is most useful for reports that filter out transactions, for example using matching criteria. You can also change a memorized report and then rememorize it with the changes.

Memorizing a report

1 **Create and display a report as described in "Creating a report" on page 236.**

Or press Ctrl+M

2 **Click Memorize on the Report button bar.**

Or choose Memorize Report from the Edit menu. .

If you use the same title as an existing memorized report, Quicken warns that you are about to overwrite an existing memorized report.

This option is available only if you selected a preset date range in the Create Report window.

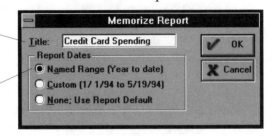

3 **(Optional) Change the title of the memorized report.**

For example, you could enter a more specific title such as "Inv. Transactions - Current Quarter."

4 **Choose an option for report dates.**

Named Range. (Available only if you used a preset date range when creating the report.) Instead of memorizing actual dates, Quicken will calculate the dates, depending on when you recall the report. For example, if you memorize a report with the date range "Month to date," the report will cover the period from the beginning of the current month to the day when you recall the report.

Custom. Quicken memorizes the actual dates that were used in the report.

None. Quicken will use the preset starting and ending dates that appear in the Create Report window when you recall the report. (To change the preset starting and ending dates for all reports, see "Changing report preferences" on page 250.)

5 **Click OK to memorize the report.**

Quicken adds the report to the Memorized Report list.

Recalling a memorized report

After you have memorized a report, you can recall it. When you recall a report, it's really the report definition you are recalling (including all the settings and sort criteria you've specified).

To recall a report, use either of the following two methods (as described on pages 236 to 238):

- Click the Reports icon in the iconbar, select Memorized as the report family, then select a memorized report from the list.

  OR

- Choose Memorized from the Reports menu, select a report from the list of your memorized reports, and click Use. At the Create Report window, click OK.

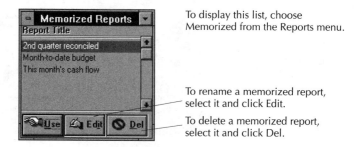

To display this list, choose
Memorized from the Reports menu.

To rename a memorized report, select it and click Edit.

To delete a memorized report, select it and click Del.

Quicken searches for transactions and prepares the report as usual.

If you change the settings for a memorized report, you can rememorize it with the same title or you can give the altered report a new title and memorize it again. If you don't rememorize a report whose definition you have changed, it retains the original definition the next time you recall the report.

Changing report preferences

You can change certain aspects of Quicken's reports from the Preferences menu.

1 **From the Edit menu, choose Preferences (or click the Preferences icon on the iconbar).**

2 **Click the Reports icon.**

This illustration shows the preferences that are selected when Quicken is installed.

Click a button to select it.

Click a checkbox to select or clear it.

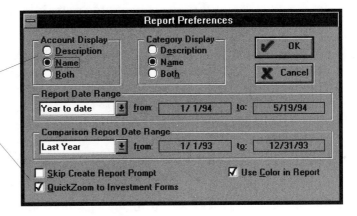

3   **Choose the preferences you want to use and click OK.**

Quicken updates all opened reports so you can see your changes immediately.

Quicken displays report text on your screen in Helvetica and uses Times Roman for its report headings. These display fonts can be modified only by editing your QUICKEN.INI file. Instructions for changing the fonts you see displayed onscreen in reports are in Help. (Press F1 and then click Contents. Click "Customizing Quicken," click "How to...," and then click "Changing the font in reports displayed onscreen.")

Report preference	Effect on reports
Account Display	**Description** shows the account description only. If an account has no description, Quicken uses the account name. **Name** shows the account name only. **Both** shows both the name and description.
Category Display	**Description** shows the category/class description only. If a category or class has no description, Quicken uses the category or class name. **Name** shows the category/class name only. **Both** shows both the name and description.
Report Date Range	The initial date range for all reports (which you can change when creating a report). Select the date range you use most often for your reports. If you want to use some other date range that isn't listed, see "Setting up your own default date range" next.
Comparison Report Date Range	The second default date range for comparison reports. Select the date range you use most often for comparison reports.
Skip Create Report Prompt	Select to create reports from the Reports menu without first displaying the Create Report window. The default date range shown in this window will be used. If necessary, you can change any settings by clicking the Customize button on the report button bar after the report is created.
QuickZoom to Investment Forms	From an investment income or investment transactions report, QuickZoom to the entry forms instead of to the investment register.
Use Color in Report	Select to display text in blue and negative amounts in red.

Setting up your own default date range

In the Report Preferences window, you can select the date range that you want Quicken to use as the starting (or "default") date range when you create reports. However, if the date range you most often want to report on isn't in Quicken's list, you can set up your own default date range. Quicken then displays that as the starting date range each time you create a report.

1 **In the Report Preferences window, click the drop-down button in the Report Date Range field.**

2 **Select Custom Date at the bottom of the list.**

3 **Select From and To dates from the drop-down lists.**

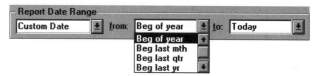

These lists contain more dates than are available from Quicken's preset date ranges. If you select a From date such as "May 1," Quicken always uses the previous May 1. For example, if you set up a date range of May 1 to August 1, and run a report on January 20, 1994, the report will run from May 1, 1993 to August 1, 1993.

4 **Click OK to record your changes.**

Note: A memorized report will not remember your own default date range as "floating" dates

If you memorize a report after using your own default date range to create the report, Quicken does not offer you the date range as a "Named Range" (see page 249). For example, if you set up a default date range of "Beginning last month" through "Today," Quicken converts this to (for example) 4/1/94 through 5/19/94 when you create the report. If you memorize the report, you can memorize only the fixed custom dates 4/1/94 through 5/19/94 or the report default options.

Transferring report data to other programs

Using the Copy to clipboard feature when you have a report displayed on your screen, you can easily transfer Quicken data to other programs, such as Microsoft Excel for Windows, Lotus 1-2-3 for Windows, other spreadsheet software, or a word processor.

1 **In Quicken, display the report with the data arranged exactly as you would like to copy it to the other program.**

Customize the report if necessary, as described in this chapter.

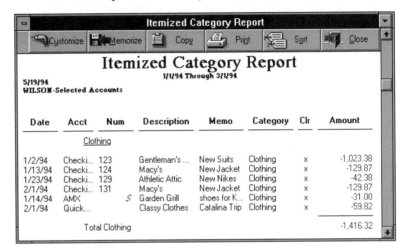

The report data is copied in a tab-delimited format compatible with many spreadsheet programs.

2 **Click Copy.**

3 **Switch to the other program.**

Click in the other program's window if it is visible, or press Alt-Tab to select the program. If it wasn't already running, start it now.

4 **Position the cursor where you would like the data to be read in.**

5 **Use the program's Paste function to copy the Quicken data in.**

The Paste function is usually found in the Edit menu. The data is read from the clipboard into the program.

This example shows a Microsoft Excel worksheet.

If you paste the report data into a word processor document, you may need to set tabs in the document to format the report attractively. The figures in the Quicken report are separated by tabs. However, you may prefer to print the report to an ASCII file on disk (as described on page 266), and then import the file into your document. When printed to an ASCII file, the report columns are separated by spaces.

16

Creating graphs

Quicken can display your data as pie charts and bar graphs. Creating and displaying graphs helps you visualize your finances more effectively than viewing numbers in an account register or a report.

Use graphs to help analyze your income and expenses, develop better budgets, determine your net worth, and evaluate your investment portfolio.

About graphs

Graphs are helpful if you're looking for a visual summary of your finances. If you need more detailed information about an item you see in a graph, you can get it quickly using a feature called *QuickZoom* to move to another, more detailed graph.

Quicken creates four types of graphs:

- Income and Expense
- Budget Variance
- Net Worth
- Investment

It takes Quicken about the same length of time to create a graph as it takes to create a comparable report.

You can create graphs for all the data you have entered in Quicken, but it's best to limit the date range. Graphs may be too cluttered and difficult to understand if you enter a date range longer than a year.

Creating graphs

1   From the Reports menu, choose Graphs.

Or click the Graphs icon on the iconbar.

(Optional) Change the dates in the date range.

Choose the type of graph you want to create.

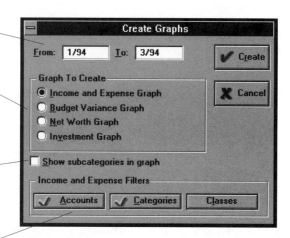

(Optional) Select Show Subcategories in Graph if you'd like the graph to show the extra detail that subcategories allow you.

(Optional) Click the filter buttons if you'd like the graph to include or exclude specific accounts, categories, or classes (or securities for the investment graph). The checkmark on the button tells you when some items are being excluded.

Unless you specify otherwise, the graph includes all categories and classes. The selection of items for graphs works the same way it does when you customize reports. You can select accounts, categories, and classes for income and expense, budget variance, and net worth graphs. You can select accounts and securities for investment graphs. When the Select Items To Include window appears, mark the items you want to include.

2   Complete the Create Graphs window and click Create.

You can print the graph. From the File menu, choose Print Graph. See Chapter 17, *Printing reports and graphs,* beginning on page 263.

Viewing graph windows

Each segment of a graph is shaded with a different color (or pattern if you do not have a color monitor). Legends identify the meaning of each bar, line, or pie slice.

Quicken comes set to display two graphs in one window. If you prefer to view the graphs in separate windows, you can change this setting. See "Changing graph preferences" next.

In bar graphs Quicken displays dollar amounts on the y-axis and months, accounts, or categories on the x-axis.

The title of each individual graph appears above the graph.

In pie charts, if you have more than ten categories, Quicken displays the largest ten categories first. It groups the rest of the categories in the eleventh slice of the pie, called "Other." To see the rest of your categories in a pie chart, click Next 10 or double-click the "Other" slice.

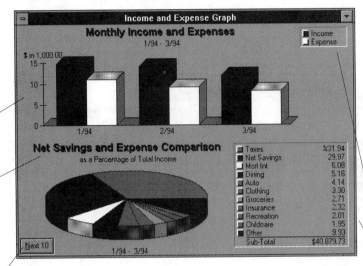

If you have a color monitor but prefer to view patterns instead of colors, you can do so. See "Changing graph preferences" next.

A legend to the right of each graph shows what the patterns or colors represent.

Changing graph preferences

If you are using a color monitor and some of the colors in your graphs are very similar to other colors, turn up the brightness or contrast on your monitor. Each color becomes vivid and distinct.

You can change three graph display settings.

1 **From the Edit menu, choose Preferences and then click the Graphs icon.**

Select this preference to display patterns instead of colors. (If you have a monochrome monitor, Quicken turns this option on automatically.)

Select this preference to display each graph in its own window instead of two graphs per window.

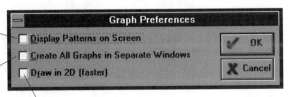

Select this if your computer takes a long time to display three-dimensional graphs.

2 **Select the preferences you want to use and click OK.**

Investigating items in graphs

You can investigate the information you see in a graph in three ways. Whenever you see the arrow cursor turn into a magnifying glass, you can see more information about the item under the magnifying glass. Or you can remove the item from the graph to look more closely at other items.

QuickZoom. As with Quicken reports, you can QuickZoom from a graph to examine transaction details in a report. To get more information about a particular element in a graph, double-click any pie slice or bar. Double-click again to see even more detail in a report.

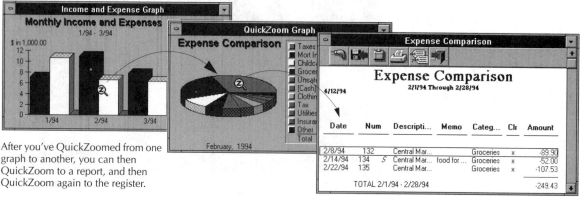

After you've QuickZoomed from one graph to another, you can then QuickZoom to a report, and then QuickZoom again to the register.

Data labels. To see the exact value of a pie slice or bar, click and hold down the right mouse button.

Whenever you see the mouse pointer turn into a QuickZoom magnifying glass, you can see the exact value of the element that is below the magnifying glass by holding down the right mouse button.

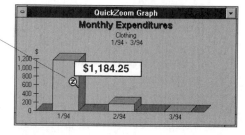

Hide data. To hide a pie slice or bar from the graph, shift-click the left mouse button. To *unhide* an item, create the graph again.

In the first graph, the Taxes and Mort Int categories make the largest slices of the pie. You can hide these categories so that you can see other pieces of the pie more clearly.

Hiding categories is not the same as filtering them. When you filter categories, Quicken doesn't include them in its analysis. When you hide them, Quicken still calculates their value in the graph, but does not display the value.

After *hiding* the tax slice, Quicken displays a subtotal instead of a total at the bottom of the legend.

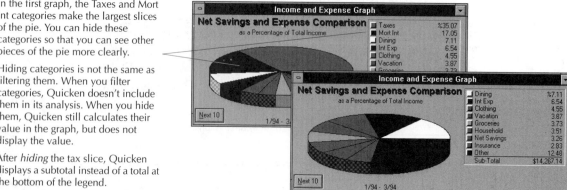

Analyzing income and expenses

Income and expense graphs can help you spot spending patterns, highlight your top ten expenses, warn about overspending, and provide comparisons of historical data.

Quicken creates these graphs using the categories you assign when you enter transactions. Quicken ordinarily includes the value of any subcategory within its parent category; however, when you create the graph, you can select the Show Subcategories in Graph checkbox to break down the graph into subcategory amounts.

Income and expense graphs help you answer these financial questions:

- Is my income changing over time?
- Is my income covering my expenses?
- Where does my money come from?
- Where does my money go?

The bar graph compares income and expense over time.

This example shows that income was greater than expenses for most months in the first half of the year. Both income and expenses fluctuate from month to month in this household.

If your income was greater than your expenses in the time period covered by the graph, this pie chart shows your top ten expenses relative to (as a percentage of) your total income. Quicken displays the difference between your income and expenses as "Net Savings." The Net Savings slice represents the amount of money that you received and did not spend.

If your expenses were greater than your income in the time period covered by the graph, this pie chart will show your top ten expenses as a percentage of your total expenses and the Net Savings slice will not appear in the graph. (Graphs do not display negative amounts.)

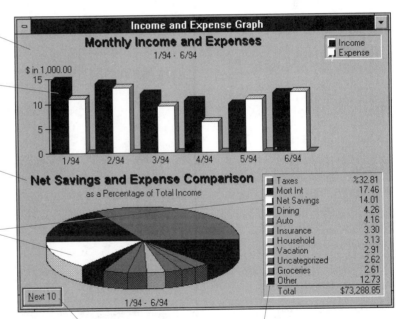

When you click the Next 10 button, Quicken replaces this "top ten" graph with the next ten highest expense categories.

When you double-click Other in the legend, Quicken creates a QuickZoom graph of the next ten highest expense categories.

Understanding budget variance

Budget variance graphs compare actual spending and income with budgeted spending and income. Quicken calculates the difference in dollars between the two so you can see how you are actually doing compared with your budget.

You can create budget variance graphs that quickly alert you to potential problem areas such as expenses that are over budget or income that is under budget. Determining how successfully you budgeted this year can help you prepare next year's budget. (If you have not already set up a budget, Quicken cannot create budget variance graphs.)

Budget graphs help you answer these financial questions:

- Am I staying within my budget from month to month?
- How well do I estimate what I will earn and spend?
- In what categories do I overspend or underspend?

Favorable means that either actual income was more than budgeted income or actual expenses were less than budgeted expenses.

Unfavorable means that either actual income was less than budgeted income or actual expenses were more than budgeted expenses.

The top graph shows actual net income less budgeted net income.

This example shows the budget variance in January and March as favorable.

The bottom graph shows the five categories that are furthest from budget (both over and under).

Using the information in this graph, you can pursue the reasons for overspending or underearning by category.

Because of what you learn, you may be able to budget better for these categories in the next six months or next year.

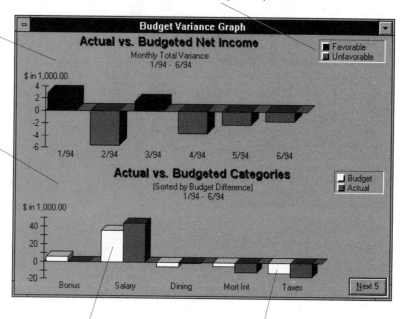

Income categories appear above the x-axis. Expense categories appear below it.

Analyzing net worth

Net worth graphs are similar to income and expense graphs, except they use account balances rather than category data. Net worth graphs are also similar to account balance reports you may create in Quicken.

Create net worth graphs to show the balance of your credit cards or other debts and your bank accounts or other assets over time, or to show if your net worth is changing.

Net worth graphs help you answer these financial questions:

- Do I own more than I owe?
- In what assets do I have most of my money?
- What are my largest debts?
- How is my net worth changing over time?

The graph shows your assets in bars above the x-axis and your liabilities in bars below the x-axis.

Your net worth is the difference between your assets and liabilities.

This example shows that net worth is positive (above zero) and increasing slightly over the first half of the year.

You can double-click a liability bar to see a liability comparison graph as of that month to see a breakdown of your individual liabilities as a percentage of your total liabilities.

Double-click an asset bar to see an asset comparison graph as of that month. The QuickZoom graph shows a breakdown of your individual assets as a percentage of your total assets.

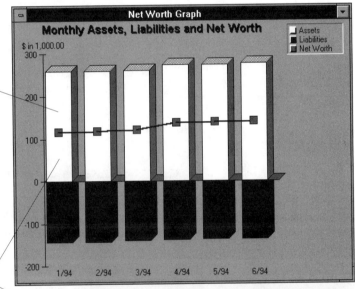

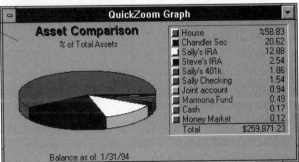

Evaluating investment performance

Investment graphs display information that helps you to evaluate your investment portfolio and the price history of your securities.

Four portfolio value graphs summarize the market value of each security you own, either by type (such as bond, CD, or mutual funds), goal (such as college, retirement, growth, or income), security (such as IBM, Exxon, AT&T, or Intuit), or Quicken investment account (such as Steve's IRA, Sally's IRA, or Merrill Lynch).

The average annual total return graph is a measure of how well your securities are performing.

The price history graph, available from the Portfolio View window, displays the trends in the prices and market value of a particular security. For how to update security prices, see "Updating the values of your investments" on page 199.

Investment graphs help you answer these financial questions:

- Is my portfolio value increasing?
- How is my portfolio allocated?
- How are my stocks and bonds doing?

The monthly portfolio value graph shown here is summarized by security. To see the graph summarized by security type, goal, or account, click the appropriate button.

This graph summarizes the market value of each security you own.

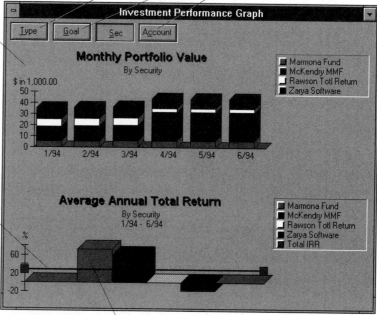

The total internal rate of return (IRR) is shown on this line. IRR is the annual total return of your securities during the time period you specified for the graph. This value takes into account dividends, interest, and other payment you receive, including increases and decreases in the market value of your securities.

The average annual total return graph measures how well your securities are performing. Taller bars indicate better performance.

Printing reports and graphs

Quicken enables you to print your reports and graphs to many kinds of printers and offers several styles of printing, depending on the capabilities of your printer. You can also print a report to a disk file in one of several different formats.

Before you print reports or graphs, you need to set up your printer.

Setting up your printer

Before you print a report, you need to select the printer you're going to use. Depending on the capabilities of your printer, you can also select options for printing reports, including fonts, paper size, and page orientation (that is, the horizontal or vertical direction in which text is printed on the page).

When you set up a report printer,* Quicken remembers your settings and uses them whenever you print a report. Printer settings for reports have no effect when you print checks and vice versa. However, Quicken uses your report printer settings when you print graphs and budget spreadsheets.

1 From the File menu, choose Printer Setup and then choose Report/ Graph Printer Setup.

Select your printer.

Quicken can automatically detect whether your printer is continuous-feed or page-oriented.

Click Settings to select the paper size and page orientation.

Select this checkbox if you want to print negative report amounts in red and graphs in color (if you have a color printer).

To indent your printed text, enter the margins here.

Click Head Font or Body Font to select the fonts Quicken uses when it prints your reports.

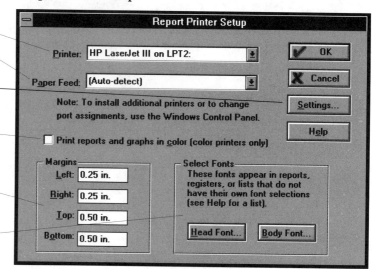

2 Select the printer you want to use from the Printer drop-down list.

If your printer is not listed, use the Windows Control Panel to install the printer driver for your printer. See your *Microsoft Windows User's Guide* for instructions on installing a printer.

3 (Optional) Change the paper-feed option for your printer in the Paper Feed drop-down list.

With Auto-detect selected, Quicken automatically detects whether your printer is continuous-feed or page-oriented. However, you can force Quicken to use one or the other by selecting another option.

---

* Setting up your printer and changing the fonts affect printed reports, not reports as they are displayed onscreen. Quicken displays report text on your screen in Helvetica and uses Times Roman for its report titles. You can modify report display by editing your QUICKEN.INI file. Instructions for changing the fonts you see displayed onscreen in reports are in Help. (Press F1 and then click Contents. Click "Customizing Quicken," click "How to...," and then click "Changing the size of the font in reports onscreen.")

4   **To allow more space or less space between the printed text and the edges of the paper, change the margin measurements.**

5   **To change the font settings for report titles and headings, click Head Font, select the settings you want to use, and then click OK.**

The fonts you can use in your Quicken reports are determined by the fonts available to your printer.

Quicken displays this window when you click Head Font in the Report Printer Setup window.

Select the font, font style, and size you want to use for report titles and headings.

For the best printing results, select a font with either a printer icon or a True Type icon (TT) next to it.

The Sample box shows the currently selected font and size.

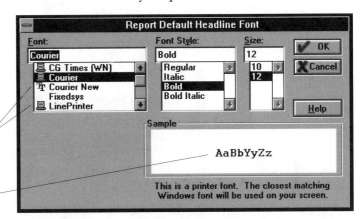

6   **To change the font settings for report and graphs text, click Body Font, select the settings you want to use, and then click OK.**

When you click Body Font, Quicken displays the Report Default Font window. Select the report text font settings in the same manner that you selected the report heading font settings.

7   **(Optional) To change the settings for paper size and page orientation, click Settings, select the settings you want to use, and then click OK.**

The options you see on your screen may be different from this illustration, depending on the type of printer you are using.

Use the Paper Size drop-down list to set up the correct size for the paper you want to use.

If you see a Fonts button, you can click the button to install fonts for your printer. (Then click Help for instructions.)

These options appear only if your printer provides a choice of page orientations. Click Portrait to print your report across the width of the page. Click Landscape to print across the length of the page (which is useful for wide reports).

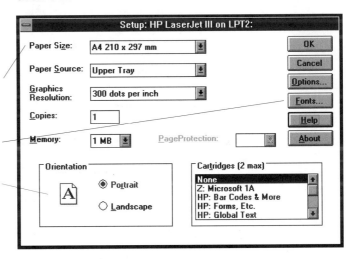

8   **Click OK to save the settings for printed reports and graphs.**

Printing reports

Print a report when you want a paper copy or when you want to save the report in a file on your disk.

1   **If you're printing on paper, check that your printer is turned on, is set to online, and is loaded with paper.**

2   **Create the report you want to print.**

Or press Ctrl+P

3   **Click the Print button on the report button bar.**

Or, from the File menu, choose Print Report.

4   **Select the options in the Print Report window.**

Select Printer to print the report on your printer.

Or print to:

A file on disk that you can read into your word processor or other program.

A tab-delimited disk file that can be read by spreadsheets (such as Microsoft Excel).

A comma-delimited disk file that you can read into Lotus 1-2-3 and other spreadsheets.

Your screen, to see a preview of how the printout will look on paper.

Enter a page range if you don't want to print all pages.

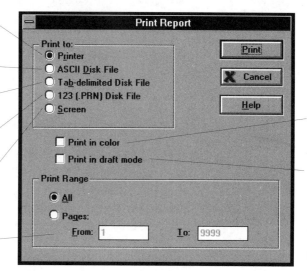

Select this if you have a color printer and want negative amounts to print in red.

Select draft mode for faster but less atttractive printing.

(You also see this window if you are printing your budget spreadsheet.)

5   **Click Print.**

Printing wide reports

Some reports have too many columns to print completely on a single sheet of paper. Depending on the capabilities of your printer, you may be able to fit the report on a single page by selecting different report printer options:

•   Select a smaller font size for the report text.

•   Select landscape orientation to print horizontally on the page.

See "Setting up your printer" on page 264 to change report printer options.

Printing graphs

When you print a graph, Quicken uses the same settings you selected for printing reports. It prints the text in your graph using the report text (body) font settings.

Your printer needs sufficient memory if it's to print a graph successfully at a resolution of 300 dpi (dots per inch) or higher. You may want to set your printer's resolution to 150 dpi or lower to avoid errors from insufficient memory. To set the resolution, see "Setting up your printer" on page 264 to change the printer driver settings (step 7). Note: This procedure displays the printer driver window, but you may need to go to an auxiliary window to change the resolution. For example, you may need to click an Options button in the printer driver window to display the auxiliary window.

1 **Make sure your printer is turned on, is online, and is loaded with paper.**

2 **Create the graph you want to print.**

Or press Ctrl+P 3 **From the File menu, choose Print Graph.**

Quicken prints the graph. Note: A printed graph typically looks a little different from the onscreen graph.

Printing graphs in color

If you have a color printer, select the option Print Reports and Graphs in Color in the Report Printer Setup window, as described on page 264.

☑ Print reports and graphs in color (color printers only)

If you have a color monitor but do not have a color printer, leave the option Print Reports and Graphs in Color unselected. Quicken prints fill patterns to distinguish between different segments in the graph. However, if you prefer, you can print shades of gray instead of fill patterns by selecting the option.

If monochrome graph printing seems very slow:
If you have a monochrome printer and it takes a very long time to print a graph (more than 20 minutes), try selecting the Print Reports and Graphs in Color setup option. With some printers, this speeds up graph printing.

Report and graph printing problems and solutions

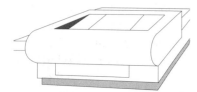

This section describes some common report and graph printing problems and their solutions. If you continue to have problems, see your printer manual or call Intuit's technical support group. (See "Phone numbers" on page 372.)

Problem Printer doesn't print.

Solution Check your equipment.

- Make sure your printer is turned on and is online.
- Make sure the cable connection between the printer and the computer is secure.
- From the File menu, choose Printer Setup and then Report/ Graph Printer Setup. Make sure the correct printer is selected.
- Press Ctrl+Esc to display the Windows Task List window, and then select Print Manager from the list. Check the Print Manager window to see if your printer has stalled; if it has, select your printer and then click Resume.
- Try to print a Windows Write document. Look for Write in the Accessories Program Group. Open it and type a few words. Then, from Write's File menu, choose Print. If the document prints OK, the problem may lie with your report printer setup.

Problem Printer prints strange characters instead of report text.

Solution From the File menu, choose Printer Setup and then Report/ Graph Printer Setup. Make sure the correct printer is selected.

Problem Printer prints blank pages instead of report text.

Solution Check your settings.

- From the File menu, choose Print Report. Make sure draft mode is not selected.
- If you are using Adobe Type Manager, turn it off.

Problem Large fonts are not aligned on the report page.

Solution Use the same style and size fonts for the headings and the body text.

Problem Printer error occurs before the graph is completely printed. (The printer may report an "out of page memory" error or error 20; Windows may report an "out of paper" error.)

Solution Change your graphics resolution setting to 150 dpi (dots per inch) or less. This setting is in the printer driver window. See "Setting up your printer" on page 264. Note: This procedure displays the printer driver window, but you may need to go to an auxiliary window to change the resolution. For example, you may need to click an Options button in the printer driver window to display the auxiliary window.

Preparing your income taxes

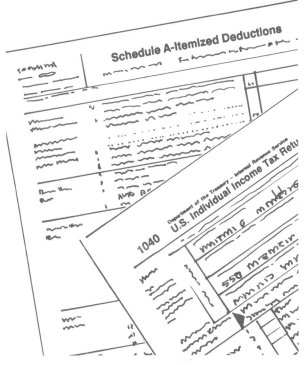

Quicken can simplify the preparation of your federal income tax return and related tax schedules. Using Quicken helps whether you use dedicated tax preparation software, prepare your returns manually, or gather the information to turn over to a tax preparation service.

You can produce a tax schedule report and capital gains report that list the exact amounts to fill in for your tax forms and schedules.

You can also export the reports to tax preparation software such as TurboTax for Windows.

Preparing your personal income taxes

Quicken can greatly simplify the preparation of your Federal Income Tax Return (Form 1040) and related tax schedules. Using Quicken helps whether you prepare your own returns or gather the information to submit to a tax preparer. Even if you use a tax preparer, documenting your income and tax-related expenses used to take hours. But if you categorize your transactions with Quicken income and expense categories throughout the year, you can create reports with the tax information you need in seconds.

You can also transfer Quicken data directly to Windows or DOS tax software programs, eliminating the need to re-enter financial information when you prepare your taxes. See "Transferring Quicken data to tax preparation software" on page 273.

Setting up categories with tax time in mind

You can set up your income and expense categories in several ways, depending on how you want to report your tax information.

To get these kinds of reports	Set up your category like this
Tax summary reports that group and subtotal transactions in your accounts by tax-related category.	Mark the category as tax related.
Tax schedule reports and capital gains reports that group and subtotal your transactions by tax schedule line item.	Make sure you're set up to use tax schedules and then assign the category to the correct tax schedule line item.
Both tax summary and tax schedule reports.	Mark the category as tax related AND assign the category to a tax schedule line item.

Quicken's standard home and business categories are already set up with appropriate tax schedule assignments. Whenever you create a new category, you may need to assign it to a tax schedule line item.

1 **If you want to create tax schedule reports, make sure you've set Quicken to use tax schedules with categories.**

From the Edit menu, choose Preferences and then choose General.

Make sure that the Use Tax Schedules With Categories checkbox is selected. If it is not selected, click the checkbox.

2 **From the Lists menu, choose Category & Transfer.**

Or click the Cat List icon on the iconbar.

3 **Select the category or subcategory that you want to be tax related and click Edit.**

If the category is not already in the list, click New.

The tax schedule line items Quicken uses include these forms and schedules:

Form 1040
Schedule A
Schedule B
Schedule C
Schedule D
Schedule E
Schedule F
Form 2106
Form 2119
Form 2441
Form 3903
Form 4137
Form 4684
Form 4952
Form 6252
Form 8606
Form 8815
Schedule K-1
W-2
1099R

4 **If you want to create tax summary reports, select the Tax-related option.**

5 **If you want to create tax schedule reports, select the tax schedule line item for that category from the Form drop-down list.**

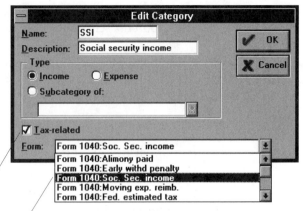

If you want to create tax summary reports, select the Tax-related option.

If you want to create tax schedule reports, select the tax schedule line item that the category should report to from the Form drop-down list.

6 **Click OK.**

Creating tax summary reports

When you want a report that shows the total amount of tax-related income and expenses, create a tax summary report. See "Tax summary" on page 213 for a sample tax summary report. This report initially includes all accounts in the current file except tax-deferred investment accounts (such as 401(k) and IRA accounts).

See Chapter *15, Creating and customizing reports,* beginning on page 235, for full details of running reports.

Creating tax schedule reports

The tax schedule report lists the exact figures you need to fill in on your 1040 tax form and schedules, with these qualifications.

You must:

- Check the figures against any limits defined by the IRS, for example, the maximum deduction allowed for IRA contributions. The Quicken tax schedule report simply gives you your personal totals.

- Have already recorded all relevant transactions in Quicken. (If you assign the investment categories _DivInc and _IntInc to Schedule B, the tax file subtotals the amount for each category by investment account but not by security.)

The report gathers figures from all accounts in the current file except tax-deferred investment accounts (for example, 401(k) and IRA accounts) and from all categories that have been assigned to a tax form and line. Several categories or accounts can contribute to the same figure in the report. For example, the line "Salary" on Form W-2 can include both regular salary and bonuses.

You can run this report at the end of each year or tax period. You can also export tax schedule reports to tax preparation software.

1   **Click the Reports icon on the iconbar.**

2   **Enter a date range that covers the tax period.**

3   **Choose Home and then choose Tax Schedule.**

4   **(Optional) To restrict the report to certain accounts, click Customize and then click Accounts.**

Select the accounts you want to use. You may need to do this if, for example, your file contains checking accounts for you and your spouse and you are filing separate tax returns. If you exclude an account for which you defined tax form information (for example, your IRA account), the report still lists transfers made into or out of the account if the account at the other end of the transfer is included.

5   **Click OK to create the report.**

The resulting report lists your transactions, subtotaled for each tax line on each tax form.

See "Tax schedule" on page 215 for a sample report.

See "Transferring Quicken data to tax preparation software" on page 273 if you are using software to prepare your tax return.

Creating capital gains reports for Schedule D

If you have investment accounts with realized capital gains (following buy and sell transactions), the tax schedule report does not show these realized gains. To obtain figures for your realized gains, run a capital gains report. To get income by security, run an investment income report as described on page 221.

The capital gains report lists your long-term and short-term capital gains transactions in a format suitable for Schedule D.

You can also export capital gains reports to tax preparation software.

1 Click the Reports icon on the iconbar.

2 Enter a date range that covers the tax period.

3 Choose Investment and then choose Capital Gains.

4 Click Customize.

5 In the Report Layout section, select "Short- vs. Long-Term" in the Subtotal By box.

6 Click OK.

See "Capital gains" on page 220 for a sample report.

See "Transferring Quicken data to tax preparation software" next if you are using software to prepare your tax return.

Transferring Quicken data to tax preparation software

If you use Windows or DOS tax software to prepare your Form 1040, you can use data from Quicken's tax schedule or capital gains report in the program that calculates your tax and prints completed tax forms.

Exporting Quicken for Windows tax data to TurboTax for Windows

If you use TurboTax for Windows, you do not need to create the tax schedule report or capital gains report or export it into TurboTax. TurboTax for Windows can read and import Quicken for Windows data without any work on your part. See the *TurboTax for Windows User's Guide*.

If you use another type of tax preparation software, you need to follow the next steps.

Exporting Quicken for Windows data to other tax preparation software (including DOS TurboTax)

Quicken writes your tax data to a TXF (Tax Exchange Format) file with a standard format compatible with several major tax preparation programs. Exporting your Quicken tax schedule report or capital gains report to a TXF file eliminates the need to re-enter financial data when you prepare your taxes.

1 Display the tax schedule or capital gains report as described earlier in this chapter.

2 Click the Export button on the Report button bar.

3 **Enter a filename for the tax schedule or capital gains report in the File Name field.**

The filename must follow the usual DOS rules for filenames (maximum eight characters).

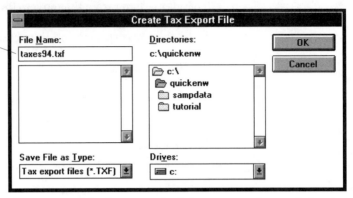

If you created both a tax schedule report and a capital gains report, you must print each report to disk so that you have a separate TXF file for each report.

4 **Click OK.**

Quicken writes the data to the file and closes the Report window. See the instructions that accompany your tax preparation program to use the data file.

Updating your tax form information

Occasionally the IRS changes the information required on IRS tax forms and schedules. When this happens, Intuit provides an updated list of tax form assignments (the TAX.SCD file) to the manufacturers of tax preparation software.

Most changes to IRS tax forms occur in January and very often affect only specialized forms that most people do not need to file. If the IRS makes any changes to the forms you file, however, you will need to obtain a new copy of the TAX.SCD file.

If you are a TurboTax for Windows user, your Final Edition will include an updated TAX.SCD file in time for you to file your annual returns. If you are not a TurboTax for Windows user, you can call the Intuit Customer Assistance (software upgrades) number listed on page 372 to obtain an updated version of the TAX.SCD file.

All you need to do is copy the file to your Quicken directory. (The directory is QUICKENW if you used Quicken's Express Installation to install Quicken.)

19

Planning with Quicken – an overview

Taking control of your finances begins with thoughtful planning. Planning for your mortgage payments, planning for the vacation you hope to take next summer, planning for retirement.

Quicken doesn't just track where your money's been going. It also gives you a clear picture of your financial future.

This chapter introduces Quicken's planning tools and helps you decide which to use for your own situation. The following chapters describe each of the planning tools in more detail.

Introducing Quicken's planning tools

We all make plans to some extent, although different people have different planning methods and different needs.

Some people want only to see what expenses are coming up next month. Other people like to plan 20 years ahead to their retirement, or to putting their children through college. Some people like to spend an evening analyzing their budget for the next year. Others just want a simple reminder to pay the rent.

Whatever your planning needs, Quicken is designed to help you. Quicken offers a complete suite of planning tools, from quick loan calculators to planning graphs that can project your account balances for years ahead.

Read what tools are available here, and then decide which would benefit you the most by following the guidelines in "Deciding which tools to use" on page 278.

Financial planning calculators

Type in the numbers and Quicken instantly shows you the significance. The five calculators let you try out "what-if" scenarios for loan planning and refinancing, investment savings planning, college planning, and retirement planning. See Chapter 20, *Using financial planning calculators,* beginning on page 281.

Budget spreadsheet

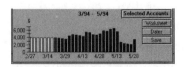

To keep track of where your money goes, set up a budget spreadsheet. Enter estimates of your income and expenses, and later compare your actual income and expenses against your plan. A budget lets you plan a whole year ahead at a time. Special graphs and reports show how well you are keeping to your budget. See Chapter 21, *Budgeting your income and expenses,* beginning on page 289.

Financial planning graph

Nothing makes your financial future clearer than a picture. Quicken projects your spending patterns forward up to two years, and displays your account balances in a graph. Now you can make the right medium-term decisions such as when to buy a new car, when to invest money, and how large a home loan you can afford. See Chapter 22, *Projecting the future,* beginning on page 301.

Other Asset:
Vacation 94

Savings goals

If you like to put aside some of your earnings for a vacation or other major purchase, you can set up a special type of account called a savings goal account, in which you track how much you have saved. See "Setting up savings goals," beginning on page 297.

Loan and mortgage tracking

Quicken amortizes your home or car loan and shows you the complete payment schedule. You can see how much interest and principal you are paying, and can track the varying payment amounts on an adjustable-rate mortgage. Quicken even records the payments in your register each month if you set up the payment as a scheduled transaction. See Chapter 23, *Tracking loans and mortgages*, beginning on page 315.

Financial Calendar

The calendar on your wall can't record your bill payments for you, and it can't project your mortgage payments forward into the future. Quicken's Financial Calendar can. You can schedule once-only future transactions on your Financial Calendar, or recurring transactions such as your paycheck deposit or your house payment. Make the Financial Calendar an integral part of how you enter transactions in Quicken, and see exactly what's coming up and what your short-term expenses are looking like. See Chapter 8, *Scheduling with the Quicken Financial Calendar*, beginning on page 93.

Reports and graphs

It may not be obvious, but your best aid in planning the future is to know all about what's already happened. Use Quicken's reports and graphs liberally to help you understand your present situation. Then use the other planning tools with insight. See Chapters 14, 15, and 16.

Deciding which tools to use

You can use some, or all, or even none of Quicken's planning tools. Everyone's financial situation is different, so you should decide which tools are helpful and which are not.

If you're the type who likes to experiment, go ahead and try out all of Quicken's planning options. They're flexible (but unbreakable!), so you'll get the most out of them by experimenting.

A good starting point is to decide what it is you want to get out of Quicken. Try and answer these questions:

- Over what sort of period am I interested in planning? A month? A year? Ten years?

- Do I need to make a detailed analysis of the period ahead? For example, would I like to differentiate between household expenses and leisure expenses? Or is it just the overall financial picture I'm interested in?

- Do I want to improve my money management, for example to plan to make a regular transfer to a mutual fund or savings account?

- Do I have specific goals in mind, such as:
    - saving toward a home loan down payment
    - affording a higher monthly rent
    - putting my children through college
    - planning my investments for retirement?

The table on the next page will help you get the most out of Quicken with the least time and effort. It describes some typical aims of planning, and how best to use Quicken to achieve those aims.

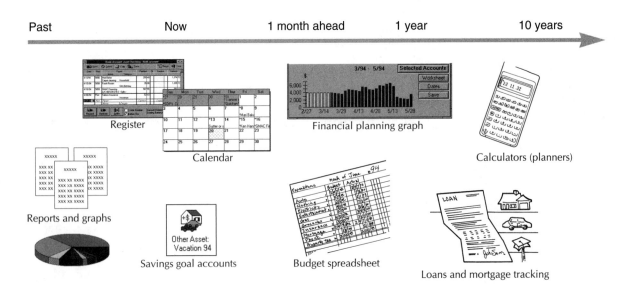

Past   Now   1 month ahead   1 year   10 years

Register

Calendar

Financial planning graph

Calculators (planners)

Reports and graphs

Savings goal accounts

Budget spreadsheet

Loans and mortgage tracking

To do this	Use Quicken in this way
Decide what you can afford over the next year or so	Keep your **registers** up to date. Use the **budget spreadsheet** to plan your spending for the next year. Schedule major income and expenses on the **Financial Calendar**; use the **financial planning graph** and **worksheet** to view your account balances.
Determine what size loan you can afford	Use the **Loan Planner** (calculator) to play with the numbers. You can also set up the loan in the **View Loans window** and see the effect of your loan payments on the **financial planning graph**. For an adjustable-rate loan, try adjusting the rate for future dates, to see the effect on the payment schedule.
Estimate how much you can set aside each month for long-term investment	Enter figures in the **financial planning worksheet** and see the results on the **financial planning graph**. Select only your cash flow accounts (bank, credit card, and cash accounts). Save different **scenarios** to compare spending and saving habits. Also try using the **Investment Savings Planner** (calculator).
Save towards a specific medium-term goal, such as a car, a vacation, or a down payment on a house	Use the **financial planning graph** to predict when you will have the money available, or to estimate your spending allowance. To track how much you are managing to put aside, set up a **savings goal account**.
Save towards a specific long-term goal, such as retirement or putting your children through college	Use the **financial planning calculators** to see how much you need to save now.
Automate entry of future transactions as much as possible	Set up recurring **scheduled transactions** for all regular deposits and expenses such as paychecks, rent, insurance. Set up **loans** for all amortized loan payments. **Memorize** any other transactions to ease transaction entry (see Chapter 7, *Memorizing special transactions,* beginning on page 85).
Enter transactions in advance; remind yourself to pay bills	First set up amortized **loans** and recurring **scheduled transactions** as described above. Enter once-only future transactions on the **Financial Calendar**.
Leave reminders for yourself (not necessarily finance-related)	Attach notes to the **Financial Calendar**.
Compare current spending to past spending patterns	Create a **comparison report** to compare two periods on a dollar or percentage basis (see page 217 for an example). If you previously set up a budget spreadsheet, create a **monthly budget report** or a **budget variance graph**.

Using financial planning calculators

Quicken's five financial planning calculators enable you to try out "what if" scenarios for loan planning and refinancing, investment savings planning, college planning, and retirement planning.

About financial planning calculators

Quicken has five financial planning calculators that enable you to do "what if" calculations. You work with each financial planning calculator in the same way; only the information and calculations are different.

You can use the financial planning calculators to answer questions such as:

- If I take out a mortgage with a 9.25% interest rate, what will my monthly payments be?
- Is it worth my refinancing my mortgage if I plan to move within five years?
- If I invest $10,000 of my savings and receive an annual yield of 12%, what will the value be in 5 years?
- If I set aside $3,000 each year until my child is 18, will I have enough to pay for a good four-year college?
- If I retire in ten years and put $2,000 into my IRA account every year until then, how much money will I have available?

1   From the Activities menu, choose Financial Planners and then choose the calculator you want to use.

2   Enter information into the appropriate fields.

If you need more information about entering data, press F1.

Enter amounts in these fields. Press Tab or click the next field to move to the next field.

Whenever you move to another field, Quicken calculates the result and displays it in the CALCULATED area.

The field containing CALCULATED tells you which amount Quicken will compute. Click a button here to select the amount you want computed.

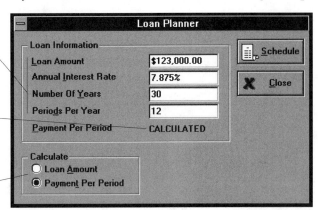

The formulas Quicken uses to calculate values for the Financial Planning Calculators are in Help. (Press F1 and then click Contents. Click "Technical information about Quicken" at the end of the Contents, and then click "Quicken's financial planning formulas.")

3   Click Schedule to view a payment or deposit schedule.

Quicken displays a payment schedule for the Loan Planner, and a deposit schedule for the Investment Savings Planner, College Planner, and Retirement Planner.

Calculating loan payments and principal

When the Calculate Payment Per Period button is selected, Quicken calculates what your payments would be for a loan of a given amount.

For example, if you want to take out a second mortgage on your home to complete some remodeling, you can learn how much your payments would be if you borrow $20,000 for 30 years at a 9% interest rate.

From the Activities menu, choose Financial Planners and then choose Loan. Quicken displays the Loan Planner window.

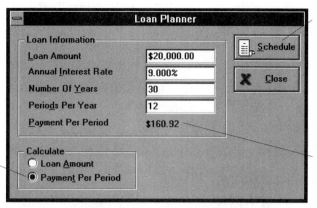

Click to display a payment schedule.

Quicken calculates the payment and displays $160.92 in the Payment Per Period field.

If you select the Calculate Loan Amount button, Quicken calculates how much you can afford to borrow, given a particular payment amount and interest rate.

For example, if you want to buy a new car and you think you can afford to pay $300 a month on a car payment, you can learn how much the total amount (not including a down payment) will be if you borrow for 5 years at a 10.125% interest rate.

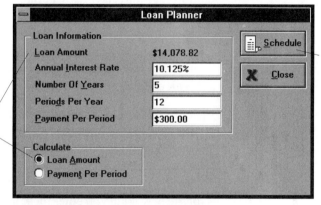

You can see how much of your payment is interest and how much is principal by clicking Schedule to display the payment schedule.

Scroll in this window to see more of the schedule, or press PgUp or PgDn to move up or down one screen.

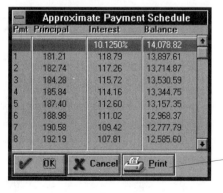

Click this button to print the complete payment schedule.

How many more loan payments?

If you prepay the principal on a loan, you may wonder how long it will take to pay off the loan. Follow the next steps to to find out how many years are left.

- On the Approximate Payment Schedule, scan down the Interest column until you find the interest amount that most closely matches the interest due on your next payment.

- Notice the number of that payment.

- Subtract that payment number from the number of the last payment to get the number of payments left.

- Divide by twelve (Periods Per Year) to get the number of years remaining.

Calculating the cost of refinancing a loan

From the Activities menu, choose Financial Planners and then choose Refinance.

Quicken's refinance planner helps you determine whether it makes sense to refinance your current mortgage. Although the new mortgage may have a lower interest rate, you also need to look at the cost of the new loan—the points charged by the lender, as well as other closing costs—and how long you plan to stay in the house. If you plan to stay only one more year, the lower interest rate may not offset the cost of getting the new loan. (In other words, you won't break even on your investment.)

For example, suppose you are currently paying $1,750 each month, and you want to apply for a new mortgage with an 8% interest rate. The lender is charging 1.75 points (1.75%), and your loan broker has estimated closing costs of $3,000. You plan to stay in the house at least two more years. To find out when you would recoup the costs of the new loan, you enter these figures into the refinance calculator.

Quicken compares your current mortgage with the new mortgage and tells you how long it will take to break even—that is, recoup your costs.

Enter your total payment here, including any impound or escrow amount.

Click Print to print the contents of this window.

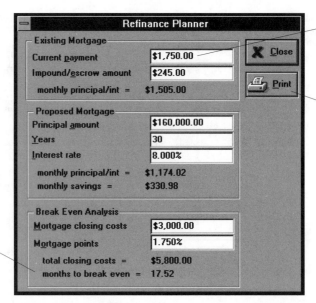

Quicken calculates that it would take you 17.52 months to break even. Because you plan to be in the house for at least 24 months, the refinancing looks like a good deal.

Planning your investment savings

From the Activities menu, choose Financial Planners and then choose Savings. Quicken displays the Investment Savings Planner window.

If you select Opening Savings Balance, Quicken calculates how much money you need to begin with to reach a financial goal.

If you select Regular Contribution, Quicken calculates how much you need to contribute to your savings to reach your goal (the number you enter in the Ending Savings Balance field).

If you select Ending Savings Balance, Quicken calculates the future value of your savings, given a certain period of time, a consistent level of contributions, and an expected inflation rate.

Click to display a deposit schedule.

Quicken calculates the contributions on a weekly, monthly, quarterly, or yearly basis.

When Quicken calculates your investment's future value (the Ending Savings Balance), it also shows what that amount is worth in today's dollars. Because of the effects of inflation, ten dollars buys more today than ten dollars will buy thirty years from now.

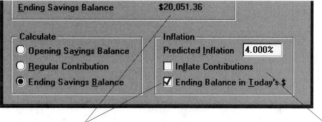

For example, if you currently have $10,000 saved and you contribute $1,000 to your account each year (with a 7% yield), your investment grows to $27,441.66 in eight years. However, if you estimate that inflation will average 4%, that amount will buy only $20,051.36 worth of goods (in today's terms).

The rate of inflation affects what each of your contributions is really worth. To counteract the effects of inflation on your contributions, you may want to increase your contributions to the investment account by the same rate of inflation. Click Inflate Contributions.

After clicking Inflate Contributions, click Schedule to see how the contributions are adjusted. To keep up with a projected 4% inflation rate, you must increase your $1,000 contribution every year to $1,315.93 by the end of eight years.

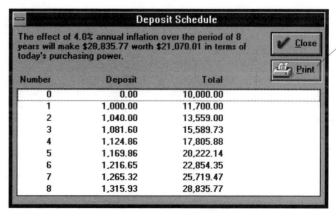

Click this button to print the complete deposit schedule.

Planning for college expenses

From the Activities menu, choose Financial Planners and then choose College. Quicken displays the College Planner window.

If you select Annual College Costs, Quicken calculates the level of tuition you can afford given your present savings and the number of years until your child goes to college.

If you select Current College Savings, Quicken calculates what you need to have put away already today given a certain tuition, annual yield on your investment, and the number of years until your child attends.

If you select Annual Contribution, Quicken calculates how much you need to save each year to pay college expenses when your child is ready to attend.

For example, suppose your child is four years away from attending college. You have $12,000 already saved and figure that, in the next four years, you can contribute a total of $20,000 more to the college fund. Enter these numbers into the College Planner and Quicken calculates that you can afford an annual tuition of over $13,000 in today's dollars.

The Deposit Schedule shows the deposits you need to make while your child is in high school and in college.

All of Quicken's calculations are conservative: this Deposit Schedule assumes that each deposit is not made until the end of the year, and that each tuition payment is made at the beginning of the year.

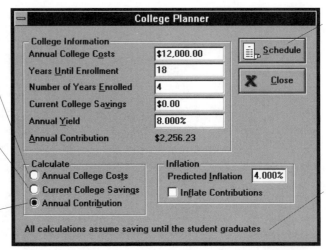

Click to display a deposit schedule.

Note that Quicken expects you to continue saving while the student is attending college.

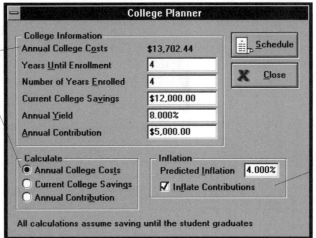

Quicken can inflate contributions in the College Planner the same way it does in the Investments Savings Planner. See "Planning your investment savings" on page 285.

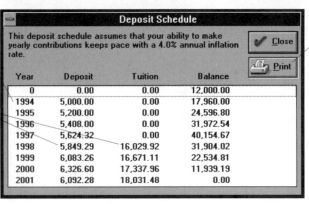

Click this button to print the complete deposit schedule.

Saving for retirement

From the Activities menu, choose Financial Planners and then choose Retirement. Quicken displays the Retirement Planner window. The Retirement Planner lets you look at one retirement account at a time to project how much income that account will provide in your retirement.

You need to provide tax information for Quicken to perform its calculations.

If this retirement account is tax-sheltered (for example, an IRA or Keogh account), click Tax-Sheltered Investment. Quicken presets the Retirement Tax Rate at 15%.

If it is not tax-sheltered, click Non-Sheltered Investment. Quicken presets the Retirement Tax Rate at 15% and the Current Tax Rate at 28%.

If you select Current Savings, Quicken calculates the amount you need to start with to meet your projected retirement-income goals.

If you select Annual Contribution, Quicken calculates how much you need to contribute to your retirement account each year to meet your goals.

If you select Annual Retirement Income, Quicken calculates how much a particular investment will be worth given your estimated tax rate and all contributions.

For example, suppose you are 38 years old and plan to retire at age 65. Your IRA account currently has $20,000 in it and you plan to contribute $2,000 to it annually until you retire. You've inherited genes for long life, so you plan to withdraw from the account until age 85.

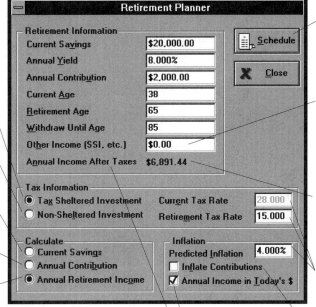

Click to display a deposit schedule.

Enter the annual (not monthly) amount of other retirement income you expect to receive.

Quicken shows the after-tax income in today's dollars.

You can change these preset percentages.

Quicken can inflate contributions in the Retirement Planner the same way it does in the Savings Planner. See "Planning your investment savings" on page 285.

Clear this bottom checkbox to show the income in future dollars.

When Quicken calculates your pre-tax income, it shows the amount in future dollars. Because of the effect of inflation, each dollar you receive in the future is worth less (has less buying power) than a dollar you receive today. Consider this when you are planning retirement income. What sounds like a huge sum of money may be reduced to a moderate sum when you account for inflation.

This approximate schedule shows how your contributions grow and how much income you can withdraw given your estimated life span.

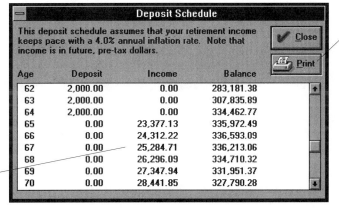

Click this button to print the complete deposit schedule.

Budgeting your income and expenses

You can use Quicken to budget all of your income and expenses or just a few of them. To *budget* means to plan your income and expenses and then later to compare your actual income and expenses against your plan.

A Quicken file contains the budget for only the current year, even if you have more than one year's worth of data in the same file.

This chapter also tells you how you can set up savings goals to put money aside for specific purposes, such as a vacation, even though the money stays in your checking accounts.

Setting up a budget

When you set up a budget in a Quicken file, you set monthly budget amounts for some or all of the categories and subcategories you use. (You can also set budget amounts for transfers.) Budget amounts for each category can be the same for each month. Or, if you know your income and expenses for a category will change, you may want to enter different budget amounts for different months in the year. For example, if you pay property taxes twice a year, you can budget the amount only in the two months in which you make payments. You can enter and change monthly budget values at any time.

◆ **Set up home or business income and expense categories.**
(See "Setting up categories and subcategories" on page 9.)

◆ **Categorize transactions.**
(See "Assigning categories to transactions" on page 22.)

◆ **Set up budget amounts.**
You can enter data into a blank budget (see below) or you can have Quicken create a budget automatically using actual data from your accounts and then edit the budget amounts (page 292).

◆ **Create budget reports or graphs.**
(See "Monthly budget" on page 211, and "Budget" on page 233. To create reports, see "Creating a report" on page 236. To create graphs, see "Understanding budget variance" on page 260.)

Entering amounts in a blank budget

1 **From the Activities menu, choose Set Up Budgets.**

Depending on the number of categories you use, you probably need to scroll to see the entire list. But you can hide unbudgeted categories to shorten the list (see the next page).

Your income categories appear at the top of the list of categories. Your expense categories appear below (not shown here).

Category Name	Jan	Feb	Mar	Apr	May	Totals
INFLOWS						
Bonus	0	0	0	0	0	0
Div Income	0	0	0	0	0	0
Gift Received	0	0	0	0	0	0
Int Inc	0	0	0	0	0	0
Invest Inc	0	0	0	0	0	0
Other Inc	0	0	0	0	0	0
Salary	0	0	0	0	0	0
_DivInc	0	0	0	0	0	0
_IntInc	0	0	0	0	0	0
Total Inflows	0	0	0	0	0	0
Total Outflows	0	0	0	0	0	0
Difference	0	0	0	0	0	0

The total budgeted amounts for all categories each month are in the Total rows at the bottom of the window.

The total budgeted amounts for each category are in the Totals column on the right side of the window.

2 **Use the Budget button bar near the top of the Set Up Budgets window to change the budget display to your liking and to edit budget amounts.**

For example, do you want to budget by month, by quarter, or simply for the entire year? Do you want to break down your budget by subcategory?

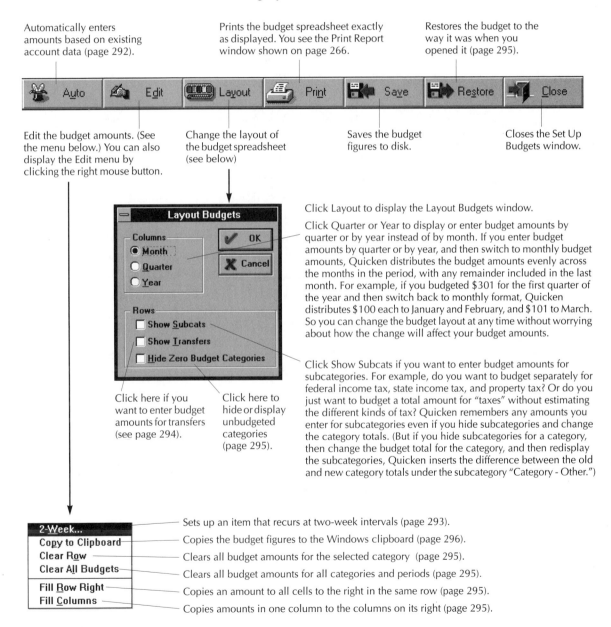

Automatically enters amounts based on existing account data (page 292).

Prints the budget spreadsheet exactly as displayed. You see the Print Report window shown on page 266.

Restores the budget to the way it was when you opened it (page 295).

Edit the budget amounts. (See the menu below.) You can also display the Edit menu by clicking the right mouse button.

Change the layout of the budget spreadsheet (see below)

Saves the budget figures to disk.

Closes the Set Up Budgets window.

Click Layout to display the Layout Budgets window.

Click Quarter or Year to display or enter budget amounts by quarter or by year instead of by month. If you enter budget amounts by quarter or by year, and then switch to monthly budget amounts, Quicken distributes the budget amounts evenly across the months in the period, with any remainder included in the last month. For example, if you budgeted $301 for the first quarter of the year and then switch back to monthly format, Quicken distributes $100 each to January and February, and $101 to March. So you can change the budget layout at any time without worrying about how the change will affect your budget amounts.

Click Show Subcats if you want to enter budget amounts for subcategories. For example, do you want to budget separately for federal income tax, state income tax, and property tax? Or do you just want to budget a total amount for "taxes" without estimating the different kinds of tax? Quicken remembers any amounts you enter for subcategories even if you hide subcategories and change the category totals. (But if you hide subcategories for a category, then change the budget total for the category, and then redisplay the subcategories, Quicken inserts the difference between the old and new category totals under the subcategory "Category - Other.")

Click here if you want to enter budget amounts for transfers (see page 294).

Click here to hide or display unbudgeted categories (page 295).

Sets up an item that recurs at two-week intervals (page 293).

Copies the budget figures to the Windows clipboard (page 296).

Clears all budget amounts for the selected category (page 295).

Clears all budget amounts for all categories and periods (page 295).

Copies an amount to all cells to the right in the same row (page 295).

Copies amounts in one column to the columns on its right (page 295).

3   **To change the amount budgeted for a category, select the amount and enter the new amount.**

For information about shortcuts for setting up budgets, see "Editing budget amounts" on page 295.

Use these keys to enter or edit budget amounts.

Key	Action
Home	Move cursor to the beginning of the current cell
End	Move cursor to the end of the current cell
Enter	Move down one category (same period)
Shift+Tab, Left Arrow	Move left one column in the same category
Tab, Right Arrow	Move right one column in the same category
Ctrl+Left Arrow	Move left by page within the budget data
Ctrl+Right Arrow	Move right by page within the budget data
Home+Home	Move left to the first column in the same category
End+End	Move right to the last column in the same category
Up Arrow	Move up one category in the same column
Down Arrow	Move down one category in the same column
Ctrl+Home	Move up to the first category in the same column
Ctrl+End	Move down to the last category in the same column
PgUp	Move up by page within the budget data
PgDn	Move down by page within the budget data

4   **When you have finished entering budget amounts, click Save in the Budget button bar to save your changes, and then click Close.**

Windows tip
Double-click the Control-menu box to close the window.

(Or just click Close. Quicken prompts you to save before closing the Set Up Budgets window.)

After you've estimated your income and expenses, you're ready to create budget reports or graphs to compare what you've actually earned and spent with your budget. See "Creating budget reports and graphs" on page 296.

Using data from your accounts to set up a budget

You might want to set up a budget more quickly than you can by entering all the figures into a blank budget. You can do this by having Quicken automatically enter actual income, expense, and transfer amounts into the budget. Quicken uses data that you've already entered into your account registers. You can extract these amounts from any time period in the current Quicken file and then copy the amounts to the current year's budget. You can also select which categories you want to copy amounts for if you want to fill in only some of the categories in your Set Up Budgets window.

> **Caution:**
> If you use data from your accounts to set up a budget, Quicken will overwrite any budget amounts you have already entered for the selected categories.

1   **Click Auto in the Budget button bar.**

2   **Enter information in the AutoCreate Budget window.**

(Optional) Change the date range. The preset dates include all transactions from the previous calendar year.

(Optional) Change the value for rounding dollar amounts. You can round off values to the nearest $10 or $100 instead of $1.

Click one of the lower two buttons to show Quicken how to copy the amounts:

Click Use Monthly Detail to have Quicken copy the actual income, expense, and transfer amounts from any number of months up to 12 to the same months in the budget. If you are budgeting by quarter or year, Quicken copies the actual monthly amounts to their corresponding periods. For example, Quicken copies actual data for January, February, and March to Q1 of a quarterly budget.

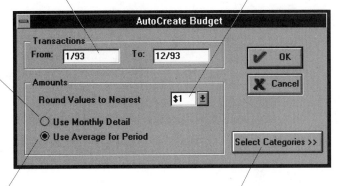

Click Use Average for Period to have Quicken compute monthly averages for income, expense, and transfer amounts based on the months you specified in the date range. If you are budgeting by month, Quicken enters the average amount in every month. If you are budgeting by quarter (or year), Quicken enters three (or 12) times the monthly average in every period.

(Optional) Click here if you want to enter budget amounts for only some categories. Select the categories in the drop-down list. If you don't select categories, Quicken copies amounts for all categories.

3   **Click OK to copy data from your accounts into the budget for the categories you selected .**

Quicken overwrites any budget amounts you entered with data from your accounts. However, you can restore the budget to the way it was when you first opened the Set Up Budgets window by clicking Restore in the Budget button bar.

Setting up an item that recurs at two-week intervals

You may have a special category or transfer item that you enter into Quicken every two weeks. For example, you might record the deposit of your paycheck in a bank account every other week. Quicken can budget your salary income at the correct two-week intervals.

1   **Select an amount in the appropriate category row (of any month) for the item that recurs at two-week intervals.**

2   **Click Edit in the Budget button bar and choose 2-Week.**

Make sure the correct income or expense category is displayed. If not, click Cancel and go back to step 1.

Enter the amount you receive or spend every two weeks.

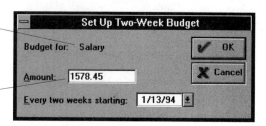

3   **Enter the amount you want to budget in two-week intervals for the selected category.**

4   **Enter the starting date for the first two-week interval.**

If you are setting up Salary as a two-week budget category for the rest of the year, enter the date of your next payday. If you want to budget at two-week intervals for the entire year, enter the date of the first payday in January.

5   **Click OK.**

Quicken fills in budget amounts calculated at two-week intervals from the starting date to the end of the year in the same row.

Setting up budget amounts for transfers

The Set Up Budgets window can include the names of all your accounts under both INFLOWS and OUTFLOWS, in case you want to budget transfer amounts as well as income and expense categories. For example, you might want to budget for items such as mortgage payments and transfers to 401(k) and IRA accounts.

To turn on the display of transfers, click Layout on the Budget button bar and then select Show Transfers. (To turn off the display of transfers, clear Show Transfers.)

You don't have to budget transfer amounts, but budgeting transfers can give you a more complete picture of your cash flow. For example, if you want to budget a monthly transfer of $200 from checking to savings, you should enter 200 for INFLOWS from [Checking] and the same amount for OUTFLOWS to [Savings].

Enter or edit transfer amounts in the Set Up Budgets window just as you would budget income and expense amounts.

Editing budget amounts

Use the commands on the Budget button bar to enter or change the amounts that you see in the Set Up Budgets window.

- If you've hidden zero-budget categories, redisplay them to budget amounts for them (clear Hide Zero Budget Categories).

- To copy the amount from the current cell to all cells to the right in the same category, select the amount you want to copy, click Edit, and choose Fill Row Right.

To display the Edit menu, either click Edit on the button bar or click the right mouse button anywhere.

- To copy each of the amounts in the current column to all the columns to the right, place the insertion point in the column to be copied, click Edit, and choose Fill Columns. For example, you can copy all amounts for January to the rest of the months of the year when you click Fill Columns. If your insertion point is in the March column when you click this button, the amounts in January and February will not be affected.

- To erase all amounts for the currently selected category, click Edit, and choose Clear Row.

- To erase all amounts for all categories, and start with a blank budget, click Edit, and choose Clear All Budgets.

- To restore the budget to the way it was when you first opened the budget, click Restore.

Reviewing budget amounts

Quicken provides two ways to help you review amounts in the Set Up Budgets window more easily.

QuickScroll. Use the scroll bar to move through the window. When you drag the scroll box in the scroll bar, you'll see a box in which the names of categories appear and disappear as you scroll. When you see the category name you want in the box, release the scroll bar. The category row will appear at the top of the window.

QuickScroll displays categories in your budget as you drag the scroll box.

Category Name	Jan	Feb	Mar	Apr	May	Totals
Books, Music	32	32	32	32	32	384
Charity	57	57	57	57	57	684
Childcare	200	200	200	200	200	2400
Clothing	354	354	354	354		1148
Computer	36	36	36	36		32
Dining	240	240	240	240	240	2880
Entertainment	42	42	42	42	42	504
Gifts	0	100	50	50	50	1006
Groceries	288	288	288	288	288	3456
Home Rpair	200	0	0	200	0	743
Total Inflows	12947	12947	12947	12947	12947	155364
Total Outflows	10580	10480	10430	10630	10430	126309
Difference	2367	2467	2517	2317	2517	29055

Hide. Click Layout on the Budget button bar and select Hide Zero Budget Categories to condense the budget display by hiding unbudgeted (zero amount) categories.

Quicken hides only unbudgeted categories that have no subcategories. If you turn on the display of subcategories, transfers, or both, Quicken doesn't hide them, even if they are unbudgeted. To turn off the display of subcategories and transfers, click Layout on the Budget button bar and clear Show Subcats and Show Transfers.

Copying budget figures to another program

Once you have set up your budget, you can very easily copy the amounts into another Windows program such as Microsoft Excel for Windows or Lotus 1-2-3 for Windows. Click the Edit button and choose Copy to Clipboard. The data is copied in a tab-delimited format compatible with many spreadsheet programs. Switch to the other program and use the program's Paste function to copy the data in. (The procedure is the same as copying report data to another program, as described on page 253.)

Creating budget reports and graphs

To use budget reports and graphs, you must first categorize your transactions (see "Assigning categories to transactions" on page 22), set up budget amounts for the categories that you wish to track (see "Setting up a budget" on page 290), and enter transactions with those categories.

You can print the budget spreadsheet by clicking Print on the Budget button bar.

You can also print a budget report or graph that compares the amounts you entered in the budget with the actual amounts you've spent or received.

Quicken has two types of budget reports.

Budget report (Custom)	Monthly budget report (Home)
Is a variation of the basic summary report	Is a variation of the basic budget report
Compares the money you spend and receive in a specific date range with your budget amounts for each category and transfer account	Compares the money you spend and receive in a specific date range with your budget amounts for each category and transfer account
Calculates the difference between the actual and budgeted amounts for each category and transfer account	Calculates the difference between the actual and budgeted amounts by month
Does not subtotal by month	Subtotals by month
Includes all accounts	Includes only bank, cash, and credit card accounts
Organized by income and expense	Organized by cash flow

A monthly budget report is illustrated on page 211. A budget report is illustrated on page 233. See also Chapter 15, *Creating and customizing reports*, beginning on page 235.

Quicken also uses the budget data you enter to create a budget variance graph. For more information about budget variance, see "Understanding budget variance" on page 260.

Setting up savings goals

Quicken offers budgeting of a different kind through its savings goal accounts.

As you survey the balance of your bank account, you may like to mentally set aside a portion of it for something you need to save for—your vacation, for example, or a new car, or even a house down payment. Although the money is in your bank account, you want to mark it as unavailable for other spending purposes. And if you spend some money on your specific savings goal, you want to know how much you still have set aside in your account to spend on that goal.

You can track this money you are putting aside in a special type of asset account called a savings goal account. When you put the money aside (mentally), you transfer it into this account. When you spend the money, you transfer it out of the account. The account's balance tells you how much you still have left available for this specific goal.

The important property of a savings goal account is that it does not represent a real account and there is no real money in it! It's just a way of keeping tab, with a specific purpose in mind, on money that is sitting in other accounts.

You can display the balances of your checking accounts with or without the money you've set aside.

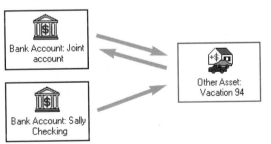

The savings goal account is like an imaginary account. The money you "transfer" into and out of it does not really leave the other bank accounts.

Setting up a savings goal account

See also:
"Setting up additional Quicken accounts" on page 2.

1 **From the Activities menu, choose Create New Account.**

2 **In the Select Account Type window, select Asset Account and click OK.**

3 Enter a name for the savings goal account and an opening balance of zero.

4 Select the Savings Goal Account checkbox.

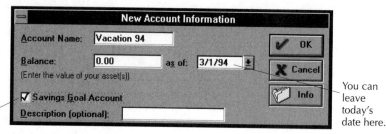

Make sure this checkbox is selected.

You can leave today's date here.

5 Click OK to set up the account.

Setting money aside

Decide how much you can afford to put aside, and then "transfer" it out of your checking account to the savings goal account.

This example shows $2,000 being put aside for a vacation in Egypt.

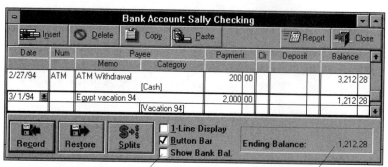

Transferring money to a savings goal account does not affect your overall net worth (as shown in a net worth report).

This extra checkbox appears when the account contains a transfer to a savings goal account.

When the Show Bank Bal checkbox is clear, the Ending Balance shows how much money is left available in the checking account for spending.

Notice that the checking account Register window now includes an extra checkbox called Show Bank Bal.

With the Show Bank Bal checkbox clear (as shown above), Quicken displays the account balance including transfers to any savings goal accounts. *The Ending Balance is then not the true balance of your checking account* (because the money has not really left the checking account). Instead, it shows you how much money is available in the account once you have put aside money for your savings goal. To stay on target for your savings goals, you shouldn't let this balance fall below zero.

Click the Show Bank Bal checkbox. The Ending Balance changes. When the Show Bank Bal checkbox is selected (as shown next),

Quicken hides the transfer to the savings goal account, and displays the true Ending Balance for the checking account.

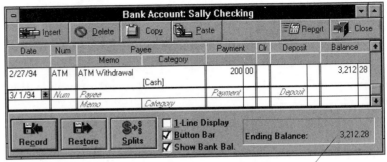

When the Show Bank Bal checkbox is selected, any transfers to the savings goal account are not displayed. (They are not "real" transactions.)

When the Show Bank Bal checkbox is selected, the Ending Balance shows the account's true balance.

Spending money for your savings goal

When you spend money from your checking account toward your savings goal, you need to do two things: transfer the money back from your savings goal account into the checking account, and then record the payment transaction in your checking account.

For example, let's say you buy tickets for $820 for your vacation.

First, transfer the money to be spent back to your checking account.

(Note that you can transfer money from more than one account into the savings goal account, as shown here.)

Date	Ref	Payee / Memo	Category	Decrease	Clr	Increase	Balance
3/1/94		Egypt vacation 94	[Sally Checking]			2,000 00	2,000 00
3/5/94		Egypt vacation 94	[Joint account]			600 00	2,600 00
3/15/94		Retrieve money for tickets	[Sally Checking]	820 00			1,780 00

Other Asset: Vacation 94 — Ending Balance: 1,780.00

The Ending Balance in your savings goal account shows you how much money you still have put aside for this goal.

Second, record the expense transaction in your checking account as you normally would.

The net result of these two transactions (here dated 3/15/94) is to decrease the balance of your savings goal account by $820, and to decrease the *true* balance of your checking account by $820 (click Show Bank Bal to see the true balance).

Date	Num	Payee / Memo	Category	Payment	Clr	Deposit	Balance
3/1/94		Egypt vacation 94	[Vacation 94]	2,000 00			1,212 28
3/15/94		Retrieve money for tickets	[Vacation 94]			820 00	2,032 28
3/15/94		King Tut Travel / 2 tickets	Vacation	820 00			1,212 28

Bank Account: Sally Checking — Ending Balance: 1,212.28

When your savings goal account has served its purpose (for example, you've been on vacation), simply delete the account. Quicken removes all the transfer transactions from your checking account(s), and the checking account Ending Balance figure once again shows the true balance.

Do not record payments in a savings goal account
Quicken does not let you spend directly from your savings goal account. As the previous example illustrates, you must transfer the money back to a regular bank account first, and then spend it from the bank account.

Reporting on your savings goals

If you just want to check how much you have saved toward your goal, look at the Ending Balance of your savings goal account. You can see the balance in the Account list.

If you keep several savings goal accounts, you can run a net worth report to show how much you've saved toward each goal.

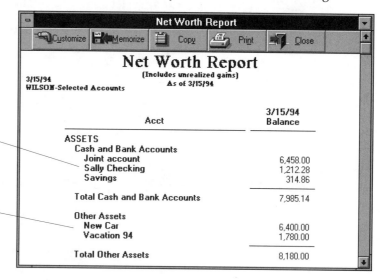

In reports, the balances of your checking accounts do not include the money you've set aside (transferred to the savings goal accounts).

The money you've set aside for savings goals is shown separately under the asset accounts.

Projecting the future

A key feature in Quicken's planning system is the financial planning graph. Quicken can forecast how your account balances will look for months, or even years, to come.

You can use this feature in a number of ways, depending on what you want the graph to show you. Be sure to read this entire chapter to get the most out of the planning graph.

Projecting your account balances

You've kept your Quicken registers up to date with your past transactions. You're using the Financial Calendar to keep track of upcoming bills and receipts. With this information, you're now ready for the "big picture," the illuminating view of how your financial future is shaping up. (This is not for the faint of heart...)

The financial planning graph projects forward the balances of your accounts on the basis of two sources of information:

- Your income and spending behavior up to today (Quicken gets this information from your registers, or from your budget spreadsheet, or from estimates you enter manually)

- Any additional transactions you have scheduled on your Financial Calendar; recurring transactions are projected forward for the range of the graph

For example, Quicken can display what your checking account is likely to do for the rest of the month, as shown here. Or you can display the combined balances of several accounts.

On the Financial Calendar for this month, you've marked income and expenses coming up. (For information on how to use the Financial Calendar, see Chapter 8, *Scheduling with the Quicken Financial Calendar,* beginning on page 93

The bars on the graph show your account balance for each day of the month ahead.

You can match up rises and falls in the graph with transactions you've entered on the Financial Calendar.

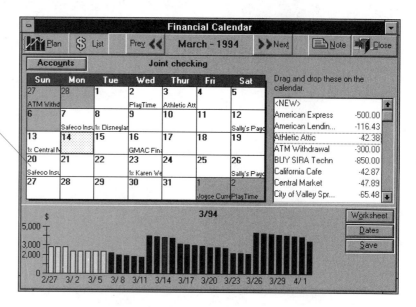

Quicken can also show your account projections beyond the current month, up to two years ahead. With the ability to look forward, you can:

- See when you'll be able to afford the new jacuzzi, motorbike, or skiing trip.

- Look for danger zones when your accounts might fall below zero.

- Plan your spending and map out your savings more clearly.

You can also experiment with Quicken's projections to do "what-if" planning. For example, you can alter the rent amount and see what happens to your account balance over the next six months, to find out what level of rent you can afford.

Displaying the financial planning graph

Quicken's projections will be as accurate as *you* make them. The graph can include average income and expense amounts to cover all the transactions not scheduled on your Financial Calendar. This chapter shows you how to build the greatest accuracy into your financial planning graph.

1 Choose Financial Calendar from the Activities menu.

Or click the Calendar icon on Quicken's iconbar.

2 Click Plan at the upper left of the Financial Calendar button bar.

Quicken changes the Financial Calendar display to include a financial planning graph below the Financial Calendar. The graph shows you the balance of the selected accounts for the currently displayed month. You can display previous or future months by clicking Prev or Next on the Financial Calendar button bar, or you can change the range of the graph by clicking Dates.

Click List to make more room for the scheduling days.

Select which accounts you want to project.

Financial Calendar

| | Plan | $ List | Prev ◀◀ | March - 1994 | ▶▶ Next | 📄 Note | Close |

Accounts   Sally checking\Joint checking

Sun	Mon	Tue	Wed	Thur	Fri	Sat
27 ATM Withdrawal	28	1 Joyce Currell	2 PlayTime	3 Athletic Attic	4	5
6	7 Safeco Insurance	8 1x Disneyland	9	10	11	12 Sally's Paycheck
13 1x Central Motors	14	15	16 GMAC Financing	17	18	19
20 Safeco Insurance	21	22	23 1x Karen Weiss	24	25	26 Sally's Paycheck
27	28	29	30	31	1 Joyce Currell	2 PlayTime

3/94

Worksheet
Dates
Save

$2,992.61

$ 5,000 — 3,000 — 2,000 — 0 —   2/27   3/2   3/5   3/8   3/11   3/14   3/17   3/20   3/23   3/26   3/29   4/1

The graph shows a projection of the state of your accounts for the selected month.

Balances before today are shown in yellow (lighter).

Projected future balances are shown in blue (darker).

The green bar indicates which day is selected on the Financial Calendar.

Click the right mouse button to see the exact balance.

Click Dates to change the period covered by the graph, for example to show the next six months.

Typically, a planning graph will show a gradual rise or decline in the balance, due to your underlying financial trend, disturbed by sharp jumps and falls resulting from your scheduled transactions.

For example, the sharp jumps on the graph shown here represent the regular deposit of Sally's paycheck, which has been set up as a recurring scheduled transaction. The gradual underlying decline is caused by the ongoing living expenses.

When you first display a planning graph, you may not see a gradual rise or decline like that in our example. Your graph may rise unrealistically, because you have not yet set Quicken up to account for your underlying income and expenses. Before doing that, though, as described on page 307, read through the next important section on selecting accounts to display.

Selecting accounts for your graph

It's important to realize at this point that the financial planning graph does not necessarily show the balance from just one account, though you can set it up that way if you wish. Which accounts you decide to include in the planning graph depends on how you use your accounts and what you want the planning graph to show you.

Broadly speaking, you can use the financial planning graph in two different ways:

- To forecast individual account balances, such as your checking account so you know when to transfer money in to cover your check payments

- To forecast cash flow, so you can see how much money is readily available, and can make investment decisions such as when to buy a new car or when to invest a sum in mutual funds

For the second option, you may want the graph to show you the aggregate of all your cash flow accounts—your bank accounts, cash account, and credit card accounts combined. This is how the graph is initially set up, as it gives you a more meaningful picture of the state of your finances than to depict just one account.

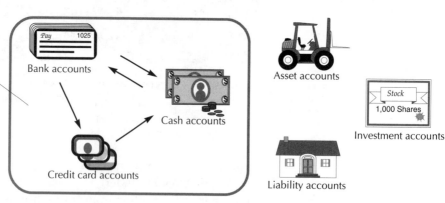

Your cash flow accounts are where you track your income and spending. Because you often transfer money between these accounts, you probably want to include all, or most, of these accounts in your planning graph.

Bank accounts

Cash accounts

Credit card accounts

Asset accounts

Stock
1,000 Shares

Investment accounts

Liability accounts

In general, you should use the graph to project your *income and spending* trends. Most people use more than one checking account for spending. When you visit the supermarket, you may pay with your credit card or by writing a check. So it makes sense to include both your credit card account and your checking account in the projection, to give an overall picture of your cash flow. In this way, for example, a transfer from your checking account to your VISA account, to pay off your VISA bill, does not show up as a dip in the planning graph.

You may want to exclude certain savings accounts. If your savings accounts are fairly stable, because you do not use them for spending or income deposits, you probably do not want their balances to swamp the variations in the graph. On the other hand, if what you want to use the graph for is to track your available funds (for example, you deposit your paycheck into a savings account), you probably do want to include your savings accounts.

Read through the following illustrations to help you decide what you want to get out of Quicken's projections, and then select your accounts accordingly.

Single checking account: David C. Miller has a checking account and a credit card. However, he is slowly paying off a large loan on his credit card, so doesn't use it for regular spending. He needs to keep a close watch on his checking account to make sure he doesn't bounce any checks. He selects only his checking account for Quicken's planning graph, so that Quicken shows him a running account balance, and he can see when he might be able to transfer money to his credit card account.

Projecting a single account shows you a running account balance, and warns you when you might be going into the red.

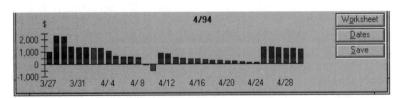

Cash flow: Peggy Smith likes to put money into mutual funds when she has enough left over from her month to month spending. She needs to know the total worth of her spending accounts, so that she can plan for investing in funds. She selects her bank accounts, her credit card accounts, and her cash account. The planning graph shows her that by next month she will have enough to put $5,000 into a mutual fund.

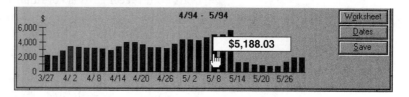

Projecting all your spending accounts helps you time your investments better.

When Peggy schedules the transfer to the fund, the graph falls by $5,000 because the mutual fund account is not included in her projection setup.

Total available funds: John and Mary are hoping they'll have enough for a down payment on a house by the end of the year. They estimate they'll need $20,000. What interests them is the value of their available funds. For their projection, they select all their Quicken accounts, including their savings account and their CD. However, they exclude Mary's 401(k) asset account, as they don't want to disturb that. The planning graph shows a gradual improvement in their funds, and reveals they'll be able to start looking for a house by the fall.

Projecting all your available funds helps you make big investment decisions, such as buying a house, a car, or taking a vacation.

For a long-term picture, select a one-year or two-year view.

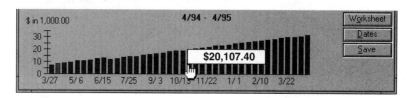

1   **To change the accounts that are included in your projection, click Accounts above the Financial Calendar.**

2   **Mark the accounts to include and click OK.**

To mark or unmark an account, double-click it, or select it and then click Mark or press the spacebar.

Note that you are selecting accounts for both the financial planning graph and the Financial Calendar.

You cannot select investment accounts.
The financial planning graph is designed to help you manage your spending. It does not take into account the market value of your investments in stocks, mutual funds or other investments, and you can not select Quicken investment accounts to include in the financial planning graph. If you want to see how your net worth changes over time, including the value of your investments, create a net worth graph as described on page 261.

Estimating your average income and expenses

The financial planning graph includes transactions you have scheduled on your Financial Calendar, but these alone are not enough to give an accurate projection for the months ahead. You also need to give Quicken an estimate of all the other income and expenses not scheduled on the Financial Calendar, such as your grocery bills, car fuel, and trips to the movies. You do this in the financial planning *worksheet*.

To set up the planning graph quickly, you can group these miscellaneous amounts into just two figures, an Other Monthly Income and an Other Monthly Expense. Later, you may decide to break the figures down by category, to get a more detailed analysis of your financial projections, as described on page 309. But the graph works well with just the two Other figures, so begin by entering these as described next.

Before you enter figures in the worksheet, be sure you have selected the right accounts for your planning graph, as described in the previous section, starting on page 304.

---

1   **With the financial planning graph displayed, click Worksheet (to the right of the graph).**

Quicken displays the Financial Planning Worksheet window. This window shows you all the figures that go into the planning graph.

Your Other amounts are initially 0. You need to enter realistic figures.

These are the transactions you scheduled on your Financial Calendar.

As you enter monthly figures, Quicken calculates the yearly equivalents and the totals.

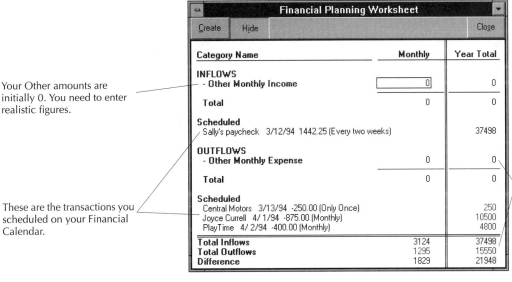

The table shows your income (INFLOWS) and your expenses (OUTFLOWS). For each, you can see listed the transactions you have scheduled on your Financial Calendar. Above each of these is an Other amount, which is initially 0. You can now enter figures for your other monthly income and other monthly expenses, which are your best estimates for all your income and expenses not scheduled on the Financial Calendar.

For example, Other Monthly Income might be any bonuses or investment income. (If your bonuses are paid twice a year, you may prefer to schedule them on your Financial Calendar instead.) If you have not scheduled your salary deposit as a recurring transaction on your Financial Calendar, you would include this amount too. In the example shown, Sally's paycheck is already scheduled, so the Other figure would not include this.

The same is true of monthly rent and insurance payments. If you scheduled these on your Financial Calendar as recurring transactions, do not include them in the Other Monthly Expense figure.

2   **Enter an Other Monthly Income figure and an Other Monthly Expense figure.**

Press Up Arrow and Down Arrow to move between the fields, or click in a field.

3   **Click Close.**

4   **Click Yes to confirm that you want to save your changes.**

Now the planning graph reflects your worksheet figures and should give a more accurate projection of your account balances. You can modify the figures in the worksheet as often as you like. See "Modifying your worksheet" on page 311.

Caution:
The figures you enter in the worksheet must be realistic for the account or accounts you have selected for the planning graph. You can not simply select different accounts without modifying the worksheet figures to match.

Entering more detail in your worksheet

If you like, you can break down the figures in your worksheet category by category to help you estimate your monthly income and expenses and give a more accurate projection in the graph. (New users: we recommend that you instead enter just the two Other figures, as described in the previous section.)

You can enter category estimates manually if you wish. But, if you have been using Quicken for some months already, use AutoCreate to read figures from either your registers or your budget spreadsheet. This is not only faster but probably a more accurate way of setting up. You can manually adjust any figures that AutoCreate reads in (for example, to allow for amounts that are already included as scheduled transactions, as described later).

AutoCreating figures for your worksheet

1   **With the Financial Planning Worksheet window displayed, click Create (at the left side of the window's button bar).**

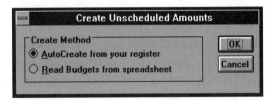

Quicken can read in data from either your historical register transactions or your budget spreadsheet, if you have set one up. Quicken reads in a category by category breakdown of your income and expenses, and uses this as your projection data. You can modify the figures at any time later.

2   **Choose the register or the budget option and click OK.**

If you choose the budget option, Quicken reads data in from your budget spreadsheet and displays it in the worksheet. Skip to step 5.

3   **If you choose the register option, enter the date range of the register transactions from which Quicken should take the figures.**

Enter dates that cover what you think is a good, representative period in your Quicken accounts. The longer the period, the more accurate will be your figures. Six months is a good timeframe for most people.

(Quicken looks at all the registers for the selected accounts.)

- (Optional) Change the rounding value.

- (Optional) Click Select Categories if you want to omit certain categories from your worksheet. By default, Quicken uses any categories it finds in the register, and we recommend that you leave it this way the first time through.

4   **Click OK.**

Quicken analyzes all the transactions in your registers for the date range you specified. It sorts the figures by category (much as an Itemized Categories report does) and reads the results into your worksheet.

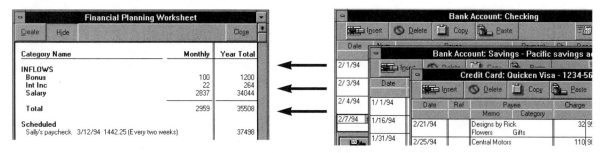

5   **Now a corrective step. If any category amounts include amounts listed under Scheduled, edit the category figures to exclude these scheduled amounts.**

Your worksheet may contain some duplicate amounts. These will be recurring amounts such as your paycheck and rent that you scheduled on your Financial Calendar. Because they are on your Financial Calendar, they are listed under "Scheduled." But because they appear in your register or in your budget, they are probably also now listed under their respective categories. The corrective step is to deduct those amounts from the categories section, so that the amounts for your categories are all *other* income and expenses, those not scheduled on your Financial Calendar.

An example of a completed projection summary is shown on page 311.

6   **Click Close and then click Yes at the confirmation message to save your worksheet figures and return to the planning graph.**

Continue reading at "Modifying your worksheet" on page 311.

Entering worksheet figures by hand

1   **With the Financial Planning Worksheet window displayed, click Hide on the button bar.**

The worksheet now displays all your income and expense categories.

2   **Enter a figure for each category.**

Remember to exclude from the category estimates any amounts already scheduled on the Financial Calendar as recurring transactions, as listed under Scheduled.

3   **When you have entered all the figures you need to enter, click Hide again to hide any categories with zero amounts.**

4   **Click Close and save your changes.**

Modifying your worksheet

Now you have reasonable data in your worksheet. Your worksheet might look something like this one. If you entered just two Other figures instead of breaking down the figures by category, your worksheet will be much simpler.

The financial planning worksheet shows all the amounts, some scheduled on your Financial Calendar and the rest estimated, that go into the planning graph.

Note: the figures you enter in the worksheet affect *only* the planning graph. They have no effect whatsoever on your Financial Calendar, your registers, or your budget spreadsheet.

Click Create to read in data from your registers or budget.

Click Hide to display zero amounts (to add amounts for hidden categories).

Click Close to close the summary window.

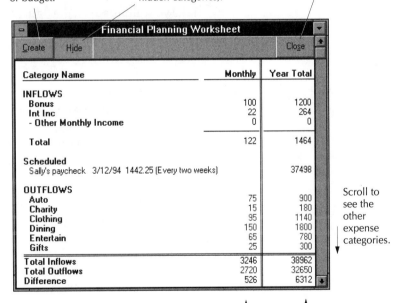

Scroll to see the other expense categories.

This column shows average monthly amounts, (including averages for scheduled amounts).

This column shows total amounts on a yearly basis.

You can change any figures in this summary at any time (apart from the scheduled ones), and see the result immediately in the planning graph by clicking Close (and then Click Yes to confirm that you want to save your changes). You cannot change scheduled amounts here—change those on the Financial Calendar.

Remember two rules when making changes:

- If you schedule a recurring transaction on your Financial Calendar, remember to display the worksheet and subtract the same amount from the appropriate category or Other figure. This amount is now scheduled, and must not appear in both places. For example, if you have set up your paycheck deposit as a recurring transaction on the Financial Calendar, Salary under INFLOWS should be set to 0.

  (Note that if you schedule a *one-time* transaction on your Financial Calendar, Quicken's financial planning graph includes this amount *in addition to* the monthly unscheduled amount you entered in your worksheet.)

- The Other fields are "remainder" jars, where you can add amounts that don't fit in any of the other categories. Whenever you add an amount for a category that was previously zero, remember to subtract the amount from the "Other" field to compensate.

Quicken's financial planning graph is a feature to experiment with. Take your time, adjust the figures in the summary, and click Close to see the results in the graph. You can't do any harm, so play with this feature until you feel comfortable with your setup.

Saving a projection

After a month or two, you may want to compare what has *actually* happened to your account balances with what you *thought* was going to happen. Quicken lets you save a financial planning graph's projection so that you can look back at it later and see how accurate it was.

Or you may save different projections to compare, so that you can do "what-if" analysis. For example, how would your accounts look if you bought that new car?

When you have finished setting up your planning worksheet, so that you believe the graph shows your best guess at the future, save the projection as follows.

1   **With the graph displayed, Click Save.**

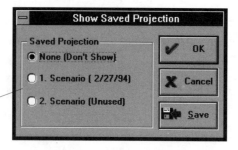

You can save two different projections, as Scenario 1 or Scenario 2.

Use this window to save a projection or to retrieve a previously saved projection.

2   **Select one of the Scenario buttons.**

3   **Click Save, and then click OK.**

Quicken saves the projection as either scenario 1 or scenario 2. Now notice the additional line on the graph—this is your saved projection.

To get rid of the line from your graph, click Save, and then select None and click OK.

Let's say you now wait a month and want to see how close to reality your saved projection was. To retrieve your saved projection:

1   **Click Save.**

2   **Select the scenario button where you saved your projection and click OK.**

Quicken superimposes your previously saved projection over the actual history of your account balances.

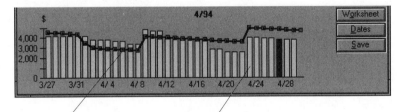

The line of dots shows your previously saved projection

The bars show what actually happened to your account balances, or your latest projection of what you think will happen.

You can overwrite a saved projection with an updated one by saving the new projection to a scenario button that's already used.

23

Tracking loans and mortgages

Use Quicken to keep a close watch on your loans, such as your house mortgage or your car payments.

Quicken automatically tracks the amortization of a loan, showing you how much interest you are paying (for tax purposes), how much of the principal you have left to pay off, and how long your payment schedule has left to run.

Quicken can handle many different aspects of a loan, including variable interest rates, balloon payments, and negative amortization. You can also use Quicken to calculate and track payments you receive for a loan.

Tracking loan amortization

Amortization is the gradual reduction of a loan by periodically paying off the principal as well as the interest. Although your total payment each time is the same, the split between principal and interest is always changing.

For example, if you make a steady payment of $1,000 each month, you will pay a little less interest with each payment:

Payment	Principal	Interest
1	$671.21	$328.79
2	$675.69	$324.31
3	$680.19	$319.81
4	$684.72	$315.28
5	$689.29	$310.71
6	$693.88	$306.12
7	$698.51	$301.49
etc.	etc.	etc.

Eventually, the interest part of the payments falls towards zero, and your loan is paid off.

For each of your loans, Quicken calculates a schedule of payments like the one above, including the principal/interest split. If the interest rate changes, or you prepay part of the principal, or you refinance your mortgage, Quicken immediately recalculates the schedule.

With your loan set up, Quicken automates the entry of payment transactions. You can set up your loan payments as a memorized transaction or as a scheduled transaction (or as a CheckFree fixed payment if you use CheckFree). When you enter a loan payment in your checking account register, Quicken fills in the principal and interest automatically, and updates your payment schedule.

Setting up a loan

When you set up a loan in Quicken, Quicken creates a liability or asset account (depending on whether you are borrowing or lending) to track the principal remaining on the loan.

Upgraders: Quicken sets up an account for you.
If you used Quicken's amortization feature in a previous version of Quicken but did not use an account for tracking the principal, you may have noticed that Quicken sets up the account for you. This happened when you first started Quicken after installing Version 3 for Windows. Quicken entered the correct opening balance and current balance according to the amortized state of your loan. The loan is already in your loan list.

The examples in this manual show a straightforward house mortgage being set up. For your own setup, you might want to browse through the section "Handling different types of loans" on page 322 first for details of particular types of loan setup.

1 From the Activities menu, choose Set Up Loans.

You see the View Loans window. This is your main information window for all your loans. It is described in detail later in this chapter (on page 321).

2 Click the New button in the upper left corner of the window to set up a new loan.

Click New. ———————————

3 Fill in the loan account information and click OK.

If this is a loan you have taken out, click Borrow Money.

If this is a loan you have made to someone else, click Lend Money.

Enter a new account name or select an existing account. Quicken will use this account to track the principal remaining on the loan. The account name also becomes the loan name in your loan list.

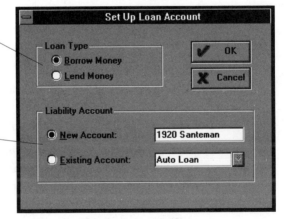

Note: These figures show a sample loan setup to help you see what to enter.

Using an existing principal account:

If you have been manually tracking a loan in Quicken (that is, you've been entering payments for the loan by copying the principal and interest amounts from your loan statement into the split transaction of the payment, and tracking the principal in a liability or asset account), you can use your existing principal account in the loan setup. Quicken will use the ending balance of your principal account as the current loan balance on which it bases its amortization calculations. Be sure that, in your principal account register, the ending balance and the date of the last transaction correctly reflect your most recent payment.

---

4   **Enter information in the Set Up Loan window and click OK.**

This example shows a 15-year mortgage for $100,000 that was taken out on 6/5/89. The current balance (on 6/4/94) is $77,412.67.

If you make monthly payments, enter 12 here.

Enter today's balance (the amount of principal remaining). If you are setting up a brand-new loan, leave the Current Balance blank.

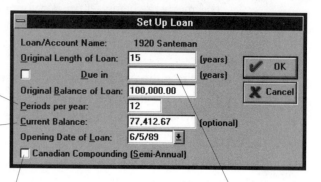

For more information on what to enter in each box, press F1.

🍁 **Canadian users:** Make sure Canadian Compounding is selected, so that Quicken calculates interest on the basis of semi-annual compounding as used in Canada.

If your loan includes a balloon payment, click the Due in checkbox and enter the total number of years in which the loan must be paid off (that is, counting from the beginning of the loan). See page 324 for more advice.

There are two common scenarios for setting up a loan:

- You are describing a brand-new bank loan. In this case, enter the loan amount in the Original Balance box, and leave the Current Balance blank. Quicken inserts today's date as the opening date of the loan, but you can change it if necessary.

- You are describing an existing bank loan, but are setting it up in Quicken as of today. (You do not want to enter all previous loan payments into Quicken.) Enter the Original Balance of the loan and the Opening Date on which you first took out the loan. Also enter the amount of principal remaining today in the Current Balance box.

If you are describing an existing bank loan and want to keep a complete record of all previous payments, you must complete this loan setup procedure, and then enter all previous payments in your checking account. However, we do not recommend such a detailed setup, as Quicken's payment schedule works perfectly well without historic data.

Quicken displays the Set Up Loan Payment window. In this window, you enter details of the loan payments you make (or collect).

For more information on what to enter in each box, press F1.

Enter today's interest rate.

Quicken uses the interest rate to calculate the regular payment amount (principal plus interest).

To include impound items such as insurance and property tax in your regular payments, click Split.

Type: select Chk if you want to write checks with Quicken for the loan payments, or Pmt if you don't. Select Epmt if you use CheckFree to make payments. If you collect payments, the Type is set to Deposit.

If you select Chk, you can enter the payee's address by clicking the Address button (far right).

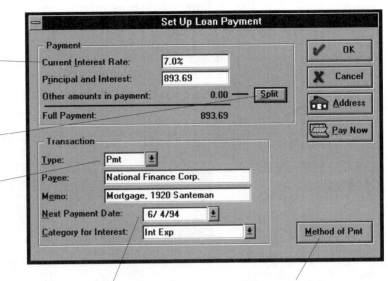

Enter the date when you must next make a payment.

Quicken sets up the payment as a memorized transaction unless you specify otherwise.

5   **Enter the payment details.**

If your loan has an adjustable (variable) interest rate, enter the current rate. You can change the rate in Quicken whenever your interest rate changes (as described on page 322).

Using the interest rate and the information you entered in the Set Up Loan window, Quicken calculates how much your regular payments should be (principal plus interest). You can change the actual payment amount each time you enter a payment in your register (page 326). You can change the regular payment amount in this window, but, if you do, Quicken recalculates the length of the loan. (Adjusting it a few cents up or down should make no difference to the length of the loan.)

6   **(Optional) To include impounded fees such as homeowner's insurance and property tax in your regular payments, click Split and enter the details of the impound items. Then click OK to return to the Set Up Loan Payment window.**

Anything you enter in the Splits window will be included in the transaction written into your register.

For more information about split transactions such as this one, see "Splitting transactions" on page 28.

	Splits		
🔲 Insert	⊘ Delete	🗑 Clear All	
Category	Memo	Amount	
01 Insurance	Impound account	55 00	
02 Tax:Prop	Impound account	96 00	
03			

7 **Enter transaction information in the Set Up Loan Payment window.**

These are the transaction details that Quicken will write into your register.

8 **(Optional) Click Method of Pmt to specify the method by which Quicken should enter the payment transaction in your register.**

Unless you change the setting, Quicken sets up the payment as a memorized transaction.

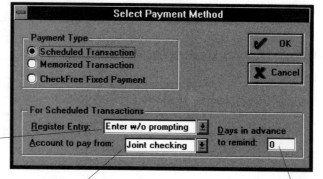

Scheduled transactions only:

Quicken can enter the transaction in your register with or without asking you to confirm first. (See page 97 for more details.)

Select the account into which the transaction should be entered.

Quicken can record the payments in your register ahead of time if you want. (Otherwise, enter 0 here.)

See also:
"Scheduling transactions," beginning on page 95.

- If you specify Scheduled Transaction, Quicken will automatically enter the payment transaction in your register (or in the Write Checks window if you entered Chk as the transaction Type). It knows when to do this from the Next Payment Date and the Periods Per Year that you've already entered. This is a great time-saver, especially if you make your loan payments through automatic drafting set up at your bank.

  Fill in the lower part of the window too for a scheduled transaction.

See also:
Chapter 7, *Memorizing special transactions,* beginning on page 85.

- If you specify Memorized Transaction, you can manually recall the transaction and enter it in your register (or in the Write Checks window) whenever you make the payment.

See also:
"Amortizing a fixed payment" on page 120.

- If you use CheckFree to make your payments, you can set up the payment transaction as a fixed (recurring) payment. To do this, click CheckFree Fixed Payment and select a payee from the drop-down Fixed Payee list that appears.

9 **Click OK to return to the Set Up Loan Payment window.**

10 **(Optional) Click Pay Now if you want to enter the first payment in your register now.**

After you specify the account to enter the payment transaction in, Quicken opens the register with the transaction selected. Click in the View Loans window to see your loan payment schedule.

11 **From the Set Up Loan Payment window, click OK to return to the View Loans window.**

Your loan is set up and your View Loans window should now look something like this one.

This example shows a loan named "1920 Santeman.")

You can display the payment details of any of your loans by selecting the loan from the drop-down list.

The upper payment window shows the payments already made on this loan. (Quicken gets this information from the transactions in your principal account.)

The lower payment window shows the payments to be made next.

Click Show Running Totals to see the accumulated principal and interest payments.

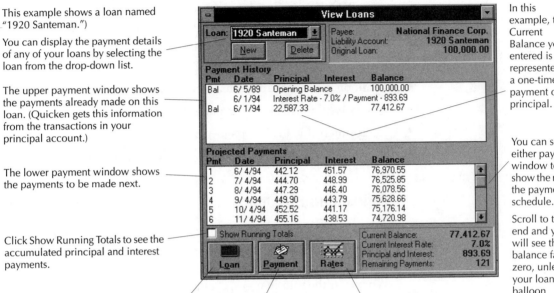

In this example, the Current Balance you entered is represented by a one-time payment of principal.

You can scroll either payment window to show the rest of the payment schedule.

Scroll to the end and you will see the balance fall to zero, unless your loan is a balloon payment type.

To change the loan details at any time, click Loan.

To change the regular payment details, click Payment.

To change the interest rate, click Rates.

Each time you make a loan payment (or deposit) in your checking account register, Quicken updates the past and future payment schedules shown in the two payment windows.

You can also change the details of any of your loans at any time from this window. However, if you want to work out "what if" scenarios with your loan, you may find it quicker to use the Loan Planner instead, as described on page 283. Also, Quicken's Refinance Planner will come in useful if you're considering refinancing a loan—see page 284.

Handling different types of loans

Quicken can handle many different types of loans. For example, you can use Quicken to track adjustable-rate loans or loans with balloon payments. In this section, you'll find guidelines for setting up several different types of loans. Refer to these guidelines as you follow the procedure under "Setting up a loan" (starting on page 316). If your loan involves several different features (for example, an adjustable-rate loan with negative amortization), follow all of the guidelines that apply.

- "Adjustable-rate loans" on page 322
- "Balloon payments and nonamortized loans" on page 324
- "Negative amortization" on page 324
- "Zero-interest loans" on page 325
- "Loans for which you receive payments" on page 325

Adjustable-rate loans

An adjustable-rate loan has a variable interest rate. When the rate changes, the scheduled payment amount also changes. When you set up your loan in Quicken, enter the current interest rate. Whenever the rate changes, change the rate in Quicken. You can do this in either of two ways. If the rate change is effective today, before your next payment date enter a new Current Interest Rate in the Set Up Loan Payment window. You can access this window:

- From the View Loans window by clicking Payment
- From the Memorized Transaction list if you set up the payment as a memorized transaction (select the payment transaction and click Edit)
- From the Scheduled Transaction list if you set up the payment as a scheduled transaction (select the payment transaction and click Edit).

Alternatively, you can program a rate change in Quicken on some other date as follows.

1   **From the Activities menu, choose Set Up Loans.**

2   **In the View Loans window, click Rates.**
    Quicken displays a history of loan rate changes.

3   **In the Loan Rate Changes window, click New.**

4   **Enter the new interest rate and the effective date, and click OK.**

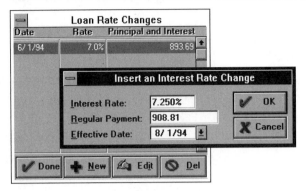

The Loan Rate Changes window lists the history of your interest rates as they change up or down.

5   **Click Done in the Loan Rate Changes window.**

When you change the interest rate, Quicken uses the new rate to calculate the new regular payment amount. Quicken keeps the length of the loan constant.

However, if you increase the Regular Payment amount, Quicken reduces the length of the loan accordingly. If you decrease the Regular Payment amount, Quicken does not change the length of the loan but adds the extra remaining principal to the last payment.

Quicken indicates the interest rate change in the Payment History section of the View Loans window, and adjusts the principal and interest amounts in the projected payment schedule to match.

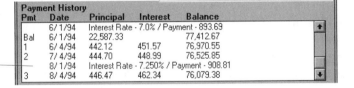

You can see when the interest rate changed.

Through the Loan Rate Changes window, you can also enter an interest rate change effective on some future date; Quicken then recalculates the projected payments shown in the View Loans window. If you like, you can enter several future rate changes to create "what-if" scenarios. By entering your best guesses at how interest rates may change through the years to come, you can estimate your future payments.

Balloon payments and nonamortized loans

In a loan with a balloon payment, the principal is not fully repaid when the regular payments stop, so the balance of the loan (the "balloon payment") is due at the end of the payment period. In this case, the loan is amortized over a longer period than the period of payments. For example, if you have a "30 due in 7" loan, your payment is amortized over 30 years. But at the end of seven years, you must either pay off the balance or refinance the loan.

You can define this type of loan in Quicken when setting up the loan. In the Set Up Loan window, click the Due in checkbox and enter the period of regular payments in years.

Enter the period over which the loan is amortized.

Enter the period over which loan payments will be made.

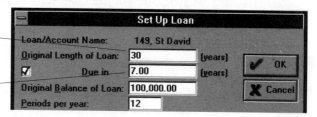

In some balloon payment loans, each payment covers only the accrued interest (no principal), and the original loan amount is due at the end of the repayment period. For such a nonamortized, or "interest-only" loan, do not use Quicken's loan tracking feature. Instead, create a regular memorized transaction for the payment and categorize the entire payment amount as interest. See "Memorizing and recalling transactions" on page 87 to create a regular memorized transaction.

Negative amortization

Negative amortization happens when your payment is less than the interest on the loan. Not only is no principal paid off, but the unpaid part of the interest is added to the loan balance, increasing the principal. Often, this is an agreed and temporary arrangement, usually for the first part of the loan only.

While setting up the loan in Quicken, enter the length of the loan (the period over which you are making payments) as the Original Length of Loan in the Set Up Loan window. In the Set Up Loan Payment window, after entering the interest rate, modify the Principal and Interest amount to be the amount you are actually paying. If this is not enough to cover the interest on the loan, the payment schedule will initially show you that you owe more at the end of the payment period than the original amount of the loan.

If you know when your repayment amount is due to rise, you can enter this change through the Loan Rate Change window. From the View Loans window, click Rates and then click New to enter a new Regular Payment amount and effective date. The payment schedule now shows a reduced, or zero, ending balance on your loan.

(You can also adjust the repayment amount on a one-time basis in the Confirm Principal and Interest window when entering a payment in your register, as described in step 3 on page 326).

Zero-interest loans

If you have a zero-interest loan, you do not incur any interest expenses. Your entire payment (excluding other charges such as impound payments) is principal.

In Quicken, enter an interest rate of zero while setting up the loan. In the View Loans window, click Payment and clear the Category for Interest box, so that zero amounts don't show up on reports.

Loans for which you receive payments

If you hold a loan note and receive payments on a loan, you can set up your loan for amortization in Quicken. Quicken creates a memorized loan deposit (instead of a payment) and uses an asset account (instead of a liability account) as the principal account for tracking how much the borrower still owes you.

In this window:	And in this box:	Enter this:
Set Up Loan Account	Loan Type	Lend Money
Set Up Loan Payment	Type	Dep
	Payee	Name of the borrower
	Category for interest	Name of an income category

Making a loan payment

If you set up your loan payment as a memorized transaction, you can now recall it to record a payment in your checking account register. If you set up the loan payment as a scheduled transaction or as a CheckFree fixed payment, the entry is made automatically; for a scheduled transaction, if you specified Prompt Before Entering you will see a prompt for the total payment amount when you first start Quicken.

When you enter the payment, Quicken updates the loan balance in the View Loans window.

Recalling a memorized loan payment

1   **Open the register or the Write Checks window for the bank account from which you will make the loan payment.**

2   **Start typing the Payee name. When QuickFill completes the full name, press Tab to recall the memorized payment.**

(If QuickFill is turned off, click the drop-down payee list and select the memorized loan payment. Or choose Memorized Transaction from the Lists menu, select the memorized loan payment, and click Use.)

Quicken asks you to confirm the principal and interest amounts, and gives you a chance to modify them.

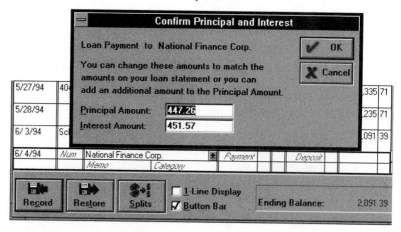

Any impound items (such as escrow and insurance fees) that you set up will be recorded in addition to the principal and interest amounts shown.

3   **Change either figure if necessary and click OK.**

If you change the amount of principal or interest, you are changing the figure for this one payment only. (To change the amount for all future payments, edit the transaction in the Memorized Transaction list or in the Set Up Loan Payment window, as described on page 322.)

- If you increase the amount of principal, you are making an additional payment of principal. Quicken recalculates the payment schedule in the View Loans window accordingly, which may shorten the term of the loan.

- If you decrease the amount of principal, you are not fully paying what is due on the loan. Quicken keeps the length of the loan fixed, which means you may have an extra balance to pay off at the end of the repayment period.

4   **Click Record.**

If you open the split for this transaction, you will notice that Quicken has included any impound items you set up.

The first line of the split is a transfer of the principal amount to the liability (or asset) account that tracks the principal.

The second line is your interest payment.

Below the second line are any impound items you set up.

	Category	Memo	Amount	
01	[1920 Santeman]	Mortgage, 1920 Santeman	447 26	
02	Int Exp		451 57	
03	Insurance	Impound account	55 00	
04	Tax:Prop	Impound account	96 00	
05				
06				

Splits window: Insert, Delete, Clear All

Each time you record an amortized loan payment, Quicken updates the payment schedule in the View Loans window to show you the new state of your balance. The transfer to the liability (or asset) account on line 1 of the split reduces the remaining balance on your loan and keeps your net worth up to date in reports and graphs.

Additional prepayments of principal

By making prepayments, you pay off the loan balance sooner and pay less in interest than if you pay only the scheduled payment amount.

- To include an additional prepayment of principal with your regular payment, adjust the principal amount in the Confirm Principal and Interest window, as described in step 3 on page 326.

- To make a separate prepayment of principal, do not recall the memorized payment transaction. Instead, enter a separate payment (or deposit) transaction in your checking account register. In the category field, enter a transfer to the liability (or asset) account that tracks the principal:

Date	Num	Payee / Memo	Category	Payment	Clr	Deposit	Balance	
6/ 5/94	5057	Western Financiers		1,000 00		*Deposit*		
		Prepayment	[149, St David]					

Enter the name of the principal account in the Category field.

When you make an additional prepayment of principal, Quicken recalculates the payment schedule, and the term of the loan may be shortened. You can see the new schedule in the View Loans window.

Undoing a mistaken loan payment

If you accidentally record an extra loan payment in your register, simply delete it from the register. Quicken automatically removes the payment from the View Loans window. Similarly, if you edit the principal or interest amounts in the split, Quicken reflects your changes in the View Loans window.

Reporting on your year-to-date loan interest

For tax purposes, you may want to know how much interest you've paid on the loan since the beginning of the year. You can run any one of several reports to find this information. For example, create an itemized category report.

1   **Click the Reports icon on the iconbar.**

2   **Confirm that the date range is from January 1 through today.**

3   **Select the Itemized Categories report in the Home report family and click OK to create the report.**

    The report contains the interest figures under EXPENSES-Interest Expense, but you can narrow down the report further first.

4   **Click the Customize button and then click Accounts.**

    Or double-click the header line in the report that tells you which accounts are selected—this is a shortcut to select which accounts to include.

5   **Select only the account from which you make loan payments.**

6   **Click Categories/Classes and select only the Int Exp category.**

    If you used some other category for your loan interest payments, for example Mort Int, select that category instead.

7   **Click OK to create the report again.**

The total for Interest Expense shows you how much interest you have paid so far this year.

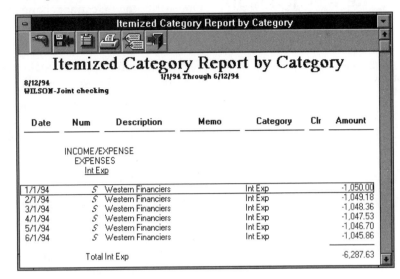

Forecasting interest payments for the entire year

You can look ahead to forecast how much interest you will pay for the entire year by clicking Show Running Totals in the View Loans window.

For example, at the start of the year, you had paid a total of $3,915.17 in interest.

By the end of the year, you will have paid a total of $15,580.95 in interest.

Total interest for the year is $15,580.95
                               –$ 3,915.17
                               =$11,665.78

Click Show Running Totals to show the cumulative principal and interest.

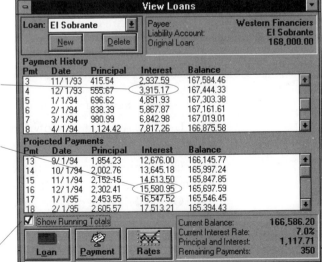

Changing the details of a loan

See the instructions for filling in the loan windows under "Setting up a loan," beginning on page 316.

You can edit any of the loan setup information at any time. To change the interest rate, see "Adjustable-rate loans" on page 322. One attribute you cannot change through the View Loans window is the name of the principal account; see "Editing account information" on page 5 to change the name of an account.

- To change loan setup information, display the View Loans window and click Loan, Payment, or Rate/Amt.

- To change payment information, you can also select the payment transaction in the Memorized Transaction list or the Scheduled Transaction list and click Edit.

Deleting a loan

Delete a loan from the View Loans window when you have finished paying off the loan. When you delete the loan, Quicken removes it from the loan list in the View Loans window, the Memorized Transaction list (and any transaction groups that contain it), Scheduled Transaction list, or Electronic Payee list.

1   **In the View Loans window, select the loan and click Delete.**

2   **Click OK to confirm the deletion.**

However, Quicken does not delete the loan's principal account, as you may want to keep the account for your records. If you want to delete the account, see "Deleting an account" on page 6.

Refinancing a loan

See "Setting up a loan," beginning on page 316, for a complete description.

If you refinance a loan that you've been tracking in Quicken, follow this procedure to set up the new loan and "pay off" the old loan. (To help you determine whether you should refinance, see "Calculating the cost of refinancing a loan" on page 284.)

1   **Set up your new loan.**

- Set Up Loan Account window: Create a new liability account with a name that's different from the one for the old loan.

- Set Up Loan window: Enter the total term of the new loan in the Original Length of Loan box. Enter the amount of the new loan in the Original Balance of Loan box.

2   **Adjust the balance of the liability account for the old loan to zero.**

Open the liability account. Choose Update Balances from the Activities menu, and choose Update Cash Balance. Enter an amount of 0.

3   **(Optional) In the View Loans window, delete the old loan from the drop-down loan list.**

See "Deleting a loan" on page 330.

Managing your data files

This chapter describes how to set up and use additional Quicken files. You'll also learn how to rename and delete files.

If needed, you can copy files, copy data between files and accounts, and set up passwords to protect your data from unauthorized access.

Setting up additional files

Your Quicken accounts are grouped in one or more Quicken files. A Quicken account is **not** the same as a Quicken file. Each file is separate and distinct, unrelated to any other Quicken file. Reports show data from only one file at a time. Accounts in the same file, on the other hand, are related to each other and do share some data.

Each Quicken file can contain up to 255 related accounts, although most people will have no more than about ten accounts. All the accounts in a single file share the same categories, classes, and memorized transactions. Reports can show data from all or selected accounts in a file. And you can transfer amounts from one account to another within the same file. *Most people need only one Quicken file.* For most people, this file is QDATA, the one Quicken automatically creates during installation.

You may want to have more than one file for either of the following reasons:

- To keep your home finances separate from your business finances for tax reasons

- To keep a separate file for each year's accounts

1   **From the File menu, choose New.**

If you want to set up a new account within your existing Quicken file instead, click New Account and click OK. See "Setting up additional Quicken accounts" on page 2.

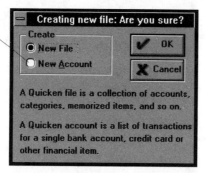

2   **Click OK if you are sure you want to create a new file.**

Enter a DOS filename (up to eight characters) for your new Quicken file right before the .QDT extension. If you delete the .QDT extension, Quicken replaces it again.

Quicken will create the file on this drive and in this directory. If you want the file to be created elsewhere...

...double-click the directory you want in this list (you can double-click c:\ to see other directories on the C: drive)...

...or first select the drive you want from this drop-down list.

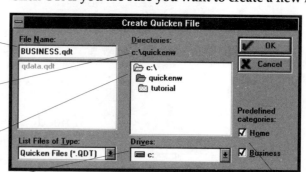

Quicken is set to give you predefined home and business categories. Clear the Home and/or Business checkboxes if you are sure you don't want to use these predefined categories.

3 **Enter a name for your new Quicken file.**

Don't enter a different extension or delete the .QDT extension that Quicken automatically creates.

4 **Select the drive and directory for your new Quicken file from the Drives and Directories lists.**

5 **(Optional) Clear the predefined Home or Business categories checkbox.**

Quicken provides predefined home and business categories so you can identify transactions by income or expense type (for example, salary income or mortgage expense). By using categories, you can also produce meaningful reports with your Quicken data.

Selecting predefined categories now does not limit you in any way, as you can always add, edit, or delete categories later. However, if you do not want to use predefined categories with your file, clear the checkbox for either or both category types.

6 **Click OK.**

Quicken creates a new file with the name and location you specified and opens the Select Account Type window.

Set up accounts within this file as described in "Setting up additional Quicken accounts" on page 2.

Choosing a file

When you start Quicken, it opens the last file you used in the previous session. To work in another file, open it.

Or press Ctrl+O

1 **From the File menu, choose Open.**

Enter the name of the Quicken file you want to open. Don't delete or type over the .QDT extension.

Or, select the file from this list to automatically enter its name in the File Name box.

If the file you want to open is not in this directory or drive...

...double-click the directory you want in this list (you can double-click c:\ to see other directories on the C: drive) or first select the drive you want from this drop-down list.

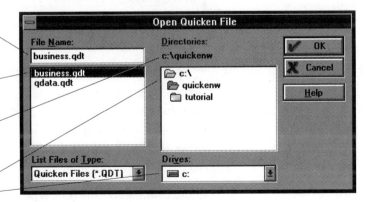

2 **Select the file you want to open.**

All Quicken data files have the .QDT extension after the filename.

Windows tip
You can double-click the
filename in the file list instead
of selecting it and clicking OK.

3   **Click OK.**

4   **Enter a password if you have assigned one to this file.**

5   **Click OK.**

Quicken closes all the open account windows of the current file
before it opens the new file.

Assigning a password to your file.
You can assign a file password to your Quicken file to prevent unauthorized access. For more information, see "Requiring a password to open
a file" on page 344.

Creating icons for additional files

If you use more than one Quicken file (for example, one file for your
personal accounts and one file for your business accounts), you can
set up a Windows icon for each file you have. When you double-
click the icon to open it, Quicken takes you directly to that file. If you
set up icons for each of your files, you won't need to use the File
Open command to move between your files.

1   **From Windows, click the Quicken 3 for Windows icon to select it.**

2   **From the File menu in the Program Manager window, choose
     Properties.**

This is the current name of the
Quicken icon.

This is the command line Windows
uses to start Quicken.

The working directory is where
Quicken will look first for its data
files.

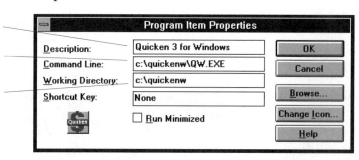

3   **In the Description box, enter a name for the first Quicken icon you
     want to create.**

For example, if you enter Personal Accounts, Windows changes the
name of this icon from Quicken 3 for Windows to Personal
Accounts.

4   **In the Command Line box, type a space after the existing text, and
     then enter the name of your Quicken data file with the .QDT exten-
     sion.**

For example, if you named the Quicken file for your personal
accounts PA and stored it in the working directory (in this example,

the QUICKENW directory on the C: drive), type a space after C:\QUICKENW\QW.EXE, and then enter PA.QDT.

This is the new label for one of your Quicken icons.

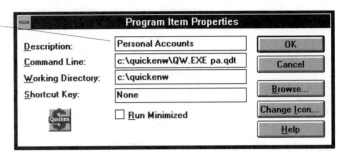

Program Item Properties

Description:	Personal Accounts	OK
Command Line:	c:\quickenw\QW.EXE pa.qdt	Cancel
Working Directory:	c:\quickenw	Browse...
Shortcut Key:	None	Change Icon...
	☐ Run Minimized	Help

5 **In the Working Directory box, enter the drive and directory where your Quicken data file is located.**

6 **Click OK.**

The Quicken 3 for Windows icon is now labeled with the name you entered in the Description box. (In this example, the Quicken icon is now called Personal Accounts.)

7 **To create another Quicken icon that opens a different Quicken file (for example, your business accounts), select the icon you just created.**

Windows tip

Instead of using the Copy command, you can hold down the Shift key and drag the Quicken icon to the group where you want the copy to be located.

8 **From the File menu in the Program Manager window, Choose Copy.**

The Copy Program Item window appears.

9 **Use the drop-down list to select the group where you want the new Quicken icon to be located and click OK.**

Now you have two Quicken icons with the same name in Windows.

10 **Click one of the Quicken icons to select it.**

11 **From the File menu in the Program Manager window, choose Properties.**

12 **In the Description box, enter a name for the new Quicken icon you want to create.**

For example, if you enter Business Accounts, Windows changes the name of this icon to Business Accounts.

13 **In the Command Line box, enter the name of the other Quicken data file with the .QDT extension.**

For example, if you named the Quicken file for your business accounts BA.QDT and stored it in the working directory (in this example, the QUICKENW directory on the C: drive), type a space after C:\QUICKENW\QW.EXE, and then enter BA.QDT.

Change the name of the data file (and, if necessary, the Working Directory).

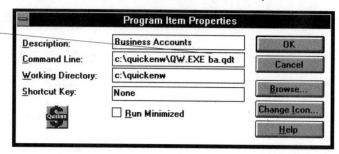

14 **In the Working Directory box, enter the drive and directory where your other Quicken data file is located.**

15 **Click OK.**

(In this example, the Quicken icon is now called Business Accounts.)

Renaming a file

When you first installed Quicken, Quicken named your data file QDATA (for "Quicken data") unless you changed that preset name. If you like, you can change the name of QDATA. For example, if you keep your personal data in QDATA and you set up an additional file named BUSINESS for your business data, you may want to rename QDATA to PERSONAL or another more meaningful name.

When you rename a Quicken data file, you actually change the names of the five DOS files that make up the Quicken file (or six DOS files if you use CheckFree). You must not change the extensions of these DOS files when you rename the Quicken data file, so use Quicken's Rename command (not DOS or Windows commands) to rename files.

---

1 **From the File menu, choose File Operations and then choose Rename.**

Enter the name of the Quicken file you want to rename. You don't need to enter the .QDT extension.

You can select the file from this list to automatically enter its name in the File Name box.

If the file you want to rename is not in this directory or drive...

...double-click the directory you want in this list (you can double-click c:\ to see other directories on the C: drive)...

...or first select the drive you want from this drop-down list.

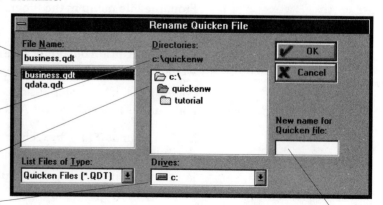

Enter the new name for the file.

2   **Use the files, directories, and drives lists to select the file you want to rename.**

The file to be renamed appears in the File Name box.

3   **In the New Name For Quicken File box, enter the new name for the file.**

Don't enter an extension for the file. Quicken automatically gives the file the extension QDT, even if you enter a different extension.

4   **Click OK.**

Quicken displays the renamed file with its new name in the file list. To see the file list: from the File menu, choose Open.

Deleting a file

Deleting a Quicken file permanently removes all of the records in that file from your disk. Once you've deleted records, there is no way to get your account data back except by using your backup disk. Be certain you want to delete a file before doing so.

1   **From the File menu, choose File Operations and then choose Delete.**

2   **Use the files, directories, and drives lists to select the file you want to delete.**

Windows tip
You can double-click the filename in the file list instead of selecting it and clicking OK.

3   **Click OK.**

Quicken warns you that you are about to permanently remove the accounts in that file.

4   **If you are sure that you want to delete the selected file, type** YES **and click OK.**

To keep the selected file, click Cancel to return to the Quicken window.

Copying part or all of a file

You can copy all or part of a file to create a new file. (Do not confuse copying a file with copying an account. If you want to copy transactions in one account to another account, see "Copying data from one account to another" on page 340. Or, if you want to copy your Quicken data file from one computer to another, see "Moving a Quicken file between computers" on page 347.)

You might want to copy part of a Quicken file for one of the following reasons:

- You want to copy transactions within a certain date range to start a new file for a new fiscal year.

- Your data disk is full.

- You want to copy your scheduled transactions, memorized transactions, transaction groups, and categories to a new file without copying any transactions.

- You want to increase the maximum number of accounts that can be created in the file to 255.

  Quicken does not change the original file in any way.

1   Open the file you want to copy.

2   From the File menu, choose File Operations and then choose Copy.

See "How Copy treats prior uncleared transactions" on page 339 before selecting or clearing this checkbox.

This option appears only if you have investment accounts in your file.

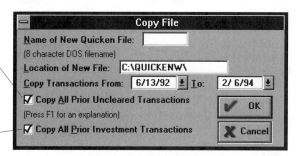

3   Enter a name for the new Quicken file.

4   Enter the directory location for the new file.

5   (Optional) In the Copy Transactions From and To boxes, enter the date range of transactions to be included in the new file.

By default, Quicken copies all transactions in the file by entering the dates of the oldest and newest transactions in the current file as the date range of transactions to be included in the new file. You can change these dates if you want to copy only some transactions.

If you want to create a new file that contains only your scheduled transactions, memorized transactions, transaction groups, and categories (but no transactions), enter dates that are later than the last transaction in the existing file. You must also perform steps 6 and 7.

6   **(Optional) Clear the Copy All Prior Uncleared Transactions checkbox to *exclude* from the new file all transactions that occurred before the date range but haven't yet been cleared or reconciled.**

For more information, see "How Copy treats prior uncleared transactions" below.

7   **(Optional) If your file includes investment accounts, clear the Copy All Prior Investment Transactions checkbox to *exclude* from the new file all investment transactions that occurred before the date range.**

8   **Click OK.**

9   **Choose the file you want to work in now.**

How Copy treats prior uncleared transactions

Prior uncleared transactions are transactions that occurred before the date range but haven't yet been cleared or reconciled (marked with an asterisk or X in the Clr (Cleared) column).

If you include prior uncleared transactions when you copy a file, Quicken transfers the information to the new file as follows:

- For each account in the original file, Quicken summarizes (that is, sums the amounts of) all prior cleared transactions. Quicken then uses this total amount as the opening balance of the corresponding account in the new file.

- Quicken copies all prior uncleared transactions from each account in the original file to the corresponding account in the new file.

When should you copy prior uncleared transactions?

Copy prior uncleared transactions to the new file if you use Quicken to do any of these tasks:

- Reconcile bank or credit card accounts

- Track assets

- Track business payables and receivables

For such tasks, it's important to include uncleared transactions in the new copy of the file, even when those transactions occur before the beginning of the current period. To include these transactions, make sure the Copy All Prior Uncleared Transactions checkbox is selected in the Copy File window.

If your cash, asset, or liability account contains prior cleared transactions, Quicken does not copy these transactions to the account in the new file. Instead, Quicken summarizes the transactions and uses this sum as the opening balance of the account in the new file.

Remember that transfer transactions are special because they may include cases where one side of a transfer has cleared, but not the other. For example, a check to VISA might have appeared on a bank statement, but not on a VISA statement. In this example, if you include prior uncleared transactions when you copy and the check date is prior to the beginning date you specify, Quicken summarizes the bank account side of the transfer and copies the credit card account side. This partial summary is not harmful, but it does cause Quicken to display the message, "Transfer not present" if you use the Go to Transfer (Ctrl+X) command in the VISA account transaction. Also, the TOTAL TRANSFERS line item in a summary report might not be zero.

When should you exclude prior uncleared transactions?

You should exclude prior uncleared transactions from the new file only if you perform none of the tasks listed in the previous section using Quicken. You want the new file to include only transactions in the date range for the current period, regardless of their cleared status. To exclude prior uncleared transactions, clear the Copy All Prior Uncleared Transactions checkbox in the Copy File window.

Copying data from one account to another

There are two ways of copying transactions from one account to another.

To copy transactions one at a time, use the Copy and Paste buttons in the registers:

- Select a transaction
- Click Copy to copy the transaction data to the Windows clipboard
- Go to the second account (which could be in a different file)
- Select an empty transaction

- Click Paste to copy the transaction data in

If you don't select an empty transaction, Quicken replaces the selected transaction with the copied transaction details.

If you want to copy many transactions at once, it's quicker to use the Export and Import commands. Export copies data into a special file called a QIF file (for "Quicken interchange format"). A QIF file is a DOS file. Import copies the data from the QIF file into your account. You can export and import transactions within a date range only; you cannot specify individual transactions.

You might want to copy many transactions for these reasons:

- To merge transactions from two accounts into one account. For example, you may have been using Quicken on two different computers, and now want to combine your data.

- You originally set up an account with the wrong account type. To rectify this, create a new account of the right type, and then copy all the transactions from the old account to the new.

- You want to move an account from one Quicken file to another. To do this, set up a new account in the second file, and then copy all the transactions from the old account to the new.

Copying a range of transactions from one Quicken account to another is a two-step process:

◆ Export the transactions from the source account to a QIF file. See page 342.

◆ Import the QIF file into another account in the same Quicken data file or in a different Quicken data file. See page 343.

Copying your lists

If you copy data from an account to a different file, you can include more than just the account transactions. You can also include any or all of the associated data:

- Category& Transfer list
- Class list
- Memorized Transaction list
- Account list

You can choose which lists to copy over. When you import all this information to a new file, Quicken adds the categories, classes,

To set up a new file with your existing lists, use Export and Import to copy everything *except* the transactions from an existing file. After copying the list information, you can make changes to the lists at any time.

memorized transactions, and account names to the new file's lists. It copies all the transactions from the account you exported to the chosen account in the new file, but it does not copy all the transactions from the other accounts; it copies just the transfers that were made to or from the copied account. For example, if you export data from a Checking account that contains transfers to a Cash account and then import that data into a new file, Quicken creates a Cash account in the new file's account list. This new Cash account is empty except for transfers from Checking.

Exporting transactions from an account to a QIF file

1 **Open the account you want to export data from.**

2 **From the File menu, choose Export.**

Quicken displays the QIF Export window.

3 **In the QIF File to Export box, enter the directory path and name of a DOS file to receive the exported data.**

You can append a filename to the directory path Quicken enters in the box, or you can specify a different path. You don't have to give the file any particular extension, but if you enter the extension .QIF, it will remind you what the file is for. If you want to change the directory location, you can click Browse to choose a new location.

Enter the directory path and name of a file to receive the exported data.

Or click Browse to specify a directory location and filename.

In this example, the filename is JOINTACC.QIF. The file is to be created in the directory C:\QUICKENW.

This is the account you are exporting transactions from.

Select what you want to export. Unless you select the lists, Quicken will export only transactions. When you select the Category list, Quicken also exports the Class list.

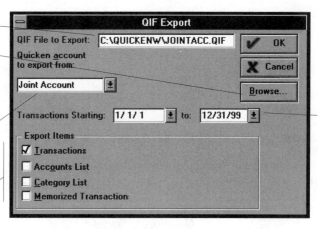

Leave these default dates to export all transactions.

Or enter the starting and ending dates of the transactions to be exported.

4 **Enter the dates of the first and last transactions to be included in the exported text file.**

You can specify only a date range, not specific transactions.

5 **Select the items you want to export.**

You can export transactions, account names, categories (including classes), and memorized transactions.

More information about QIF files is in Help. (Press F1 and then click Contents. Click "Technical Information about Quicken" at the end of the Contents, and then click "Information about Quicken's QIF format.")

6   **Click OK to export the transactions to a text file.**

Now you are ready to import the QIF file you just created into the destination account, as described next.

Importing the transactions from the QIF file to an account

1   **If the account you want to import data into does not yet exist, set up the account.**

See "Setting up additional Quicken accounts" on page 2.

2   **From the File menu, choose Import.**

Quicken displays the QIF Import window.

3   **In the QIF File to Import box, enter the name of the QIF file (including the extension) that contains the exported data.**

Enter the directory path and name of the QIF file you are importing data from.

Or click Browse to specify a directory location and filename.

Select the account you are importing transactions into. Click the underscored down arrow to drop down the list. Click the down arrow to scroll the list. Then click the account you want.

Select what you want to import.

If you want to import from several QIF files into several different accounts, select this checkbox to prevent Quicken from duplicating transfers.

4   **(Optional) From the Quicken Account To Import Into drop-down list, change the account you want to import the data into.**

By default, Quicken selects the current account as the account to import data into, but you can select a different account.

5   **Select the items you want to import.**

6   **Decide how to treat transfer transactions, and use the Special Handling For Transfers checkbox to indicate your preference.**

Select this checkbox only if you have exported from a number of Quicken accounts in the same file (to several QIF files) and will be using import to re-create all the transactions (by importing from several QIF files). By selecting this checkbox, you instruct Quicken to omit transfer transactions that do not increase your net worth. This special handling helps prevent duplicate transfer transactions when you import data from both the "to" and the "from" accounts involved with transfers.

7   **Click OK.**

Quicken imports the transactions from the QIF file into the current account. If you choose to import any of the lists, Quicken copies the complete lists into the current file. See "Copying your lists" on page 341. If the category list, class list, or any of the transactions contain categories or classes not already in the current file, Quicken asks you to confirm that it should add these items to the current file's lists.

If the current account has a different name from the account you exported from, Quicken offers to create a new account with the same name as the exported account.

- Click Yes to create the new account and import the transactions into the new account, or

- Click No to import the transactions into the current account.

Setting up passwords

You might want to protect all or some of the transactions in a Quicken file from unauthorized changes. You can set up two different types of password in Quicken:

- You can discourage unauthorized access to your Quicken data by requiring a file password before your file can be opened.

- You can also set up a separate transaction password that protects all transactions before a certain date.

Requiring a password to open a file

Use a file password to protect an entire file. After you set up a file password, you cannot open your Quicken file unless you enter the password correctly. A file password does not protect your file from being copied, deleted, or renamed. However, if your file is renamed, the password is still in effect. If your file is copied, the copy has the same password.

When you set up a password, it protects only the current file. Make sure that the current file is the one you want to assign a password to.

Be sure that you write down the password and keep the written password in a safe place in case you forget it.

1   **Open the file you want to protect with a password.**

2   **From the File menu, choose Passwords and then choose File.**

As you enter your password, Quicken displays an asterisk (*) in place of the character you typed to ensure privacy.

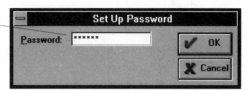

3   **Enter a private password that is easy for you to remember and click OK.**

You can enter up to 16 characters, including spaces. It doesn't matter whether you type upper- or lower-case characters (capitals or noncapitals) when you set up or later enter a password.

4   **Enter the password again to confirm it and click OK.**

From now on, Quicken prompts you for the password before allowing you to open this Quicken file.

Changing or removing the file password

You can change or remove a password from a file if you want to allow access to it by other individuals.

1   **Open the file whose password you want to change or remove.**

2   **From the File menu, choose Passwords and then choose File.**

3   **In the Old Password box, enter the current password.**

4   **In the New Password box, enter a new password, or leave the box blank to remove the password for the file.**

5   **Click OK and enter the new password again to confirm it.**

6   **Click OK.**

Quicken activates the new password or removes the current password immediately.

Requiring a password to change earlier transactions

Use a Transaction password to protect transactions within a date range from inadvertent change. After you set up a Transaction password, you cannot make changes to transactions prior to a given date unless you enter the password correctly. For example, you might want to *close* an accounting period so that no changes can be made inadvertently to transactions in it.

When you create a Transaction password, you specify the password you want to use and a date. The date you specify is the date of the last transaction you want this password to protect.

1 **From the File menu, choose Passwords and then choose Transaction.**

As you enter your password, Quicken displays an asterisk (*) in place of the character you typed to ensure privacy.

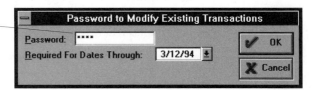

2 **In the Password box, enter a private password that is easy for you to remember.**

You can enter up to 16 characters, including spaces. Quicken passwords are not case-sensitive.

3 **(Optional) Enter the date of the last transaction you want the password to protect.**

Quicken presets the date to today's date.

4 **Click OK.**

5 **Enter the password again to confirm and click OK.**

From now on, Quicken prompts you for the password before it allows you to record changes to any of the transactions dated on or before the date you specified.

Changing or removing the transaction password

You can change or delete a password from a range of transactions if you want to allow access to it by other individuals. You can also change the date of the last transaction protected by the password.

1 **From the File menu, choose Passwords and then choose Transaction.**

2   **In the Old Password box, enter the current password.**

3   **In the New Password box, enter a new password to change the password, or leave the box blank to remove the Transaction password, or enter the current password if you want to change the protected date range.**

4   **(Optional) Change the date of the last transaction you want the password to protect.**

Be sure to enter the current password in the New Password box as well.

5   **Click OK.**

Quicken activates the new password, removes the current password, or changes the protected date range immediately.

Moving a Quicken file between computers

More information about QIF files is in Help. (Press F1 and then click Contents. Click "Technical Information about Quicken" at the end of the Contents, and then click "Information about Quicken's QIF format.")

If you need to move a Quicken file from one computer to another (for example, from your home computer to your business computer), you can move data using Quicken's Backup and Restore commands.

One Quicken data file actually comprises five DOS files (six DOS files if you use CheckFree). When you use the Backup and Restore commands, Quicken finds all of its files quickly and easily, and then backs up and restores the DOS files together. Don't try to back up and restore the DOS files individually.

1   **Install Quicken on any computer that does not already have Quicken installed on it.**

Use the *Getting Started Guide* for complete installation instructions.

2   **On the first computer, back up the Quicken file you want to move.**

See "Backing up your Quicken files" on page 350.

3   **On the second computer, restore the Quicken file you backed up.**

See "Restoring a Quicken file" on page 352.

Backing up and archiving your data files

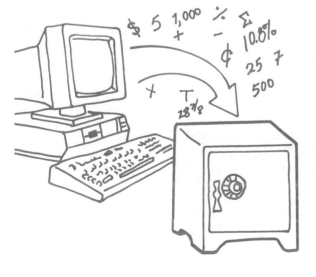

Your Quicken file represents a lot of your time. It is very important to make backups. At least once a month (once a week if you use Quicken frequently) you should make a backup copy of each of your Quicken files to guard against accidental loss of data. Quicken does the backup for you in seconds.

This chapter tells you how to back up and restore your Quicken data. If you need to close out your accounts at the end of the year, this chapter also describes Quicken's two archive options.

Backing up your Quicken files

It's always a good idea to back up your work each time you use Quicken. Backing up is important because, if you accidentally lose data, you can use the copy of the file stored on the backup disk.

Caution:
The most unfortunate calls our staff in Technical Support get are from people who have lost their only copy of Quicken data because of hard disk failure. In this situation, there's nothing we can do to help. Your data is valuable—back it up to a floppy disk.

You can put a Backup icon on the iconbar to make this task more convenient. See "Adding an icon to the iconbar" on page 359.

Quicken automatically offers to back up your data for you. Every so often, you'll notice Quicken prompting you to back up your current file before leaving Quicken. We recommend that you let Quicken do it.

Important: When you back up your work, *use a separate floppy disk,* even if you have a hard disk. Although they have lots of space, hard disks can fail. The first time you make a backup copy, you should have two sets of blank, formatted disks on hand before you begin. For subsequent backups, alternate between the two sets of backup disks.

Or press Ctrl+B

1 **From the File menu, choose Backup.**

2 **Insert your backup disk.**

3 **Select the drive containing the backup disk from the Backup Drive drop-down list.**

4 **Select the file you want to back up from the File to Back Up box and click OK.**

Click this option to back up the file you are currently using. Then click OK and skip to step 6.

Click this option to select another file to back up.

5   **(Optional) If you clicked the Select From List option in step 4, select the Quicken file you want to back up and click OK.**

Double-click the directory containing the Quicken file to be backed up. The line above the Directories list changes to show you the full pathname of the directory you have selected.

This list shows all Quicken files in the selected drive and directory. You probably have only one Quicken file. When you find it, select it so that it appears in the File Name box in the top left corner.

Select the drive containing the Quicken file to be backed up from this drop-down list.

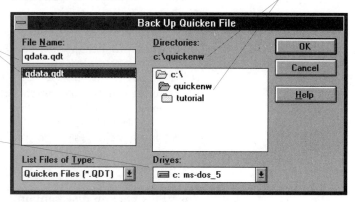

6   **If the file is larger than the space available on the backup disk, select the backup option you want, replace the backup disk with another disk, and then click OK.**

If you select this option, replace the backup disk with one that has enough space for the entire file to be backed up.

If you select this option, replace the backup disk with an additional disk on which to back up the remainder of the file. The backup file will span multiple disks.

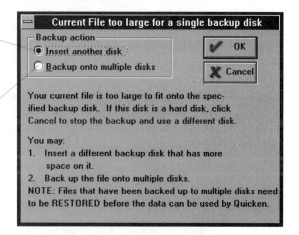

7   **When Quicken tells you that the backup is complete, click OK and remove the backup disk.**

Store the disk (or disks) in a safe place.

8   **Repeat steps 1 through 7 to make a second backup copy.**

Once you have made a backup copy of your file, you should update it at least once a month. Alternate between the two sets of backup disks each time you back up your work.

Restoring a Quicken file

If your hard disk ever accidentally loses data, you'll need to restore your files from your backup disk. In this event, first reinstall Quicken; then restore your files as described below. (See the *Getting Started Guide* for installation instructions.)

If you need to move a Quicken file from one computer to another (for example, from your home computer to your business computer), you can use Quicken's Restore command to restore files on one computer that you've backed up on another computer.

Restoring replaces your current data.
When you restore from a backup file, Quicken overwrites your current Quicken file with the file stored on the backup disk. Be aware that you will lose any changes you have made to your file since the backup was made.

---

1   **Insert the backup disk containing the file you want to restore.**

2   **From the File menu, choose Restore.**

3   **In the Restore Quicken File window, select the drive containing the backup disk from the Drives drop-down list.**

4   **Click on a filename to select the file you want to restore.**

Make sure the filename is shown in the File Name box.

This list shows all Quicken files in the selected drive and directory. Select the one you want to restore so that it appears in the File Name box in the top left corner.

If necessary, first double-click the directory containing the Quicken file to be restored in this list. The line above the Directories list changes to show you the full pathname of the directory you have selected.

If the Quicken file to be restored is on a single disk, it has a .QDT extension. If the file spans multiple backup disks, it has a .QB1 extension.

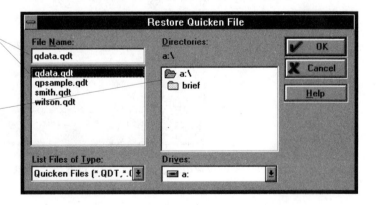

Windows tip
You can double-click the file in the file list instead of selecting it and clicking OK.

5   **Click OK.**

6   **If you are restoring the current file, click OK to overwrite it.**

Archiving your Quicken files

Many people think you need to "close out your accounts" before continuing to the new year. "Closing out accounts" is required by many accounting packages. It means you save all the information about completed transactions from the previous year in one file, and continue the new year with only those transactions that are still uncleared.

Quicken does not require you to close out accounts at the end of a year, or at the close of any fiscal period. In fact, if you do "close out" a Quicken file, you forgo easy access to reports covering several years. In many cases, the only reason people close out a year is to protect their data from changes. If you're worried about protecting your data, you can protect a range of transactions by date with a password. (See "Requiring a password to change earlier transactions" on page 346.)

However, if you still want to close out a file, Quicken offers two options, depending on how you want to organize your historic files: Archive and Start New Year.

Archiving the previous year's data

The Archive option makes a copy of all transactions in the current file dated earlier than the current year. You give the file copy its own name (for example HOME93) and this copy is for archiving only. The current file is untouched and remains your working file—it still contains all your past transactions.

If you select the Archive option once a year, you will eventually have a series of archive files, each containing all transactions up to the end of a certain year. You can give these archive files appropriate names.

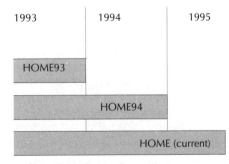

1 **From the File menu, choose Year-End Copy.**

2 **Click Archive in the Year End Action box and click OK.**

3   **Change any entries you want in the Archive File window and click OK.**

Quicken appends last year's date to the filename to create the archive filename.

Quicken presets the location for the archive file to your current Quicken directory.

By default, Quicken archives transactions through the last day of the previous year.

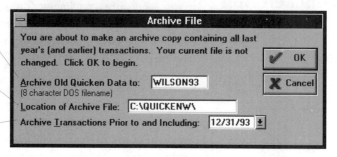

Quicken creates the archive file and copies the historic transactions to it. When the copy is finished, Quicken asks you which file you would like to use, the current file or the archive file. The archive file appears in your list of files.

You should never need to make changes to an archive file. To ensure that nobody makes changes inadvertently, you can set a transaction password that lets you view (or "read") the file but not make changes without entering the password. (See "Requiring a password to change earlier transactions" on page 346.) Or you can set a file password so that nobody else can view the file or make changes to it. (See "Requiring a password to open a file" on page 344.)

Reviewing the year

Quicken provides many reports for reviewing yearly finances. When creating reports with a date range, specify the entire year.

- To see how activity varies from one period to another, create a summary report (page 231) for the year with column headings set to the time period you prefer, for example, Half Month, Month, or Quarter.

- To review how funds have moved in and out of categories and asset or liability accounts, create a cash flow report (page 210) for the year.

- To see changes in your net worth during the year, create a net worth report (page 214) with columns for the intervals you want to examine.

Starting a new year

You can start a new file each year, so that your current file contains only this year's transactions. The Start New Year option saves a copy of your current file, and then deletes any transactions in the current file that are not of the current year. In other words, your current file will go back no further than January 1 of this year. However, investment transactions and uncleared transactions are not deleted, regardless of how old they are. (If you have never used Reconcile, the Start New Year option will not work well, as your old transactions will not be cleared.)

If you select the Start New Year option at the beginning of each year, you will eventually have a series of archived files, each containing the transactions for just one year.

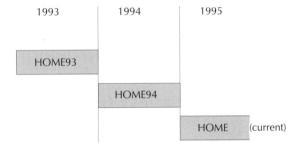

If you use IntelliCharge to update your credit card accounts, Intelli-Charge's use of Payee information may also affect your decision whether to use the Start New Year option. Start New Year removes the previous year's transactions from your accounts (including payee information). When payee information is removed, Intelli-Charge may not be able to match payees and categories correctly the next time you update your register.

If you want to start using this method part way through a year, use Archive first and then use the Start New Year option, using your current file in both instances. Archive creates an archive file without any of the current year's transactions, and then Start New Year deletes previous years' transactions from your current file, except for investment transactions and uncleared transactions. Start New Year also creates an intermediate file containing all transactions: you can delete this file.

1   **From the File menu, choose Year-End Copy.**

2 **Click Start New Year in the Year End Action box and click OK.**

Enter the name of a DOS file to copy your current file to. Quicken puts the copy in your current Quicken directory.

The preset start date is the first day of the current year.

Quicken keeps your current file in the current Quicken directory, but you can move your current file to another directory if you want.

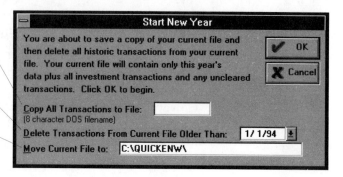

3 **In the Copy All Transactions To File box, enter a name for the copy of your current file.**

For example, you could enter HOME93. Do not include an extension.

4 **(Optional) Change the start date and location for the current file (this year's file).**

5 **Click OK.**

Quicken makes a copy of your current file, and then deletes all transactions in the current file earlier than the "Older Than" date. However, it does not delete any investment transactions or any uncleared transactions.

6 **In the File To Use box, select the file you want to use and then click OK.**

Click this option to use the copy of your original file with all transactions intact.

Click this option to use your current file, which now contains only this year's transactions, plus all investment transactions and uncleared transactions.

Did Start New Year work as you expected? If not, it could be because you have not reconciled your previous year's transactions. Start New Year does not delete any transactions that are not cleared. You can clear a transaction by entering an x in the Clr field. See also Chapter 6, *Balancing your checkbook*, beginning on page 69.

Customizing the iconbar

You can use Quicken's iconbar just as it is, or you can change the display and behavior of the iconbar to your liking.

When you customize the iconbar, Quicken saves your changes in the current Quicken file.

(For an introduction to using the iconbar, see "Clicking icons on the iconbar" on page 24 of the *Getting Started Guide*.).

Rearranging the icons

To rearrange the order of the icons in the iconbar, simply drag and drop each icon using the *right* mouse button. For example, to move the Register icon so that it appears to the right of the Graphs icon:

1. Click on the Register icon with the right mouse button and hold the mouse button down.

2. Move the skeleton icon over the Graphs icon and release the mouse button.

Quicken shifts the other icons to the left or right to make room.

Removing an icon from the iconbar

To permanently remove an icon that you don't use, shift-click the icon using the left mouse button. (You can also remove it by clicking Delete in the Customize Iconbar window—see below.)

If you decide you want to reinstate the icon to the iconbar, see "Adding an icon to the iconbar" on page 359.

Changing the iconbar display

Each icon is usually composed of a graphic and a label. You can display just the graphic, or just the label, or neither if you want to hide the iconbar altogether.

1   From the Edit menu, click Preferences.

2   Click the Customize Iconbar icon (labeled Iconbar).

Quicken displays the Customize Iconbar window.

3   Click Show Icons or Show Text, and then click OK.

To turn off the icons in the iconbar so that only text appears on the buttons, clear the Show Icons checkbox.

To turn off the text in the iconbar, clear the Show Text checkbox.

To turn off the iconbar entirely, clear both checkboxes. To display the iconbar again, select one or both checkboxes.

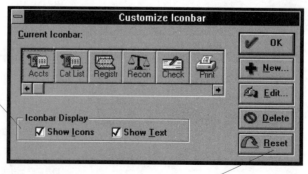

Click Reset to reset the iconbar back to the way it was set when Quicken was first installed. Caution: Quicken has no way to restore your custom settings if you reset them in this way.

Adding an icon to the iconbar

In addition to the icons you initially see in the iconbar, Quicken has a store of other icons you can add to the iconbar, each with its own specific action.

1   **From the Edit menu, click Preferences.**

Or hold down the Ctrl key and click in an empty position on the iconbar.

2   **Click the Customize Iconbar icon (labeled Iconbar).**

3   **Click New.**

Quicken displays the Add Action to Iconbar window.

4   **From the Icon Action list, select the action you want the icon to take when you click it.**

For example, select File Backup from the list.

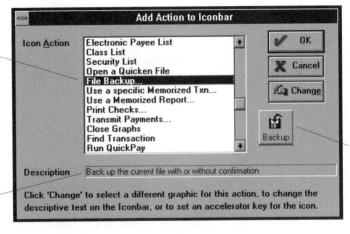

Quicken shows you the icon for the selected action here.

Quicken displays a description of the selected icon here.

5   **(Optional) Click Change to change the graphic, label text, or Speed Key for the icon.**

Click an appropriate icon if you don't want to use the icon that Quicken has assigned for the action.

For example, if you were setting up a transaction that involves a credit purchase, you might click one of the credit cards in the list of graphics.

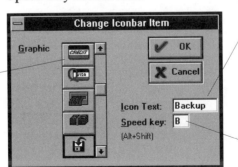

You can change the icon's text label here.

You can also set up a Speed Key here, so that you can perform this action either by clicking the icon or by pressing the Speed Key.

In this example, pressing Alt+Shift+B has the same effect as clicking the icon.

- (Optional) Scroll up or down through the list of graphics and select an appropriate icon (there are over 70 to choose from).

- (Optional) Enter or change the text for this action in the Icon Text box.

- (Optional) Enter a letter for this action in the Speed Key box.

- Click OK to close the Change Iconbar Item window.

6 Click OK to close the Add Action to Iconbar window.

7 Click OK to close the Customize Iconbar window.

When you click the new icon (or press the assigned Speed Key combination, if you set one up), Quicken performs the action; for example, Quicken prepares to back up your file.

Editing the icons in the iconbar

You can change the action of any icon in the iconbar, or change the icon associated with an action. (You are really choosing a new action and icon for the position in the iconbar.)

Or hold down the Ctrl key and click an icon on the iconbar to edit it.

1 From the Edit menu, click Preferences.

2 Click the Customize Iconbar icon.

3 Select an icon and click Edit.

4 Continue at step 4 on page 359.

Opening a specific account

Instead of displaying the account list to open an account, you can set up an icon to open an account you use frequently. For example, you can set up the Use Account icon so that it opens a credit card account named "American Express." Or you can set up an icon to open an investment account with the Portfolio View window displayed instead of the register.

1 Click the Use Account (UseAcct) icon on the iconbar.

Quicken displays a message describing how to set up the icon.

2 Click OK.

Quicken displays the Assign Account to Icon window.

Windows tip
Click the underscored down arrow to display the drop-down list. Then click the down arrow at the bottom of the scroll bar.

3 Scroll the Account to Load drop-down list to see all available accounts and select the account you want to set up.

4 Select an option for the type of window you want to open for this account from the Register, Reconcile/Pay Credit Card, Write Checks, or Portfolio View options.

Windows tip

If a menu choice is gray, it is not available and you can't select it.

Not all options are available for all accounts. For example, on a credit card account you cannot write checks or see an investment portfolio, so those options are dimmed for a credit card account.

Scroll the Account to Load drop-down list to select the account.

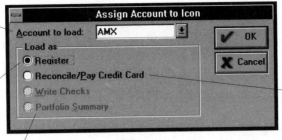

Select Reconcile/ Pay Credit Card if you want the reconcile window to open when you click the icon.

Select Register if you want the account register to open when you click the icon, or choose one of the other available options.

You may prefer to open an investment account with the Portfolio View window displayed, so that you can immediately update security prices.

5   **Click OK.**

Now the icon is set up so that when you click it, the account you selected opens and displays the window you specified.

To set up an additional icon to open another specific account, add a new icon to the iconbar as described in "Adding an icon to the iconbar" on page 359, and select the action "Use a Specific Account" from the Icon Action list.

Changing the Use Account icon setup

You can get back to the Assign Account to Icon window in order to change the account assignment via the Customize Iconbar icon.

1   **From the Edit menu, click Preferences.**

2   **Click the Customize Iconbar icon (labeled Iconbar).**

3   **Select the Use Account icon (UseAcct) and click Edit.**

4   **With "Use a Specific Account" selected, click OK.**

Quicken displays the Assign Account to Icon window and you can change the setup as described in the previous steps.

Entering a specific transaction

The example that follows shows you how to set up the Use Transaction icon so that, when you click it, Quicken enters a transaction you use frequently (such as an ATM withdrawal for $300) into your checking account register. The transaction must already be in your Memorized Transaction list.

1   **From the Edit menu, click Preferences.**

2   **Click the Customize Iconbar icon (labeled Iconbar).**

3   **Click New.**

4   **From the Icon Action list, select "Use a Specific Memorized Txn" and click OK.**

Quicken displays the Assign Memorized Transaction to Icon window.

5   **Scroll the Memorized Item drop-down list to select the memorized transaction you want to set up.**

6   **Scroll the Target Account drop-down list to select the account in which you usually enter this transaction.**

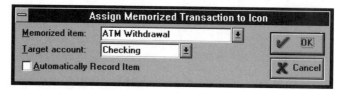

7   **Click OK twice to close the Customize Iconbar window.**

Now the icon is set up so that, when you click it, the register for the account you selected opens and Quicken inserts the memorized transaction you selected into the register. All you have to do is check the amount and change it if necessary, and click Record.

> When you click the icon Use Tx or press the assigned Speed Key combination (see how to create Speed Keys on page 359), Quicken enters the memorized transaction.

Date	Num	Payee		Payment	Clr	Deposit	Balance
		Memo	Category				
3/16/94	ATM	ATM Withdrawal		300 00		*Deposit*	
			[Cash]				

If you want to change the transaction assigned to the Use Transaction icon, follow the procedure described in "Changing the Use Account icon setup" on page 361 (but select the Use Transaction icon in step 3.)

To set up an additional icon to enter another specific transaction, add a new icon to the iconbar as described in "Adding an icon to the iconbar" on page 359, and select the action "Use a Specific Memorized Txn" from the Icon Action list.

Ordering supplies and other Intuit products

Other timesaving products   366

Other Intuit software products   367

All Intuit products help you complete your financial chores faster and with far greater ease than paying bills by hand.

The Intuit Check Catalog is the best place to learn about these products because it has pictures, more information, and an order form. This appendix answers some common questions about our products. If you have more questions about checks or if you no longer have the catalog, call us. See "Phone numbers" on page 372.

When you're ready to place an order, use the order form in the catalog or choose Order Supplies from the Activities menu to print an order form on your printer.

Intuit checks

The only way to take full advantage of Quicken is to allow the system to print your checks. After all, Quicken already does most of the work to prepare checks. Why duplicate work by writing checks by hand when printing is so easy? You will save hours of valuable time, avoid clerical errors, and prevent unnecessary financial hassle every month.

Intuit offers a complete line of checks and envelopes to meet both personal and business needs. You can order Intuit checks for continuous-feed printers and page-oriented printers such as laser printers and inkjet printers. With Intuit's automatic alignment system, you can easily align checks in any printer.

Intuit's Three-Point Guarantee

All Intuit checks are triple guaranteed. We guarantee that:

- Your checks will be accepted by your bank.
- Your checks will work with your Windows-compatible printer.
- Your check order will be printed as you submitted it.

If we fail to meet these three conditions, please call right away. We will quickly replace your order or refund your money, whichever you prefer.

Why should I print checks with Quicken?

You should print checks with Quicken for two reasons:

- Using Intuit checks in conjunction with Quicken will save you the maximum amount of time. Once you've entered your data into the program, you can press a button to print checks in just seconds.
- Checks printed with Quicken are legible and attractive, which will help you look more organized and professional.

Is it OK to order checks from Intuit instead of my bank?

ABSOLUTELY. Intuit checks are guaranteed to be accepted EVERY-WHERE your checks are accepted now. They're printed to the exacting standards of the American Banking Association and are pre-approved by all banks, savings and loans, credit unions, and brokers across the U.S. and Canada.

How do I write checks away from home?

For checks you might write away from home, such as at the grocery store, just use the paper checks you already have or handwrite a Quicken check. Then the next time you use Quicken, simply enter the transactions into your Quicken check register. When you order your Intuit checks, select a starting number that is considerably greater than your personal check numbers. That way, you avoid any confusion or possible duplication of numbers.

For example, if your personal check numbers are in the 1000 range, begin your Intuit checks at 3001.

Is having two sets of check numbers a problem?

NO. Quicken can easily manage two sets of check numbers in one account. Moreover, the bank has no concerns about which numbers you use on your checks. Check numbers are for your own records.

Should I have the check number printed on my Intuit checks?

YES. Check numbers are printed with magnetic ink along the bottom of the check where they can be read electronically. When you place a stop payment on a check, the bank's automated equipment reads the check numbers to find and stop payment on the requested check. Some people have requested that check numbers not be printed on checks to avoid problems in case their printer misprints a check. However, with Quicken's automatic check alignment system, misprints are minimized.

Where do I get Intuit checks?

You can order Intuit checks through Intuit. The enclosed Intuit Check Catalog will give you a complete description of the available check styles and colors. We've also enclosed an order form in the Quicken package for your convenience. If you need more order forms, Quicken will print them for you. Choose Order Supplies from the Help menu. Order today and Intuit checks will be in your hands in less than three weeks. For faster service, FAX your order anytime to Intuit. See "Phone numbers" on page 372.

What is the Logo Service?

Intuit has a selection of hundreds of standard logos that you can print FREE on your Intuit checks. Just order by number from the catalog. If you want a custom logo, enclose black-and-white, camera-ready artwork with your order. There is a one-time $35 setup fee for custom logos. If touchup, typesetting, or rearrangement is required, additional charges may be incurred. Custom logos cannot be ordered by FAX.

Don't forget that you can use Quicken to print your own artwork on your checks without using our Logo Service. See "Setting up continuous-feed printers" on page 51 or "Setting up page-oriented printers" on page 59.

Other timesaving products

These products are also described in the Intuit Check Catalog.

Intuit double-window envelopes

Window envelopes save even more time by eliminating hand addressing of envelopes. Each envelope has two windows. The upper window shows the return address printed on the check and the lower one shows the mailing address that Quicken prints on the check for you. All you do is sign the check and then drop it in the envelope.

Single Sheet Forms Leaders

These prevent wasted checks. If you have a page-oriented printer that does not have an envelope feed, you need a Forms Leader if you are using standard three-to-a-page checks and want to prepare partial sheets (one or two checks at a time). The Forms Leaders are not recommended for wallet-size checks.

Deposit slips

Intuit deposit slips are preprinted with your account number and name and address. They are available in two books of 100 each. When ordering, be sure to enclose one of your current deposit slips.

Endorsement and return address stamps

To reduce the time it takes to endorse checks and write addresses, use Intuit's endorsement and return address stamps. These pre-inked stamps are good for over 25,000 impressions. They measure 2 3/8 inches x 3/4 inch, with plenty of space for five imprinted lines. To ensure accuracy when ordering an endorsement stamp, enclose a voided sample check from your checking account.

Other Intuit software products

To order any of these products, call our Customer Assistance number for software products, listed on page 372.

Intellicharge

Use a Quicken VISA Gold card and you won't need to type any more credit card purchases into Quicken. The transactions are delivered to you every month on disk or by modem, and Quicken reads them into your account automatically. Details of this feature are given in "Using IntelliCharge," beginning on page 140. You must apply for a Quicken VISA Gold card before you can use this feature.

Quicken Companion™

The Companion comprises three programs that enhance your financial planning capabilities with Quicken.

- With the Quicken Tax Estimator, you can estimate your income taxes.
- Quicken Home Inventory keeps track of your household belongings and other possessions, so you can plan for insurance and track your total net worth.
- With Quicken Quotes™, you can receive immediate updates on stock prices by modem.

All three programs are fully integrated with Quicken. The package also contains our popular Quicken Tips book, in which experts share their knowledge of the most efficient and novel ways to use Quicken.

Quicken Business User's Guide

This book contains advice on how to use Quicken in your business. It explains how to set up your accounts for cash-basis or accrual-basis accounting, how to track liabilities and accounts receivable, how to use Quicken for payroll, how to get the most out of Quicken's business reports and graphs, and more.

QuickPay

For business users. By adding QuickPay to Quicken, you can integrate your payroll and business accounts into one financial system. QuickPay processes your payroll by storing details of your company and employees, and calculating all withholdings from its built-in tax tables. When you write the payroll checks, QuickPay automatically updates your Quicken accounts and keeps track of your payroll liabilities. The Tax Table Update Service ensures that you keep abreast of any tax rate changes.

QuickInvoice™

For business users. With QuickInvoice, writing invoices is as easy as writing checks with Quicken. QuickInvoice stores the details of your customers and your sale items for easy completion of invoices. It helps you track your receivables in Quicken, retrieve information about your receivables, and create complete business reports.

QuickBooks®

The complete solution for small businesses, QuickBooks is a full-fledged bookkeeping system with Quicken's ease of use. With QuickBooks you can write checks and invoices, view an invoice's payment history, and maintain customer and vendor lists. When you use QuickBooks for accounts receivable and accounts payable, you can view reports and graphs that show aging of unpaid invoices and bills. You can record loans, liabilities, assets, and credit card transactions. QuickBooks is the simplest way to manage your business.

Like Quicken, QuickBooks works with QuickPay. QuickBooks can also use any business data you've created in Quicken and QuickInvoice.

Contacting Intuit

As an Intuit customer, you have full access to technical support at no charge for help with any Quicken problems you can't solve yourself. To register for this support, fill out your customer registration card on the first page of this book and mail it to Intuit.

This appendix suggests ways to save yourself time and long distance charges by checking for the easy answers yourself. If you try these suggestions, you may not need to call or, if you do need to call, the support specialist may be able to help you faster because you will have ruled out common problems already.

Saving a phone call

If you have a question about the way Quicken works, the best way to get an accurate, immediate answer is to try looking here:

Help. Press F1 to get instant onscreen information while you're working in Quicken. If you want information about a specific task, make sure the window for that task is open and active. You can also look up topics by name in the Help Contents and get trouble-shooting tips. See "Getting Help" on page 26 of the *Getting Started Guide* for more information.

Index. Check the index in this *User's Guide* beginning on page 373 for the topic you need. We've worked hard to make the index useful.

Problem-solving tips. These tips are located at the end of some chapters in this book. Look for common symptoms that you may be experiencing and solutions that you may not have thought of. If you are trying to:

- Print checks, see "Check printing problems and solutions" on page 67.

- Print reports or graphs, see "Report and graph printing problems and solutions" on page 268.

- Send payments to CheckFree, see "CheckFree problems and solutions" on page 132.

README.TXT. This is a text file included on the Quicken Install Disk #1 that describes installation, printing, and other problems and their solutions. Open the file using Windows Write or any other word processor or text editor, or use the DOS command TYPE.

If you still have a problem using Quicken, the best way to solve it is to try these self-help approaches first:

1 Exit from Quicken, and then start running Quicken again.

(You should always choose Exit from the File menu or close the Quicken window to exit.)

When you start running Quicken again, you may see a message explaining that Quicken is maintaining or reconstructing your index file. Quicken maintains an index file to improve access to your financial data. Sometimes Quicken does not have a chance to save the index file before you exit. By restarting, you give Quicken the opportunity to reconstruct its index file.

2 Explore the problem a bit before you call.

When you call Intuit with a problem, the support specialist leads you through steps to identify and solve the problem. You can do some of this exploration yourself to eliminate possibilities that don't

---

If an error message tells you to reindex:

Quicken normally reindexes automatically whenever it's required. You can make Quicken reindex a file as follows:

1 From the File menu, choose Open.

2 Select the Quicken file to reindex.

3 Press Ctrl+Z.

Under some circumstances, this procedure can help you to recover a damaged file, but don't do this unless a Quicken error message tells you to.

require technical expertise. The key to troubleshooting is trying the most basic approach first.

- Try the procedure again, starting at the beginning.

    Examine the windows where you entered information to be sure you are using the appropriate window and are choosing the correct options for what you want.

    For example, if a report does not include the information you want, check the date range and restrictions in the Create Report window.

- Try a related procedure.

    For example, if you have a printing problem, check that the printer is working by trying to print a Windows Write document. (Windows Write is a word processing program that is available on any personal computer that uses Windows.)

    If you have trouble printing checks, try printing a report. If you can't print from Quicken, try printing from a word processor. If nothing prints, you know the problem is related to the printer, not the software. Check the printer connections and the name of the printer selected in the Windows Control Panel.

- If something used to work, think about what has changed.

    For example, if Billminder doesn't work, did you move BILLMNDW.EXE to a different location from QW.CFG? Both files must be in the same directory for Billminder to work.

Look for Write in the Accessories Program Group. Open it and type a few words. Then, from the Write File menu, choose Print.

3   **If you call, be at your computer with Windows and Quicken running, and have the following information handy:**

- Exact wording of the error message if you received a message

- Quicken version number (from the Help menu, choose About Quicken to see the version number)

- Hardware type and model and amount of memory (RAM) installed

- DOS version number and Windows version number

- Monitor type

- Printer manufacturer, type, and model (if relevant to your problem)

- Network configuration, if any

    You can also write our Technical Support Department. Include the information listed above, your day and night phone numbers, the best time to call, and a FAX number if available. Send your letter to:

    Technical Support Department, Quicken for Windows
    Intuit
    P.O. Box 3014
    Menlo Park, CA 94026

Phone numbers

If you would like	Contact	At this number	During these hours
Assistance using: **Quicken 3 for Windows**	Intuit Technical Support	**415-858-6003**	Monday - Friday 5 am - 5 pm Pacific time
To order: **Software upgrades** **Intuit software products** **Quicken Business User's Guide**	Intuit Customer Assistance	**800-624-8742** (in the U.S. and Canada) **USA 415-858-6095** (outside the U.S. and Canada)	Monday - Friday 7 am - 5 pm Pacific time
Assistance using: **Intuit checks and invoices** **Supplies**	Intuit Customer Service	**800-433-8810** (in the U.S.)	Monday - Friday 6 am - 5 pm Pacific time
		800-268-5779 (in Canada)	Monday - Friday 8 am - 8 pm Eastern time
To order: **Intuit checks and invoices** **Supplies**	Intuit Supplies	**FAX: 415-852-9146** **Mailing Address:** Intuit Supplies P.O. Box 51470 Palo Alto, CA 94303	Anytime
To get an application form for: **Quicken credit card**	Intuit Customer Assistance	**800-756-1855**	Monday - Friday 7 am - 5 pm Pacific time
Assistance using : **IntelliCharge statement disks or** **modem use**	Intuit Technical Support	**415-858-6070**	Monday - Friday 5 am - 5 pm Pacific time
Assistance with: **Quicken credit card limits** **Billing inquiries and other** **Quicken credit card issues**	Primerica Bank	**800-772-2221**	Monday - Friday 8 am - 9 pm Eastern time
Assistance with: **A lost or stolen credit card**	Primerica Bank	**800-426-2441**	Anytime

Assistance with:
24-hour Quicken credit card
  balance or last payment amount
  and date received
	Primerica Bank's
	Automatic Response Unit
		800-262-9323
		Call from touch-tone phone, and
		enter your Personal Identifica-
		tion Number)
			Anytime

Assistance using: **CheckFree** **Payment processing**	CheckFree Technical Support	**614-899-7500**	Monday - Friday 8 am - 8 pm Eastern time
Assistance using: **TurboTax for Windows**	ChipSoft Technical Support	**602-295-3090** or **FAX: 800-374-7057**	Monday - Friday 8:30 am - 5 pm Pacific time (extended hours during tax season)

Index

custodial fees, shares redeemed for, 185

custom reports, *see* standard reports, 229–234

Customer Assistance, Intuit, phone number, 372

customers, A/R report by customer, 224

customizing Quicken, *see* preferences

D

damaged file, reindexing, 370

data
    budgeting automatically from, 292
    Quicken, how organized, GS-7

Date field printing too high or low on check, 55

dates
    Canadian or European, setting style, 42
    changing style, 42
    graphs, 256
    reports
        changing default range, 252
        preset start and end, 251
        range in, 236
        sorting by, 241
    scrolling to, 32
    shortcuts to enter, 22, 395
    style when printed, 48
    viewing the scheduled payment date, 131
    writing checks dated after today, 47

Decrease column in asset register, 157

deferring taxes, setting up investment accounts
    for, 165

definitions of terms are in Help, GS-26

Delete Transaction command, 38

deleting
    account, 6
    categories, 10
    classes (same as categories), 11
    investment goals, 168
    memorized reports, 250
    memorized transactions, 90
    merchants, 129
    payee (CheckFree), 129–130
    Quicken file, 337
    scheduled transaction groups, 101
    security, 167
    security price, 201
    security types, 167
    subcategories, 11
    transactions, 38

demoting category names in the list, 11

departments in income/expenses report, 225

deposits
    add in register, 18
    bank may summarize, 79
    college savings, 286
    paycheck, how to enter, 31
    recording deposit less cash, 150
    reports, limiting to deposits, 244
    slips, ordering, 366
    transfers, 24

depreciation in asset account, 157

desktop settings, saving, GS-28

destination account, transfers, GS-8
    defined, 24

dialing, checking tone or pulse setting, 132

Difference amount
    defined, 77
    equals zero, 76
    not zero, 77

disks
    file larger than backup disk, 351
    full, copying data to new file, 338
    printing a report to file, 266

displaying register in 1 or 2-line mode, 33

disputed items, IntelliCharge, how to handle, 147

dividends
    entering in investment account, 184
    investment income report, 221
    reinvestment, entering, 184
    tax-free bond income, 190

dollars in reports, display only (no cents), 242

DOS Quicken
    changing Enter key action, 42
    updating security prices (*see* footnote), 201

drafting, automatic
    paying loans or mortgages, 320
    setting up as a scheduled transaction, 95

draft-quality reports, 266

drop-down lists
    turning on or off, 41
    using, 20

duplicate
    CheckFree payments, 123
    payee, distinguishing in list and reports
        (CheckFree), 120

E

earlier transactions, adding to reconcile, 83

earmarking money, *see* savings goal accounts, 297–
    300

editing
account name or description, 5
budget amounts, 292
category names, 10
memorized reports, 250
merchants, 129
payee (CheckFree), 129–130
transactions in register, 37

electronic payment
payee list, adding to, 117
settings, 115
stopping, 128

Electronic Payment, on Write Checks screen, 122

Enabled, means account is set up for CheckFree, 117

end of year, *see* **year-end procedures, 355**

ending balance
in Register window, 19
in Write Checks window, 44
postdated checks, 47
postdated transactions included, 122

endorsement stamps, ordering, 367

Enter key, changing its action, 42

entering transactions using an icon, 362

envelopes, window, ordering, 366

E-PMT, for transmitted payments, 127

equal sign (=), used as match character, 246

equipment, tracking depreciation, 157

equipment needed to run Quicken, GS-12

equity, balance sheet and, 228

erasing, *see* **deleting, 38**

errors
correcting in register, 37
messages during CheckFree transmission, 126
reconcile finds wrong transaction, 75

estimated income, displayed in Portfolio View, 197

exact match character (=) for matches, 246

Excel, Microsoft, transferring Quicken data to
budget amounts, 296
report data, 266

excluding transactions from reports, 246

existing account, set up for CheckFree, 116

exiting from Quicken, GS-29

expense categories, 7–14
defined, 8
see also categories

exporting
categories to another file, 341
data to QIF files, 343
Quicken data to tax software, 273

F

Favorable, budget graphs, 260

FAX, ordering checks, 365

features, new with this version, overview, GS-32

federal income tax return, 270

fees
bank, add in register, 18
entering in investment account, 182, 183
IRA custodial, entering in investment account, 185

fields
filling in from drop-down lists, 20
settings for automatic entry features, 41

File password
changing or removing, 345
setting up, 344

files
archiving, 353
backing up, 350
choosing, 333
closing, 353
copying, 338
copying categories into, 341
deleting, 337
icons to represent, 334
making a backup copy of, 350
maximum is 255 accounts, 332
new file using categories from old, 342
new year option, 355
opening Quicken data created in other versions, GS-15
printing reports to disk, 266
Quicken file, defined, 332
reindexing, 370
renaming, 336
restoring from backup, 352
saving, 338
setting up passwords, 344
when to have more than one, 332

filters
matches in reports, 246–247
saving report instructions (*see* memorizing reports), 249

finance charges in credit card accounts, 138

Financial Calendar, 94, 102–108
accounts, selecting, 103
financial planning graph, 301–313
font, changing, 102
notes and reminders, adding to, 108
past transactions, entering, 105
scheduling transactions on, 104
viewing, 102

itemized category reports, 212
  see also reports

J

job costing, suggested method, 15
job/project reports, 225
  see also reports

K

Keoghs, type of account for, 161
keyboard shortcut lists, *see the back cover*
keys
  changing Enter key action, 42
  date shortcut, *see the back cover*
  editing budget amounts, 292
  using Quick Keys, GS-24
  using Speed Keys, 359

L

landscape printing, reports, 265–266
laser printers and checks, 364
LaserWriters, printing checks on, 59–66
late charge, contacting CheckFree about, 127
legends, graphs, 257
lending loans, 325
liabilities
  balance sheet and, 228
  defined, 156
liability accounts, 155–158
  account register, 157
  mortgages, tracking, 317
  sample uses, 156
  updating, 158
  using to track accounts payable, 155
lists
  account, 5
  Category & Transfer, 9
    using in register, 22
  class, 16, 27
  drop-down lists
    turning on or off, 41
    using, 20
  font, changing, 40
  keyboard shortcuts in, 21
    see also the back cover
  memorized transactions,
    adding to manually, 88
    changing, 90
    printing, 88

printer, 51, 67
scrolling items in lists from within fields, 21
using items without opening, 21
loads, entering in investment account, 182
loans, 315–330
  additional payments of principal, 327
  adjustable rate, 322
  amortization, 316
  balances, 156
  balloon payments, 324
  calculating amortization for, 316
  interest-only loans, tracking, 324
  liability account illustration, 157
  Loan Planner, using, 283
  mortgage balances, 156
  payments, recording, 326
    undoing a mistake, 328
  prepayments, 327
logos, printing on checks, 366
  adding your own artwork, 52, 61
lots, securities, selling, 183
Lotus 1-2-3 for Windows, transferring Quicken data
  budget amounts, 296
  report data, 266

M

magnifying glass, cursor becomes in graphs, 258
mail
  mailing list, using the Electronic Payee List, 117
  receiving from CheckFree, 131
  to CheckFree about payment, 130
  to CheckFree (not specific to payment), 131
  U. S., CheckFree uses for payments, 125
margin interest expense, entering in investment register, 187
market value
  defined, 197, 203
  of investment account, viewing in register, 173
  of investments, in net worth report, 214
  portfolio value graphs, 262
  updating in Portfolio View window, 199–201
Match If drop down list, searching for transactions, 35
match transaction, *see* Find command, 35
maximizing windows, GS-29, 33
Memorize Transaction command, 87
memorized transactions, 85–90
  amortized loan payments
    recalling, 326
    setting up, 320
  assigning to a transaction group, 99, 101
  copying to new file, 338

R

RAM, minimum required for Quicken, **GS-12**

rate of return, in graphs, **262**

README.TXT, on install disk, reading, **GS-15**

real estate
  investment trusts, type of account for, 161
  types of account for, 161

realized gains, explained, **203**

rearranging categories in the list, **11**

recalling
  memorized reports, 250
  memorized transactions, 90
  transactions, automatic setting, 41

receipt, for CheckFree payment, **125**

receivables, *see* accounts receivable

Receive column in cash account, **153**

reconciling, **69–84**
  adding earlier transactions, 83
  benefits of, GS-9
  correcting transaction errors, 75
  entering earlier transactions, 83
  first time, 70
  interest earned, 73, 78
  investment register, 206
  marking a range of check numbers, 74
  missing transactions, 75
  opening balance difference, 71, 77
  report, 76
  service charge, 73, 78
  updating opening balance, 81

recurring transactions
  CheckFree, 118
  groups, 99
  see also scheduling

refinancing a mortgage, **284**
  recording in Quicken, 330

register, **17–42**
  automatic sorting in, 19
  cash account, 153
  condensing to 1-line mode, 33
  deleting transactions, 38
  displayed as an icon, 33
  entering earlier transactions, 83
  finding a transaction, 34
  font, changing, 40
  illustration, 19
  keyboard shortcuts, 32
  liability account, 157
  maximizing, 33
  moving around in, 32
  printing, 39
  reporting on payees, 35

resizing, 33
  returning to report, 248
  scrolling in, 32
  searching for a transaction, 34
  updated automatically (CheckFree), 112
  view options, 33
  x in cleared field, 76
  1-line display, 33

Register command, **18**

Register Entry field, what it means, **97**

regular investment account, defined, **162**

reindexing a Quicken file, **370**

reinvestments, entering in investment
  account, **184**

REITs, type of account for, **161**

reminders
  in Financial Calendar, adding notes to, 108
  memos in investment register, 191
  Reminder, turning off, 110

renaming
  accounts, updates transfers, 26
  memorized reports, 250
  Quicken file, 336

rent, scheduling as a recurring transaction, **94**

reports
  account balances, 234
  accounts payable, 224
  accounts receivable, 224
  balance sheets, 228
  benefits of, GS-6
  budget, 233
  budget, two types, 296
  button bar, 237
  capital gains, 220
  cash flow, 210
  category QuickReport, 13
  category/class descriptions or names in, 251
  changing settings, 239–247
  class QuickReport, 16
  comparison, 217
  creating, basic steps, 236
  customizing, 239–247
  date range, changing default, 252
  deleting memorized, 250
  editing memorized, 250
  filtering, 246
  fonts on screen, changing, 251
  fonts, selecting for printing, 265
  INF, means infinity, 217
  investment reports, summarized, 202, 218
  investment income, 221
  investment performance, 219
  investment transaction, 222
  itemized category, 212
  job/project, 225

using
onscreen Help, GS-26
Quick Keys, GS-24
Speed Keys, 359

U.S. Savings Bonds, redeeming, 188

V

variable-rate loans, 322

vendors
accounts payable report, 224
printing addresses and phone numbers, 117

viewing the register, 1 or 2-lines per transaction, 33

voiding a transaction, 37

voucher checks
categories printed on, 48
printing categories on, 48
selecting the paper size, 68

W

Wallet checks, selecting the paper size, 68

wash sales, in capital gains report, 220

where is transaction?
disappears when entered, GS-22
Find command, 34

wildcard characters (.. and ?) for matches, 246

Window menu, shows open accounts, 4

Windows, version needed for Quicken 3, GS-12

windows
resizing, GS-29, 33
saving positions, GS-28

word processors, copying Quicken data to, 253

Write Checks window
finding a transaction, 34
illustrated, 44

writing checks, 43–47

X

X in the Cleared field, 76
IntelliCharge register, 146

x-axis, displays months, accounts, or categories, 257

XMIT, for payments to be transmitted, 123, 127

Y

y-axis, displays dollar amounts, 257

year-end procedures

archiving last year's file, 353
copying transactions to a new file for new year, 338
starting new file, 355

years, budgeting by, 291

year-to-date
and reconcile, 83
transactions, reconciling, 83

Z

zero-coupon bonds, 189

zoom, *see* **QuickZoom, 248**

Symbols

* (asterisk)

( ) parentheses, entering in phone numbers, 116

{ } (braces), characters in payee name, 120
cash balance of investment register, 173, 176
phone system symbol, 132

.. (two periods), match character, 246

= (equal sign), match character, 246

? (question mark), match character, 246

~ (tilde), match character that excludes, 246

/ (forward slash) separator in Category field, 27

_ (underline), in investment category names, 9, 166, 175

Numbers

3-dimensional graphs, turning off, 257, 267

401(k) retirement plans, types of account for, 161

403(b) retirement plans, types of account for, 161